Marketing Analysis and Decision Making

Text and Cases with Lotus 1-2-3®

The Scientific Press Marketing Software Series

- **Applying Marketing Management: Four PC Simulations,** John R. Hauser (MIT). These simulation games allow students to try various strategies to develop an intuitive sense for marketing concepts of positioning, competitive strategy, new product development, and life cycle forecasting.

- **Marketing Management: Analytical Exercises with Lotus 1-2-3,** Gary Lilien (Penn State), approximately 260 pages, paperbound, to be published in Spring 1988. This book/template package includes Lotus 1-2-3 programs for exercises and cases that expand and elaborate on the concepts developed in Kotler's new Marketing Management textbook.

- **Marketing Analysis and Decision Making: Text and Cases with Lotus 1-2-3,** Darral Clarke (Brigham Young), 440 pages, hardbound, 1987. This text/template package analyzes Harvard cases in marketing management. Its four sections proceed from early new product development to pre-test testing and product modification, to test marketing, to marketing mix management.

- **Marketing Mix Analysis with Lotus 1-2-3,** Gary Lilien (Penn State), 206 pages, paperbound, 1986. This text/template package is best described as an MBA version of the Kotler/Lilien models book for the Ph.D.—the computer now does the mathematics.

- **Electronic Questionnaire and Design with CAPPA,** Paul C. Green (Wharton School) and John Liefeld (University of Guelph). This is a revised and simplified version of the questionnaire and design portion of CAPPA's earlier and larger version. The analysis portion has been replaced by a utility disk tying completed questionnaire data to the most prominent statistical packages.

And a Lotus 1-2-3 Tutorial

- **The Lotus Tutorial,** Philip Dybvig (Yale University), 146 pages, paperbound, 1987. This concise tutorial/template package contains everything one is expected to know about Lotus 1-2-3 that is used in macro-based courses and can be covered in class or self-learned in a few days.

Marketing Analysis and Decision Making

Text and Cases with Lotus 1-2-3 ®

Darral G. Clarke

National Advisory Council Professor of Management
Brigham Young University

▲*The Scientific Press*

507 Seaport Court, Redwood City, CA 94603, (415) 366-2577

Marketing Analysis and Decision Making:

Text and Cases with Lotus 1-2-3®
Darral G. Clarke

Copyright (c) 1987 by The Scientific Press. All rights reserved. No part of this book may be reproduced, stored in a retrieval system, or transcribed in any form or by any means without the prior written permission of the publisher, The Scientific Press.

The copyright on each case in this book, unless otherwise noted, and the software listed below is held by the President and Fellows of Harvard College and they are published herein by express permission. Permissions requests to use individual Harvard copyrighted case material should be directed to the Harvard Business School, Boston, MA 02163.

Case material of the Harvard Graduate School of Business Administration is made possible by the cooperation of business firms and other organizations, which may wish to remain anonymous by having names, quantities, and other identifying details disguised while maintaining basic relationships. Cases are prepared as the basis for class discussion rather than to illustrate either effective or ineffective handling of an administrative situation.

Software copyrighted by Harvard College includes:

Syntex Laboratories I, Darral G. Clarke (1985) 6-585-129

Johnson Wax I and II, Darral G. Clarke (1985) 6-585-150

Optical Distortion, Inc., Darral G. Clarke (1985, 1987)

Printed in the United States of America
10 9 8 7 6 5 4 3 2
ISBN 0-89426-083-9

Text and cover design: *Rogondino and Associates*
Technical illustration: *Pat Rogondino*
Typography: *Sally Edgecombe with Colleen Moyer*

For information on this book/software package,
call or write:

The Scientific Press
507 Seaport Court
Redwood City, CA 94063
(415) 366-2577

To Vicki

Contents

Editor's Foreword

The Series

The technological advances in personal computers and their rapid diffusion have generated the need for software-based texts that integrate computer capabilities with marketing concepts, methods, and findings. The objective of The Scientific Press Marketing Software Series is to provide microcomputer packages that allow marketing educators and professionals to apply state-of-the-art marketing technology to real-world marketing problems. This is a need that has not previously been met by traditional texts and standard mainframe statistical packages.

The series can be divided into two major areas:

1. Marketing research and modeling tools that can be applied to a variety of marketing situations (for example, electronic questionnaire design and analysis, conjoint analysis, and new product forecasting)

2. Products related to marketing strategy (such as marketing management with Lotus 1-2-3, marketing mix analysis, market segmentation, product positioning, product portfolio analysis and strategy, and competitive analysis)

The series is designed to provide a new set of tools that can be of value to the marketing practitioner as well as to the marketing student and professor. The computer software packages allow easy, user-friendly implementation of the most sophisticated concepts, tools, and findings available in marketing, and are intended to advance the state of marketing practice.

Marketing Analysis and Decision Making: Text and Cases with Lotus 1-2-3

Darral G. Clarke, National Advisory Council Professor of Management at Brigham Young University, has developed an extremely useful set of cases, with accompanying text and decision analysis software, that can help users effectively employ marketing research and models as part of a marketing decision support system aimed at improving marketing decisions. The unique characteristics of this advanced and easy-to-use package are:

1. Excellent state-of-the-art exposition of research and modeling for marketing analysis and strategy. The book focuses on the critical role marketing research and modeling can play in supporting marketing decision making.

2. Among the many marketing research and modeling approaches illustrated and included in the book are:

ASSESSOR: A pretest design for forecasting the market for new consumer products.

Trade-off analysis: A forecast demand model for forklift trucks in Brazil.

BehaviorScan: Space-age test market technology that makes use of electronic information from supermarkets and home television.

Sales force allocation: A model that determines optimal sales force size and allocation of effort across products and customer segments for a pharmaceutical company.

3. A large selection of Harvard cases that allow the user to explore the use of the latest research and modeling methods in real-world situations.

4. Clearly written expository chapters that explain the various research and modeling approaches, including marketing decision support systems and their role in management decision making.

5. A truly "user friendly" text and accompanying spreadsheets that are of value to the novice as well as the sophisticated student, researcher, and manager.

These features offer significant advantages over conventional marketing management texts. The package offers a practical set of tools for students, professors, and marketing research practitioners, and clearly demonstrates the value of analytical decision making in marketing.

It is my hope that this set of tools will enhance the quality, efficiency, and effectiveness of marketing analysis and decision making. It is designed to take advantage of the benefits of microcomputers—respondent involvement, flexibility, and speed—and introduces analytical thinking and tools to tomorrow's marketing managers.

The book offers to students, professors, and practicing managers a much-needed set of concepts, cases, and software that are useful and fun to work with.

Jerry Wind   *Philadelphia, January 1987*
Series Editor

Preface

In the last few years a number of important developments in marketing research, marketing science, computer hardware, and computer software have significantly improved the ability of technically trained specialists to do marketing analysis. The marketing research staffs of major corporations and commercial marketing science consultants routinely analyze data using methodologies that could only have been dreamed of a few years ago, even with computer systems that only the federal government could afford. I was fortunate enough to know a number of successful marketing science consultants that introduced me to their clients, and with the generous support of the Division of Research at the Harvard Business School, it was possible for me to interview managers at companies for whom a number of extensive marketing research studies had been completed. This afforded me an unusual opportunity—not only to study how the research studies were undertaken, which was my original intent, but also to observe the impact of the studies after the consultants had completed their work. The managers generally thought that the research studies had been helpful, and in a number of instances had done the same kinds of research a number of different times. Despite this improved technical support and the managers' expressed satisfaction with it, however, I noticed that in most of the situations the manager's mode of analysis remained the same as I observed in other situations where no technical support was available. The research results, if they were available at the time they were needed to make the decision, were intuitively integrated with the rest of the factors the manager was considering, and the research had only an informal impact on decision making.

This observation was reinforced when I taught the cases. Student evaluation of the early versions of the course reported that studying the cases improved their ability to analyze business situations, but didn't help them make better decisions. I had assumed that better analysis would automatically lead to better decision making, but it became apparent to me that this was not true, and that analysis and decision making are quite different things. The fact that marketing scientists have concentrated on analysis and neglected its integration with decision making has kept marketing science from having the impact on management that marketing scientists have long believed it deserved.

Through interviews with the consultants who did the marketing research studies, the managers for whom they were done, and the students who studied the cases, I began to understand how sound analysis could be integrated into the decision-making process. The field study interviews and the teaching process finally led to the conceptualization that appears in this book—how the impact of marketing research and marketing science on decision making could be increased. I hope that the reader, by the conclusion of the book, will be convinced that a manager who knows how to use the powerful marketing science support tools that are available can make better decisions than he or she could make without them. Happily, learning to use these tools is well within the reach of managers without technical training if they are willing to make the effort.

There are a few basic skills that a manager must acquire in order to increase his or her analytical powers and improve decision making. The first of these skills is the ability to do sound, rigorous business analysis that explicitly integrates marketing plans, market response, and financial consequences. The second skill is the ability to interact with the technical support staff to define objective information needs and interpret the implications of research results. The final skill is more an attitude than a tool: the willingness to accept necessarily incomplete analysis, evaluate its contribution, compensate for its shortcomings, and explore its implications.

The key to providing the decision maker with objectively based decision support lies in the development of, and experience in using, management-oriented decision support systems that I call *decision models*. A decision model consists of two components:

1. An explicit, mathematical expression of the manager's existing quantitative decision framework in a financial spreadsheet model
2. A market response function, embedded in the financial spreadsheet, that relates marketing action and market response

A further requirement for a decision model to impact decision making is that it must be oriented toward the manager's approach to the decision situation, and it must be both available and suitable for the decision maker's *personal* use.

Decision models can be developed using most financial spreadsheet models, not only on mainframe computers or time sharing, but also on personal computers using spreadsheet models such as Lotus 1-2-3. This book contains a number of decision models to assist the student in analyzing the cases. For the most part, these decision models are quite simple and provide an example of how a modest but insightful programming effort can greatly increase the value of marketing research.

Students that carefully analyze the cases using the decision models will be surprised to see how much more useful the research is to them than the consultants' research reports were to the decision makers in the cases. This demonstrates the point that the objective of research should not be merely to provide a written report or recommendation, but rather to give the decision maker the ability to personally analyze the marketing situation in three areas:

To find out what happened (*status*)

To find out why it happened (*explanation*)

To ask "What if...?" in order to explore the *implications* of the research

Status, explanation, and *implications* are the critical components of managerial decision support. Marketing science has made great leaps forward in the realms of status and explanation, but the major hinderance to making research more valuable in decision making has been the failure of researchers to provide managers with simple decision models that provide a "What if" capability.

In order for a decision maker to benefit from the use of a decision model, he or she must have at least an intuitive understanding of the decision model and be able to evaluate its validity. These skills can be developed without extensive technical training if the decision maker learns to evaluate response functions and data quality. To evaluate response functions, a manager must be sensitive to three major considerations:

Specification—the shape of the response function

Data foundation—the character of the data from which the response function is developed

Estimation—the process by which the specific values in the response function are developed

A manager evaluating data quality must deal with three major considerations:

Bias—systematic errors in the data

Control—the elimination of factors that corrupt the data by introducing extraneous influences

Information content—the information conveyed by the data

There are, of course, a multitude of technical details involved in each of these areas, and few decision makers could find the time to develop sufficient expertise to do their own research or develop their own models, but a decision maker who has become sensitive to these considerations and applies common sense can competently evaluate the appropriateness of decision models. The objective of this book is to teach managers how to interact with marketing scientists in defining, evaluating, and utilizing marketing research, rather than to teach them to do the research themselves.

Outline of the Book

The analytical approach to marketing decision making is developed in the first two chapters, followed by a sequence of four chapters of text and case studies. The concluding chapter restates the analytical approach and illustrates its implementation with examples from the case discussions.

Chapter 1: The Problem and the Opportunity introduces the problem of why marketing research and marketing science have not had as great an impact on decision making as the quality of their results would warrant. It also describes the confluence of recent conceptual and technological developments that provide a unique opportunity to benefit from marketing science.

Chapter 2: An Introduction to Analytical Decision Making introduces the basic concepts of the decision maker's existing quantitative decision framework, the market response function, and the decision model. It develops the decision model concept and outlines the analytical process that forms the basis of our approach to marketing analysis and decision making. It also discusses the new product development process that provides the organizational framework for the order of the case studies.

Chapter 3: Early New Product Development describes the research similarities that are common to early new product development situations. CableShop, the first of two cases in this chapter, illustrates the need for our analytical approach. In this case, despite the results of an extensive research effort and the development of a financial planning model, many critical planning issues remain unresolved and the research provides very little decision support. The second case, Optical Distortion Inc., demonstrates how the development of a simple decision model, even in the absence of extensive research, can lead to considerable decision support.

Chapter 4: Pre-Test Market Testing and Product Modification–describes the pre–test market stage of the new product development process. Pre–test market tests and concept testing have been developed to reduce the risk inherent in test markets and new product introduction. The Johnson Wax cases describe the use of AS-SESSOR, a pre–test market procedure for consumer products, in developing a new hair conditioner. The Clark Equipment cases describe the use of trade-off analysis in planning the Brazilian product line strategy for an international heavy equipment manufacturer.

Chapter 5: Test Marketing describes the test market stage of the new product development process and focuses attention on advertising research and advertising management. The cases follow the development in test marketing methodology over the last decade and a half. The UDIA case describes an inter-city experiment to find the best advertising budget for cheese; analysis of variance (ANOVA) is used to analyze the data. AdTel, Ltd. describes a test market to determine the better of two advertising budgets for a peanut butter brand, using the AdTel split-cable testing system. Recent technological developments have made feasible the development of a test marketing facility in which households are individually targetable and purchase histories are gathered electronically at the individual purchase level. The Information Resources, Inc., case describes this system, called BehaviorScan, and invites students to develop a strategic plan for the company. G. D. Searle I describes the BehaviorScan test for Equal low-calorie sweetener, one of the most successful new consumer products in recent years.

Chapter 6: Marketing Mix Management describes marketing research studies intended to improve the effectiveness of various marketing mix elements for products subsequent to introduction. The advertising emphasis of the previous chapter continues in the first two cases. The General Foods case uses an application of econometric model building. In Convection Corporation, the ADVISOR model, a multi-company cross-sectional study of advertising budgeting practices, is applied to the allocation of the communication budget across three industrial products. Sales force management is the focus of the Syntex Laboratories cases, where a normative decision calculus model is used to determine the optimal sales force size and allocation of effort across products and customers. G. D. Searle II, the final case in the book, provides a close look at promotion and addresses the broader issue of planning a marketing strategy when research results are available about most of the relevant parts of the marketing mix.

Chapter 7: An Approach to Analytical Marketing Decision Making restates the analytical process presented in the first two chapters and shows how the approach is validated by the decision-making experiences presented in the cases.

Using the Text

The subject matter included in this text does not fall neatly into any one course presently offered in most MBA and doctoral programs. It is designed for a second-level marketing management course; it assumes that the student requires only a brief reminder of basic marketing management principles. The book is written for a managerially oriented course that develops skill in marketing analysis. It seems to me that most current advanced marketing management courses only put the student in the position of the marketing vice president rather than that of a product manager. They don't provide additional tools or a more sophisticated decision framework. This book has been written to increase the analytical power and improve the decision making of marketing (or financial) managers, regardless of their level in the company.

Many of the case situations are at the strategic planning level and would be appropriate for a strategic marketing or strategic planning course, where they would provide an opportunity for greater in-depth analysis than is generally available. A general problem that I have observed in strategic marketing cases is that, although extensive quantitative detail is given in the cases, there is no means to make this detail accessible to students. The spreadsheet decision models in these cases make it possible for the average student to utilize the quantitative detail in the cases. The material is also appropriate for supplementing a course in marketing models because it provides extensive experience in the design and use of models. A number of the cases could be used to develop application skills in a marketing research course that stresses survey methodology. Finally, individual cases are of interest to various functional marketing courses such as advertising, new product development, product policy, sales force management, and so on.

It is the author's opinion, of course, that the concept of making quantitative analysis accessible to decision makers is much needed in the MBA curriculum, and I would hope that teachers who initially use the book to enrich existing courses will find the material sufficiently valuable to develop a course devoted to it.

Cases appropriate for inclusion in various existing courses are listed below:

Marketing Models: Chapters 1, 2, and 7; ODI, Johnson Wax I and II, Clark Equipment I–III, AdTel Ltd., General Foods, Convection Corporation, Syntex Laboratories I and II, G. D. Searle II.

Marketing Research: Chapters 1, 2, and 7; CableShop, Johnson Wax I and II, Clark Equipment I, UDIA, AdTel Ltd., Information Resources Inc., Convection Corporation, G. D. Searle I.

Strategic Marketing: CableShop, ODI, Johnson Wax I and II, Clark Equipment I–III, Information Resources Inc., G. D. Searle I and II, and Syntex Laboratories I and II.

New Product Development: Chapters 2–5.

Acknowledgments

The development of this book has extended over a number of years and I have benefited from a number of favorable influences over that time period. The most obvious group of contributors is, of course, the company case sponsors and consultants whose generosity made the cases available. More obvious to me, but perhaps not as apparent to the reader, is their influence on my development of the conceptual scheme. Although I cannot name them individually in order to preserve confidentiality, I want to thank them for the stimulation of their insight and the pleasure of their association. Without exception I have the utmost respect for their efforts to expand the frontiers of management practice. Suggestions I have made for improving the usefulness of the research in their situations are highly dependent on technological developments that were not available to them at the time and should not be construed as critical of their performance.

Several people were instrumental in providing introductions to these case sponsors, including James Findley and Gerald Eskin of IRI, Curtis Jones of the John Morton Company, and Richard Johnson of Sawtooth Software. I would like to recognize the contribution of the students who have so diligently and intelligently attacked these cases. The observation of their motivation and goals played an extremely important role, not only in the development of individual decision models, but also in the development of the concept itself. I cannot recognize their contributions individually, but if in reading the book they should see something familiar, they should rightly ascribe it to their influence on me. If they could see the teaching notes that accompany this volume, they would even more clearly see their contributions to the effort.

A number of academic colleagues have made important contributions to this effort. My thanks to E. Raymond Corey, Theodore Levitt, and Walter Salmon of the Harvard Business School, who in their official capacities made time and financial resources available to me as only HBS can, as well as for their personal support. Robert D. Buzzell of HBS whose willingness to try something this new in an HBS executive program was little short of courageous. John Hauser, John D. C. Little, and Glen Urban of MIT; Subrata Sen of Yale University; J. Morgan Jones and David Hughes of the University of North Carolina; Gary Lilien of the Pennsylvania State University; John Quelch of the Harvard Business School; and Leonard Lodish and David Reibstein of the Wharton School all contributed significantly to this effort.

I also enjoyed the support of two extremely capable secretaries, Marie Castro and Jane Barrett, whose organizational efforts contributed as much as their exceptional typing. The word processing centers of the Harvard Business School and the Brigham Young University performed yeoman duty through the many drafts and revisions that my random work process necessitated.

Elaine Fritz, editor of the book, provided constant encouragement and good humor, in addition to expert editing. She was a pleasure to talk with, and it was always exciting to see how she skillfully sculpted the rough manuscript I sent her.

Last, but certainly not least, my family has provided the safe haven from which I dared to venture forth on this voyage of discovery. Vicki, my wife and best friend, has supported me in this effort with love, patience, and encouragement. I cannot conceive of having completed this effort without her. My son Steven has helped with programming, graphics, and answers to numerous personal computer operating system questions. (Thank goodness the book was completed before he left home for college.) Finally, my daughters Stacey, Elizabeth, and Margaret have cheered me up on numerous occasions. There's nothing like a hug from a loving daughter to keep you going.

Provo, Utah
September 20, 1986

The Problem
and the Opportunity

This book is designed to help marketing managers learn to use marketing research and marketing science to better understand their markets and make better decisions. It is also useful for marketing researchers and marketing scientists who would like their research to have more impact on the decisions made in their organizations. It is not intended to provide sufficient background either for a manager to become a marketing scientist or for a marketing scientist to become a manager; but rather to help each to interface more effectively with the other.

To do this, the book provides a number of case situations in which marketing research and marketing science have been applied by major corporations in important marketing decision situations. The case situations, with one or two exceptions, reflect good research practice as well as interesting decision situations.

Marketing science will be loosely defined as the application of the scientific method to marketing problems. It will refer to the process of developing specific, quantifiable hypotheses about marketing phenomena; of obtaining measurements of those phenomena where possible; of building mathematical models; and of using mathematical models to test the hypotheses and forecast the phenomena. *Marketing research* deals primarily with survey research to measure various aspects of the marketing environment. Although marketing research and marketing science represent two somewhat different disciplines, it is tedious always to refer to both, so I will use the term *marketing science* to represent both areas and *marketing scientist* to refer to a practitioner of either discipline.

My original intent when I began this collection of cases was to provide examples of the types of marketing science applications that were being used by American businesses in the 1980s. I was initially encouraged to find that companies had accumulated considerable experience in using recently developed methodologies and techniques, but it soon became apparent that the actual impact of marketing science on managerial decision making was far less than either researchers or managers wanted. Discussions with managers revealed that they lacked confidence in their ability to use the insights provided by research. Discussions with researchers sometimes revealed disappointment that their work had not had more impact; while in some other instances, the researchers greatly overestimated the impact of their work and had an unrealistic view of the role it had played.

It was in the process of teaching with the materials at the Harvard Business School, however, that I began to see a number of reasons for this lack of impact. Even in situations in which the research practice was sound and the results were interesting to the students, they had to work much too hard to use the results in making decisions. Few decision makers can be expected to be motivated to expend as much effort as the students did to use the results. While observing how these highly motivated students tried to use the research, I could see a number of good reasons why the managers in the cases had not utilized the results to a greater extent, and why marketing science has not reached its potential in affecting managerial decision making. I began to develop the concept about how these powerful tools could be made more useful for decision makers. This concept, which is outlined in Chapters 1 and 2 and summarized in Chapter 7, underlies the organization of these cases.

The Problem

Managers face three important problems in making more effective marketing decisions: (1) obtaining the information they need from the flood of data that are available, (2) interpreting the information, and (3) determining what action should be taken. Even though the factors that influence the sales of a product are generally understood by marketing managers in principle, determining an effective course of action in any particular situation is difficult. There are many variables to consider and the variables interact, so their complex effects on demand are difficult to conceptualize.

Direct measurement of what a consumer buys—let alone *why* it is purchased—is economically infeasible on a broad scale, even in those situations where it is theoretically possible. The information available to managers is incomplete, subject to statistical error, and difficult to interpret. Furthermore, decisions always seem to be required before the information is available or an analysis can be completed.

Managers and marketing scientists react to the complexity and uncertainty of the marketing situation in very different ways. Typically, managers try to overcome the uncertainty inherent in marketing decision making by acquiring an extensive, detailed institutional knowledge about their products and their markets, from which they form an intuitive model of how these many factors influence sales volume and market share. They know myriads of details about their products and competitors, and have an explanation for every phenomenon.

The same conceptual complexity and uncertainty also concerns marketing scientists, but they react quite differently. Marketing scientists typically try to reduce this complexity by focusing attention on a mathematical abstraction of the decision situation. They eliminate all but a few major factors and express the relationships between these factors in explicit, mathematical terms. These mathematical relationships are then used to find a "best" solution to the abstracted mathematical problem in the hope that this solution will also be a good solution to the real problem.

These methods of dealing with the complexity and uncertainty of a marketing situation are diametrically opposed to each other, and in the past neither managers nor marketing scientists have been comfortable with each other's approach. However, in those situations in which this discomfort has been overcome long enough to support a joint effort, the strengths of the two approaches have proven to be complementary and a powerful synthesis has resulted.

Marketing science *has* been used in many major corporations, but there's been a lot more good analysis done—by consultants, academics, and in-house research staffs—than has been effectively used by managers. Even in the case histories in this book, which represent the best applications of marketing science that the author could find, the research results were not fully utilized by managers.

One of the major difficulties for managers is that of interpreting the information they receive about their products and markets. It would seem that this flood of information should provide a basis for sound decision making, but it isn't necessarily so. An interesting experiment illustrating the difficulty of acquiring useful information and using it to obtain a competitive advantage was done by Robin Hogarth and Spyros Makridakis [1981] when they entered computer teams to compete with human teams in a business game being run at a well-known European business school. Each of the computer teams was a computer program containing a set of explicit mathematical rules that enabled the computer to fill out the decision forms without any further human input. The rules developed by the reseachers were not particularly insightful, since neither of them were marketing or game-playing experts, but nevertheless their computer teams beat about half of the human teams.

The comparative performance of the computer and human teams illustrates the need for better marketing decision-making skills, because the computer teams could neither analyze the ongoing results of the game nor change their strategy, while the human teams had the opportunity to observe period-by-period results, determine trends and relationships, and change strategy to exploit competitive advantage. These results don't indicate that the computer teams were smarter than half of the student teams, because the computer teams were not smart at all—they could neither learn nor adapt. The point is that, in a complex decision-making environment requiring the acquisition, interpretation, and analysis of information as well as the formulation of strategy, nearly half of the human teams were unable to do better than a computer program that could do none of these things!

If intuitive learning, effective analysis, and the adaptive development of better strategies is difficult in a business game, imagine how much more difficult it must be in the real business world. In such a complex environment, even the value of experience is questionable. The spirit of the marketing mix concept is that it is the joint result of marketing action that produces results, so for any event there are always many possible causes. The problem is not only to determine what is wrong when a product is doing poorly, but also what is right if a product is doing well; and it is never clear whether a product that has done well might not have done even better with a different strategy.

The key point to this discussion is that:

In a complex marketing decision making environment, using intuitive insight and managerial experience alone, it is nearly impossible to consistently (1) learn, either from one's successes or mistakes, (2) correctly attribute cause and effect, or (3) devise effective strategy to exploit competitive advantage.

There are a number of important factors that have restricted managers' ability to utilize marketing science to improve their decision making, limiting them to using intuitive insight. Managerial dissatisfaction with intuitive decision making is widespread and has been for many years. The existence of this collection of cases indicates the desire of managers in major corporations to improve the quality of their decision making, and it is not for lack of intent that the research in the cases was not more fully utilized. For the managers in the cases, there were a number of very real problems that limited progress in making their marketing decision-making more scientific.

1. The cost of computer hardware and software was so substantial that marketing managers and marketing scientists could not afford their own computer systems and databases. This limited them to the use of databases that were intended for the accounting function of the firm.

2. The data available for marketing decisions was limited to company operations data, survey research, and commercial audits at an aggregate level.

3. Utilization of computer systems required substantial training, and the time taken from question to useful answer was unreasonably long. Direct managerial use of computer systems was not a reasonable expectation for most managers, who were not technically trained.

4. Marketing science was oriented toward research projects and making recommendations rather than toward the delivery of analytical tools for managerial use.

5. The managers lacked training in the evaluation and use of research.

The good news that comes from the research that went into this book is that many important conceptual and technological limitations have recently been overcome, and the skills that need to be developed by both managers and marketing scientists are now well within reach of those who want to become more analytical in their decision making.

The Opportunity

The problems that have kept marketing science from being more useful to managers are both conceptual and technological. Important technological developments over the last decade have made the managerial use of marketing research and marketing science feasible on a broad scale for the first time. Important technological developments in computer hardware and software, data recovery systems, and communications have greatly increased the quality of the computer systems available to managers, and improved databases are now commercially available. An accumulation of research findings have strengthened the conceptual basis for understanding how marketing works and how decisions should be made. These developments have made it possible for the first time to put the results of marketing research and marketing science studies in the hands of the operating marketing manager in a usable and useful form.

When Columbus made his historic journey in 1492, a number of developments in navigation and ship and sail design, and the accumulated experience of expanded trade in both the Mediterranean and around the coast of Africa to Asia, provided an environment in which both a new continent and the true size and scope of the world were discovered. These developments, which had been in process for hundreds of years, concurrently reached levels of development that provided an environment in which man's concept of his world was forever changed. In describing this dynamic time, Daniel S. Boorstin stressed the fact that when the necessary technological developments were in place:

> The great obstacle to discovering the shape of the earth, the continents, and the oceans was not ignorance but the illusion of knowledge. Imagination drew in bold strokes, instantly serving hopes and fears, while knowledge advanced by slow increments and contradictory witnesses. [*The Discoverers*, p. 86]

The next ten years may well be as pivotal in the development of our understanding of how marketing works and how products should be managed as the fifteenth and sixteenth centuries were to geography. A number of important developments, each spanning decades in process, have simultaneously reached a useful degree of completion. Developments in the fields of statistics, mathematical marketing models, and marketing research have advanced by slow increments over the years to provide finally a meaningful, critical mass of useful knowledge. Parallel developments in computer technology, computer software, and commercially available software, which have advanced at a fantastically rapid rate, have converged to provide an analytical capability for marketing managers that could only have been dreamed of ten years ago. In terms of both its power and accessibility, these developments have the potential to greatly expand the manager's knowledge of how the marketplace works, explode old myths, and increase the manager's ability to develop strategies to exploit this knowledge. A partial list of some of the most important of these developments includes:

1. Powerful marketing research techniques and marketing science models have been developed.

2. The cost of computer hardware has been reduced to the point where marketing and marketing research departments can design and maintain databases for their own purposes.

3. Sophisticated, commercially available databases and research techniques have been developed.

4. The decision support system (DSS) concept and its commercially available realization have provided a powerful tool to increase the quality and timeliness of marketing research and to make it available to managers in a useful form.

5. The personal computer and easy-to-use spreadsheet programs finally provide a manager-friendly interface with the computer and marketing science.

The illusion of knowledge, however, may well be the last major obstacle in the discovery of a new world of marketing management, just as it was the final obstacle to understanding the nature of the earth in the fifteenth century. Managing a product is every bit as intensive and complex an activity as exploration in the fifteenth century. The constant bombardment of new information combined with the need for decisions in the face of uncertainty require that a marketing manager develop a conceptual model of the marketplace, and most surviving marketing managers have been successful in doing so. The obstacle to improving marketing management above this intuitively insightful level is not ignorance; but rather, the illusion of knowledge.

The necessity for making rapid decisions while deluged with abundant but uninterpreted information has required that the marketing manager's understanding of the market also be drawn "with bold strokes, instantly serving hopes and fears." Marketing decision makers have seldom had the time to wait for the results of marketing research and marketing science studies that would advance their knowledge by "slow increments." The result is that most marketing managers base their decisions on conceptual models of the marketplace that are part fact and part imagination. Like Christopher Columbus, who died believing that the island of Cuba was the east coast of Asia, the misconceptions of marketing managers will never be corrected by monitoring the same data in the same way as they have in the past.

Marketing Science Developments

Powerful marketing research methodologies and promising marketing science models have been developed for a broad range of marketing activities and companies now have a great deal of experience in using them to improve the quality of their marketing decision making. Many companies have perceived sufficient value in the application of marketing science that they have established support groups to do in-house studies or work with consultants. The author's experience indicates that the percent of companies involved and the breadth of the research efforts by the technical support groups and external consulting firms in the 1980s is increasing significantly. The disappointing aspect of all this technical progress is that, although there is ample evidence that a body of useful tools has been developed, its effect on decision making in many situations is minimal.

The study of marketing science models and research techniques has been greatly facilitated in the past five years by the publication of two very good textbooks. We will not attempt here to duplicate their coverage of this material, which provides the basis for the marketing science applications in these cases. Readers with substantive interest in the technical details of the models should read one of the following:

Lilien, Gary L., and Philip Kotler. *Marketing Decision Making: A Model Building Approach.* New York: Harper and Row, 1983.

Urban, Glen L., and John R. Hauser. *Design and Marketing of New Products.* Englewood Cliffs, NJ: Prentice Hall, 1980.

In addition, a spreadsheet disk/book package is now available for modeling marketing mix analysis:

Lilien, Gary L. *Market Mix Analysis with Lotus 1-2-3.* Palo Alto, CA: The Scientific Press, 1986.

Computer Hardware Development

Another key development is the availability of computer hardware that delivers adequate computational power at a much lower cost. When the minicomputer was introduced in the 1970s, the cost of obtaining adequate computer power for many marketing management needs was decreased significantly. It became feasible to develop a marketing database separate from the corporate databases that were maintained primarily for accounting purposes. Marketing managers could now determine what data to include in the database, the form in which they were to be stored, and how they should be accessed. The importance of freeing marketing data from the accounting system of the corporation should not be underestimated.

More recently, the microcomputer has provided adequate computational power so that smaller companies and divisions can get control of their own computer systems at a cost of less than $100,000. The personal computer has also increased the capability of an individual manager to interact directly with the marketing computer systems to analyze the implications of research results. The personal computer is a crucially important development, and in fact provides an impetus for the analytical approach developed in this book.

Commercial Databases

Data about the performance of one's own as well as competing products have always been of great interest to marketing managers. The complex distribution channels of many consumer products make it impossible to determine from factory shipment data alone how a product is doing in the field, and these data provide no comparison with other products. The need to know what is happening at the retail and intermediate channel levels, as well as how competitors are doing, has been the impetus behind the emergence of the A.C. Nielsen Company and SAMI as the largest marketing research organizations in the U.S. Most major consumer product firms buy data from one or both of these companies. The same data needs have led to various industry organizations within specific markets.

In recent years a number of other new databases and research methodologies have greatly expanded the type and quality of information that are available. Just as the microscope and the telescope expanded the range of phenomena that could be observed in medicine and astronomy, recent developments in marketing measurement may prove just as important to marketing management and marketing science. A number of these databases are encountered in the cases.

Marketing Decision Support Systems

In the previous section we discussed the importance of a number of recent developments in marketing research, marketing science, and computer technology in providing an environment in which the analytical power available to a marketing manager can be significantly increased. It is the power of a unifying concept, however, that transforms these developments from academically interesting diversions and expensive machinery into a practical management and research tool. The concept of a Marketing Decision Support System is important because it changes the nature of the interaction between manager and researcher from one of limited communication with each other into a cooperative, interactive environment. A Marketing Decision Support System (MDSS) is defined as:

> A coordinated collection of data, systems, tools, and techniques with supporting software and hardware by which an organization gathers and interprets relevant information from the business and environment and turns it into a basis for marketing action. [Little 1979, p. 11]

The particular strengths of an MDSS when compared with older concepts are the degree to which flexible inquiry of a database is supported, the analytical power that can be directed at research questions, and the degree to which the results of database inquiries and research studies can be focused on a decision situation (see Lilien and Kotler, 1983, ch. 20). The MDSS provides the manager with personal, direct access to important market information for a wide variety of simple inquiries. It also provides researchers with a powerful research tool to address more complicated questions.

One practical difference between an MDSS and older business system concepts is the degree to which a decision support system provides components that help interpret information as well as merely retrieve and present it. Little's conceptualization of an MDSS (Exhibit 1.1) is a flexible system that allows a manager to address a wide variety of questions in what is called a "semi-structured environment," and receive answers that are not merely predesigned reports. The components of the MDSS are *models, statistics, data,* and an *optimization capability.* This configuration has proven to be a valuable tool for marketing researchers and management scientists in applications ranging from quick and accurate responses to a marketing manager's questions about product performance to extensive research projects requiring substantial database manipulation and sophisticated statistical analysis. Commercial MDSS systems have progressed in simplifying the interaction between the MDSS and the user to the point that straightforward database inquiries are feasible for managers as well as researchers. Two interesting descriptions of the use of MDSSs in consumer and industrial products companies can be found in Struse [1985] and Lillis and McIvor [1985].

Recently, managerial interest in financial planning models has led suppliers of marketing DSSs to include financial planning capabilities, graphics, and the ability to do both sensitivity and scenario analysis. At the same time, suppliers of financial planning systems are increasing the database management and statistical capabilities of their systems.

Despite the analytical power resident in a powerful MDSS, the conceptualization of its role in managerial decision making has been somewhat weak. In Exhibit 1.1 the interaction between the manager and the MDSS is in the form of question and answer, but this doesn't adequately describe what a manager requires to increase his or her analytical capability and receive decision-making support.

The requirements that an MDSS must fulfill in order to support managerial decision making requires more careful consideration. On the one hand, decision support from an MDSS includes much more than the mere provision of information, and leaving the manager to decide what it means and how to use it. On the other hand, decision support doesn't include making decisions—that is the role of the manager. Therefore, the response of a decision support system to a manager's question should not be limited to just providing information, nor should it provide a decision; but rather, it should provide a capability that enables the decision maker to make a better decision.

Exhibit 1.1   Marketing Decision Support System (MDSS) Components

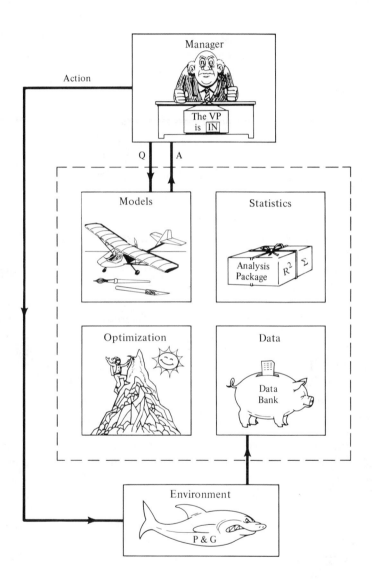

Source: John D. C. Little, "Decision Support Systems for Marketing Managers," *Journal of Marketing,* Vol. 43, No. 3 (Summer 1979), p. 10. Used with permission.

Managerial decision making would be supported if the manager were provided with a *capability* to determine *what* is happening, *why* it is happening, and *what* would happen if a particular action were taken. In other words:

*Decision support should provide a manager with the capability of determining the **status** of products and markets, an **explanation** of what is happening, and the capability to explore the **implications** of proposed actions or anticipated changes in the marketplace.*

This is a key concept, and we will be referring to these three levels of decision support throughout the book.

Market Response Functions

One of the most important contributions that marketing decision support systems make is the ability to develop mathematical relationships between market conditions, marketing actions, and market results such as sales or market share predictions. Such relationships are called *market response functions*, and they form the foundation of quantitative analysis of market situations. Although the development of market response functions has been a primary focus of marketing science in the past and a number of useful insights have resulted, the impact of this research on managerial decision making has been far less than the results have warranted. This is due primarily to two factors: (1) the researcher may not recognize the manager's need to explore the managerial implications of the market response function; and (2) there has not been a good interface between the manager and response functions. What has been needed is a manager-friendly computer model that incorporates the market response function in a quantitative framework that directly addresses the manager's decision situation and success criteria. As compared to the general MDSS, such models provide a more focused analytical capability in a particular decision situation. We will call such limited-scope MDSSs *decision models* and they will be discussed in more detail later in this chapter.

The relationship between these three elements can be summarized as follows: A powerful analytical tool called a *marketing decision support system* greatly increases, among other things, researchers' ability to develop *marketing response functions* or mathematical relationships between market conditions, marketing actions, and market share or sales. Marketing response functions are integrated into a computer model that expresses the manager's quantitative decision-making framework to produce a powerful decision support tool called a *decision model*.

Making Marketing Science Useful for Decision Making

Despite the many potentially useful marketing models and marketing research techniques, their explicit use in marketing decision making is rare because the results have not been made available to decision makers in an acceptable form. Results are usually presented in the form of hard-copy research reports including a recommendation, and the integration of the results into the decision-making process is left to the decision maker. Since the manager can only use the results intuitively, the impact of most marketing research and marketing science studies on decision making has been, at most, informal and intuitive.

Customarily, marketing scientists assume that providing a technical report and a recommendation is providing decision support, and decision makers insist on receiving a recommendation. The problems implicit in this practice are illustrated in the following situation.

The Marketing Science Dilemma

Suppose a marketing scientist has been asked to analyze a situation and provide the manager with a recommendation. After completing the analysis (possibly using an MDSS), the marketing scientist prepares a report that includes both a recommendation and supporting analysis. If the recommendation is different than the manager had expected, it doesn't matter how well the analysis was done or how thoughtfully the marketing scientist prepared the recommendation—the manager will question the result. The decision maker will soon find an aspect of the problem that has not been considered or a situation in which the recommendation would be questionable, so the recommendation will appear to the decision maker to be seriously flawed. Even if the decision maker *agrees* with the recommendation, the insights gained in the study will only be used informally in the decision-making process. Since the decision still has to be made, it is made without any rigorous input from what might have been a valuable study. The decision maker has behaved rationally, but still wishes that somehow the uncertainty in the decision process could have been reduced.

The marketing scientist correctly observes that in this study everything went quite well until a recommendation was made, and so resolves in the future not to present one, but rather to provide a set of reasonable alternatives so that the decision maker can choose his or her own recommendation! But at the presentation, the decision maker presses the marketing scientist to endorse one alternative or another, until the marketing scientist finally makes a recommendation. The presentation has now degenerated into the previous unproductive format, with the same result.

Both the manager and the marketing scientist want marketing science to work, but despite their favorable inclinations, it doesn't! The marketing scientist's analysis cannot possibly include all of the important factors the manager believes should be considered—so the marketing scientist can't expect to make an acceptable recommendation, and the manager can't ignore personal experience and accept an inadequate recommendation, even while respecting the analysis that went into it.

> *The marketing science dilemma is that there appears to be no way for marketing science to ever impact marketing decision making even though both the manager and the marketing scientist want it to work.*

The solution to the dilemma is found in changing the nature of the research output. As long as decision makers insist on getting answers and marketing scientists supply them, all the analytical tools of marketing science will have only a minimal impact on decision making. However, if the marketing scientist produces an analytical tool rather than an answer, then the decision maker, or the decision maker and the marketing scientist working in concert, can develop and evaluate alternatives and explore the implications of various decisions. The manager then makes the decision while still benefiting from the marketing scientist's insight and analysis.

This logical solution is more easily said than done, of course, and there are a number of very good reasons why it hasn't been accomplished more often. The next section discusses in more detail how marketing scientists have attempted to make marketing science more useful to managers in the past, and why it hasn't been successful. This is the central dilemma of marketing science as well as the problem that provides the basis for the analytical approach proposed in this book.

Indirect Decision Maker Access to the MDSS

The interaction between marketing management and marketing science in the marketing science literature has been envisioned by most marketing scientists as a pair of one-way communications preceding and following a research study. This is also the form that most marketing research projects have followed in practice. In the MDSS conceptualization in Exhibit 1.1, the impression is that the manager poses a question to the MDSS and gets an answer—there is nothing to suggest a dialogue. This is not Little's intention. He has been instrumental in the development of a commercially available MDSS that is designed to promote dialogue as much as possible.

Even when MDSSs are designed to facilitate communication between the decision maker and the MDSS, this dialogue, when it occurs at all, has been almost exclusively at the *status*, or basic data inquiry level. In situations in which more extensive or sophisticated analysis was necessary, interaction between the decision maker and the MDSS has occurred through a technical research specialist in the form of a research project that begins with a question posed to the marketing

Exhibit 1.2   Researcher-Oriented MDSS

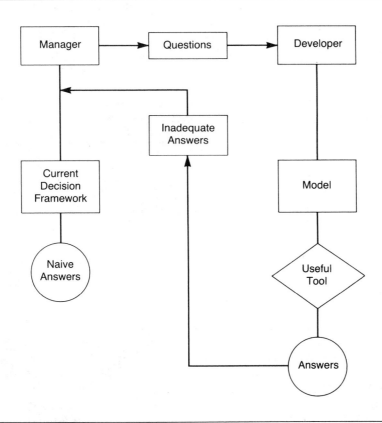

scientist and ends with a formal written report, often including a recommendation.

The marketing scientist is the interrogator of the MDSS, and the decision maker has no direct contact with the MDSS. This has often been necessary because the nature of the inquiry requires more technical training and time than a decision maker could be expected to have. In the hands of a technical specialist, the integrated database, flexible inquiry capability, statistical library, and the simulation and optimization capabilities of the MDSS have made it a powerful research tool, but the presentation of the results to the decision maker has resulted in the marketing science dilemma presented in the previous section.

Even when the decision maker has found the results of the research project and the recommendation to be potentially useful, it has been difficult for the research results to impact decision making. Exhibit 1.2 graphically depicts the problem. We see that the interaction begins with the definition of a problem that started a research effort by the marketing scientist. In order to address the problem, the marketing scientist develops a mathematical model or does some kind of quantitative analysis (ideally within an MDSS), and arrives at some research findings or a recommendation. The recommendation is transmitted to the decision maker. However, the decision maker receives no support in integrating these findings into his or her existing quantitative decision framework, and the recommendations and insights can only be used informally by the decision maker. In particular, the research results cannot be used to explore their implications for various alternative courses of action. As a result, the insights derived from the research provide inadequate answers to managerial questions. Most decision makers lack the necessary skill to explicitly incorporate the results of the research into their own quantitative decision framework.

Although many MDSSs provide the software to do so, few marketing scientists seem to understand the importance of integrating research results into the decision maker's existing decision framework. The result is that, although the results of the analysis may have been important, the decision maker receives, at best, intuitive decision support.

Time-Sharing Access to the MDSS

Recognizing that the MDSS provided a powerful analytical tool for developing both an understanding of a decision situation and a recommendation, the natural thing for the marketing scientists to do was to provide the decision maker with access to the same analytical system (Exhibit 1.3). Until recently, because of technological limitations and high cost, this approach occurred primarily through time-sharing on large mainframe computers, whether an in-house computer or an external consultant's. While this solution has an immediate intuitive appeal, it has not proven to be very effective for a number of reasons, not the least of which is that, until recently, the interaction protocols with mainframe computers were complex, tedious, and unattractive—in other words, not manager-friendly.

A further reason for the lack of success of the time-sharing approach lies in the fact that the marketing scientist and the decision maker are not necessarily interested in the same issues, even when addressing the same problem. Marketing scientists are interested in optimal solutions to restricted mathematical problems, efficient means of obtaining them, and the statistical properties of the solutions. An MDSS that supports their efforts typically utilizes complex mathematical procedures that efficiently seek out an optimal solution to the mathematical problem. The user interface is often esoteric, difficult to adapt, poorly documented, and sometimes only usable by its developer. Developing attractive, flexible, and generally foolproof interfaces requires considerable time and effort, and the manager-friendly interface has not been important for the marketing scientist's personal use of the MDSS or decision models.

Exhibit 1.3   Researcher-Oriented MIS with Manager Access to Model

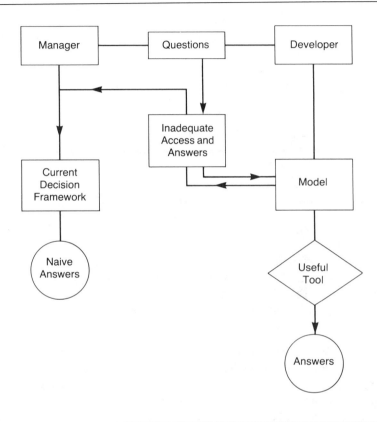

Decision makers, on the other hand, are seldom interested in optimal solutions to a precisely defined mathematical problem, because all of the aspects of
the real-world managerial problem are not included in it. Usually they need a decision model that allows them to examine alternatives that are not optimal solutions to the abstract mathematical problem, but nevertheless make sense in the
manager's broader context. The user interface for a manager needs to be much
more flexible than that for a marketing scientist, and it needs to require little or
no understanding of how the MDSS or decision model works. This type of interface is much more demanding to develop than most marketing scientists have
been willing or able to produce on time-shared mainframe computers.

Finally, the output of the marketing scientist's model within the MDSS seldom includes the exact data or deals with the exact situation that the decision
maker needs to address his own quantitative analysis. This leaves the manager
with the same familiar problem: even though the manager has the benefit of di-

rect use of the MDSS, he or she still lacks the skill to integrate the results explicitly into the existing decision making framework. The result has been that when decision makers have personally accessed an MDSS through time-sharing, it has been for *status*, or basic data retrieval. Some *explanation* has taken place, but the results of such insight have only been used informally in decision making, and the decision maker has been unable to explore the *implications* of the research results on alternative decisions.

Decision Maker Access to a Decision Model

A number of commercially available MDSS systems are capable of providing a suitable interface for a manager to address the MDSS for the purposes of determining status. The same systems also provide the opportunity to develop easy-to-use programs, or *decision models*, that access an MDSS so that a manager can explore the implications of research results.

The "What if....?" capability of decision models is usually much smaller in scale than the general-purpose MDSS, and if a suitable MDSS is not available, the use of spreadsheet software such a Lotus 1-2-3 on a personal computer provides a convenient vehicle to develop a "What if....?" capability incorporating research results for problems of a fairly substantial size. A decision model differs from a full-blown MDSS in a number of ways:

> It is designed to address a more limited and specific set of questions rather than to provide flexible inquiry of the entire database.

> It incorporates the *results* of a research project, (usually in the form of a response function), rather than being a vehicle for doing more research.

> It explicitly expresses the manager's existing quantitative decision framework.

> It integrates the response function, or other results of the research with the quantitative decision framework.

It is much easier to develop decision models within an MDSS that includes a financial planning capability, because the financial planning module provides a relatively easy-to-use managerial interface similiar to the spreadsheets that marketing managers are accustomed to using in planning and reporting.

The use of a decision model by a decision maker is presented in Exhibit 1.4, but before discussing its use, let's discuss its components. Most managers have a quantitative decision framework they use to evaluate plans and report performance to top management. One of the problems we've seen in the previous two sections is that this framework has not been explicitly expressed in a spreadsheet, or if it has, the results of the research have not been integrated into it, and research has had only an informal and inexplicit role in decision making. A managerially useful MDSS *must* explicitly include the decision maker's decision

Exhibit 1.4   Manager-Oriented MDSS

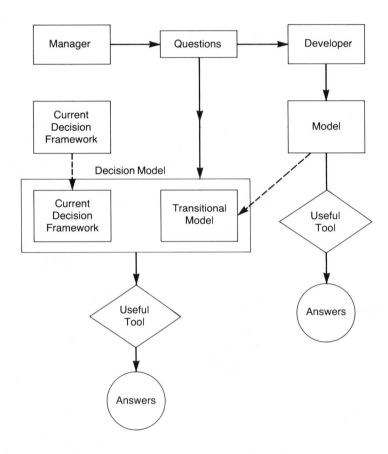

framework in the decision model, and the response function or other research results *must* be explicitly integrated with it. If this isn't done, then the decision maker must again manually extract values from the research results and informally try to apply them, and this approach will be just as ineffective as the other approaches we've considered.

Since the manager's use of a decision model may not be consistent with the intent of the marketing scientist's it may be necessary to modify the marketing scientist's research model. This modified analytical model needs to capture the essence of the relationships in the marketing scientist's model, but it may need to be directed at a different set of questions. We will call this modified analytical model a *transitional model*, since it provides a transition between the marketing scientist's research-oriented models and the explicit expression of the decision maker's existing quantitative framework.

Sometimes the transitional model will just be the market response function that resulted from a research project, and its inclusion in a spreadsheet format is very simple. In other situations, the transitional model must have a very different character than the researcher's model. The intention of the decision model is to provide the decision maker with an analytical tool rather than an answer, and thereby solve the marketing science dilemma.

> When the marketing scientist provides this tool to the decision maker, the decision model becomes a starting point from which the decision maker and marketing scientist can work together to formulate a recommendation that embodies both of their unique competencies.

The decision maker may develop the capability to personally use the MDSS in many instances, but may still wish to rely on the marketing scientist to do more extensive analysis or to investigate new scenarios that require additional technical expertise.

The delivery of a decision model, as well as the willingness of the marketing scientist and decision maker to work together to arrive at a recommendation, results in objective marketing research having an impact on decision making, and provides a solution to the marketing dilemma.

The Importance of Financial Spreadsheet Models

A decision model can be developed from most commercially available MDSSs that feature a financial planning module and/or the capability of developing menu-driven application programs for managerial use. The main reason this hasn't been done more often is that the direct users of current MDSS systems are, by and large, researchers rather than managers. A number of manager-oriented MDSSs have been developed on mainframes or mini-computers. For example, the market simulation analysis model in the Clark Equipment cases in Chapter 4, and the sales force strategy model in the Syntex Laboratories cases in Chapter 6 were both made available to the companies for which they were built through time-sharing on the consultant's computers.

Easy-to-use personal computer spreadsheet models have greatly decreased the amount of computer expertise required to use a computer, and a Lotus 1-2-3 or similar spreadsheet is a much more attractive and easy-to-use interface for a decision maker than those available on most mainframe computers, either in-house or through time-sharing. It's easy to transport a small decision model on a personal computer from one location to one in another. A final advantage of spreadsheet programs on personal computers is that it's easy to develop models like the ones found in this book—after all, the author wrote these, and he's not a programming expert by any means. In other words, if you have learned or are willing to learn to use a personal computer spreadsheet model in order to do financial analysis, the development of decision models incorporating marketing response functions is not a difficult additional step.

In Chapter 2, we will take a closer look at analytical decision making and its role in product development, and we'll outline the commonly used types of models, with an introduction to the Lotus 1-2-3 spreadsheets in this book.

References and Background Readings

Amstutz, A. E. *Computer Simulation of Competitive Market Response*. Cambridge, MA: M.I.T. Press, 1967.

Barabba, Vincent P. "Steel Axes for Stone Age Men." In Robert D. Buzzell's *Marketing in an Electronic Age*. Boston: Harvard Business School Press, 1985.

Bass, Frank M., et al. *Mathematical Models and Methods in Marketing*. Homewood, IL: Irwin, 1961.

Bass, Frank M., Charles W. King, and Edgar A. Pessemier (eds.). *Applications of the Sciences in Marketing Management*. New York: John Wiley and Sons, 1968.

Debruicker, F. Stewart, and David J. Reibstein. *Cases in Marketing Research*. Englewood Cliffs, NJ: Prentice Hall, 1983.

Hogarth, Robin M., and Spyros Makridakis. "The Value of Decision-Making in a Complex Environment: An Experimental Approach." *Management Science*, Vol. 27, No. 1 (January 1981), pp. 93–106.

Lilien, Gary L., and Philip Kotler. *Marketing Decision Making: A Model Building Approach*. New York: Harper and Row, 1983.

Lillis, Charles M., and Bonnie J. McIvor. "MDSSs at General Electric: Implications for the 1990s from Experiences in the 1970s and 1980s." In Robert D. Buzzell, *Marketing in an Electronic Age*. Boston: Harvard Business School Press, 1985.

Little, John D. C. "Decision Support Systems for Marketing Managers." *Journal of Marketing*. Vol. 43, No. 3 (Summer 1979), p. 11.

Montgomery, David B., and Glen L. Urban. *Management Science in Marketing*. Englewood Cliffs, NJ: Prentice Hall, 1969.

Parsons, Leonard J., and Randall Schultz. *Marketing Models and Econometric Research*. New York: Elsevier North Holland, 1976.

Schultz, Randall L., and Andris A. Zoltners. *Marketing Decision Models*. New York: Elsevier North Holland, 1981.

Struse, Rudolf W. III. "The Four P's of Marketing Decision Support Systems: Promises, Payoffs, Paradoxes, and Prognostications." In Robert D. Buzzell's *Marketing in an Electronic Age*. Boston: Harvard Business School Press, 1985.

2

An Introduction to Analytical Decision Making

The extensive marketing research and marketing science literatures have presented today's manager with a broad range of mathematical models and statistical tools with which to interpret data. Commercial data sources now provide the manager with marketing information of greater breadth, accuracy, and significance than yesterday's managers would have dreamed possible. The *marketing decision support system (MDSS)*, when combined with the new data sources, has provided marketing researchers with an extremely powerful tool for investigating how marketing actions affect marketing phenomena. One of the major benefits of the MDSS is the increased analytical power it provides researchers for developing explanations of the market's response to marketing actions. These measures of *market response* may vary from a few measurements—for example, the proportion of potential consumers that will try a new product—to explicit mathematical relationships that we call *market response functions*.

In Chapter 1 we said that marketing science has not had an impact on decision making commensurate with its potential, because most researchers have been content to provide insight on the status of markets, explanations of marketing phenomena, or recommendations, and have not provided managers with tools that would enable them to examine the implications of the research findings. We introduced the *decision model*, which is a less general version of a manager-oriented MDSS focusing directly on relating research findings to the manager's existing quantitative decision framework.

In this chapter we will propose an approach to analytical decision making that begins with the manager's analysis of the decision situation and ends with the development of a decision model with which the manager can personally explore the implications of marketing research and make his or her own decisions. This approach is intensely pragmatic rather than scholarly, and the goal is to enable valuable research to make an impact on decision making.

Every effort has been made to make the decision models in this casebook as simple as possible. One of the main messages of this approach is that the impact of most marketing research efforts, no matter how sophisticated their design, can be significantly increased if they are integrated into simple spreadsheet models for marketing managers to use in their decision making.

An Approach to Analytical Decision Making

The biggest problem in utilizing marketing science to its full potential is that the manager's analysis of the decision situation is often inadequate to define either the dimensions of the problem or what information is required to make the decision. The crucial first step in good *quantitative* analysis is a sound *qualitative* analysis of the managerial issues in a decision situation. The approach to analytical decision making presented here can be summarized in these seven steps:

1. Carefully analyze the managerial decision situation.
2. Conceptualize the underlying marketing process.
3. Develop and use a simple spreadsheet model for sensitivity analysis to identify critical information needs.
4. Design a marketing research study to obtain the information identified as critical.
5. Develop a decision model that integrates the marketing research findings with the quantitative decision-making framework.
6. Do sensitivity and scenario analysis using the decision model to understand the decision situation.
7. Make the decision using the insights developed through the analytical process.

The cases in this book deal with the efforts of major American corporations to use marketing research and marketing science. Most of these companies used state-of-the-art applications that represent reasonably good practice. The cases do not provide examples of managers and researchers following the decision framework recommended here, but they do represent what typically happens when a consultant presents the results of a marketing research study to the client. It is not presently standard practice for consultants to provide decision models to clients, but only the results of the study.

The research efforts in the cases were well done, but the author contends that the use of the above analytical procedures could have: (1) improved the applicability of the research, (2) increased the satisfaction of the client with the consultant's work, and (3) increased the impact of the research on decision making. The decision models that accompany the cases were developed by the author independently from the companies in the cases. They are intended to demonstrate how simple decision models—which can be developed in a few hours—can make good research more useful.

Managerial Benefits of the Analytical Process

The most apparent managerial benefit of such an analytical process is that it results in better decisions, but the reasons for this are not as obvious as it might at first seem. Probably the most important benefit is the increased depth of the manager's understanding of the decision situation, which results from participating in the analyses and research processes and in the development and use of the decision model. Through participation in the development and use of a decision model, a decision maker can expect a number of benefits:

1. An increased understanding of a decision situation through the analytical rigor that is required in order to make an explicit statement of important factors and the relationships between them

2. An increased capacity to understand the relative importance of multiple factors and a lessened tendency to believe that a single factor controls the situation

3. An increased capacity to consider and evaluate alternative marketing programs

4. An increased capacity to analyze alternatives more completely

5. A final decision drawn from the total analytical experience rather than the adoption of a specific alternative evaluated using the decision model

A decision maker only receives these benefits by supervising the research and the development of the decision model and being personally involved in its analytical use. Since most decision makers have neither the technical training nor the time for extensive involvement in model development and analysis, some compromises must be made. The personal involvement of the decision maker is most crucial at the initial stages of designing the marketing research and decision model, and in the early stages of scenario definition and analysis. Involvement at these two critical stages is not only necessary to assure that the research and decision model address the important managerial issues, but also for the decision maker to enjoy the benefits listed above.

Managerial Roles in the Analytical Process

Once the direction of the research and modeling effort is firmly established with the involvement of the decision maker, a period of extensive effort and analysis follows that frequently requires more technical expertise and almost certainly more time than most decision makers are able to provide. Supervision of the development process beyond this point consists primarily of meetings to review progress and assure that the goals of the model developers are still congruent with those of the decision maker; this should not require large amounts of time or technical expertise.

> *A manager without technical training can effectively evaluate decision models and understand marketing research projects by using common sense to evaluate three elements: the **decision situation** itself, the **market response model**, and the **data** being used.*

Let's define and then take a closer look at these three key elements.

> *Decision situation evaluation.* Make sure that the decision model addresses the managerial considerations and that the analytical technique chosen is appropriate to the decision situation.

> *Market response model evaluation.* Acquire intuitive understanding of both the potential and the limitations of the market response model.

Data evaluation. Evaluate data quality and appropriateness by paying careful attention to the details of how the data are defined and the procedures used to collect them.

These three considerations provide the basis for evaluating advanced analytical techniques in marketing decision making. The following sections provide an overview of each area.

Decision Situation: New Product Development

The new product development process and subsequent profit management after the product is introduced provide a convenient organization for a discussion of decision situations, and Chapters 3 through 6 are organized around this sequence. There are a number of new product development processes in the literature, but a modification of the new product decision process presented in Urban and Hauser (1980, p. 33) closely fits the research approach in most of the cases here. Their book is an excellent reference work containing an extensive explanation of many of the marketing models and research techniques found in the cases.

The new product development process subjects each new product concept to a series of tests—preliminary economic analysis, market research studies, more extensive economic analysis, and test marketing—in order to reject weak product concepts as early in the process as possible. Only the surviving new product concepts are passed on to the next, more expensive step. While the expected cost of introducing one successful new product is minimized through such a process, the danger of rejecting other potentially successful products is high. Since many of the cases span more than one stage in this new product development process,

Exhibit 2.1 New Product Development Process

Opportunity Identification and Product Design
    Market definition
    Product positioning
    Product engineering
    Forecasting sales potential
Pre–Test Market Testing
Test Marketing and New Product Introduction
Profit Management

Source: Modified from Urban and Hauser 1980, p. 33.

Exhibit 2.2   Estimated Time and Investment for Development of New Products ($000's)

| | Consumer Goods | | Industrial Goods | |
	Time	Cost	Time	Cost
Opportunity Identification	5 months	$ 100	NA	$ 50
Design	6	200	NA	620
Testing	12	1,050	NA	290
Introduction	4*	5,000	NA	1,270
Total	27 months	$6,350		$2,230

*Time to set up the introduction

Source: Adapted from Urban and Hauser 1980, pp. 47 – 52.

it is convenient to group Urban and Hauser's stages into the more condensed classification scheme shown in Exhibit 2.1.

The basic assumptions of this new product development process are:

1. The introduction of new products is such a major undertaking that few companies have the resources for more than one at a time.
2. The likelihood that a new product idea will develop into a successful new product is quite small.
3. The new product development process can be broken down into a number of logical steps requiring various degrees of effort and commitment.
4. The cost of introducing a successful new product can be minimized by eliminating weak new product candidates as early in the process as possible.

The Expected Cost of a Successful New Product

The financial resources and time required for developing new products are substantial for both industrial and consumer products. The drain on a company's creative energies and managerial capabilities is also so substantial that even large companies find their human resources as severe a constraint as their financial limitations in terms of the number of new products they can afford to introduce. Exhibit 2.2 provides an estimate of the average time and investment required for the development of new products.

As substantial as these costs are, they do not present an accurate picture, because they do not reflect the cost of other new product proposals that were developed, carried through at least part of the development process, and then rejected. Since it is impossible to know at the beginning of the process which products will be introduced and through how many stages a concept will progress before it is rejected, one must consider that the true cost of one successful new product includes the total cost of evaluating *all* the company's new product ideas.

According to Urban and Hauser, the average new consumer product introduction costs about $5 million, and only about one out of five new consumer product introductions in the U.S. are successful (0.19). Such products have usually undergone a fairly rigorous evaluation of some sort prior to introduction, so one should not assume that if a company casually arrived at five new product ideas, one would be successful. An average company with a goal of one successful new product introduction each year—would have to expect to introduce about five new products each year, and the *expected* cost of this one successful new product introduction would also have to include the cost of the four introductions that failed. More precisely, the expected cost of introducing one successful new product per year would be:

average cost per introduction/probability of success, or

$5 million / 0.19 = $26.3 million/year

Suppose, however, that a consumer product company instigates a new product development process that includes the steps introduced above with the following average costs and results:

1. An *opportunity identification* procedure costing $100,000 is instigated to perform a preliminary estimation of the economic potential of a particular new product idea. This step includes a preliminary economic analysis.

2. A design analysis procedure costing $200,000 is used that reduces by 50 percent the number of new product designs or ideas receiving further consideration. This step includes a more rigorous economic analysis.

3. A *pre–test market test* is used that costs about $50,000 and results in only 60 percent of the new products tested progressing to the test market stage.

4. Finally a *test market* costing $1 million is performed, with the result that only 80 percent of the new products tested are introduced.

5. The result of this process is that 85 percent of the *introductions* of new products surviving this process are successful in the marketplace.

The expected probability of a successful new product emerging from this new product development process is still roughly 0.19 (.5 ∗ .6 ∗ .8 ∗ .85), but the expected cost of introducing one successful new product using this new product development process is much less because potential new products are eliminated earlier in the process. See Exhibit 2.3 for a summary of these costs.

The expected net benefit from this new product development process is $26.3 million − $8.56 million = $17.74 million, a substantial savings that provides ample evidence of why new product development processes similar to this have been adopted by so many major innovative firms. Executing this type of program

Exhibit 2.3   Expected Cost Using the New Product Development Process

	Average Cost ($000)	Probability of Success	Expected Cost ($000)
Opportunity identification	$ 100		$ 100
Design	200	0.50	980
Testing			
Pre-test market	50	0.60	123
Test market	1,000	0.80	1,471
Total development cost			$2,674
Introduction	5,000	0.85	5,882
Total expected cost			$8,556

Source: Urban and Hauser, p. 57.

in practice is complicated by the self-interest of individuals whose personal success and failure are tied to specific product opportunities, even though the need for, and the benefits of, such a process from the standpoint of the company are quite generally understood.

The steps in the new product development process provide a convenient framework for organizing the chapters and cases in this book, since marketing science applications at similar stages in the process address similar problems, pursue similar goals, and provide similar opportunities.

Opportunity Identification and Design

An attractive new product opportunity requires not only an interesting new product concept but also the existence of a sufficiently large number of potential customers to justify the effort of developing, producing, and marketing the product. Exploiting an interesting product opportunity calls for creativity, careful planning, and effective implementation. The most difficult of these activities to analyze is creativity, but this does not necessarily imply that quantitative analysis is antithetical to creativity. There is a great benefit in requiring creative people to be analytical in the evaluation of their ideas, because the criteria that business uses to evaluate ideas is not whether or not they are creative, but whether or not they make money. The need to both identify and quantify the market potential of a product concept imposes a necessary discipline on the evaluation of creative ideas and provides the means of objectively choosing between alternatives.

Several activities are involved in opportunity identification and product design:

Market definition is the determination of the customer population that will be potential customers for the new product. The market definition provides a foundation for matching buyer needs to product benefits. A fundamental consideration in market definition is the idea of market segmentation, or the splitting of the customer base into relatively homogeneous subpopulations. Markets are commonly segmented by demographics, psychographics, product benefits sought, price sensitivity, and so on. The set of customers for which a product is intended is called the *target market*. The target market provides a definition of the potential customers for the product that can be used to quantify the magnitude of the market opportunity.

Product positioning is the determination of the benefits that will be stressed in offering the product to the target market. The product position also specifies how it compares to competitive products and the rest of the company's own product line. Advertising copy is a key vehicle for communicating the product position of a product.

Forecasting market potential is the process of quantifying the results of marketing a new product. The term *market potential* is frequently used to refer to two quite different quantities: the total quantity of a product that might be demanded in the absence of any marketing considerations, or the level of sales that a product could attain with the maximum marketing resources that could be expected from a particular marketing strategy. Both of these quantities are useful to know. The first is particularly valuable at the early stages of product planning because it can be used as a ceiling for determining the appropriate level of investment in the new product. The latter is useful for evaluating the potential of a particular marketing strategy as well as the quality of execution of the strategy.

Product engineering is the process of converting the abstract product position into a viable product or service. The product should be perceived by the potential customers in the target market as the embodiment of the product position. This is much easier said than done, and making sure this matching of product perception and product position occurs is one of the frequent goals of market research and market testing.

Pre–Test Market Testing

A pre–test market test is an integrated series of careful measurements and analyses in a controlled environment. According to Levine [1981], the objectives of a pre–test market research program are:

1. To develop volume estimates for test market planning
2. To provide a disaster check, since this is the first time a total marketing plan is exposed to the consumer
3. To provide information for modification of marketing programs prior to test marketing
4. To obtain diagnostic information on product performance, the impact of advertising, and pricing [p. 286]

Pre–test market testing has become quite common in recent years and it has been estimated that more than 1300 pre–test market tests had been done by the early 1980s. Pre–test market testing is intended to increase the effectiveness of test marketing. However, the success of pre–test market testing procedures has led some managers to rely heavily on them, and in some cases test markets are skipped. In fact, until recently, more progress had been made in pre–testing than had been made in test marketing, and some managers have more confidence in the pre–test markets than in the test markets. An interesting managerial issue that will emerge in the cases in Chapter 4 is whether or not a successful pre–test market test is an adequate substitute for a test market.

Test Marketing and New Product Introduction

The most commonly held view of test marketing is that it is intended to replicate the new product introduction plan, or some important part of it, on a smaller, more manageable scale. In reality this ideal can seldom be reached because the accurate measurement of the effect of one part of the marketing plan is best done by controlling the effects of other parts of the marketing plan. For example, if one wishes to determine the appropriate advertising level in a test market, it is usually considered essential to force distribution of the product so it will be available for purchase. Clearly, this masks the measurement of advertising's effect on distribution and the ability of the sales force to gain distribution.

Although test markets are costly and time consuming, they result in a substantial reduction in the expected cost of the new product introduction. They are often considered necessary because the damage done to a company's reputation by a poorly conceived national introduction extends beyond the cost of the failed introduction to include the loss of an opportunity to introduce another product and damage to the company's reputation with its distribution channels.

This loss is so substantial that one would expect most companies to be so conservative that no product would be introduced without sound market testing. In fact, many products are introduced without testing because the test market itself has risks associated with it that must be weighed against the risk of new product failure. First of all, there is no guarantee that a test market will provide accurate results. Test markets have frequently produced inconclusive results, so that the time and expense of the testing do not contribute to a resolution of the uncertainties involved. In other cases, the testing results are actually misleading, and a potentially good product may be rejected because its potential was underestimated, or a poor product may attain sales levels in the test market that can't be sustained in the marketplace. Since the test market is also a public display of the new product and the company's marketing plans for it, there is also a risk that competitors may steal the concept and introduce a competing product with much less development time and cost. Chapter 5 includes a more complete discussion of test marketing.

Profit Management

After the new product has been introduced, marketing programs must be developed and implemented that maintain a level of sales, growth, and net contribution to profit that justifies the continued commitment of company resources to it. The introduction of competitive products may require that the product be modified, or there may be an opportunity for the company to expand its product line and introduce companion products. Advertising copy and budgets must be continually analyzed, evaluated, and changed if necessary. Promotional programs must be planned and implemented. The necessary level of sales force effort must be determined and obtained from sales management with internal competition from the company's other products. The product's price in relationship to other products in its product line and competitive products must be carefully determined and coordinated across various levels of distribution.

The profit management of existing products is the heart of introductory marketing management courses; this text assumes that the reader is well acquainted with the basic concepts, and we will not attempt here to summarize these important considerations. The interested student is encouraged to use one of the numerous good marketing management texts as a reference or source of review.

The profit management cases in Chapter 6 deal with advertising, promotion, and sales force management for new products. Product policy and pricing are dealt with in Chapters 4, 5, and 6.

In summary, there are three major reasons for organizing the cases around the stages of new product development:

1. It is the intention of the author to emphasize applications and decision making.

2. It emphasizes that the initial step in the sound application of advanced analytical techniques is a good managerial case analysis. Without this foundation, it is unlikely that marketing research or marketing science will impact decision making no matter how sophisticated or elegant the technical accomplishment.

3. It groups cases of similar research methodology and approach together and minimizes the amount of new learning needed for each case.

Elements of Decision Models

The stages in the new product development process determine to a large extent the appropriate types of analysis to do as well as the degree of effort and resources that should be invested. Not only should new product ideas be rejected as early in the process as possible, but also the marketing research, model development, and analysis appropriate for an early stage should be both less costly and less time consuming than at a later stage.

This seems to make so much sense that it is obvious, but it is a very important point in developing, using, and evaluating decision models. Two errors are commonly made:

1. The research is more extensive than is appropriate and the results are not available when the decision must be made. The cost of such studies needlessly increases the cost of new product development and the results play no role in decision making.

2. The analysis and models used may be appropriate for the decision stage in terms of scope, time, and expense, but are not as complete or empirically based as most researchers and managers would like them to be. Although simple models are very useful at an early stage of new product development, they are frequently rejected by decision makers because some potentially important factors are omitted.

Two keys to the successful application of marketing decision models are to develop models appropriate to the timing and nature of the decision, and to train decision makers to use them for scenario and sensitivity analysis. This preliminary analysis is necessary to identify the level of risk and the factors that are critical to the decision.

Another key to successfully applying marketing decision models is to understand *market response functions,* which are the explicit, mathematical links between the marketing plan, research results, and the financial decision-making criteria of the decision maker.

Market Response Functions

The insightful product manager invests a lot of time in a search for cause and effect in reports of the product's sales performance. The data retrieval and report generation capabilities of an MDSS, which can compare marketing programs with market performance on a region-by-region or product-by-product basis, is a powerful tool that many managers use to great advantage.

The statistical techniques used within an MDSS to develop marketing response functions provide a mathematical explicitness that augments the manager's intuitive understanding of the factors affecting a product's market performance. Market response functions are useful because, to the extent that the manager believes they capture the relationship, they provide a more explicit explanation of how the market works, and they can be used to forecast the sales and market share that will result from a change in the marketing plan.

Market response functions vary considerably from one application to another. A broad variety are presented in the cases, ranging from very simple ones to some of considerable complexity, but it is beyond the scope of this book to attempt a complete taxonomy of market response functions.

*There are three aspects of a market response function that are critical for managers to understand, at least intuitively: the **specification** (shape or functional form) of the market response function; the character of the **data foundation** from which the parameters (or coefficients) of the market response function were estimated; and the **estimation procedure** that was used to estimate the parameters of the market response function.*

Even without technical training, a marketing manager that pays attention to these three aspects of marketing response functions can adequately understand and evaluate a market response function.

Specification

Some market response models are very simple and can be easily graphed so that the shape of the market response function can be seen. If the manager has a graph of the market response function in which the coordinate axes are labeled with the magnitudes of the relevant marketing variables and the response, he or she can develop an adequate understanding of how the market response function relates market response to marketing action. For example, consider market response function A in Exhibit 2.4, which relates sales and advertising. This response function is a simple linear relationship between sales and advertising over a specified advertising range, with no response either below or above that advertising range.

Knowing the mathematical equation for this simple market response function wouldn't add much to the intuitive understanding that comes from looking at the graph. The same is true for market response function B in the same exhibit: the incremental effect of additional advertising expenditures on sales decreases as the advertising level increases. These two market response functions would lead to quite different optimal advertising budgets, but with an appropriate decision model, these two models can easily be evaluated by an insightful manager,

Exhibit 2.4 Two Response Functions

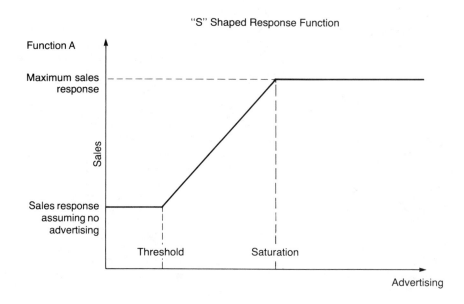

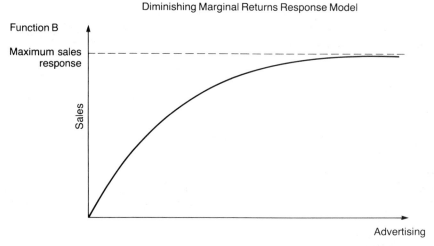

even if the exact mathematical equations are not available. Using the decision model to estimate the response to various levels of advertising, the manager can soon determine which, if either, provides the most reasonable results. Other market response functions are more complicated, may not be graphed, or may not have a single, precise mathematical specification. Such response functions are best understood through simulation and sensitivity analysis.

Estimation

We must all face the fact that our educational choices and past experience place limitations on what we can understand, and other demands on our time limit the investment we're willing to make in studying unfamiliar concepts. This means that the marketing scientist must accept that he will not understand the details of the decision maker's marketing situation as completely as the decision maker does. It also means that the decision maker may not understand in detail how the marketing scientist developed a response function. The place where the decision maker will be most limited and have to rely on the marketing scientist the most is in the estimation procedures used to derive market response functions. This does not mean that decision makers must have blind trust in marketing scientists, for by understanding the shape of the relationship and through hands-on use of the market response function in the decision model to do sensitivity and scenario analysis, they can be satisfied that a market response function is reasonable.

If something is wrong, sensitivity and scenario analysis procedures will show that the market response function is not making reasonable predictions, indicating that the specification is wrong, the data are bad, or the estimation procedure isn't delivering proper parameter estimates. It's the marketing scientist's job to sort out where the problems lie, but the involvement of the decision maker can be very helpful in eliminating specification and data as the culprits.

If the problem lies in the estimation procedure it may require an expert statistician or econometrician to sort things out, since the technical difficulties that are often encountered in marketing applications are not covered in the training that students receive at the MBA or master's level in either of these specialties.

Data Foundation

Another way that market response functions differ is in the types of data from which they are estimated. For managerial purposes it is initially adequate to consider data as one of two basic types:

Objective/Empirical Data.   These data are obtained through objective, quantitative measurement of one type or another. Examples of empirical data that appear in the cases are market surveys, Nielsen and SAMI sales audits, factory shipment records, advertising expenditures, the number of sales representatives, and so on. It is very important for both the marketing scientist and the decision maker to know the definitions of the data measurements and the procedures employed to gather the data. The fact that the data are empirical does not guarantee that they are not subject to *bias*—systematic errors related to the definition and method of measurement. Empirical data also have a random, or statistical, error associated with them. There are statistical procedures that estimate the amount of error in data due to randomness, but bias can only be determined by thoughtful analysis of procedures.

Subjective/Judgmental Data. These data are derived from managerial judgment rather than direct observation and measurement. Subjective or judgmental data are opinions about empirical phenomena that either have not been, or could not be, objectively measured. Examples of judgmental data that appear in the cases include managerial estimates of sales response to future sales force effort, predictions of the level of awareness that an advertising campaign might attain, or the likelihood that the prime interest rate will drop as low as 5 percent in the next five years, and so on.

Market response function A in Exhibit 2.4 is an example of the use of both types of data. The linear part of the response function was estimated from empirical sales and advertising histories, while the turning points were managerial estimates—judgmental data. Judgmental estimates must also be used when managers are considering changing marketing programs, and the company has no experience that provides relevant data.

There is a tendency among marketing scientists to consider empirical data to be superior to judgmental data; while I agree with this in spirit, it sometimes leads to abuse in practice. In order to base an analysis on empirical data, a marketing scientist with this attitude may redefine a problem in a way that neglects important managerial issues. This is much like looking for a lost item where the light is best, rather than where it was lost. Another reason to avoid the conclusion that empirical data is necessarily superior to judgmental data is that the value of data is dependent on its appropriateness for the intended purpose as well as its objectivity, and both empirical and subjective data are subject to various types of biases.

> *It is important to realize that the development of decision models almost always requires the use of both empirical and judgmental data, and the skillful gathering, use, and interpretation of judgmental data are indispensable skills in the design and implementation of effective decision models.*

Although researchers try to replace judgmental data with empirical data as much as possible, it should nevertheless be apparent that the use of judgmental data is indispensable at the early stages of model development and often may be the only data available when a decision has to be made.

Data Evaluation

A further element in the use of data in the development of decision models is data evaluation. The manager's ability to evaluate data quality is critical to the successful use of marketing research information. Since data provide the foundation for estimating the parameters of the response functions, they play a fundamental role in determining the appropriateness of the estimated response to marketing effort. A correctly specified model that is appropriately estimated and insightfully integrated into a decision support system will still not provide acceptable results if it is based on bad data. Understanding the details of the statistical properties of data requires considerable technical sophistication, but a thoughtful manager who is not technically trained can do an adequate job of evaluating data quality and limitations. What is required is that the manager understand a few key data characteristics and be very careful about the nonmathematical details of the data description. These are the major questions that the manager should ask about data:

1. How are the data variables defined?
2. What are the details of the procedures with which the data were collected?
3. What factors were controlled and not controlled in obtaining the data?
4. What are the statistical properties of the data?
5. In what direction will data problems bias the results?

Surprisingly, these questions are not difficult to answer. If the manager asks insightful questions and develops a sensitivity to potential problem situations, a very adequate job of evaluation can be done. Managers should be careful to avoid either blindly accepting data or rejecting it at the first sign of a problem. It is axiomatic that all data are subject to errors of one kind or another—the trick is to understand what the errors are, estimate the effect of the errors, and glean what information one can.

While each case deals with a particular decision situation and one decision model, all of the cases include more than one type of data, and it was not possible to isolate one type of data, or even one set of data considerations. However, the cases dealing with advertising and test marketing do provide a thorough look at the problem of evaluating the *information content* and *statistical control* considerations that are so important in developing the ability to evaluate data quality.

Information Content of Data.   While it might seem strange to talk about the information content of a number—after all, a number is a number—it is a very important consideration. Take the number *five*, for example. The number *five* has a very different meaning if it is used to denote the number of fingers on my right hand, or a rating for the physical attractiveness of members of the opposite sex, or the fifth category out of a list of seven possible groups of occupations, or an estimate of the likely proportion of consumers that will try a product if they are exposed to advertising for it. Each of these number fives utilizes a different definition relating it to some real-world phenomenon, each has different amounts and types of error associated with it, each supports different kinds of arithmetic, or the degree to which it is capable of reproduction by a different observer. All of these properties of numbers are important in understanding the information a number conveys—what we call its information content.

Statistical Control of Data.   The concept of control deals with the degree to which extraneous factors are allowed to affect the measurement of the phenomenon we are studying. The meaning of the numbers that result from an experiment or study are affected by the control that is exerted in their measurement. For example, a sales value of 150, when related to high advertising and price levels, has a very different meaning if it is derived from a controlled experiment than it does if it is a sales audit value from a sales district.

Overview of Market Response Function Types

The complexity of the market response functions in the cases increases as the book progresses—the more simple market response functions are found in the early cases, and the more complex models are introduced after the reader has gained some experience in their use.

The first market response functions we will encounter are the simple estimates of an important value derived from a market research survey. Survey results are often used to provide estimates of the size of markets or market response. Most of the cases include at least some peripheral use of survey results. Financial spreadsheets provide the foundation for our decision model development because they represent the manager's decision-making framework and provide a convenient interface to market response models. The market response function and the spreadsheet are combined to produce a decision model. The decision models in the cases incorporate the following types of models:

> Naive financial spreadsheet models
>
> Naive statistical models
>
> Heuristic models
>
> Decision calculus models
>
> Experimental models
>
> Econometric models

This sequence of decision models is in order of complexity, but does not necessarily express a model development process; that is to say, one shouldn't infer that every heuristic model should necessarily grow up to be an econometric model if the time and resources are available. However, it does make sense to develop simple models as a means of determining what is important enough to require the further development of more complex models.

Naive Financial Spreadsheet Models

The term *naive* will be used to designate a financial spreadsheet model that does not include explicit relationships between marketing actions and marketing re-

Exhibit 2.5   Initial Budget Plan

	Quarters				
	1	2	3	4	Total
Revenue	$6,720	$6,720	$6,720	$6,720	$26,880
– Cost of Goods	$5,040	$5,040	$5,040	$5,040	$20,160
Gross Contribution	$1,680	$1,680	$1,680	$1,680	$6,720
– Advertising Expense	$200	$200	$200	$200	$800
Net Contribution	$1,480	$1,480	$1,480	$1,480	$5,920

sults. This is not meant to imply that the financial modeling involved in the spreadsheet is unsophisticated or lacking in valuable insight, but rather that it provides very little help to a marketing manager in analyzing a marketing decision situation.

Naive financial spreadsheet models are very important to our conceptual approach to the development of managerially oriented marketing decision support systems. The manager's existing quantitative framework, which is one of the two fundamental components of the decision model in Exhibit 1.4, is very likely to be a naive financial spreadsheet model. In the next section we will discuss the importance of integrating market response models into the manager's existing quantitative framework. Perhaps the easiest way to see how a financial spreadsheet can be transformed into a decision model and the difference it makes analytically is through a simple example.

Decision Model Example.   Suppose that the product manager for product X uses a very simple spreadsheet for planning marketing programs. The spreadsheet includes revenue, cost of goods sold (COGS), and advertising expense to compute net contribution to profit. Product X currently sells for $12.00/case and the COGS is $9.00/case. The definitions of the entries in the spreadsheet are as follows:

COGS = 0.75 * revenue

gross contribution = revenue – COGS

net contribution = gross contribution – advertising

where revenue and advertising are input values

The product manager's budget plan (all values are in $1000s) for the year is shown in Exhibit 2.5.

Exhibit 2.6   Revised Forecast Showing Shortfall

		1st Q	2nd Q	3rd Q	4th Q	Total
				Quarters		
Revenue		$6,516	$6,516	$6,516	$6,516	$26,064
Cost of Goods	75%	$4,887	$4,887	$4,887	$4,887	$19,548
Gross Contribution		$1,629	$1,629	$1,629	$1,629	$6,516
Advertising Expense		$200	$200	$200	$200	$800
Net Contribution		$1,429	$1,429	$1,429	$1,429	$5,716

Now suppose that through three quarters product X hasn't been achieving its forecast. When fourth quarter performance is projected to be like the rest of the year, the manager foresees a contribution shortfall of $204,000 (see Exhhibit 2.6).

Realizing that unit sales are running 543,000 cases/quarter, the manager decides that it will be necessary to take some action to reach the target. Advertising could be cut to $50,000 in the fourth quarter and the case price raised by $0.50/case. The manager then forecasts the results shown in Exhibit 2.7.

Since this scenario exceeds the net contribution target, the manager now feels much better. Unfortunately, she is in for a big disappointment, because in this market both advertising and price affect the case volume, even though this isn't reflected in the spreadsheet or in the estimates that she has put into it.

Fortunately, the marketing research staff has recently completed a study that helped them develop a market response function that quantifies a relationship between price, advertising, and case sales, and they now incorporate it in the manager's spreadsheet to provide a simple decision model. The decision model looks similar to the spreadsheet the manager has been using, but it has some important differences:

$$\text{case sales} = 320 \left[1 + \left(\frac{\text{advertising}}{250{,}000} \right)^{1.5} \left(\frac{\text{price}}{12.00} \right)^{-0.9} \right]$$

$$\text{revenue} = \text{case sales} * \text{price}$$

$$\text{COGS} = \$9.00 * \text{case sales}$$

where $9.00 = .75 * $12.00, the base selling price advertising and price are input values

The manager inputs her intuitive plan, and sees that the decision model explains the revenue during the first three quarters very well, but that she is still headed for a disappointment. The proposed plan will be a disaster, it will be $413,000 short (see Exhibit 2.8).

Exhibit 2.7   Revised Forecast Showing Fourth Quarter Revisions

	Quarters				
	1	2	3	4	Total
Revenue	$6,516	$6,516	$6,516	$6,788	$26,336
- Cost of Goods	$4,887	$4,887	$4,887	$5,091	$19,752
Gross Contribution	$1,629	$1,629	$1,629	$1,697	$6,584
- Advertising Expense	$200	$200	$200	$50	$650
Net Contribution	$1,429	$1,429	$1,429	$1,647	$5,934

Exhibit 2.8   Second Revision of Forecast

$$\text{Unit Sales} = 320 *(1 + (\text{Adv}/250))^{1.5} *(\text{Price}/\$12)^{-0.9}$$

	1st Q	2nd Q	3rd Q	4th Q	Total
Unit Sales	549	549	549	348	1995
Price	$12.00	$12.00	$12.00	$12.50	
Revenue	$6,588	$6,588	$6,588	$4,345	$24,108
Cost of Goods $9	$4,941	$4,941	$4,941	$3,128	$17,951
Gross Contribution	$1,647	$1,647	$1,647	$1,217	$6,157
Advertising Expense	$200	$200	$200	$50	$650
Net Contribution	$1,447	$1,447	$1,447	$1,167	$5,507

Next she tries a number of alternative plans and finds that the net contribution target can be made by either

Maintaining price at $12.00/case and increasing advertising to $240,000 in the fourth quarter, or by

Maintaining advertising at the $200,000 level and raising price to $12.25/case.

The value of the market response function and the decision model in this simple example is obvious, but what about the real world? Do market response functions exist in the real world? Can we discover what they are? The answer to both of the questions is *yes*.

Market response functions do exist in the real world, but they are seldom as simple as this one. Marketing science has made great progress in estimating market response functions due to the development of better data sources and better methodology, but estimating market response functions is expensive, time consuming, and the results are subject to statistical uncertainties. A number of cases in this book are in a series of two or three, dealing with a sequence of marketing efforts. The first case in most of the case series deals with a research effort directed at the measurement of some aspect of a market response model. The others in the series deal with the application of the research to decision making and the use of a decision model to make the market response function available for use in decision making.

Naive Statistical Models

Statistical models that include the results of marketing surveys and estimated market response functions can also be termed *naive* if they have been developed without an explicit decision orientation and without a direct link to the existing quantitative decision framework. All too frequently market surveys are undertaken without a clear idea of how the results will be integrated into decision making. Some minimal involvement in market surveys just to "understand who our customers are and what they want" is probably essential in a sophisticated competitive environment, but the results of this type of market survey seldom provide more than intuitive input to managerial decision making. On the other hand, marketing research done to acquire information that has been identified as crucial to a decision is very likely to have a major impact on decision making. Most studies fall between these extremes, of course, but many companies do more of the first type than is necessary and far too little of the second.

An elementary decision model in which a conceptual marketing structure is integrated into a naive financial spreadsheet can be used to learn which factors are critical to success and need to be measured with research, even though many of the values used in the model are just educated guesses.

Heuristic Models

Heuristic models are market response models that are based as much on an intuitive concept of how marketing actions affect market response as upon economic or marketing theory. Heuristic models are pragmatic mathematical rules of thumb that form quantitative representations of how marketing works. The major criteria for evaluating a heuristic model is whether it quantifies a manager's understanding of how the market works in a particular situation, rather than whether it represents a broadly applicable marketing theory.

The reason for this apparent eschewal of theory is to encourage the use of mathematical models that are only an expression of the manager's or researcher's intuition as an initial step in creating a model. Such models play an extremely important role in making intuitive concepts more complete and precise, because they help to crystallize a manager's thinking. This conceptual rigor frequently indicates the need for additional data, more sophisticated methodology, and more soundly based theoretical concepts. Heuristic models are frequently useful as a preliminary step along the way to more sophisticated models that are better grounded in theory.

In situations in which a decision needs to be made right away and with minimal expense, a simple heuristic model is probably the most sophisticated model that should be developed and may be the only model that *can* be made available when time is short. The decision model in the Optical Distortion case in Chapter 3 is a heuristic model—it is a simple conceptualization, based primarily on available data and management judgment which allows the manager to quantify his or her intuitive feelings about the most important factors affecting the success of the product.

Decision Calculus Models

Decision calculus models also represent pragmatic attempts to quantify managerial judgment and intuition. It has been somewhat cynically alleged that the difference between a heuristic model and a decision calculus model is that a decision calculus model is a heuristic model that has been published. To the extent that publication implies that a model has been reviewed by experts for theoretical soundness and applicability in a wide variety of situations, this definition may be functional.

Decision calculus and heuristic models play the important role of providing a quantitative bridge between marketing science theory, the empirical results of marketing research, and the manager's quantitative decision-making framework. We will consider two types of decision calculus models: a *normative decision calculus model* is one in which an optimal solution for the mathematical problem is computed; an *evaluative decision calculus model* is one in which the model does not provide an optimal solution, but does allow the user to compare alternatives and choose the best one.

Neither evaluative nor normative decision calculus models assure the user that the alternative chosen is the optimal solution to the *managerial* problem, since the mathematical problem that all decision calculus or heuristic models consider is necessarily an abstraction of the managerial problem. Some detail is necessarily omitted in defining the mathematical problem, and therefore the optimal mathematical solution to the problem may not be the best—or even an attractive—solution to the managerial problem. This necessary and unavoidable abstraction requires that managerial judgment be employed in applying any marketing research results. This is also one of the primary reasons for the decision maker to be personally involved in the use of the decision model.

Experimental Models

The branch of statistics known as *research design* provides an extremely powerful methodology that includes sophisticated manipulation of the experimental conditions, data collection, and mathematical models used in order to isolate the effects of one or more experimental variables. The most commonly used models of this type are the ANOVA, or analysis of variance, models. The primary purpose of experimental models is to establish *causality*—that x caused y; rather than merely *association*—that x and y occurred concurrently. The use of these models is a mainstay in many hard science and social science fields where it is important to control the effect of variables that are not included in the experiment and thus calculate the effect of the variables that are being studied.

As a simple example, suppose that an experiment has been designed to isolate the effects of advertising and price on sales—no other factors interfere. Let's ignore for the moment how this might have been done and concentrate on what the results would tell us. Suppose that we are interested in two prices and three advertising levels, and that the results of the experiment were as follows:

		Advertising		
		Low	*Medium*	*High*
Price	*Low*	75	125	175
	High	50	100	150

It is readily apparent that a graph of the results of this experiment would show that both advertising and price have an effect on sales and that the effects are independent (the slopes of the two lines are the same). Because no other factors are allowed to play a role, it is possible to say that advertising and price *cause* the level of sales.

Although experiments of this type have been the mainstay of research in a number of scientific fields, their application in complex, ongoing competitive marketing situations has been problematic. The problems, however, lie more with controlling data collection than with the mathematical models used to analyze the data. The development of various systems to overcome these difficulties and provide solid experimental control is one of the most interesting stories in marketing research, and the cases in Chapter 5 present a glimpse of that history.

Econometric Models

In a properly designed experiment, the observed results can be related to the experimentally tested variables because the effects of other variables have been removed. In the previous example—in which all factors except price and advertising were controlled—we could both attribute causality to advertising and price and measure the magnitude of their effects. But if another, extraneous factor that wasn't controlled were present in the experiment we would be unable to reach these conclusions. This is precisely the problem that faces the manager who wants to determine the effect of a marketing program by observing the ongoing sales and advertising reports of the product's performance. Observed sales could be the result of any particular part, or combination of parts, of the marketing program, as well as external market or competitive factors. In this uncontrolled environment it is impossible to attribute cause and effect in a scientific sense, and even determining the magnitude of apparent associations requires fairly complex statistical methodology.

Although determination of strict causality is impossible in such an uncontrolled environment, we do know that the sales of a product are the result of a number of ongoing factors that change over time, and that we can establish relationships between market factors and market results. If we found various levels of price and advertising occurring in a number of different sales periods, we could hope to be able to separate mathematically the effects of advertising from those of price, just as in the experimental situation.

In fact, let's use the data in our previous example to illustrate the difference. Suppose that we obtained the data from six different sales districts in a given month instead of from our carefully controlled experiment. We would have the same apparent results, but our conclusions would be much different. If the company allocated advertising expenditures according to the size of the sales district, it wouldn't be at all clear whether advertising affected sales or if the sales level had determined advertising. Or suppose that the high price was charged during a slow season for the product and the low price was charged during the peak season. Under these conditions we wouldn't know what effect to attribute to price.

In actual market situations there are a number of factors affecting each sales observation that will not be measured or even identified. A manager observing factory sales data or sales data from other audit sources cannot determine causality from a scientific point of view. From a managerial point of view, however, we would be satisfied with a relationship between marketing actions and results that was practically useful and probably true, whether or not a scientist would accept it. But with so many things going on in the marketplace at the same time, determining relationships between variables from observation of the raw data alone is problematic. This kind of a situation is very common, especially in economics.

Econometric analysis is the branch of statistics that was developed by economists and statisticians in order to observe and test economic theories empirically. It was precisely the existence of many uncontrollable economic variables interacting with each other over time that required the development of statistical tools to develop relationships between various economic variables that necessarily are observed outside of experimental conditions. It is not within the reach of most practicing marketing managers or MBA students to develop an expertise in econometric modeling that is adequate to analyze time series data measuring the sales, advertising, and pricing histories for competing products. Nevertheless, common sense, attention to detail, and insisting on incorporating the market response function derived from econometric analysis into a decision model will enable most managers to use econometric models appropriately.

Using the PC Spreadsheet Models

The personal computer spreadsheet models that accompany the cases are very easy to use, but still provide an unusual opportunity to analyze the cases in depth using decision models such as those described in this chapter. Each model is designed to integrate the market response insight drawn from the research and the manager's existing quantitative decision framework. This research insight in some cases consists of only a few important measurements of key demand elements such as trial and repeat, or even just the size of the potential market; in other cases the research yields an explicit market response function that has been integrated into the financial spreadsheet model. Most of the decision models are quite simple—in fact they were purposely made as simple as possible in order to make the point that marketing research and marketing science can be made much more useful to the decision maker through the development of simple programs that transform research reports and naive financial spreadsheets into decision models.

The spreadsheet models are written in Lotus 1-2-3® and are extremely easy to use, even for someone with little or no personal computer experience. They have a very simple menu structure that makes it easy for the novice to use the spreadsheets as they are, but there is also flexibility for users who know enough about Lotus 1-2-3 to modify the programs.

In order to use the spreadsheet models you will need the following:

1. An IBM/PC or PC-compatible personal computer
2. A Lotus 1-2-3 system diskette, version 1.A or later, using DOS version 2.0 or later

---

®Lotus and 1-2-3 are registered trademarks of Lotus Development Corporation.

3. The diskette of spreadsheets that is inside the back cover of this book

4. A formatted diskette on which you can save your own versions of the spread-sheets

Before turning on the computer, you should be aware of a few keys on the keyboard that are essential to using Lotus 1-2-3. Take a look at the keyboard shown in Exhibit 2.9. On the right-hand side of the keyboard there is a cluster of nine keys that have both numbers and arrows on them. The four keys with arrows on them are used to move the cursor—a little blinking bar—around the screen. The cursor is used to point to areas of the spreadsheet where you want to perform functions or to enter numbers. (These keys are not ordinarily used to enter numbers into the computer.) The **9** key is also labeled **PgUp**—page up—and moves the cursor a full screen at a time. Similarly, **PgDn** on the **3** key moves the cursor a full screen down. Numbers are entered into the spreadsheet with the numerical keys across the top of the keyboard. After a number has been typed that is to be entered into the spreadsheet, or the cursor has been placed on a command that you wish to execute, the return key [◄—┘] is pressed to signify the end of your input. The return key is the large vertical key on the right side of the keyboard with the bent arrow on it. Its role is like the pilot saying "Over and out" in old World War II airplane movies.

The other two keys that are important are the **/** and the **Alt** keys. Lotus 1-2-3 has a large number of preprogrammed functions that are accessed through menus that appear at the top of the screen. To call up the menu, press the **/** slash key found at the lower right side of the keyboard. After the menu has been raised, move the cursor to the function you want to choose, using the arrow keys, and choose the function by pressing the return key. More advanced users simply type the slash, then the initial letters of commands. For example, **/fr** for **File Retrieve**. It's a snap, and not nearly as confusing to do as it is to read about.

Each of the spreadsheets accompanying the cases has a menu specific to that spreadsheet. These menus are used in most of the cases to help you find your way around the spreadsheet and to print the spreadsheet on your printer. These special menus are raised by pressing the [Alt] key and holding it down while pressing the [M] key. To print a spreadsheet, hold the [Alt] key down and press the [P] key. To use the programs as they are written, that's about all that you need to know. You'll probably get so interested in 1-2-3 as you go along that you'll want to learn more about it from the 1-2-3 manual, and you might have a couple of questions, so keep the manual handy.

Introduction to a Simple Spreadsheet Model

Let's use one of the spreadsheet models now to see how it works. The simple spreadsheet and decision model that we discussed earlier in this chapter will serve as an introduction. First, boot up the program, using the follwing instruc-

Exhibit 2.9   The IBM Personal Computer Keyboard

Function Keys   "Typewriter Part"   Direction/
                                                             Numeric Keypad

Special Keys In Typewriter Part

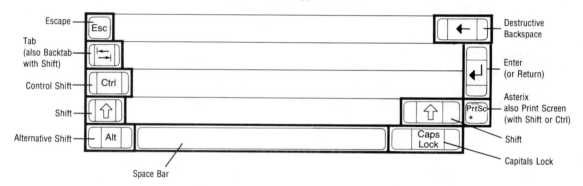

Function Key Meanings In 1-2-3

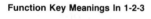

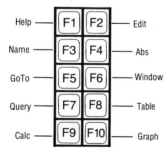

Help — F1 F2 — Edit
Name — F3 F4 — Abs
GoTo — F5 F6 — Window
Query — F7 F8 — Table
Calc — F9 F10 — Graph

**Direction Keys
Numeric Lock, And
Scroll Lock (Break)**

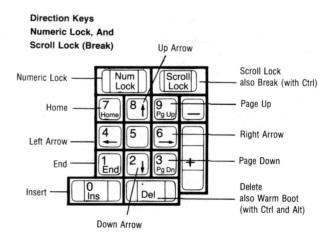

tions. These instructions assume that you have already made your Lotus system disk self-booting. If you have not, refer to your Lotus manual for instructions.

Booting Up with Two Disk Drives.   Insert the Lotus system diskette in the A disk drive (the upper or left-hand drive). Insert this book's diskette in the other disk drive. Turn on the computer, and when the instruction to "press any key" appears on the screen, do so.

After a little whirring and light blinking, the title page for the book's disk will appear on the screen, and you'll see a number of program names written accross the top of the screen.

Use the arrow keys to move the cursor to CHAP_2 and press [◄─┘]. This will direct Lotus 1-2-3 to read the CHAP_2 spreadsheet from the program diskette and transfer it to the computer screen where you can work with it. (See Exhibit 2.10) If the title page does not appear, you can get it up using the normal 1-2-3 menu. Press **/** to bring up the Lotus menu, then direct the computer to the programs on drive B by moving the cursor to **File**, [◄─┘], **Directory**, [◄─┘], then type **b:** (to indicate drive B). Next, get into the book's spreadsheet menu by pressing **/**, then **File**, [◄─┘], move the cursor to **Retrieve**, then [◄─┘]. Move the cursor to AUTO123 and press [◄─┘], and this book's menu will appear on the screen.

Booting Up with a Hard Disk Drive.   If you have Lotus 1-2-3 on a hard disk, you'll need to boot up on DOS, then route to the directory where Lotus is. If you have an unprotected copy of Lotus, simply put this book's disk in the floppy disk drive and type **123**. Then type **/File Directory** and **a:** to direct the Lotus program to the floppy disk for spreadsheets. To get into the program that goes with this book, type **/File Retrieve**, then select AUTO123. Our menu will appear.

If you have a protected copy of Lotus 1-2-3, boot up in DOS and route to the directory where Lotus is. Put the original Lotus system disk in the floppy disk drive and type **123**. After the program checks to make sure you have a valid Lotus disk, the Lotus menu will appear on the screen. Direct the program to the spreadsheets on the floppy disk by typing **/File Directory** and then **a:** to direct it to the A drive. To get our menu up, type **/File Retrieve** and then select AUTO123. The menu for this book's spreadsheets will appear on your screen.

The CHAP_2 Spreadsheet.   You are now in the spreadsheet and ready to begin using it. You'll notice that there is a menu at the top left of the screen that says **Basic** and **Decision**, and that the cursor is on **Basic**. If you hit [◄─┘], the menu will go away and you'll see the cursor move to the upper left field of the spreadsheet. Use the arrow keys to move the cursor around the spreadsheet and observe how the upper left corner of the screen shows the coordinates of the cell where the cursor is, as well as the contents of the cell. After you've done this for a while, press the [Alt] and [M] keys together to get the menu back, move the cursor to **Decision** and press [◄─┘]. You'll find yourself in the decision model section of the spreadsheet. While you're there, you might as well move the cursor around a bit and see what makes this sheet tick. You'll notice that the cells on the "Unit Sales" row have a formula in them that computes sales from the advertising and price entries in the spreadsheet. After you've examined this spreadsheet a bit, print out the spreadsheets. Make sure that your printer is turned on and ready to print and that the paper is at the top of a page, then hold the [Alt] key down and press [P]. The printer will then begin to print your spreadsheet.

Exercises. The following exercises will help you get familiar with the skills that you need to use the spreadsheets:

1. Change price to $14.00 and advertising to $100,000 in the 4th quarter.
   What are 4th-quarter unit sales? (Answer: 390,000)
   Revenue? ($25,230,000)
   Total Net Contribution? ($6,193,000)

2. Suppose a new advertising campaign is planned for next year. The expected advertising budget is $300,000 per quarter. Price is expected to be $12.50/case. What will net contribution for the year be if the advertising effectiveness is:
   a. The same: advertising elasticity = 1.5? ($8,957,000)
   b. Less effective: advertising elasticity = 1.2? ($8,655,000)
   c. More effective: advertising elasticity = 1.7? ($9,167,000)

3. With advertising elasticity left at 1.7, make the following changes:

	Quarters			
	1	2	3	4
Price	$11.00	$12.50	$13.00	$10.50
Cost of Goods	$10.00			
Advertising	$225,000	$450,000	$300,000	$50,000

   What is total net contribution? ($4,828,000)

4. What is the formula for unit sales in the second quarter?
   a. Move the cursor to cell D31.
   b. Read the formula at the upper left corner of the screen.
   (Answer:)
   + B27 * (1 + ((D38/250)^D26) * (D32/12)^F26)
   The $ signs designate a cell address that doesn't change depending on the cell that addresses it. So this formula means:
   Unit sales (2nd quarter) =

$$320 \left[1 + \left(\frac{\text{Advertising (2nd Q)}}{\$250,000} \right)^{1.5} \left(\frac{\text{Price (2nd Q)}}{\$12.00} \right)^{-0.9} \right]$$

Exhibit 2.10   CHAP_2 Spreadsheet

Chapter Two Practice Exercise

Basic Spreadsheet

		1st Q	2nd Q	3rd Q	4th Q	Total
Revenue		$6,516	$6,516	$6,516	$6,516	$26,064
Cost of Goods	75%	$4,887	$4,887	$4,887	$4,887	$19,548
Gross Contribution		$1,629	$1,629	$1,629	$1,629	$6,516
Advertising Expense		$200	$200	$200	$200	$800
Net Contribution		$1,429	$1,429	$1,429	$1,429	$5,716

DECISION MODEL

Unit Sales relationship

$$\text{Unit Sales} = 320 * (1 + (Adv/250)^{1.5}) * (Price/\$12)^{-0.9}$$

		1st Q	2nd Q	3rd Q	4th Q	Total
Unit Sales		549	549	549	549	2196
Price		$12.00	$12.00	$12.00	$12.00	
Revenue		$6,588	$6,588	$6,588	$6,588	$26,351
Cost of Goods	$9	$4,941	$4,941	$4,941	$4,941	$19,763
Gross Contribution		$1,647	$1,647	$1,647	$1,647	$6,588
Advertising Expense		$200	$200	$200	$200	$800
Net Contribution		$1,447	$1,447	$1,447	$1,447	$5,788

When you are finished doing these exercises, you might want to save the results of your work to use at a later time. This is easily done using the Lotus 1-2-3
menu:

1. Make sure you are not in the program menu. If you are, just press [◄─┘] and
   you'll get out.

2. Enter the 1-2-3 menu by pressing [**/**], move the cursor to **Files** and press [◄─┘]. Then move the cursor to **Save** and press [◄─┘]. The computer will then ask you for the name you would like to give your new file. You will probably want to choose a different name than the original just so you would have it to go back to later. (The original worksheet remains unchanged unless you save to it with the same file name.) Type in the new name, say—"Junk." You have saved the file. It is probably a good idea to save your own files on a separate diskette, rather than on the disk that came with the book.

This simple exercise demonstrates the skills that you need to use most of the spreadsheets accompanying the cases. The spreadsheets are more complicated, but using them requires no more knowledge of the computer than you have used in this example.

Modifying the Spreadsheet Models

If you want to modify the spreadsheet models, I assume that you know how to run Lotus 1-2-3 reasonably well, so I will provide only the basics. Before you can modify a spreadsheet, you must disable the global protection that keeps novice users from overwriting a formula. This is done with the command **/WGPD**, Worksheet Global Protect Disable.

Watch out for the macros that run the menus which are located to the right of the spreadsheet model, usually within the first 10 to 15 rows. You'll want to be careful about inserting rows into the worksheet in this area. Also the [goto] statements in the menus might not take you to the right places anymore if you modify the spreadsheet. These are minor problems, since the menus aren't very important if you know your way around the spreadsheets well enough to modify them.

The integration of naive financial spreadsheets and the various market response models that will be presented in the cases result in the decision models that accompany the cases. A decision maker with a well thought-out naive financial spreadsheet model is in a very strong position to discuss the need for and design of marketing research, and to participate in the development of the market response functions needed for a useful decision model.

Summary

This chapter has provided an overview of the considerations that led to the approach to analytical marketing decision making that is central to the organization of the cases in the book. There are several dimensions to the conceptual structure underlying the sequence of cases in this book. This structure is more complex than one usually encounters in a case book, because we are studying a more sophisticated approach to managerial decision making, which necessarily requires simultaneous attention to mathematical modeling, data characteristics, and the managerial decision situation. Therefore the reader should keep in mind (1) the stage of the new product development process and the elements of analysis that are a common to it, (2) the appropriate level of research and the type of market response function and decision model that are both feasible and appropriate, and (3) the nature of the data that support the analysis and its limitations.

References and Background Readings

Levine, Joel. "Pre–Test-Market Research of New Packaged-Goods Products—A User Orientation." In Wind, Mahajan, and Cardozo, *New Product Forecasting*. Lexington, MA: Lexington Books, 1981.

Little, John D. C. "Models and Managers: The Concept of a Decision Calculus." *Management Science*, Vol. 16 (1970), pp. 466–485.

Urban, Glen L., and John R. Hauser. *Design and Marketing of New Products*. Englewood Cliffs, NJ: Prentice-Hall, 1980.

Wind, Yoram, Vijay Mahajan, and Richard N. Cardozo. *New Product Forecasting*. Lexington, MA: Lexington Books, 1981.

3

Early New Product Development

The three main managerial considerations in using the advanced analytical techniques that we identified in Chapter 2—decision situation, model evaluation, and data evaluation—exhibit strong similarities at the early stage of new product development. At this stage, the decisions to be made are in the areas of opportunity identification, forecasting market potential, and new product design, and these decisions are more similar across products now than at any other stage in the management of a product.

The decision situation is nearly always the same—a new product concept has been identified, and the decision maker, whether an entrepreneur or an employee of a large corporation, must decide whether or not the product concept is attractive enough to warrant further investment. An objective appraisal of the economic potential of a new product concept is one key to effectively managing a company's new product development resources. This decision usually has two phases: Is the new product concept economically attractive? Is it more attractive than other available opportunities? Advanced analytical techniques make a significant contribution to both phases of the decision, and alternatives can be more accurately compared if similar analytical techniques are used for each one.

There are also some important differences at this stage, which result from the nature of the products, the competitive situation, and those aspects of the marketing strategy about which the most uncertainty exists. Comparing the similarity and differences in the analytical approach across the cases can greatly expand the reader's sensitivity to the factors affecting successful analysis at this stage of the new product development process.

The types of data that are available also have strong similarities at this early stage: secondary data, data published by government or industry sources, and managerial judgment are often the only data available about the new product's market. The more unique a product is, the less information there will be that directly addresses the new product's potential. Consumer market surveys are often undertaken at this stage in order to obtain some information that is directly relevant to the new product.

Decision models for most new product ideas should be relatively simple in concept, quickly developed, and easily modified. Characteristically, decision models at this early stage involve a great deal of guessing because we aren't sure about anything.

The most reasonable yardstick to apply to the use of advanced analytical methods at the early stages of new product development is whether they lead to an increased understanding of the decision situation and therefore to better decisions, rather than how reliable the estimates are likely to be.

Two anecdotes will serve to illustrate this point:

A former student of mine is now involved in a venture capital firm. He tells me that almost every proposal he reviews assumes that the new product or service will achieve 5 percent of the market. No justification is given as to why the firm should be able to achieve that level—it just seems like a small share that will be accepted without question.

I was recently involved in building a new product forecasting system for new pharmaceutical products as a joint effort of six major pharmaceutical firms. When we presented the results of using the model to forecast the first year sales for about fifty recent new drugs, we stated that for most of the products our model's prediction was within 10 percent, but we missed a few by nearly 50 percent. The marketing research director for a product we'd missed by 50 percent stated that he had held a contest to forecast the sales of that product, but since the closest estimate had missed by more than 200 percent, he had declared that the contest had no winner and given everyone their money back.

These anecdotes illustrate two important considerations for the analysis of any marketing situation, but particularly for this early stage of new product development: (1) a sales forecast is not necessarily attainable just because it is small, and (2) the results of an analytical approach should be compared to what could be done without analysis, not some nonexistent perfect capability.

When a company uses objective, consistent analysis to compare alternatives, it is less vulnerable to making new product choices based more on the daring and imagination of the product concept's sponsor than on the merit of the product concept. Every successful new product has had an energetic, imaginative manager backing it—someone who was effective at presenting the most persuasive case for a new product concept and getting the company's support for its development. This is how it should be, because a manager that cannot command the resources to push a new product concept through the development process would probably not be able to successfully manage a new product introduction. The use of sound analytical methodology can be a great aid to a manager—even a very creative and subjectively effective one—in being more persuasive and winning support for his or her new product. If sound, objective analysis is the basis for choosing between alternatives, the company wins, too, because better products, backed by the more skillful managers, are more likely to succeed in the marketplace.

Managerial Considerations in Early New Product Development

New product introduction is one of the most interesting and complex branches of marketing management, and a comprehensive discussion of it could, and has, filled books much larger than this one. This discussion is not intended to be comprehensive or even a digest of the most important concepts in a new product de-

Exhibit 3.1   Classification of New Products

		Market	
		New	Existing
Product	New	Innovation	Product line extension
	Similar	New uses	Product line extension

velopment; rather, it will point out a few concepts that will be useful as a starting point in analyzing the cases in the chapter. This discussion might best be described as helpful hints. Some important managerial factors to consider in evaluating the cases in this chapter (and in analyzing the potential of new product concepts in general) are *product concept "newness," consumer market structure, competition,* and *cannibalization.*

These factors affect the size of the potential market, the design of a marketing strategy to penetrate the market, and the timing and magnitude of market response, and they also strongly affect the kinds of data that will be available and the kinds of decision models that can be developed.

Product Concept "Newness"

The most common paradigm for defining new product situations classifies them by product and market newness, both in general and for the firm (See Exhibit 3.1).

The least uncertain new product for the firm is one that is merely a modification of one in the company's existing product line; in this situation both the consumer buying process and the target markets are well understood. At the other extreme is the introduction of a very new product that does not fit into any existing product category very well; in this situation neither the consumer buying process nor the target market is understood.

One conceptual framework for the definition of product newness and its effects on the development of new product marketing strategies is found in the literature about adoption and diffusion of innovation, especially as it is applied to consumer buying behavior. In general, it has been found that a number of factors tend to slow down the speed of adoption: high product uniqueness, high perceived risk, the availability of substitutes, high cost, difficulty of trial, low com-

Exhibit 3.2   Consumer Market Structure for Nutritional Cereals

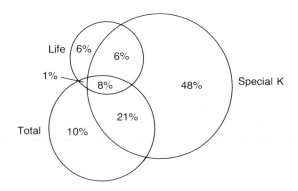

Note: The relative size of the circles is indicative of the sales volume of each brand.

parative advantage, and incompatibility with current behavior. The same literature indicates that adoption progresses more rapidly when these conditions are present: communication between potential customers, the presence of innovators, sophisticated customers, and experience with similar products.

These factors all determine the nature and effectiveness of the marketing strategy and provide an indication of how rapidly market potential will be achieved. The greater the need for information and assistance in problem solving, the more important the marketing program becomes and the more important it becomes to incorporate the timing and magnitude of market response to marketing effort in the early estimation of the market potential. It is important to know that the market potential of a new product concept is very large, but if that potential can only be achieved with great expense over a number of years, identification of the potential alone is not enough to evaluate the financial attractiveness of the concept.

Consumer Market Structure

Familiarity with the product category, brand usage experience, brand and company loyalties, existing buying patterns, exposure to media, and price sensitivity are critical factors in analyzing the buying process and determining the customer's likelihood of buying the new product. The distribution of these characteristics across the customers in the marketplace will be called the *consumer market structure,* and it is a useful concept for determining market segments, marketing strategy, and estimating market response. Exhibit 3.2 displays an example of a consumer market structure for nutritional cereals, circa 1975, based on consumer brand usage experience. It is easy to see that Kelloggs' Special K held at that time a powerful position in the marketplace, since nearly all nutritional cereal users in the survey purchased at least some Special K. One would expect that it would have been difficult (and it was) for a new nutritional cereal to enter this market without some strong differentiating characteristic. Many "me-too" nutritional cereals failed at this time until the new "natural cereals" made headway with these consumers.

There are a number of other ways to conceptualize the consumer market structure, but the basic idea is to derive an explicit representation of the strength of the relationship between customers and products—new or existing—in the marketplace. Market segmentation schemes that identify customers by their product loyalties, benefits sought, or media exposure patterns are also good first steps in developing a meaningful consumer market structure—one that is both conceptually rich and quantitatively explicit.

Competition

Competition is one of the most powerful determinants of the market's response to a new product concept, and has a number of dimensions that need to be considered. The firms offering products that will compete with the new product are considered to be the competition. Their marketing programs, whether developed in response to our marketing strategy or independent of our actions, need to be carefully considered.

The array of products that consumers might substitute for our new product is another very important dimension of competition. The brand loyalties, product satisfaction, and established relationships that form the dimensions of the consumer market structure and represent the franchise of the existing brands are the obstacles that a new brand must overcome and are the weapons that are used to compete. Advertising expenditures and price promotions play to a more favorable audience for established brands with strong market positions than they do for entering products, and represent a competitive advantage that must be overcome.

Competition can also take the form of competitors' marketing actions that are specifically directed to respond to the marketing strategy of the new brand and to defend the established brand's customer franchise. This response can take many forms—not just response in kind—such as price cuts for established products, product line extensions, special trade allowances, and so on.

One of the most important effects that competition imposes on marketing analysis is that competitive action changes the basis of comparison between strategies. Managers sometimes compare the net contribution to profit they will receive from a new alternative with that of the current market situation and decide that the new alternative does not look favorable. Often, however, competitors can be predicted to take actions that will change the market situation regardless of our action, so the new alternative should be compared with the new competitive situation rather than the old one. For example, many bankers initially declined to offer NOW accounts because they calculated that the bank's cash flow would be less favorable. They failed to consider, however, what their cash flows would be like without NOW accounts *if their competitors offered NOW accounts*. Consumers found the NOW account to be an attractive product and many switched their accounts to banks that offered them. The banks that offered the NOW accounts early enjoyed an increase in their customer base that more than compensated for the less favorable cash flow. The banks that lagged behind lost these customers, and then, in order to keep the customers they still had, they were forced to offer NOW accounts (which did offer worse cash flow performance) to a smaller customer base.

Cannibalization

The effect of a new product entry into a marketplace is felt not only by products of competing firms but also by the other products offered by the firm introducing the new product. In multi–product firms, some of a new product's sales and contribution to profit are cannibalization from other products in the company's product line, so the new product's performance cannot be looked at in isolation. The sales and contribution to profit of the new product line as a whole, relative to the performance of the old product line, is a more reasonable success criterion. But no accounting treatment of the current situation should be considered to be definitive in evaluating an addition to the product line, because longer-term competitive considerations might conflict with a short-term policy of increasing product line profitability.

The ideal new product might at first seem to be one that draws all of its sales from competitors' product franchises and none from the firm's other products, but the situation is not that simple. For example, when General Foods developed freeze-dried coffee, their new product, Maxim, was superior to its existing instant coffee brands, and the introduction of Maxim would cannibalize its existing products' customer franchise. General Foods chose a less than optimal product position in order to minimize cannibalization. The competition then introduced Taster's Choice with a superior product position, which hurt not only Maxim's sales but also cut more deeply into General Foods' other instant coffee sales. In this situation, much of General Foods coffee franchise was lost, not just cannibalized. General Foods might have been better off introducing Maxim to maximize cannibalizing of its current coffee franchise.

It might also be the case that in seeking to minimize the amount of product line cannibalization, a company might sacrifice a more favorable market position and end up with product line sales and contribution to profit that is less than would have been available with the better product position, even though cannibalization is greater.

Evaluating any of these possibilities is not a philosophical exercise, and each alternative consists of some factors that increase profitability and others that decrease it. There is no general answer to what is best, and only through detailed and quantitatively explicit analysis can alternatives be evaluated.

Data Characteristics in Early New Product Development

The managerial considerations discussed in the previous section are also important in determining the type of data needed and available to evaluate a new product. Remember that the goal of preliminary economic analysis is to identify, *before the decision has to be made and at a reasonable cost*, promising product concepts and determine the need for more extensive data gathering, market research, and mathematical modeling at a later development stage. Decision models and data used at this early evaluation stage should not involve extensive effort based on expensive empirical data.

Product concept newness exerts a number of strong influences on the data and models available to be used in a simple decision model. It is easier to define the target market for a new product that will compete in the market for the company's existing products than it is to define the market for an entirely new product concept that does not fit into any existing market. In the former case, the market size can be reasonably estimated by the size of the markets for the relevant existing products. In the latter case, volume estimates are often difficult to make and the target market is perhaps better defined in terms of the number of potential customers. Obviously, the more unique the product concept, the less direct information is available about potential sales volume.

The most difficult products for which to estimate the potential market are products that are so different from those currently used that consumers recognize no existing need for them. According to a recent TV commercial, IBM initially estimated the U.S. market for computers at only 50. The estimate was probably made by the engineers and scientists that developed the computer and was probably based on their knowledge of how many other researchers were interested in the same kinds of problems. This obviously was not a very good estimate, but a market survey of business executives, had it been done, would not have produced very different results, because neither the executives interviewed nor those asking the questions had a very good idea of what a computer could do at the time. One should not be too anxious to perform a market survey to determine the potential market for a very new product concept—certainly not before analysis based on available secondary market data has been done to get some insight into which areas of uncertainty are most important for the evaluating alternative marketing strategies.

The more nearly unique the new product, the more difference there is between the number of customers that could theoretically use the product and the number that will actually buy it, particularly during the introduction, unless there is some overwhelmingly clear comparative advantage. Because of this, product newness increases the importance of the marketing strategy in realizing the market potential; it also increases the importance of defining the marketing program and estimating the response to it over time. It is extremely unlikely that objective empirical data will be available, and managerial judgment about the response to marketing effort is perhaps the only data that can be made available before decisions have to be made.

The trick to using this kind of data is to avoid making just one estimate that you live or die by, and to perform the analysis with a number of estimates in order to ascertain the sensitivity of product success to various levels of the factors in the decision. This *sensitivity analysis* can be extremely valuable in identifying those variables for which a given level of response could mean either success or failure, and for determining the range within which success would be a reasonable expectation. Variables that do not affect success or failure within the expected range of responses do not require research to estimate the levels they will achieve in the marketplace; those that *are* critical become candidates for market research. With this approach, the role that research results will play in decision making is known in advance, and marketing research defined in this way is most likely to have a strong impact on decision making.

It is relatively easy to define the target market for new products that will compete in more or less established markets, especially when data on the sales of competitive products are available. The potential market for such a new product is a share of the market of the existing products, plus its share of any market expansion that might result from the introduction. If the growth rate of the market is not expected to be affected by the entry of the new product, then estimating the market share to be attained is the primary task.

Estimating the demand for a totally new product is not nearly so easy, however. If the sales histories of other new products are available, it may be possible to use them as an indication of how rapidly sales might grow, but it is always difficult to make analogies with previous new products. When combined with estimates of the potential market size, however, this may be a reasonable place to start. Sensitivity analysis relating the company's success criteria to the share of the potential market, and comparison with the growth rate of other, similar new products might be all that is economically desirable to do for an initial analysis. The purpose of analysis at this stage, however, should be to determine whether or not the new product concept is promising enough to justify a marketing research expenditure of $100,000 to $250,000 to estimate its market potential more accurately.

A great deal of marketing research is typically performed at an early stage of new product development to try to determine "who the consumer is and what he or she wants." Far too high a proportion of such research is done too early in the new product development process, before a preliminary marketing plan has been defined and a preliminary economic analysis has been performed. The all-too-frequent result of such premature market research is a lack of focus in the survey and the omission of critically important information from the research. The use of a huge questionnaire is by no means a guarantee that the necessary information will be obtained by blind luck. Unfortunately, Murphy's Law is a dominant factor in survey research. What most needs to be known will not be contained in the survey, no matter how large and comprehensive it appears to be, unless it was purposely put there.

Market Research and Decision Models in Early New Product Development

Analysis of new product concepts at the initial stage of new product development does not warrant large expenses for market research and mathematical model building. What *is* required, prior to commitment of substantial funds for either product development or market research, is careful attention to the new product concept, the definition of the target market, the consumers' purchase processes, and the marketing program that would be necessary to reach the market. This intuitive, subjective analysis is a basic skill of every successful marketer, but can and should be augmented by the development and use of simple decision models.

An appropriate decision model at this early stage should be based on basic marketing and economic theory, the manager's intuitive understanding of the market situation, and readily available data. Neither model development nor data gathering should be extensive. The idea is to quantify, as objectively as possible, the manager's intuitive understanding of the marketplace and thus provide a tool for sensitivity and scenario analysis. If properly done, this type of analysis provides a solid foundation for all future analysis because it helps to define what the important success factors are, what information needs are critical, and what research might be necessary. If this early managerial analysis is omitted or if it is allowed to remain subjective or imprecise, it is very likely that future research efforts will be misdirected and will not result in acquiring information that is vital for objective decision making. The obstacles to developing appropriate analysis at this stage are more likely to be the manager's personal biases, aspirations, and analytical limitations, rather than inadequate resources to fund appropriate research.

Decision models that are appropriate for the early stages of new product development are frequently criticized by managers because of the many assumptions that have been made about the size of markets and the response to marketing programs. The criticism is certainly deserved, but frequently these critics lose sight of the fact that there is really no alternative. *If a decision model is not attempted, the uncertainties don't cease to exist.* The same uncertainties exist whether they are expressed in a decision model or not, but one benefit of modeling is that important assumptions about the size of market segments, consumer response to marketing effort, and the marketing plan are explicit and are therefore considered, whereas intuitive decision making leaves many important assumptions and success factors unrecognized.

Decision Situation Overview of the Cases

The two cases in this chapter, CableShop and Optical Distortion, deal with the role of marketing research in the development of decision models at an early stage of the new product introduction process. The cases differ considerably in terms of product type, product and market newness, the importance of the marketing strategy, and the means used to estimate the new product potential. When combined with the Johnson Wax and Clark Equipment Company cases in the next chapter, a broad range of new product introduction experience is considered, extending from a very innovative product in a virtually new market to product line extensions in a familiar, established market. The product types range from hair conditioners to fork lift trucks.

The two cases in this chapter provide a graphic indication of the value of the analytical approach we propose in the book. CableShop presents probably the most expensive market research program found in any of the cases. It is also the only case situation in which the marketing manager had developed his own financial planning model. However, CableShop is also the case in which the research provided the least value to the manager.

Optical Distortion Inc., on the other hand, did the least research, yet the information gathered had a big impact on decision making. As you prepare these two cases you'll probably share this experience. A major task for the student in this chapter is to explore the reasons for the difference in usefulness of the two research approaches.

Direct competition does not play an important role in either of these new product situations because of the innovative nature of the products, but it is a very important factor in analyzing the new products in the cases in the next chapter.

Data Consideration Overview of the Cases

The cases in this chapter illustrate the use of secondary data, judgmental data, and market survey data. The CableShop case features the use of secondary and survey data in attempting to enhance the usefulness of a traditional financial planning model for marketing planning. The Optical Distortion case is concerned with the use of secondary and judgmental data to develop a conceptual model of the farmer's decision process. Together, these two cases illustrate a number of important data considerations in the estimation of new product potential.

Research and Decision Model Considerations in the Cases

Just as the data considerations in the cases span a number of different situations and illustrate some common problem areas, the two cases provide a look at different approaches to market research and decision models at an early stage in new product development. The CableShop case features a fairly standard financial planning model—a PC model similar to ours had been developed by Mr. Lambert. This financial spreadsheet model provides a baseline for much of the model building examples that follow. The model is an adequate treatment of the CableShop's cost structure, but lacks an explicit relationship between marketing actions, marketing conditions, and financial considerations. We will term such models *naive financial models* because they are naive from a marketing planning standpoint, but not necessarily from a financial standpoint. The CableShop model provides an example of the "existing quantitative framework" referred to in Chapter 2.

The Optical Distortion Inc. case features what we will call a "semi-naive" decision model. A financial decision-making structure is present and an explicit attempt has been made to incorporate a market response model of sales force effort, but some potentially important factors may have not been modeled. Be sure not to read or use the decision model until you are instructed to do so by your teacher.

CASE: The CableShop

The CableShop is a new advertising-by-request service for CATV viewers. The case provides an example of business planning and marketing research for a new service. It also provides a baseline experience that illustrates the need for the analytical approach developed in the book. Although a financial model was developed by CableShop management and a substantial marketing research project was undertaken, these efforts were not integrated and thus the research left important questions unanswered. You will probably have difficulty planning a marketing strategy for CS that is based on objective information. Try not to get too frustrated; try instead to understand the reasons for your difficulty.

Advertisers' prime sales medium—network TV—is facing increasing erosion by cable TV (CATV) for a number of reasons:

CATV, especially pay TV, will increasingly siphon off viewers from the networks.

Those attracted to pay TV will be affluent young adults— advertisers' prime prospects.

These affluent young adults have little tolerance for conventional commercials.

A strong appeal of pay TV is the absence of commercials.

Consumers give a number of reasons for disliking commercials: they intrude on programming, they're irritating . . . . and insult my intelligence, they lack depth and useful information, and they're not helpful in buying.

Trevor Lambert, vice president of corporate development at Adams-Russell, Inc., thought that these research findings reinforced his CableShop concept, a cable TV advertising service through which viewers could watch commercial messages according to a published schedule, or by requesting a message over the telephone. Lambert's concept was to offer advertising by request.

Lambert believed CableShop would be a benefit not only to consumers, but also to cable operators and advertisers. Lambert felt the research showed that CableShop had the potential to develop into a mass medium.

Company Background

Adams-Russell, Inc. (A-R) of Waltham, Massachusetts, was a multiple-product-line company with fiscal 1982 sales of just under $72 million. Telecommunications accounted for $14.8 million and operating income was $57,000. Established in 1958, the company had its roots in electronic product development for military applications, but by 1982 had diversified into telecommunications.

A-R operated cable TV systems in five states. A-R's franchised areas included 296,000 homes, a 33% increase over the previous year. A-R had launched four new cable systems in the latter half of the year, requiring a capital outlay of $15.6 million; these additions made A-R the 48th largest cable operator in the U.S.

CableShop Development

In the summer of 1980, there was considerable interest in CATV's potential to offer home information, banking, and shopping services. Lambert decided, after extensive research, that consumers' needs

---

This case was adapted by Darral G. Clarke, from two Harvard cases prepared by Christopher Patton and Darral G. Clarke.

Copyright ©1983 by the President and Fellows of Harvard College, Harvard Business School cases 9-584-065 and 9-584-066.

could be better met by providing more complete information on the vast array of product choices confronting them than by technology-intensive interactive stock information services, electronic newspapers, or information search services.

While attending a conference on new electronic media, Lambert met Garth Hallberg, a senior vice president at J. Walter Thompson (JWT), who had also been studying the effect of CATV on the advertising industry. Their discussions led to the idea of a CATV advertising service, which they subsequently named CableShop.

The CableShop concept was to offer a number of lengthy, informative commercials called "infomercials" to cable TV subscribers on both a scheduled and a request basis. The pilot test would require four channels. One channel would continuously air a schedule of infomercials to appear during the next 30 minutes. The infomercials would be aired on the other three channels. Available infomercials for a given month were described and identified by a three-digit code in a printed supplement to the monthly CATV viewing guide. For example:

Do Ahead Dishes. Learn how to relax and enjoy your guests. Be an early bird by preparing food (dips to desserts) a day or two ahead. When the telephone rings and company arrives, you won't be spending most of your time in the kitchen—thanks to Campbell's Soups.

Arrow-Man-Story. Changing times and fashions as seen through the eyes of the famous "Arrow Collar Man." Complete with music and film footage from the turn-of-the-century to the present.

Money Market Funds. What are money market funds? How can they pay such high yields? Are they safe? Can I use one like a savings account without withdrawal penalties? Get answers and a *free* financial planning guide from IDS.

A CATV subscriber could use CableShop in two ways. He or she could tune in to the CableShop message channel, check the times and channels for the infomercials, and view them as scheduled, or the subscriber could call the CableShop number shown on the message channel and ask to see a particular infomercial. A recorded voice asked the caller to dial the household's five-digit access number, and the requested infomercial's code number was taken by the computer. The computer then scheduled the requested infomercial in the next available time period, and displayed the time and channel on the message channel. Mr. Lambert considered the call-in feature to be an automatic scheduling device that obviated the need to charge different advertising rates for different day parts, thus eliminating prime-time and off-peak pricing considerations. The four- to six-minute length of the infomercials was intended to allow advertisers to create more informative, soft-sell approaches to advertising than were characteristic of traditional commercials.

JWT and A-R agreed to cosponsor a pilot project to determine CableShop's commercial viability. JWT would serve as the project's ad agency, solicit accounts, help produce infomercials, and design and supervise the research program. A-R would devote four channels of its Peabody, Massachusetts, cable system to CableShop during the ten-month test.

The CATV Industry

CATV was a means of distributing television signals from a central originating location to residences and/or businesses by way of a coaxial cable. For a basic monthly subscription price, a subscriber received a basic service that included all the local broadcast TV stations, and for additional fees, specialized entertainment channels.

By 1982, according to one source, 5,000 cable systems in 14,200 communities served 30.2 million cable subscribers, some 33% of the nation's households. The largest single cable system, Cox Cable in San Diego, California, had over 200,000 subscribers. By the fall of 1982 it was estimated that only 8 million homes were left unfranchised in the top 30 U.S. markets. Many felt that the rest of the country would be too expensive to franchise.

The industry was beginning to consolidate with the formation of multiple-system operators (MSOs). The largest MSO, Tele-Communications, Inc., had over 2.3 million subscribers, and the top 20 MSOs were responsible for almost 60% of basic subscribers and over 65% of pay subscribers.

There were three main parties to the operation of a community CATV franchise: the *cable operator, basic service programmers,* and *pay service programmers.*

The Cable Operator

The cable operator in a community, whether an individual or an MSO, serviced a franchise area according to a contract with the municipality. This contract detailed the number of channels to be provided, the programming to be offered as part of the basic service, the pay services that would be available to subscribers, and the cost to subscribers. Most cable systems in 1970 offered only 20 channels; by late in the decade, the standard new system was 36 channels. By the early 1980s, the typical system under construction had at least 50 channels, and a state-of-the-art system could provide over 100 channels.

Developing a CATV system required substantial capital investment, and most franchise agreements granted the operator a 15-year exclusive contract. New systems typically required at least two years to show a profit because of low subscriber growth rates and substantial construction costs. Industry analysts estimated that a modern franchise for 10,000 subscribers required an investment of $750–800 per subscriber. In 1980, the average operating margin was 35.7% and pre-tax income averaged 7.5% of revenues.

Basic Service Programmers

Basic CATV service was the programming provided to subscribers for the basic monthly charge. The programmers that provided these basic services, such as local TV stations, superstations, and some other cable services, derived almost all of their revenue from advertising and none from the cable operator. Some basic services compensated cable operators for carrying their service on a per-subscriber basis. However, the sports channel, ESPN, which began by compensating cable operators, had recently imposed a 10¢ per-sub-

scriber fee on the operators. In 1980, the average revenue for the basic service was $7.69 a month per subscriber.

Pay Service Programmers

Other CATV programmers produced programming that they sold to cable operators. The first pay cable service was Home Box Office (HBO). HBO changed the CATV industry in 1975 when it leased a transponder on Satcom I and became the first pay service to transmit its programming nationally. Until then, cable had been viewed only as an adjunct to broadcast TV, to be used to pick up distant channels and provide better reception. With HBO, cable became a source of original programming and an alternative to the national broadcast networks. By 1982, with the stimulus provided by HBO and other pay cable services, 33% of all TV households had become CATV subscribers, and 80% of them purchased at least one pay cable service.

Generally, the CATV operator bought the pay service from the programmer at a wholesale price per subscriber and marked it up to a retail price for sale to subscribers. As an incentive to CATV operators to market their services, pay programmers frequently offered discounts based on the percentage of basic subscribers who also subscribed to their pay service. Industry experts believed it was the leading pay services, rather than the basic services, that were taking prime-time viewers from the broadcast networks. The average pay service revenue per subscriber in 1980 was $9.13 a month.

Home Shopping Services

In 1983, a number of home shopping services were being offered, at least experimentally. These services, variously offered on CATV or through home computers over telephone lines, had attracted considerable interest, and in a number of instances had played a role in cable system franchise negotiations.

Home shopping services varied considerably in sophistication, ranging from one-way services through which consumers could order products seen on CATV programs, to two-way systems called *videotext*, through which customers could both request and receive specific product information as well as place orders.

Advertising and Cable TV

As the number of subscribers to CATV grew, interest in its potential as an advertising medium increased. According to Trevor Lambert:

Broadcast network viewing numbers used to increase annually merely as a result of population growth. But recently, slower population growth, inflation, and audience erosion due to cable, among other things, have decreased broadcast TV viewing. This has caused advertising rates to increase faster than inflation and has made cable television advertising an increasingly attractive alternative.

National and local advertising revenues on cable, according to the Cable-Television Advertising Bureau, were approximately $250 million in 1982, a 250% increase over 1981. Broadcast TV advertising revenues were $12.6 billion in 1981, and over $13 billion in 1982. One industry expert forecast CATV advertising revenues to reach $2 billion and represent 14% of total broadcast TV revenues over the next decade.

Proponents of CATV advertising pointed out that the increasing cost of broadcast TV advertising had outpaced population growth, and the decrease in network TV's share of total TV viewing had increased the cost of network TV compared with other alternatives. They also contended that the audience erosion had been especially prevalent among upscale consumers. One Nielsen report found that 7 of the top 20 shows among households without CATV were not on the list of the top 20 shows among CATV households. Households subscribing to one or more pay-cable services were more likely to include children and teenagers, to be more affluent, and have younger heads of household. According to yet another survey, 72% of cable subscribers were under 50 years of age, and 49% of households earning more than $40,000 annually were CATV subscribers.

Narrowcasting vs. Mass Audience Advertising

One prominent viewpoint was that CATV advertising, like advertising in special interest magazines and newspapers, offered a better advertising opportunity for products with a highly segmented market than for mass market product. One agency executive felt that the variety of programming that could be offered over the many channels of a CATV system provided the same opportunity to segment the market, as did, for example, *Tennis, Sports Illustrated, Bride, Working Woman,* or *Field and Stream.* This "narrowcasting" concept was not enthusiastically accepted by everyone in the CATV industry, however. For some, executives, aware of the revenues associated with heavy network TV advertisers, narrowcasting was synonymous with small audiences and a small potential market.

Proponents of the viewpoint that CATV was a mass audience advertising vehicle based their argument on the erosion of network TV's access to the upscale audience and on the rapidly growing size and favorable demographics of the CATV audience. They pointed out that young, educated, affluent men and women had always been light TV viewers, and it was precisely this kind of viewer that was turning to CATV. They further contended that these consumers were the prime advertising targets for packaged goods as well as for upscale items.

A number of cable systems had begun to develop ways to offer audience numbers approaching network TV. "Regional interconnects" were agreements between individual cable systems to form several common channels.

Advertising Agency Response to CATV

Agency response to CATV advertising was as diverse as the CATV industry's opinions of how it should best be exploited. An executive at the Ted Bates agency recommended that clients put 5% of their prime-time ad dollars into superstation advertising to counteract the effect of network viewer share erosion. A Doyle Dane Bernbach executive felt that, "CATV is still too new. I can't see spending money on CATV when I can get better numbers on the networks."

The CableShop Pilot Test

The ten-month CableShop pilot test began in March 1982 and involved 17 major national advertisers. Lambert expected the results of the research on the Peabody experiment to play a major role in evaluating the CableShop concept and demonstrating its business potential.

The Research and Planning Department of J. Walter Thompson prepared a research program to evaluate CableShop and provide information that would help in designing an introduction strategy. The purpose of the test was threefold:

To test the basic CableShop premise

To determine the effectiveness of informational advertising and

To determine consumer attitudes toward TV programming advertising

The field test consisted of five distinct and unconnected parts:

1. *Qualitative exploration* consisted of a series of discussion groups conducted in June 1981 and again in May 1982 to obtain a broad understanding of the business and research issues that needed consideration in developing CableShop marketing and research programs and to test the questionnaires.

2. *The subscriber census* was a mail questionnaire sent to 6,112 subscriber households immediately after they subscribed, but before using the service. The purpose was to provide demographic information as well as an assessment of subscriber motivations and expectations (2,244 questionnaires were completed).

3. *Call-in monitoring* of all requests for specific messages was done by the CableShop computer. The log included the time of day, the day of the week, the advertising sponsor requested, and the identification number of the household making the request.

4. *An ongoing tracking procedure* was used to track CableShop awareness, trial, frequency of use, and attitudes toward both CableShop and the advertisers throughout the test period. In ad-

dition, 225 random telephone interviews were conducted each month to acquire information about the relative proportions of requests and "browsing" (viewing scheduled commercials).

5. *Three waves of telephone interviewing* were planned to measure changes in attitude toward TV viewing in general, and to assess the perceived benefits and potential of CableShop in particular. The first wave (benchmark) was completed just before CableShop was introduced.

The timing of the various research components is displayed in Exhibit 3.3.

Pilot Test Research Findings

The research indicated that A-R's Peabody cable franchise was above the national average in the percentage of solicited households that had become subscribers (56%), the percentage of subscribers that received at least one pay channel (92%), and the average number of pay channels per subscriber (2.2). Some results that Trevor Lambert considered important are found in Exhibits 3.4 to 3.9.

CableShop Introduction Plans

Mr. Lambert's introduction plan included paying cable operators, after the first six months, $2.50 per subscriber annually for offering CableShop. A-R would install all the necessary equipment, monitor its operation remotely, and provide service as necessary, at no cost to the cable operator. Subscriber calls to CableShop and infomercial scheduling would be handled automatically by the CableShop equipment and would not require cable operator attention. "They just have to provide a place for the equipment to stand (about four square feet of floor space) and a place to plug it in, and stick in a cassette once a month, and we'll do the rest," said Lambert. "We even pay for the Cable-Shop insert in their local viewing guide!"

The rollout version of CableShop would have only two channels, instead of the four that were tested. Advertising messages would be separated by a 30-second menu break. Acknowledgment of

Exhibit 3.3   Cableshop Research Schedule

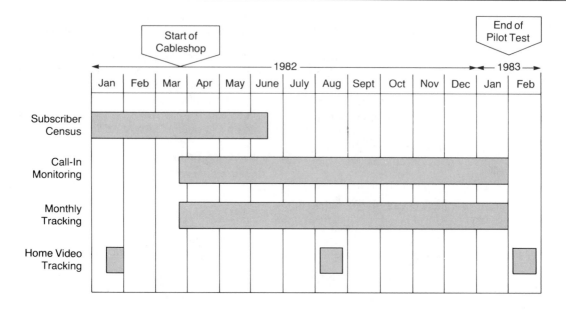

an ad request would be displayed as an overlay on whatever was currently being viewed.

Lambert anticipated some CATV operator resistance to the $2.50 subscriber fee and to the initial six-month free period.

> They'll say, "We're getting $30 per subscriber per month for entertainment. Why should we use up two channels for less than 1% of that?" But I think that the relevant comparison to make is to broadcast advertising. Approximately $13 billion was spent last year to reach 80 million households, which works out to roughly $162 per household per year. We're offering to pay the operators 2% of the entire TV industry advertising budget per household with no investment on their part at all.

Lambert's plan for introducing the CableShop was a phased rollout of CableShop services beginning with an initial subscriber base of 250,000 households in four major metropolitan areas. Sub-scribers would be added as more CATV systems were added to the CableShop network. The Cab-leShop concept he planned to use with advertisers stressed the pioneering nature of the product and its potential benefits:

> The CableShop is potentially a new mass medium for reaching sponsor-oriented viewers who are tuning out regular broadcast commer-cials but who will *choose to watch* your advertis-ing.

Lambert felt that buying access to viewers who *choose to watch* advertising was so different from buying normal broadcast advertising that potential clients would require extensive research findings to see its value. The Peabody pilot test had been a first step in providing this information and was intended to establish that there was an audience for infomer-cials. Lambert also felt that advertisers would re-quire extensive research data to confirm the suc-cess of infomercials for their own products before

Exhibit 3.4   Research Findings about Cable Subscribers

Cable Subscribers Are TV Fans

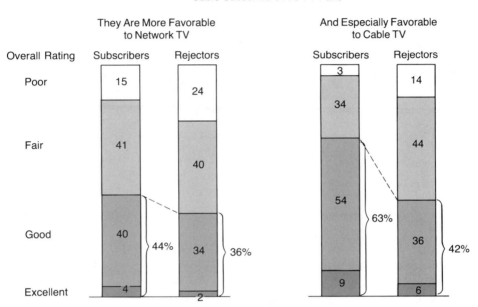

They Are More Favorable
to Network TV

Overall Rating	Subscribers	Rejectors
Poor	15	24
Fair	41	40
Good	40 } 44%	34 } 36%
Excellent	4	2

And Especially Favorable
to Cable TV

	Subscribers	Rejectors
	3	14
	34	44
	54 } 63%	36 } 42%
	9	6

Regarding Cable TV, Subscribers Are Strong Supporters

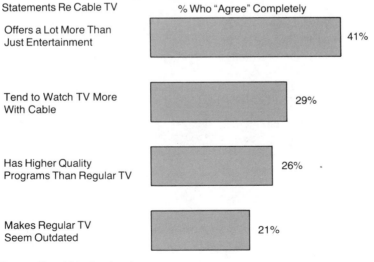

Statements Re Cable TV   % Who "Agree" Completely

Offers a Lot More Than
Just Entertainment   41%

Tend to Watch TV More
With Cable   29%

Has Higher Quality
Programs Than Regular TV   26%

Makes Regular TV
Seem Outdated   21%

Source: Home Video Benchmark

Exhibit 3.5   Research Findings about TV Commercials

Avoidance of Commercials . . . Claimed to Be an Important
Motivation for Cable Subscription

Reasons for Subscribing*   % "Extremely" Important

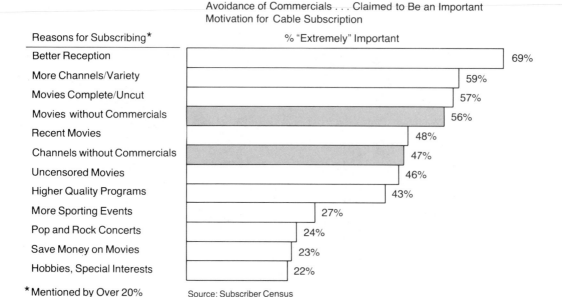

Reason	%
Better Reception	69%
More Channels/Variety	59%
Movies Complete/Uncut	57%
Movies without Commercials	56%
Recent Movies	48%
Channels without Commercials	47%
Uncensored Movies	46%
Higher Quality Programs	43%
More Sporting Events	27%
Pop and Rock Concerts	24%
Save Money on Movies	23%
Hobbies, Special Interests	22%

*Mentioned by Over 20%

Source: Subscriber Census

Cable Subscribers View Network TV Commercials
As *Irritating* and *Not Helpful in Buying*

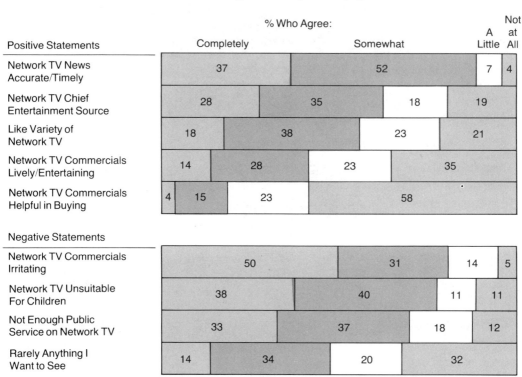

% Who Agree:

Positive Statements	Completely	Somewhat	A Little	Not at All
Network TV News Accurate/Timely	37	52	7	4
Network TV Chief Entertainment Source	28	35	18	19
Like Variety of Network TV	18	38	23	21
Network TV Commercials Lively/Entertaining	14	28	23	35
Network TV Commercials Helpful in Buying	4 15	23	58	

Negative Statements				
Network TV Commercials Irritating	50	31	14	5
Network TV Unsuitable For Children	38	40	11	11
Not Enough Public Service on Network TV	33	37	18	12
Rarely Anything I Want to See	14	34	20	32

Source: Home Video Benchmark

Exhibit 3.6   Research Findings about CableShop

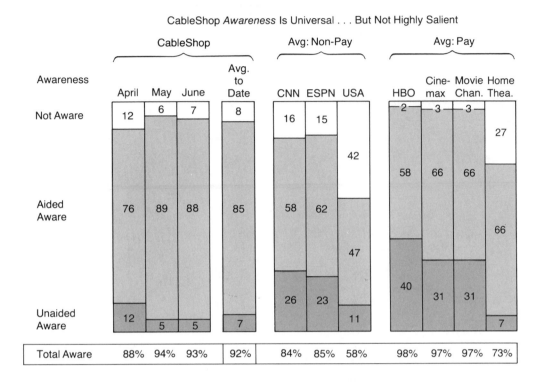

CableShop *Awareness* Is Universal . . . But Not Highly Salient

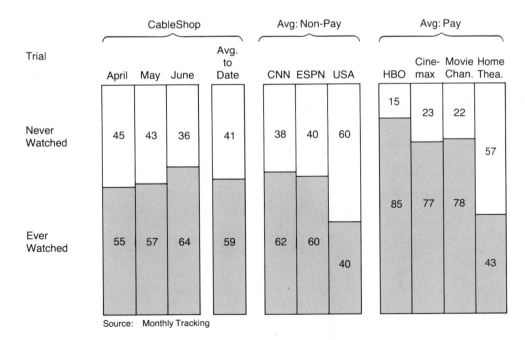

CableShop *Trial* Is Strong . . . and Building

Source: Monthly Tracking

Exhibit 3.7 Research Findings about Viewers' Watching CableShop

Among All Viewers, Watching Messages *All the Way Through* Is Increasing

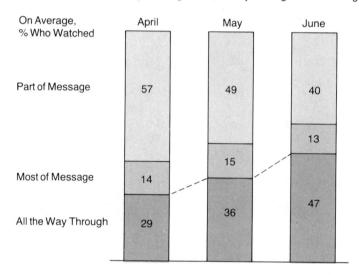

Although High . . . Levels Are Dropping For
*Viewing Frequency
*Recall of Multiple Sponsors
Probably Due to the Low Proportion of New Messages

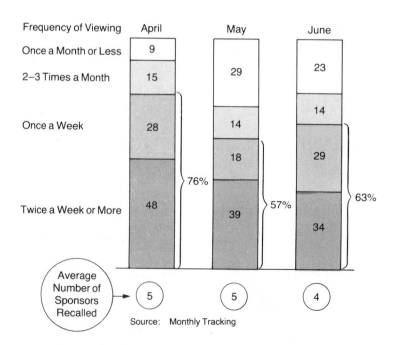

Source: Monthly Tracking

Exhibit 3.8 Research Findings about CableShop's Appeal

Overall, CableShop Has High Appeal . . . and Gains over Time

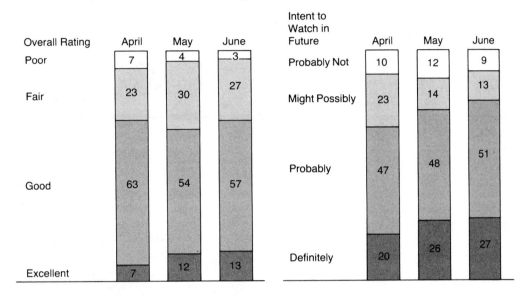

Propensity to Action* Is Substantial . . . and Building

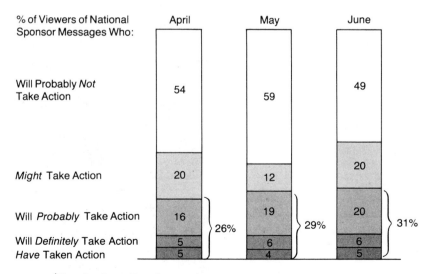

*Based on three alternative courses:
A follow-up phone call
Sending for literature
Visiting a retail store

Source: Monthly Tracking

Exhibit 3.9 Research Findings about CableShop's Messages

CableShop Messages Are Perceived as Useful

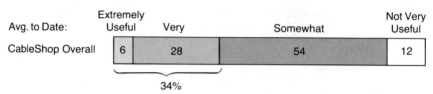

CableShop Messages Are of Far Greater Interest
Than Network Commercials

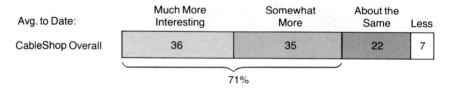

CableShop Messages Increase Favorability to
Sponsors' Products

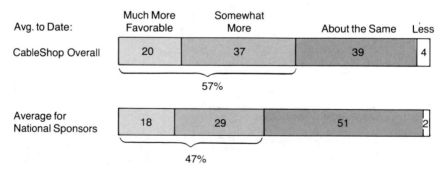

Exhibit 3.10   CableShop Sponsorship Plan

Audience
Cable systems in 250,000 cable households in
Boston
Chicago
Los Angeles
Atlanta
Other systems to be added

Programming Format
Two programming channels
Interactive dial-in capability
All programming will be 4- to 6-minute advertising messages
Each message separated by 30-second "menu break"

Telecast Frequency for Individual Infomercials
Projected average of 9 showings per day
Maximum frequency will be once hourly
Fair rotation in all day parts
No message to be aired for more than two consecutive months
Guaranteed 120 showings per month

Promotional Support
Infomercial listing with logo identification in the CableShop Guide
Local CableShop advertising campaign
Optional promotional programs in the CableShop Guide

Marketing Research
CableShop performance study
"Brand-impact" study
Customized research opportunities

committing to repeated use of CableShop. For these reasons, he intended CableShop to be marketed initially as a partnership in developing a new advertising service rather than an established advertising medium:

The CableShop Sponsorship Plan represents an opportunity for advertisers and their agencies to understand the dynamics of cable viewing, to test long-form advertising, and to help shape the future direction of infomercial advertising and interactive viewing systems as an alternative medium to the eroding position of network TV.

The CableShop Sponsorship Plan (CSP), as explained in CableShop promotional material, is found in Exhibit 3.10.

The cost of sponsorship was to be based on a rate of $25/1,000 cable households per month for a minimum of six months. A participating CSP advertiser would pay a semiannual fee of $37,500 for access to 250,000 households. In addition, the client would have to produce at least three infomercials, the cost of which Lambert estimated would be about the same as the cost of the CableShop sponsorship. Lambert had, in fact, used this production cost estimate in pricing CableShop sponsorship. "I didn't want potential clients to be constrained from buying CableShop because of unfavorable comparison with production costs," he said. Lambert felt that infomercials would "wear out" faster than network commercials and ideally should be changed monthly. Thus, a CSP advertiser's cost for

Exhibit 3.11   Pro Forma Five-Year Plan

System Description		Revenue	
Number of channels	2	Adv. fee per 1000 HH-month	$25.00
Percent of time sold	50.0%	Subscriber fee per call	$ 0.00
Infomercial length in minutes	6.5	Number of calls per 1000 HH-month	80
Broadcast hours per channel-day	24	Service charge per HH-month	$ 0.00
Showings per infomercial per day	9		

Investments		
Days receivable	60	
Hardware	45,000.00	

Expense	
Hardware maintenance/system-month	$500.00
Marketing	30.0%
General and administrative	10.0%
Tape editing per system-month	$350.00
CableShop Guide per HH-year	$ 0.60

Five-Year Plan
(dollars in thousands)

	Year 1	Year 2	Year 3	Year 4	Year 5	
System Description						
Number of systems	15	20	30	40	50	
Households per system	16,000	16,000	16,000	16,000	16,000	
Total Households	240,000	320,000	480,000	640,000	600,000	
Number of channels per system	2	2	2	3	4	
Maximum number of advertisers	49	49	49	74	98	
Number of advertisers	20	30	40	60	80	
Revenue Sources:						
Advertising fee per 1000 HH-month	$25.00	$25.00	$25.00	$25.00	$25.00	
Operator fee per 1000 HH-month	0.00	0.00	0.00	0.00	0.00	
Subscriber fee per month	0.00	0.00	0.00	0.00	0.00	
Subscriber fee per call	0.00	0.00	0.00	0.00	0.00	
Calls per 1000 HH-month	80	80	80	80	80	
Variable Expenses						
System access fee per subscriber	$ 1.25	$ 2.50	$ 2.50	$ 2.50	$ 2.50	
Operating Results						**Total**
Revenue from advertisers	$ 1,440	$ 2,880	$ 5,760	$ 11,520	$ 19,200	$ 40,800
Revenue from cable operators	0	0	0	0	0	0
Revenue from subscribers	0	0	0	0	0	0
Total revenue	$ 1,440	$ 2,880	$ 5,760	$ 11,520	$ 19,200	$ 40,800

(continued)

Exhibit 3.11 (continued) Pro Forma Five-Year Plan

	Year 1	Year 2	Year 3	Year 4	Year 5	Total
Operating Costs						
CableShop guide	$ 144	$ 192	$ 288	$ 384	$ 480	$ 0
Maintenance	90	120	180	240	300	930
Tape editing	63	84	126	168	210	651
Marketing	432	864	1,728	3,456	5,760	12,240
Cable use fee	300	800	1,200	1,600	2,000	5,900
	$ 1,029	2,060	3,522	5,848	8,750	21,209
General and Administrative Cost	144	288	576	1,152	1,920	4,080
Total Costs	$ 1,173	$ 2,348	$ 4,098	$ 7,000	$ 10,670	$ 25,289
Operating Profit	$ 267	$ 532	$ 1,662	$ 4,520	$ 8,530	$ 15,511
Depreciation)20%/year)	135	180	270	360	450	1,395
Profit Before Tax	$ 132	$ 352	$ 1,662	$ 4,160	$ 8,080	$ 14,116
Tax (49%)	65	172	681	2,034	3,951	6,903
Profit After Tax	$ 67	$ 180	$ 711	$ 2,126	$ 4,129	$ 7,213

six-month CableShop sponsorship would be between $75,000 and $112,500.

To help clients evaluate the effectiveness of CableShop infomercials, Burke Marketing Research had designed an extensive, optional marketing research program.

The Current Situation

Six months after the introduction Trevor Lambert faced a perplexing situation. Although he felt that the results of the CableShop test market showed excellent acceptance of the concept, advertisers were not buying the service. Even the advertisers who had participated in the test market had not signed contracts. Their typical response had been, "When you have 2.5 million subscribers, let us know!"

The reluctance of advertisers to buy CableShop was perplexing, especially since he thought that the Peabody test results were so favorable. Lambert concluded that advertisers were having a very difficult time comparing CableShop with more traditional advertising vehicles. In particular, it had been difficult to help advertisers make cost comparisons between media advertising and CableShop. This difficulty, in turn, was reflected in Lambert's uncertainty about how to price the product.

I think that the basic concept is sound and that the Peabody test shows there is a consumer audience for the service. But pricing such a new product is a real problem. I've tried to consider the total cost of the service and the infomercial production. And I've tried to forecast our cash flows and profitability at various price levels. An advertising price of $25/1,000 subscribers makes sense to us financially, but I don't have a really good feel right now for how much sense it makes to a potential advertiser. We'd like to provide clients with a good value for their money, but we don't want to leave money on the table!

Lambert had developed a simple spreadsheet model that would allow him to investigate the financial implications of alternative introduction plans. His analysis of the current plan is found in Exhibit 3.11.

Preparation Questions

1. Why haven't any advertisers signed up for CableShop?

2. What are the important managerial issues facing Mr. Lambert?

3. What was learned from the research about CS's attractiveness to CATV operators? Advertisers? Viewers?

4. Evaluate the research design. What questions are left unanswered?

5. How does the secondary data in the case contribute to planning the introduction strategy?

6. Develop a five-year plan for the CableShop.

The CableShop Spreadsheet Model

The five-year plan that appears in Exhibit 3.11 is a slight modification of a personal computer model that Mr. Lambert used in developing a five-year plan. Mr. Lambert's model has been rewritten in a Lotus 1-2-3 spreadsheet that you can use in developing your own five year plan. Most of the terms used in the spreadsheet are fairly standard and the definitions can be guessed directly from the row name. Of course, the definition can be derived from the formula for any cell, which can be found by moving the cursor to the cell in question and reading the formula in the upper left-hand corner of the screen.

This spreadsheet is intended to be used in deriving a five-year plan for the CableShop. You will probably notice that you have to make a lot of guesses in using the spreadsheet. Much of the guessing is unavoidable and normal in planning efforts for new products, but the CableShop case provides marketing survey results designed to investigate the attractiveness of the concept to CATV viewers and considerable secondary data has been gathered about CATV systems, advertising costs and media choices, and purchase frequency for a few product categories. One would hope that this information could be incorporated into the planning effort in order to make the guessing better informed. This is much harder to do than it might at first seem, and you will probably be somewhat frustrated. Keep track of your frustrations (the spreadsheet will display your successes) and try to determine what

role CableShop's research process plays in your experience. You should also develop a research process that you would have used if you had been in Mr. Lambert's position.

Spreadsheet Overview

The spreadsheet consists of three main parts: common inputs that apply in each period of the planning horizon; inputs that change from period to period; and a set of reports based on the inputs. These spreadsheet segments can be found using the menu (reached by [Alt] M) or, since the spreadsheet is arranged vertically, the up and down arrows, or [PgUp] and [PgDn] will get you from place to place. The initial screen that you will encounter when the spreadsheet appears on the screen as shown in Exhibit 3.12.

When you have completed your work, or just want a copy of a particular plan, you can type [Alt] P and the spreadsheet will be printed. The entire spreadsheet appears in Exhibit 3.13.

One of the variables that needs to be explained is the "Max # of advertisers"—Maximum number of advertisers. This value is a measure of the advertising capacity of the system, to which you can compare your estimate of the number of advertisers in each period—"# of advertisers." The maximum number of advertisers that the system can accommodate (M) is calculated as follows:

$$M = \frac{N * BM * 60}{L * S}$$

Exhibit 3.12   Initial CableShop Spreadsheet Screen

```
A1: PR                                                                    MENU
Common   Inputs   Rev & Costs   Profit & Inv   Summary   Quit
Common   inputs across periods
         A        B        C        D        E        F        G        H
1
2                         Cableshop System Planner
3                    (inputs per system unless otherwise noted)
4
5
6       System Description                        Expenses
7       ------------------                        --------
8       Infomercial length in min.      6.5   Hardware maint/sys.-month   $500.00
9       Broadcast hrs./channel-day       24   Marketing                     30.0%
10      Showings/infomercial/day          9   General and administrative    10.0%
11                                            Tape editing/sys.-month     $350.00
12                                            Cableshop Guide/HH-year       $0.60
13              Investments
14              -----------
15      Days receivables                 60
16      Hardware               $45,000
17
18
19
20
13-Nov-86   11:49 AM                          CMD
```

where

N	is the number of channels per system
BM	is the broadcast hours per channel-day
L	is the infomercial length in minutes
S	is the number of infomercial showings per day

This number does not enter into the calculations in the spreadsheet directly, but is used only for comparison. The number of advertisers, which is entered directly, is used in various calculations in the spreadsheet. This is important to note because if you make changes in any of the values in the formula above they will have no effect in the spreadsheet; in other words, if you change N, or BM, or L, or S, nothing will be changed in the spreadsheet except M, the maximum number of advertisers.

The revenue sources in the model also require some comment, since some of them are not discussed in the case. An attempt has been made to allow you to consider various revenue sources other than those considered by Mr. Lambert without modifying the spreadsheet. The fact that a source of revenue appears in the spreadsheet is not an endorsement that it should be used. If you don't think a source is appropriate, just put zeros in for the rate. Here are notes on the revenue sources:

Adv fee/1000 HH-month—price charged advertisers to advertise on the CableShop system

Oper fee/1000 HH-month—fee that cable operators pay to offer CableShop on their CATV system

Subscriber fee/month—fee that CATV viewers pay to subscribe to the CableShop service

Subscriber fee/call—fee that subscribers pay for each infomercial that they request

Calls/1000 HH-month—average number of infomercial requests occurring per 1000 HH in a month.

Exhibit 3.13   CableShop Spreadsheet Model

```
                    Cableshop System Planner
              (inputs per system unless otherwise noted)


        System Description                    Expenses
        ------------------                    --------
   Infomercial length in min.    6.5   Hardware maint/sys.-month  $500.00
   Broadcast hrs./channel-day     24   Marketing                    30.0%
   Showings/infomercial/day        9   General and administrative   10.0%
                                       Tape editing/sys.-month    $350.00
                                       Cableshop Guide/HH-year      $0.60

        Investments
        -----------
   Days receivables               60
   Hardware                  $45,000
```

Cableshop System Description

	(dollars in thousands)				
System Description	Year 1	Year 2	Year 3	Year 4	Year 5
Number of systems	15	20	30	40	50
Households per system	16,000	16,000	16,000	16,000	16,000
Total households	240,000	320,000	480,000	640,000	800,000
# of channels/system	2	2	2	3	4
Max # of advertisers	49	49	49	74	98
# of advertisers	20	30	40	60	80
Capacity utilization	40.6%	60.9%	81.3%	81.3%	81.3%
Revenue Sources					
Adv fee/1000 HH-month	$25.00	$25.00	$25.00	$25.00	$25.00
Oper fee/1000 HH-mnth	$0.00	$0.00	$0.00	$0.00	$0.00
Subscriber fee/month	$0.00	$0.00	$0.00	$0.00	$0.00
Subscriber fee/call	$0.00	$0.00	$0.00	$0.00	$0.00
Calls/1000 HH-month	80	80	80	80	80
Variable Expenses					
Access fee/subscriber	$1.25	$2.50	$2.50	$2.50	$2.50

Cableshop Financial Forecast

	Year 1	Year 2	Year 3	Year 4	Year 5	Total
Revenues						
From Advertisers	$1,440	$2,880	$5,760	$11,520	$19,200	$40,800
From Cable Oper.	0	0	0	0	0	0
From Subscribers	0	0	0	0	0	0
Total Revenue	$1,440	$2,880	$5,760	$11,520	$19,200	$40,800
Operating Costs						
Cableshop Guide	$144	$192	$288	$384	$480	$1,488
Maintenance	90	120	180	240	300	930
Tape editing	63	84	126	168	210	651
Marketing	432	864	1,728	3,456	5,760	12,240

(continued)

Exhibit 3.13 (continued)   CableShop Spreadsheet Model

Cable use fee	300	800	1,200	1,600	2,000	5,900
	$1,029	$2,060	$3,522	$5,848	$8,750	$21,209
Gen & Admin Cost	$144	$288	$576	$1,152	$1,920	$4,080
Total Costs	$1,173	$2,348	$4,098	$7,000	$10,670	$25,289

	Year 1	Year 2	Year 3	Year 4	Year 5	Total
Operating Profit	$267	$532	$1,662	$4,520	$8,530	$15,511
Deprec. (20%/yr)	135	180	270	360	450	1,395
Profit Before Tax	$132	$352	$1,392	$4,160	$8,080	$14,116
Tax (49%)	65	172	681	2,034	3,951	6,903
Profit After Tax	$67	$180	$711	$2,126	$4,129	$7,213

Investments

Capital Equipment	$675	$900	$1,350	$1,800	$2,250	$6,975
Receivables	237	473	947	1,894	3,156	6,707
Total Investment	$912	$1,373	$2,297	$3,694	$5,406	$13,682

Cableshop System Planner
Financial Summary per System

	(dollars in thousands)				
	Year 1	Year 2	Year 3	Year 4	Year 5
Revenue per System	$96	$144	$192	$288	$384
Cost per System	$87	$126	$146	$184	$222
Profit Before Tax	$9	$18	$46	$104	$162
Profit After Tax	$4	$9	$24	$53	$83
System Investment	$61	$69	$77	$92	$108
Operating Margin (ROS)	9.2%	12.2%	24.2%	36.1%	42.1%
Asset Turnover	1.58	2.10	2.51	3.12	3.55
Return on Assets (ROA)	14.5%	25.6%	60.6%	112.6%	149.5%
Return on Invest. (ROI)	7.4%	13.1%	31.0%	57.6%	76.4%

CASE: Optical Distortion, Inc.

ODI is a very small company seeking to introduce a radically new product that may be a viable substitute for current practice in an agricultural market. The product is contact lenses for chickens, and it is hard to imagine a more unique product concept for which to develop a business plan. The case provides an interesting contrast between its approach to marketing analysis and the approach in the CableShop. The decision model that accompanies the case is a heuristic model relating marketing effort to market response. The model is developed from managerial judgment and available secondary data. No expensive research is undertaken, yet this preliminary decision model proves to be quite useful for planning an entry strategy and defining future research needs. It is also important as an illustration of the development of a preliminary decision model, which plays an important part in our analytical process.

In late fall of 1974, Daniel Garrison, president and chief executive officer of Optical Distortion, Inc. (ODI), asked Ronald Olson, marketing vice president, to develop a marketing plan for ODI's new and only product—a contact lens for chickens.* While human contact lenses serve mainly to improve eyesight, the lens developed by ODI was made to partially blind the chickens. Garrison explained:

Like so many other great discoveries, our product concept was discovered quite by accident. In 1962 a chicken farmer in Arizona had a flock of chickens that developed a severe cataract problem. When he became aware of the problem, he separated the afflicted birds from the rest of the flock and subsequently observed that the afflicted birds seemed to eat less and were much easier to handle. So dramatic was the difference that a poultry medical detailman visiting

the farm, rather than being asked for a cure, was asked if there was any way to similarly afflict the rest of the flock. It has not proved possible chemically or genetically to duplicate the chickens' reduced vision resulting from the cataracts, but a chicken wearing the ODI lenses has its vision reduced enough to obtain the good behavior the Arizona farmer observed. This behavior has important economic implications for the chicken farmer.

By the end of 1974, the ODI lens had been tested on a number of farms in California and Oregon with satisfactory results, and Garrison was convinced that "the time has come to stop worrying about the product and get this show off the ground." While his timetable was tentative, he hoped that the ODI lens could be introduced in at least one region during spring of 1975, and that national distribution would be achieved by the end of 1977 at the latest. As he explained:

Our patent and license protection should hold off competition for at least three years, but—if we have the success I believe we will—I would

---

*Throughout this case *chicken* is used as a technical term to describe the female bird (three months old or older) raised for the purpose of egg production. Male birds are referred to as *friers* or *broilers*.

This case was prepared by Randall Wise and Darral G. Clarke.

Copyright ©1983 by the President and Fellows of Harvard College, Harvard Business School cases 9-575-072

expect the large agricultural supply firms to find a way around our patent by the late 1970s. By 1980, I would expect the big boys to have come in, and the competition to be fierce. If we are to gain the fruits of our development work, we will have to be strong enough to fight them on their own terms. To do this, we will have to be a multi-product, multimarket company that can provide effective service anywhere in the country.

Company Background

The ODI lens had been invented in 1965 by Robert D. Garrison—Daniel Garrison's father—working with Ronald Olson, the owner of a large chicken farm in Oregon. Robert Garrison conceptualized and designed the original product, and he had then worked with Olson to test and refine the lenses on Olson's chicken farm. In 1966 their efforts attracted the attention of James Arnold, a local businessman who invested approximately $5,000 in the venture. By late 1966 the three men had formed a corporation to exploit Garrison's invention.

Further testing of the lens on Olson's chicken farm during 1967, however, had identified several technical difficulties with the product. In particular, the early prototypes did not always remain in the chickens' eyes after insertion, and they frequently caused severe irritation in the last months of the chicken's 12-month laying life. Both problems were quite serious because, as Daniel Garrison explained, "No farmer is going to spend time looking into the eyes of his chickens to make sure the lenses are still there and the eyes are not bloodshot."

By 1968 ODI had solved the retention problem by modifying the size of the lens, and the company was issued a U.S. patent on the lens in December 1969. ODI found that the irritation problem could be essentially eliminated by making the lenses of a soft plastic called a hydrophilic polymer. The patents for this polymer, the same material used by Bausch and Lomb to produce soft contact lenses for human use, were controlled by New World Plastics, Baltimore, Maryland. New World's hydrophilic polymer could not be injection molded, however, and manufacturing costs using alternative production processes were far too high for the chicken market.

Since New World's hydrophilic polymer was the only such material known at the time, ODI had reached an impasse and the company became dormant.

In 1973 Robert Garrison asked his son Daniel Garrison, a student at the Harvard Business School, to contact New World Plastics and see if any progress had been made in the hydrophilic polymer. Daniel Garrison found that the hydrophilic polymer could now be injection molded and he became enthusiastic about the product's potential. With the approval of the owners, Daniel Garrison obtained a long-term license from New World for the exclusive use of hydrophilic polymer for nonhuman applications.

Under the terms of the license, New World agreed not to produce the polymer for other firms seeking nonhuman markets, nor to carry out development work on related polymers for such firms. ODI, in turn, agreed to pay New World $50,000 ($25,000 per year for the first two years), and to purchase its lenses exclusively from New World. New World would manufacture the lenses and sell them to ODI at a price of $0.032 per pair (in bulk), regardless of quantity. ODI was to supply New World with injection molds (at a cost of $12,000 each). Each injection mold had an annual capacity of 7.2 million pair, and an expected life of 15 million pairs.

During the negotiations with New World Plastics, Daniel Garrison purchased 25% of the stock of ODI from the previous owners and was elected president and chief executive officer of the firm. Having completed the license agreement with New World, he was able to raise $200,000 in the venture capital markets. About this time, Ronald Olson became vice president of marketing, and the two men began devoting a substantial portion of their time to ODI. As of late 1974, Daniel Garrison and Olson were the only full-time employees of the firm, although Robert Garrison and James Arnold remained active as stockholders and members of the board.

The Poultry Industry

Poultry and egg production had its beginnings in the family barnyard. As late as 1900, it was not unusual for a family to have its own chickens, even in

Exhibit 3.14   Chicken Census, 1880–1969

Year	No. of Farms Raising Chickens Commercially	Percent of All Farms	No. of Chickens
1880	na	na	102,272,135
1890	na	na	258,871,125
1900	na	na	233,598,085
1910	5,580,758	na	280,410,531
1920	5,839,489	na	359,607,148
1925	5,505,617	na	409,290,849
1930	5,375,559	na	379,159,783
1935	5,833,079	na	371,603,136
1940	5,152,354	84.4	338,240,109
1945	4,900,948	83.4	433,110,674
1950	4,218,857	78.3	342,956,055
1954	3,418,204	71.5	375,800,447
1959	2,172,264	58.6	351,029,294
1964	1,210,669	38.3	343,167,807
1969	471,284	17.3	371,008,459

urban areas, or to buy eggs fresh from a small local farmer. In 1921 the largest commercial egg farm in the United States was in Petaluma, California, and boasted a flock of about 2,000 hens. The eggs were picked up twice daily and loaded into a horse-drawn wagon.

In an effort to increase the efficiency of egg production, some California farmers began confining the birds to large henhouses during the 1930s and 1940s. In other parts of the United States, eggs were still being collected from haystacks until the 1940s, when henhouses became common throughout the country. Continuing their innovation, California poultrymen began to increase the utilization of henhouse space by further confining the birds in groups of three or four within multitiered wire cages, 18" x 12" in size. By the 1950s, these innovations had spread widely throughout the United States and had led to considerable concentration in the poultry industry (see Exhibit 3.14).

In 1974 the largest commercial flock of laying hens in the United States was 2.5 million birds, and 80% of the 440,000,000 laying hens in the United States were housed on 3% of the known chicken farms. California, North Carolina, and Georgia ac-

counted for 25% of the nation's chickens, while nine additional states (mostly in the South and Northeast) accounted for an additional 36% of the chicken population. Two counties in southern California contained 20 farms that housed 21 million chickens. Further details on the distribution of chicken farms in the United States are given in Exhibits 3.15 and 3.16; data on the economics of chicken farming are shown in Exhibits 3.17 and 3.18.

As might be expected from the changes in the size and number of chicken farms, the business of running a large chicken farm had changed a great deal since the 1920s. Daniel Garrison characterized the problems of managing various-sized chicken farms—small, medium, and large.

1. *Small farms* (10,000 or fewer birds). These small farms are usually family operated. They may contract their production to a larger producer, but more probably they sell their eggs locally through small grocery or milk and egg stores or at their own farm. A farmer of this size probably purchases starter pullets only once or twice a year. The birds are housed in henhouses of

Exhibit 3.15 Density of U.S. Chicken Population, 1969

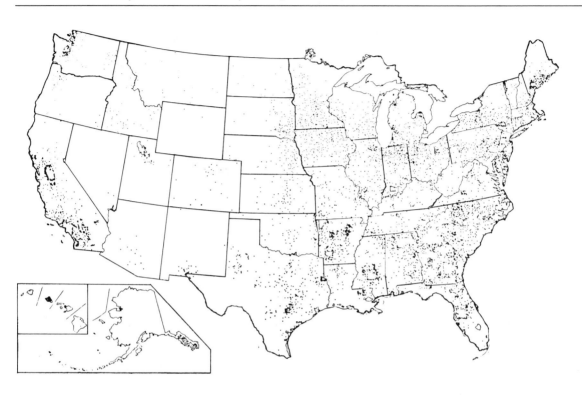

Source: Dept. of Commerce, Social, and Economic Statistics Administration, Bureau of the Census.
Note: Includes chickens three months or older. Total U.S. chicken population in 1969 was 371,008,459. One dot equals 50,000 chickens.

about 1,000–2,000 birds. The number of such farms has been declining at a rate of about 25 percent per year.

2. *Medium farms* (10,000-50,000 birds). A chicken farm of this size is typically operated professionally. Such farms are usually still owned and managed by the farmer. The farmer-owner performs administrative tasks and makes most decisions regarding the operation of the farm himself. A farm of this size requires considerable business skill as well as agricultural skill. Such an owner has yearly cash flows on the order of $375,000 to manage and would deal with large corporate

suppliers such as hatcheries, feed companies, and equipment manufacturers. The farmer most likely negotiates with a large corporate purchaser of the farm's egg production. Individual cash transactions can be as large as $35,000.

3. *Large farms* (over 50,000 birds). A chicken farm of this size is in many ways like a small manufacturing firm. Administration of the farm is sufficiently complex to require the skills and efforts of several people. The farm could employ 100 or more people and have an annual cash flow of $12 million. Such farms may mix their own feed in facilities costing up to $500,000. Their

Exhibit 3.16   Characteristics of U.S. Chicken Farms, 1969

	Total Farms (Sales over $2,500)	Chickens on Total Farms	No. of Farms	Flock Size 20,000–49,000	
				No. of Farms Reporting Flock Size	No. of Chickens*
States in Pacific Region					
Washington	1,929	5,230,575	40	20	1,090,102
Oregon	1,825	2,249,752	13	13	414,220
California	3,023,46,203,988	320	320	9,517,453	
Alaska	25	25,617	0	0	†
Hawaii	90	1,069,618	8	8	255,000
Pacific Region Total	6,892	54,779,550	381	361	11,276,775
Other Regions					
New England	2,621	17,265,305	135	128	3,660,578
Middle Atlantic	12,867	31,036,554	240	240	6,969,792
East North Central	54,429	46,650,039	339	339	9,267,919
West North Central	112,119	41,213,868	158	156	4,372,320
South Atlantic	29,971	82,176,127	860	860	24,221,265
East South Central	29,045	36,617,712	317	317	8,854,258
West South Central	31,101	46,450,783	412	412	11,876,032
Mountain	14,295	7,018,828	28	23	682,444
Total U.S.	293,340	363,208,766	2,870	2,856	81,547,775
Percent of Total	100%	100%	1%		22.4%

	No. of Farms	Flock Size 50,000–99,000	No. of Chickens*
		No. of Farms Reporting Flock Size	
States in Pacific Region			
Washington	11	11	663,378
Oregon	3	3	229,000
California	114	114	7,459,994
Alaska	0	0	†
Hawaii	4	0	†
Pacific Region Total	132	128	8,352,322
Other Regions			
New England	31	20	1,320,796
Middle Atlantic	55	55	3,419,870
East North Central	57	39	2,631,736
West North Central	34	27	1,808,508
South Atlantic	168	155	10,085,341
East South Central	62	58	3,795,730
West South Central	77	75	5,111,151
Mountain	15	0	†
Total U.S.	631	557	41,566,445
Percent of Total	0.2%		11.4%

Exhibit 3.16 (continued)   Characteristics of U.S. Chicken Farms (1969)

	Flock Size 100,000 and over		
	No. of Farms	No. of Farms Reporting Flock Size	No. of Chickens*
States in Pacific Region			
Washington	10	10	2,085,936
Oregon	6	6	848,705
California	87	87	22,952,283
Alaska	0	0	†
Hawaii	12	0†	
	—	—	
Pacific Region Total	115	103	25,886,924
Other Regions			
New England	15	13	2,974,242
Middle Atlantic	29	29	5,239,990
East North Central	22	20	3,461,252
West North Central	21	16	2,480,555
South Atlantic	70	66	12,065,486
East South Central	27	25	5,661,485
West South Central	42	39	11,264,948
Mountain	14	3	806,350
Total U.S.	345	314	74,856,267
Percent of Total	0.1%		20.6%

Note: The data in Exhibit 3.16 are not fully consistent with those in Exhibits 3.14 and 3.17 because of differences in sources and definitions.
* The number of chickens for which flock size was reported.
† Not reported to preserve confidentiality regarding individual farm flock sizes.

Exhibit 3.17   Chicken Farm Trends, 1964–1969

	Number of Farms (%)			Number of Chickens (%)		
Flock Size	1964	1969	Percent Change	1964	1969	Percent Change
Under 3,200	98.5	93.8	− 61.0	32.9	13.0	− 61.0
3,200–9,999	1.1	3.2	− 28.9	21.0	14.9	− 23.4
10,000–19,999	0.3	1.7	+ 35.6	14.1	18.0	+ 38.2
20,000–49,000	0.1	1.0	+ 82.0	18.1	22.4	+ 81.2
50,000–99,999	.001	0.2	+ 83.0	6.4	11.2	+ 89.7
100,000 & over	.05	0.1	+ 50.0	7.5	20.6	+ 189.7
Total	100%	100%	− 61.0	100%	100%	+ 6.1

Note: These data are not fully consistent with those in Exhibits 3.14 and 3.16 because of differences in sources and definitions. Totals may not add to 100 due to rounding.

Exhibit 3.18   Average Cost per Dozen Eggs Produced, 1974

	Dollars	Cost per dozen eggs* (Cents)
Laying stock		
Purchase cost per hen	$2.40	
Allocation for replacing dead birds	.21	11.9
	$2.61	
Feed		
Annual feed costs per hen	$7.04	32.0
Labor		2.4
Supplies, taxes, utilities, etc.		1.8
Miscellaneous adjustments		
Cull sales per dozen (credit)		(.3)
Laying stock value adjustment (credit)		(1.7)
Net cash and labor cost per dozen		46.1
Depreciation (15% average value of buildings and equipment)		1.2
Interest (8% on land, laying stock, and average value of buildings and equipment)		1.4
Management per dozen		1.3
		3.9
Total costs per dozen		50.0
Average price per dozen		53.0
Average profit per dozen		3.0

*Assuming 22 dozen eggs per hen-year.

egg production may be sold through complex negotiated contracts with regional offices of large grocery chains. Some may convert waste into fertilizer in their own conversion plants as a by-product. The owners purchase starter pullets (or grow their own) at least four times a year in order to smooth labor demands on the farm. On a farm of this size, a henhouse typically houses from 5,000–10,000 birds.

On the basis of various government surveys, Garrison estimated that the U.S. chicken population would grow very slowly from 1975 to 1979 as shown in Exhibit 3.19. Of these chickens, 80 percent would be on the 3 percent of U.S. chicken farms with 10,000 or more chickens. Garrison believed that a farm would have to have at least 10,000 birds to be a profitable customer for ODI, but that 50 percent penetration of such farms within five years was a realistic projection.

Cannibalism Among Chickens

Like many other fowl, chickens are social birds and chicken societies have a definite social structure. A self-selected ranking of chickens begins when chickens are about 8 to 10 weeks of age and results

Exhibit 3.19   U.S. Chicken Population, 1975–1979 (millions)

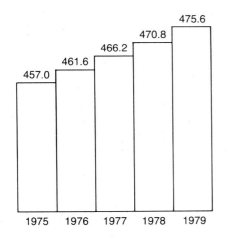

in a complete pecking order by the time the birds reach sexual maturity. According to Mark O. North, a poultry consultant, "This order is the result of the birds being able to identify other birds in the group, and through fighting and pecking, establish a hierarchical type of social organization."*

North believes that the recognition of the comb on the head of the chicken is a means of preserving the peck order, as is the position of the head. Dominant chickens carry their heads high, while submissive birds maintain a low head level. If a submissive bird raises its head too high, it is immediately pecked by one or more of its superiors until the head is lowered. Pecking can increase until the birds become cannibalistic. Submissive birds are also pecked if they enter the territory of a cage claimed by a more dominant bird. Thus cannibalism is a greater problem when more birds are

confined in cages. Cannibalism also varies with the breed of the chicken, and unfortunately the more productive strains tend to be more cannibalistic. According to Daniel Garrison, a major U.S. breeder had developed an extremely productive chicken, but "you had to put a sack over her head to keep her from killing her pen mates."

Besides the obvious loss to the farmer when a bird is killed by its pen mates, submissive birds get less time at the feeding trough and thus produce fewer eggs than the more dominant birds. Also, once the pecking order is established, replacing a dead bird seriously disturbs the pecking order.

Debeaking had been the major means of combatting cannibalism for nearly fifty years. The debeaking process did not interfere with the formation of the pecking order, but reduced the efficiency of the beak as a weapon. The debeaking operation was simple in concept: using a hot knife and an anvil, the upper and lower mandibles of the chicken's beak were cut off at different lengths. The beak was then pressed against the hot knife to cauterize the wound and prevent excess bleeding. In the debeaking operation, the chickens were subjected to considerable trauma resulting in a temporary weight loss and the retardation of egg production for at least a week; but at five months the loss was only one egg. If the beak was cut too short, the chicken would often enter a permanent regression; if left too long, the beak would grow back and become a deadly weapon again. The establishment of the pecking order among debeaked chickens took a longer time and involved greater social stress than it did among chickens with their full beaks since clear victories were rare. Experience had shown that debeaking reduced mortality due to cannibalism from as high as 25 percent for flocks of birds with full beaks to about 9 percent for debeaked flocks.

Debeaking was usually done during the first few weeks after the five-month-old hens were purchased. The farmer's own employees or a service company provided the debeaking crews, depending on the size of the farm. The cost of the debeaking operation was almost entirely labor. An experienced crew of three, each earning about $2.50/hour, could debeak approximately 220 birds per hour.

Poultry Digest, December 1973.

The ODI Lens

Daniel Garrison felt that the ODI contact lens was the first product to actually confront the cause of chicken cannibalization rather than just minimize its effects. A bird wearing the ODI lens had its depth perception reduced to about 12 inches and its visual acuity greatly reduced through an induced case of astigmatism. In this way the ability of one bird to recognize the comb of another was seriously impaired, and in order to feed, the chickens had to walk around with their heads lowered. Thus, the main visual cues for the pecking order were removed, no pecking order emerged, and cannibalism was reduced significantly.

The ODI lens was much like the soft contact lenses worn by humans except that it was slightly larger with a red tint, and it had a distortion built into the crown. When asked why the lenses were colored, Daniel Garrison responded:

It may sound like rubbish to many people, but chickens, like humans, respond psychologically to the color of their environment. We have found that changing the color of the birds' environment will affect the birds in many different ways such as altering their appetites or rate of sexual maturity, as well as affecting their cannibalistic tendencies. When birds are placed in a red-colored environment, deaths due to cannibalism are reduced. This red color, together with the distortion of the lenses, affects the chicken's ability to act out her aggressions. Our tests have shown that flock mortality is reduced to an average of 4.5% when contact lenses are used instead of debeaking.

The lens was larger than the eye opening so that when in place, the rim of the eye opening and the outer eyelid acted as retainers, keeping the lens in place. The inner eyelid, or nictitating membrane, a semitransparent membrane that flicked back and forth across the eyeball keeping it moist and clean, was under the lens and could perform its natural function.

Daniel Garrison estimated that a trained crew, similar to the debeaking crews, could install the lenses in about 225 chickens per hour. Unlike debeaking, the insertion of the lenses did not result in great trauma to the birds. The chickens were up and about within a few hours, and neither weight loss nor reduction in egg production was noticeable.

Daniel Garrison doubted that the lenses could be reused. "The lenses are harder to take out than they are to put in," he said, "and a further problem in reusing them is the fact that the melting point of the hydrophilic polymer is very close to the sterilization temperature. You could very easily end up with a mass of hydrophilic polymer rather than a potful of contact lenses."

In addition to reducing chicken mortality due to cannibalism and egg production loss due to trauma, the ODI lens had the potential of reducing a farmer's feed cost. A debeaked chicken could eat only if the feed in the trough was at least 3/8" deep (the difference in length between the upper and lower mandibles of the remaining beak). Presumably, therefore, a farmer using ODI lenses instead of debeaking the chickens would be able to reduce the depth of the feed in troughs by approximately 3/8" or more. Gil Jaeger, a University of Maine extension poultry specialist, had conducted a study suggesting that food disappearance per 100 birds per day was reduced from 24.46 pounds when the feed in the trough was 2" deep to 23.68 pounds when the feed in the trough was only 1" deep. In other words, a farmer with a 20,000–bird flock could save 156 pounds of feed per day if the depth of feed in troughs was reduced from 2" to 1". At $158 per ton for chicken feed, this would represent considerable annual savings, especially for large flocks. According to Garrison, ODI lenses would permit a farmer to reduce the depth of feed in the troughs by at least 3/8" (probably to a depth of 1") and would result in further savings because "a bird with a full beak and the ODI lenses can't see well enough to be fussy, so she doesn't bill much at all [billing throws feed out of the trough], and she doesn't drool in her food as debeaked birds do."

Although he was unaware of any broad-scale research that measured the loss of feed due to billing, Daniel Garrison felt that a farmer would find that maintaining less than a 1" food level for debeaked birds would be impractical due to more frequent trough refilling.

Exhibit 3.20   Balance Sheet at September 30, 1974

Current assets	
Cash	$200,025
Patent*	103,000
Less accumulated depreciation	(28,000)
Total Assets	$275,025
Current liabilities	0
Long-term debt	0
Stockholder's equity	275,025
Total liabilities and equity	$275,025

*At incorporation, ODI valued the contact lens for chickens patent at $103,000 and depreciated it over its 17-year life.

Developing a Marketing Program

As he began to develop the marketing plan requested by Daniel Garrison, Olson was acutely conscious of "the need to think big while recognizing that our assets are, after all, rather limited. There's no question this product has a whale of a future," he explained, "The problem is to achieve that potential as rapidly as is practical without too much strain on our limited managerial and financial resources." See Exhibit 3.20 for ODI's balance sheet as of September 30, 1974.

In discussions with Garrison, Olson had come to a number of tentative conclusions. First, it was virtually certain that ODI would enter the market via a region-by-region rollout, beginning in California. On a rough basis, he estimated that the annual costs of a West Coast regional office and warehouse would be about $196,000 per year (see Exhibit 3.21), plus about $40,000 for each salesperson (including expenses) and $35,000 for each technical representative. He felt that each salesperson should cover no more than about 80 farms, at least initially, and that there should be one technical representative for each five salespeople. The technical represen-

tatives would follow up all major sales, to make sure that the lenses were being used in such a way as to provide maximum benefits to the farmer.

Second, he and Garrison had agreed that the minimum price they should consider was $20 per box* of 250 pair, or $0.08 per pair. While this price would represent an incremental cost for the farmer (the labor costs for debeaking and insertion of lenses were approximately the same), the farmer would presumably obtain benefits much greater than $0.08 per chicken because of reduced cannibalization, less trauma, and greater feeding efficiency. Such benefits would justify a price much higher than $0.08 per pair, Olson felt, but he was not sure it would be possible to convince farmers of such benefits until after they had had considerable experience with the lenses. It was probable, he thought, that a higher price would require more intensive sales and technical coverage, which would considerably increase ODI's fixed costs. Neverthe-

*The plastic boxes would cost $0.10 each, and could be filled by ODI at $0.14 per box. Order processing and shipping were estimated at $0.18 per box.

Exhibit 3.21 Projected Costs of California Regional Office and Warehouse

Office expense	
Rent, utilities, and so forth	$36,000
Personnel	
Regional manager	30,000
Administrative assistant	15,000
Regional technical manager	22,000
3 secretaries @ $10,000	30,000
Shipping clerk	10,000
	107,000
Other expenses	53,000
Total projected annual costs	$196,000

less, he was hesitant to introduce the lenses at a low price initially in the hope of raising it later for two reasons: (1) "Chicken farmers, even the big ones, are an independent-minded breed of men who might react very unfavorably if they get the idea that they have been taken," and (2) "Because of our limited resources, we have to try to obtain maximum contribution as soon as possible."

High contribution, Olson reasoned, was critical to support the headquarters, regional office, and advertising and promotional costs inherent in a think big strategy. He and Daniel Garrison had agreed that ODI should be marketing on a national basis within two to three years, which would require four to five regional offices. Monthly advertising in the eight leading poultry industry publications would cost approximately $100,000 per year, as would participation in the most important industry trade shows. Headquarters expenses, Garrison forecasted, would rise from $184,000 per year at a volume of 20 million pair to $614,000 at 60 million

pair and $1.2 million at 120 million pair. Moreover, Garrison's strategy of becoming much more than a one-product company called for an investment of at least $250,000 per year in research and development as soon as the company could generate the funds, or become large and profitable enough to be able to obtain additional capital on favorable terms from the equity market.

"It's really a tough problem," Olson said, as he sat down at the already cluttered desk in the corner of his den. "There's a lot at stake here; more than enough potential for a big company to put fifty people on the project. There are only four of us, and none of us can yet put full time into the company, although Daniel and I are each spending at least fifty hours per week on ODI. Still, we've got to do as good a job as a big company would, and I think we can. . . . If we pull it off, we will have revolutionized the business of animal behavior in much the same way IBM revolutionized the processing of data."

Preparation Questions

1. If you were a chicken farmer, what approach would you take in considering contact lenses for your chickens?

2. What are the important managerial issues that Mr. Garrison must consider in developing a business plan for ODI?

3. What price would you set for the lenses? How large should the sales force be? How would you direct their efforts?

4. What factors should a preliminary decision model for this situation consider?

These questions are to be addressed with the ODI decision model found at the end of the case. Check with your teacher to see when these questions are assigned.

5. How well does this preliminary decision model address the managerial issues and factors that you identified in your analysis?

6. Develop a five-year plan for ODI.

7. Compare your use of the ODI decision model and the secondary data upon which it is based with the approach taken in the CableShop.

8. What additional information needs and modeling changes do you feel are appropriate for the ODI model?

Optical Distortion Spreadsheet Model

The decision model for Optical Distortion Inc. differs from the simple spreadsheet model that accompanied the CableShop case in a number of ways. The CableShop model was merely a financial spreadsheet that assumed that revenues would just happen. It contained no explicit linkages between the size of the market, the marketing expenses, and the sales of the firm. While most of the relevant cost elements of the decision were incorporated into the spreadsheet model, it was totally naive from a marketing standpoint.

The ODI model is a decision model based upon a conceptualization of the consumer's decision-making process, the composition of the marketplace, and how the market will respond to ODI's marketing strategy. The basic ideas underlying the ODI model are quite simple and should serve to demonstrate that building a useful decision model is not necessarily a highly technical endeavor. A basic idea of the model is that it is much easier to estimate the change that might result from marketing effort on a period-by-period basis than it is to estimate the size of the market at some future time period directly. The model provides an alternative to just guessing that a product will attain some small percentage of the market.

The ODI model assumes that sales will occur only as a direct result of sales effort, therefore the number of sales reps and the size of the market will be the key elements to estimate the sales that will be attained. Some of the other basic assumptions of the model are:

1. The market is broken up into three segments—large, medium, and small farms—since their purchase processes and value to ODI are expected to be different.

2. The adoption process of the farmer is expected to begin with a rather small purchase of lenses for a test. This trial phase could last from three months to a year or more. Once a farmer had accepted the contact lenses as an ongoing part of his business, he would purchase lenses for one-fourth of his flock each quarter.

3. Not only is the initial sale assumed to be difficult—no farmer will buy lenses unless sold by a sales representative—but the trial process will require attention from the sales rep or a service rep in order for it to reach a successful conclusion.

4. The size and deployment of the sales force are assumed to be the most critical success factors, both because of the importance of the selling

task, but also because of the small amount of capital available to ODI.

5. Although the price of the lenses is assumed to be an important success factor, the effect of price on the adoption process appears to be so complicated that it will not be modeled. In using the model you will have to make sure that the assumptions you make are reasonable at the price that you've chosen.

Using these assumptions, a conceptually simple decision model was developed that makes it possible to use market size estimates and estimates of the response of the market segments to sales force effort to determine the size of the sales force and allocate its effort across the various farm sizes. Repeated runs of the model provide a means of evaluating different marketing strategies and choosing the best strategy of those considered. It also provides a means of learning about the importance of various market factors in determining the success of ODI.

The ODI decision model consists of a number of models:

a model of the farmer's adoption process

a model that allocates sales effort across farms

a model that computes marketing and financial reports

The Farmer's Adoption Process

The decision of a farmer to adopt the lenses is assumed to occur in a number of steps rather than all at once. In other words, it is not reasonable to expect any farmer, even one that loves the idea, to put lenses on all of his chickens at once. The chickens already on the farm have been debeaked and the lenses provide no value on debeaked chickens. Therefore lens sales will be limited to the rate at which new pullets are added to the flock. In addition to this a farmer, at least until the lenses become more widely known and accepted, will probably be cautious about using the lenses at first and his initial response will be at most a test on a few chickens. Based on these assumptions we can conceptualize the typical farmer's adoption process as follows.

Let's start with a farmer who has not been contacted and is therefore unaware of the existence of contact lenses for his chickens. (The farmer's farm is called *Uncontacted*.) If that farmer is not visited by a sales rep he will remain unaware of the lenses, but if he is visited by a sales rep he will decide either to accept the lenses for a trial on a limited number of chickens (the farm becomes a *Trial* farm), or he will refuse to test the lenses, at least for now. (The farm becomes a *Refusal* farm.)

The model assumes that the farmer on a *Trial* farm will make a decision about the lenses after three months. The farmer could decide that:

1. The lenses are terrific and he's going to use them from now on. The farm becomes an *Adopter* and the farmer buys lenses for one-fourth of his flock every quarter from then on.

2. He needs more information before adopting the lenses but will continue to try them. (The farm remains a *Trial* farm.)

3. The lenses are not a good product and he *Rejects* them. Farmers that reject the lenses after trial rather than refuse to try them are assumed not to change their minds later.

The various stages that constitute the farmer's decision process in our conceptualization are called "states" (not to be confused with states of the union). The states in our conceptualization are shown in Exhibit 3.22.

The arrows in the exhibit's diagram indicate the possible decisions that might be made in the farmer's decision process at any given time. The model assumes that the adoption state to which a farmer will move after a decision depends on what state he was in during the previous period and whether or not he was visited by a sales rep. It also assumes that what the farmer will do is a matter of chance, but that a sales rep can affect the choice. If a farmer is visited by a sales rep can affect the choice. If a farmer is visited by a sales rep during the quarter, the chances are better that the farm will progress to a more favorable state the next quarter than it would if it had not been visited. Suppose, just for example, that the probabilities associated with the decisions of a farmer whose farm is in the trial state are as follows:

Exhibit 3.22   States in a Farmer's Decision Process

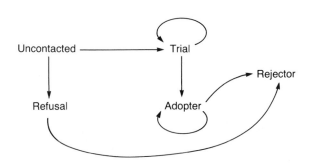

	Trial	*From trial to* Adopter	Rejector
If Visited	.70	.25	.05
If Not Visited	.60	.10	.30

Suppose now that there are 200 farms in the trial state but we only have enough sales reps to visit 100 of them. At the end of the next quarter there would be 130 trial, 35 adopters, and 35 rejectors. If, on the other hand, we had enough sales reps to visit all of the farms, in the next quarter we would have 140 trials, 50 adopters, and only 10 rejectors. Notice that in this example it makes quite a difference whether or not a farm is visited.

The probability of a farmer moving from one state to another is called a *transition probability*, and a complete set of them—the probabilities of a farm going from every state in one period to every state in the next—is called a *transition matrix*. The ODI model contains two transition matrices, one for the farms that are visited, and one for the farms that are not visited. Together, these two transition matrices form the market response function of the ODI decision model—they relate marketing action with marketing results. It is important to note that the composition of the market will change from period to period as a result of the movement of farmers from one state to another, and it is also important to know that this movement is directly affected by the size and allocation of the effort of the sales force.

The Sales Force Size and Allocation Model

The farmer adoption model computes the probability that an individual farm that is in one state in one period will be in another state in the next period depending on whether or not the farmer was visited by a sales rep. The previous example indicates that we could expect the composition of the marketplace to change over time as a result of our sales force strategy. This wouldn't be so important if there were millions of large chicken farms, but in fact there are very few so we could find that there are no reasonable prospects for a sales rep to visit after a fairly short period of time if the sales force is too large.

Naturally it would be worth a lot more money to ODI to have a farmer with 1 million chickens adopt the lenses than a farmer with only 10,000 chickens, so we need to consider the size of a farm as well as its adoption state in allocating sales effort. The sales force size and allocation model recognizes three different market segments based on farm size and defines separate adoption states for each of these segments. Transition matrices are defined for each segment separately so the probability of a sales visit moving a farm from one state to another can be different for large, medium, and small farms. In all, there are twelve "farm size–adoption state pairs" that can be visited and each can be defined to have a different financial value and response to sales effort (or the lack of it). The Rejectors are assumed not to change their minds, so they are not visited. The model removes rejectors from further consideration. The model also assumes that some proportion of the Refusers also become Rejectors.

If the size of the sales force is not adequate to visit all of the farms, a rule must be defined to determine which farms to visit with the available resources. This is done by giving a priority to each of the farm size–adoption state pairs from one to twelve. The ODI decision model will then apply the "visited" transition matrix to as many of the top priority farms (smaller number rank) as possible. If there are still some visits available after all of the highest priority farms are visited, the model uses the "visited" transition matrix on as many of the next highest priority farms as possible until no more visits are available. The farms that remain after all of the available visits have been made are then transformed using the "unvisited" transition matrix. In this way the number of farms of each size in each adoption state are computed over the planning period.

Consider an example from the model (Exhibit 3.23), which shows what happens to the initial distribution of farms after being visited by one sales rep for a quarter. The priority that the sales rep assigns to the farm size—adoption state pairs are in the first column and the number of farms of each size is given in the second column. (The transition probabilities are different from those used in the previous example.) To see if you understand, you might want to try to derive one or two of the transition probabilities from this table and compare your answers with the table of values that were actually used and are presented in the input to the model.)

Marketing and Financial Report Models

Once the number of farms in each farm size–adoption state pair has been determined for each time period, the unit sales per time period can be forecast by multiplying the number of farms times the expected average sales. The unit sales and the number of sales reps and service reps per period provide the basis for analyzing the financial implications of a particular marketing strategy. The ODI model computes two fairly standard reports: a marketing report (Exhibit 3.24) that computes share of available market, the distribution of farms across the farm size–adoption state pairs, and the number of available sales visits that couldn't be used; an income statement (Exhibit 3.25) that computes sales, costs, and contribution to profit, and so on.

It is important to recognize that the farmer's adoption process and the sales force strategy are all that have been modeled in the ODI decision model. In particular, the effect of price on the adoption process has not been modeled. If you decide to charge $100 per lens, the model will just multiply unit sales by $100 in order to get revenue, even though no farmer would pay that much for the lenses. You have to be careful with price and all of the other cost factors in the spreadsheet to make sure that they make sense—the model has no means of doing that.

The ODI model is a "semi-naive" model—some factors have been modeled and some have not. Most decision models are semi-naive in this respect, so it is always important to determine which relationships have been modeled and which have not in order to use a decision model intelligently. Don't be too hasty in condemning a model because it doesn't contain all of the important factors. There may be good reasons not to try to put them all in, for example:

1. Developing the more complex model would take more time than is available before the decision has to be made.

2. The decision to be made is not worth the additional expense that would be required to make the more complex model.

3. The incorporation of the other factors would make the model more complicated to use and possibly obscure the effects of a more important factor.

Inputs to the ODI model

The ODI model allows you to make assumptions about many factors affecting the success of ODI. We have already discussed the transition matrices and alluded to a number of these other inputs. Since the ODI business situation is one of a new start-up business for a very new product, it

Exhibit 3.23   Change in Distribution After Sales Visit

Farm Sizes and Call Priorities

| | Call Priority | Init. Farm Dist. | Quarter 1 | | |
			Visited	Not Visited	State
Small					
Uncont.	9	381	0	381	381
Trial	8	0	0	0	0
Adopter	7	0	0	0	0
Refusal	12	0	0	0	0
Medium					
Uncont.	6	132	75	57	57
Trial	5	0	0	0	23
Adopter	4	0	0	0	0
Refusal	11	0	0	0	53
Large					
Uncont.	3	105	105	0	0
Trial	2	0	0	0	32
Adopter	1	0	0	0	0
Refusal	10	0	0	0	74

| | Quarter 2 | | |
	Visited	Not Visited	State
Small			
Uncont.	120	261	261
Trial	0	0	36
Adopter	0	0	0
Refusal	0	0	84
Medium			
Uncont.	6	51	51
Trial	23	0	21
Adopter	0	0	2
Refusal	0	53	58
Large			
Uncont.	0	0	0
Trial	32	0	27
Adopter	0	0	3
Refusal	0	74	75

Exhibit 3.24   ODI Marketing Report

```
Marketing Report

                              Qtr 1     Qtr 2     Qtr 3     Qtr 4     Qtr 5
                             ------    ------    ------    ------    ------
Market
   Industry Birds (000)      17,274    17,318    17,361    17,404    17,448
   Units (000)                  248       495       751       955     1,136
                             ------    ------    ------    ------    ------
Market Share                  1.43%     2.86%     4.33%     5.49%     6.51%

Sales Calls
   Farms Visited                180       180       180       180       180
   Farms not Visited            438       438       438       438       438
   Visits Available              0         0         0         0         0

Personnel
   Salespersons                  1         1         1         1         1
   Technical Representative      1         1         1         1         1



                              Qtr 6     Qtr 7     Qtr 8     Total
                             ------    ------    ------    ------
Market
   Industry Birds (000)      17,491    17,535    17,579    17,579
   Units (000)                1,296     1,377     1,481     7,739
                             ------    ------    ------    ------
Market Share                  7.41%     7.85%     8.42%     8.42%

Sales Calls
   Farms Visited                180       180       180     1,440
   Farms not Visited            438       438       397     3,463
   Visits Available              0         0         0         0

Personnel
   Salespersons                  1         1         1         1
   Technical Representative      1         1         1         1
```

Exhibit 3.25   ODI Income Statement

Income Statement

	Qtr 1	Qtr 2	Qtr 3	Qtr 4	Qtr 5
Units (000)	248	495	751	955	1,136
Sales	$19,800	$39,569	$60,103	$76,414	$90,883
Expenses:					
Raw Materials Cost	7,920	15,827	24,041	30,566	36,353
Packaging Cost	248	495	751	955	1,136
Handling Cost	248	495	751	955	1,136
Salesperson Salaries	10,000	10,000	10,000	10,000	10,000
Tech. Rep. Salaries	8,750	8,750	8,750	8,750	8,750
Contribution Margin	(7,365)	4,002	15,809	25,188	33,508
Overhead Expense	49,000	49,000	49,000	49,000	49,000
Net Income	(56,365)	(44,998)	(33,191)	(23,812)	(15,492)

	Qtr 6	Qtr 7	Qtr 8	Total
Units (000)	1,296	1,377	1,481	7,739
Sales	$103,699	$110,179	$118,470	$619,117
Expenses:				
Raw Materials Cost	41,480	44,071	47,388	247,647
Packaging Cost	1,296	1,377	1,481	7,739
Handling Cost	1,296	1,377	1,481	7,739
Salesperson Salaries	10,000	10,000	10,000	80,000
Tech. Rep. Salaries	8,750	8,750	8,750	70,000
Contribution Margin	40,877	44,603	49,370	205,992
Overhead Expense	49,000	49,000	49,000	392,000
Net Income	(8,123)	(4,397)	370	(186,008)

Exhibit 3.26 ODI Spreadsheet Menu Trees

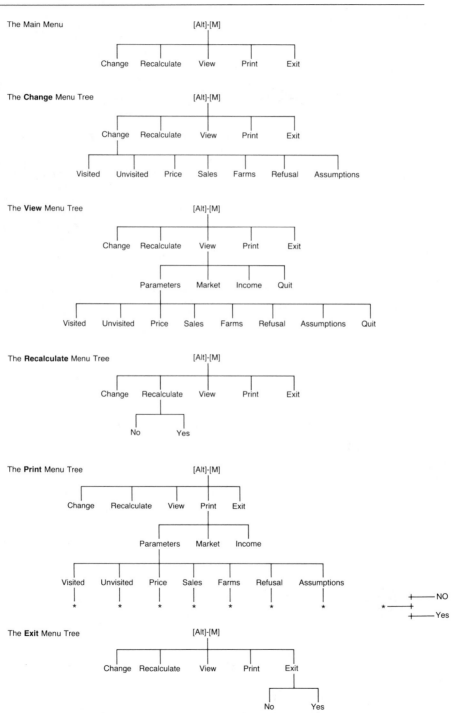

shouldn't be too surprising that most of the numbers that go into the model must be made by managerial judgment. You will probably not be too surprised to find out that there are no published sources for the transition probabilities for contact lenses for chickens, or for any other new products.

The question that is most relevant here is whether or not a conceptualization such as the one in the ODI model would give you better estimates of what you could expect to happen in the marketplace than some other *available* method. A related question is whether or not a conceptualization such as this one would help in focusing attention on the important factors to success better than some other *available* method.

In using the model you should recognize that any particular set of inputs to the model are unlikely to describe the actual situation that will exist in the marketplace, so you should look at more than one scenario to see what factors appear to be most critical.

Using the Spreadsheet Model

Although the ODI model is quite simple conceptually, programming it in Lotus 1-2-3 is quite complicated. The program requires a number of complicated macros and it is unlikely that you could figure out how to change them in the time you probably have available for this case. For this reason, and since this is the one of the first spreadsheets we'll use, the model is accessed through a menu system that makes it extremely easy to use as it was intended, but makes it very difficult to do anything else. The following documentation explains the menu structure and lists the input factors that you can change.

The ODI Menus

After pressing the [Enter] key as instructed at the opening screen of the spreadsheet, you will see the main menu. You can return to this menu at any time by pressing [Alt]M. The main menu presents you with five choices: **Change, Recalculate, View, Print,** and **Exit**. The main menu and the command trees for each of these five commands are shown in Exhibit 3.26.

The **Change** command permits you to change the transition matrix for visited and unvisited farms, unit prices and cost, sales force allocation, farm sizes and call priorities, refusal loss rates, and assumptions. **View** and **Print** permit you to display the transition matrix for visited and unvisited farms, unit prices and cost, sales force allocation, farm sizes and call priorities, refusal loss rates, and assumptions on the screen or on an attached printer respectively. Finally, **Exit** allows you to leave Lotus 1-2-3 and return to DOS.

Note that [Ctrl]-[Break], or holding down the [Ctrl] key and pressing [Break], will always cancel the underlying software within Lotus 1-2-3 spreadsheets. You should then press the [Enter] key once to clear the system, which puts you in Lotus 1-2-3 but outside the ODI spreadsheet. Press [Alt]M to return to the ODI menu.

The **Change** *Command.* Use this choice to change the transition matrix for visited and unvisited farms, unit prices and cost, sales force allocation, farm sizes and call priorities, refusal loss rates, and assumptions. See the menu tree in Exhibit 3.26.

The **View** *Command.* Use this choice to display the transition matrix for visited and unvisited farms, unit prices and cost, sales force allocation, farm sizes and call priorities, refusal loss rates, and assumptions. The **Quit** choice permits you to exit the menu system and enter Lotus 1-2-3. See the menu tree in Exhibit 3.26.

Exhibit 3.27 displays a set of sample screens obtained by selecting **View**, **Parameters**, then each of the bottom-level commands.

The **Recalculate** Command. Use this choice to recalculate the model after you make any changes to it via the **Change** command. The menu tree is shown in Exhibit 3.26. A No/Yes safety menu permits you to make sure you really want to recalculate the model, since the recalculation is time-consuming.

The **Print** Command. Use this choice to print the transition matrix for visited and unvisited farms, unit prices and cost, sales force allocation, farm sizes and call priorities, refusal loss rates, and assump-

Exhibit 3.27   ODI Screens Displayed with the View Command

```
Transition Matrix for Visited Farms


                                 Uncont.   Trial 1   Adopter   Refusal
                                 --------  --------  --------  --------
Small farms       Uncont.          0.00      0.30      0.00      0.70
                  Trial            0.00      0.85      0.10      0.05
                  Adopter          0.00      0.00      1.00      0.00
                  Refusal          0.00      0.00      0.00      1.00

Medium farms      Uncont.          0.00      0.30      0.00      0.70
                  Trial            0.00      0.85      0.10      0.05
                  Adopter          0.00      0.00      1.00      0.00
                  Refusal          0.00      0.00      0.00      1.00

Large farms       Uncont.          0.00      0.30      0.00      0.70
                  Trial            0.00      0.85      0.10      0.05
                  Adopter          0.00      0.00      1.00      0.00
                  Refusal          0.00      0.00      0.00      1.00


Transition Matrix for Unvisited Farms


                                 Uncont.   Trial 1   Adopter   Refusal
                                 --------  --------  --------  --------
Small farms       Uncont.          1.00      0.00      0.00      0.00
                  Trial            0.00      0.80      0.00      0.20
                  Adopter          0.00      0.00      0.95      0.05
                  Refusal          0.00      0.00      0.00      1.00

Medium farms      Uncont.          1.00      0.00      0.00      0.00
                  Trial            0.00      0.80      0.00      0.20
                  Adopter          0.00      0.00      0.95      0.05
                  Refusal          0.00      0.00      0.00      1.00

Large farms       Uncont.          1.00      0.00      0.00      0.00
                  Trial            0.00      0.80      0.00      0.20
                  Adopter          0.00      0.00      0.95      0.05
                  Refusal          0.00      0.00      0.00      1.00
```

(continued)

tions on an attached printer. The **Print** menu tree is displayed in Exhibit 3.26. A No/Yes safety menu permits you to check the status of your printer before actually printing. Make sure that the printer is attached to your computer, that the power is on an switched on-line, and that the paper is in the correct position for printing a new page.

The **Exit** *Command.*   Use this choice to leave Lotus 1-2-3 and return to DOS. A No/Yes safety menu will prevent you from accidentally exiting Lotus. The **Exit** menu is shown in Exhibit 3.26.

Exhibit 3.27 (continued)   ODI Screens Displayed with the View Command

Unit Cost Report

	Qtr 1	Qtr 2	Qtr 3	Qtr 4	Qtr 5
Units (000)	248	495	751	955	1,136
Unit Price	$0.080	$0.080	$0.080	$0.080	$0.080
Unit Material Cost	$0.032	$0.032	$0.032	$0.032	$0.032
Unit Packaging Cost	$0.001	$0.001	$0.001	$0.001	$0.001
Unit Handling Cost	$0.001	$0.001	$0.001	$0.001	$0.001
Unit Contribution Margin	$0.046	$0.046	$0.046	$0.046	$0.046

Demand Model
Input data for district - Pacific

Sales Force Allocation

	Personnel		Maximum
Quarter	Sales	Technical	Sales Calls
1	1	1	180
2	1	1	180
3	1	1	180
4	1	1	180
5	1	1	180
6	1	1	180
7	1	1	180
8	1	1	180

Farm Sizes and Call Priorities

		Call Priority	Initial Farm Distrib
Small	Uncont.	9	381
	Trial 1	8	0
	Adopter	7	0
	Refusal	12	0
Medium	Uncont.	6	132
	Trial 1	5	0
	Adopter	4	0
	Refusal	11	0
Large	Uncont.	3	105
	Trial 1	2	0
	Adopter	1	0
	Refusal	10	0

(continued)

Exhibit 3.27 (continued)   ODI Screens Displayed with the View Command

Refusal Loss Rates

```
        Quarter              Loss Rate
        --------             --------
           1                   0.0%
           2                   0.0%
           3                   0.0%
           4                   0.0%
           5                   0.0%
           6                   0.0%
           7                   0.0%
           8                   0.0%
```

Assumptions

```
        Base Chicken Population/4          17,231.3
        Chicken Growth Rate per Year           1.0%
        Salesperson's Quarterly Salary     $10,000
        Tech. Rep. Quarterly Salary         $8,750
        Quarterly Overhead Expense         $49,000

        Lens Purchase Rates:

            Trial :  Small farms            1,500
                     Medium farms           4,000
                     Large farms            5,000
            Adopter: Small farms            7,125
                     Medium farms          16,875
                     Large farms           58,750
```

4

Pre-Test Market Testing and Product Modification

(continued)

Pre–test market testing was introduced in Chapter 2 as a part of the new product development process intended to reduce the cost of the new product development process in two ways: by reducing the number of new products that reach the test marketing stage, and by increasing the probability that new products that survive the pre–test market test will also be successful in the test market. The form of pre–test market testing differs slightly, depending on the nature of the new product. Frequently purchased, low-priced supermarket goods that can be produced in prototype versions at a reasonable cost are candidates for pre–test procedures based upon trial purchase. Heavy industrial equipment or other products for which the development of prototype models for use in market research is not reasonable, or for which potential customers could not be expected to make the substantial investment necessary for a trial purchase, require testing based on the product concept alone. The two case series in this chapter represent extremes of these two types of products: a new hair conditioner and an automatic transmission forklift truck. Both of these new products represent product-line extensions into existing markets, and the analysis of competition is very important.

Comparison of the techniques used to pre-test new products in these two situations provides an unusual opportunity to explore the relationship between the nature of the product and the type of research that is appropriate. Although there are some obvious differences in the methodology employed in the two situations, there are also a number of similarities. Considering both the differences and the similarities will greatly increase your understanding of, and sensitivity to, the important factors that need to be considered. Since the model used in the consumer product situation is a bit simpler conceptually, we begin with the study of the pre–test market test procedure called *ASSESSOR*, which was used by the Johnson Wax Company to test Enhance hair conditioner. Following this discussion we will consider the market simulation analysis used by Clark Equipment Corporation to study the feasibility of offering an automatic transmission forklift truck in Brazil.

Pre–Test Market Testing of Consumer Products

Urban and Hauser (1980) estimated the expected cost of developing one successful new product using test marketing, but without the use of a pre–test market test, to be $9,642,000. They also estimated the expected cost of introducing a successful new product using a pre–test market procedure costing $50,000 was to be $8,556,000, a reduction of $1,086,000. See Exhibit 4.1.

The expected cost savings are a result of two factors: the rejection of some new product ideas prior to the test market (40 percent reduction) and the increase in the probability of success of the surviving new product concepts (.8 versus .45).

One might expect that these cost savings are achieved at the expense of lengthening the time involved for a product to successfully negotiate the new product development process from beginning to end, since an additional step has been included and the steps occur sequentially rather than simultaneously. According to Urban and Hauser, this is not the case, and in fact the expected duration of new product development is actually shortened by approximately six months. (See Exhibit 4.2.)

The ASSESSOR test featured in the Johnson Wax cases is just one of a number of pre–test market testing procedures that are commercially available. The first such procedure was the Laboratory Test Market (LTM) developed by Yankelovich in 1968. The BASES system developed by Burke Marketing Research has probably sold the most applications. Other systems are COMP by Elrick and Lavidge, and ESP from National Purchase Diary. In 1979 it was estimated that together these pre–test market test procedures had been used in over 1400 applications. In 1983 ASSESSOR won second place in a cross-disciplinary model application competition sponsored by the Operations Research/The Institute of Management Science societies. It is beyond the scope of this book to provide a

Exhibit 4.1   Expected Benefit from Pre–Test Market Testing

	Average Cost ($000s)	Probability of Success	Expected Cost ($000s)
Opportunity Identification	$ 100	–	$ 100
Design	200	0.50	980
Testing			
Pretest market	50	0.6*	123
Test Market	1,000	0.80	1,471
Total Development Cost			2,674
National Introduction	5,000	0.85	5,882
Total Expected Investment			$8,556

Net Benefit from Pretest Market = $1,086,000†

*Probabilities are based on actual pretest experience.
†9,642 − 8,556 = 1,086

Source: Urban and Hauser 1980, p. 57.

detailed comparison of these procedures or to attempt to determine which is better for a particular situation. We seek to provide an opportunity to explore the managerial problems and opportunities of using any one of them. The reader interested in comparisons and details will find an extensive discussion in Wind, Mahajan, and Cardozo [1981].

The ASSESSOR Pre–Test Market Procedure

ASSESSOR is designed to help management evaluate new packaged goods *before* test marketing. The system is intended to: (1) rapidly predict a new brand's long-run sales or market share at a low cost; (2) produce actionable diagnostic information that can be used to improve the product and market plan; and (3) permit evaluation of alternative marketing plans. A company that decides to do an ASSESSOR study of a new product or of some other part of the marketing strategy participates in a rather extensive research process:

Design.   The important marketing issues must be identified—for example, prototype advertising copy, relative price, target group, and potential cannibalization. An appropriate questionnaire must be written and, if necessary, a custom model is specified.

Executing the consumer research.   The laboratory field work may be carried out in anywhere from two to ten cities and requires one to two weeks to complete. The post-usage survey is conducted several weeks later, ordinar-

Exhibit 4.2 Expected Duration of New Product Development for New, Frequently Purchased Consumer Product

	Without Pretest Market Analysis		
	Average Time (months)	**Probability of Success**	**Expected Time (months)**
Opportunity Identification	5	—	5
Design	6	0.50	31
Testing			
Test Market	9	0.45	24
Total Development			60
Introduction Setup	4	0.85	5
Total Expected Time			65

Expected cost = $9,642,000

	With Pretest Market Analysis		
	Average Time (months)	**Probability of Success**	**Expected Time (months)**
Opportunity Identification	5	—	5
Design	6	0.50	29
Testing			
Pretest Market	3	0.60	7
Test Market	9	0.80	13
Total Development			54
Introduction Setup	4	0.85	5
Total Expected Time			59

Expected Cost = $8,556,000

Source: Urban and Hauser 1980, p. 58.

ily via WATS-line telephones from a central location or, in some special cases, by personal interviews.

Reporting the results. ASSESSOR results are presented in one or more preliminary technical review sessions and a final report.

According to MDS, the practice of presenting results informally to the client, specifically to those intimately involved in the study, before the final results are presented to the broader management group was instigated to reduce client resistance to the findings:

Presenting final results of an ASSESSOR study to anxious executives who were unprepared for the conclusions often resulted in an explosive meeting. We introduced the practice of first conducting a technical review session with

Exhibit 4.3   The Structure of an ASSESSOR System

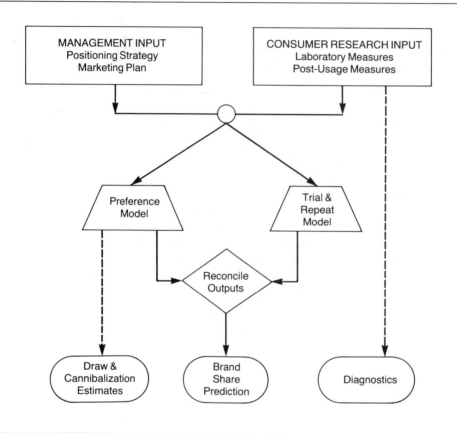

Source: Silk and Urban 1978, p. 173.

only a few representatives from the client corporation. Results are first presented in a "technical review," a low-key setting where those present can ask
challenging questions, suggest additional analyses, and gain a fuller understanding of the findings and their implications. The formal presentation to
management is usually made a few weeks later, when most of the participants
already know the share forecasts or bottom line. This procedure fosters a
more constructive meeting which focuses on the policy implications. A final
written report is issued shortly after the final report meeting, after which
management then decides whether to drop the brand, go to test market, or
attempt to improve the product. [ASSESSOR promotional material]

Structure of the ASSESSOR System

The ASSESSOR procedure was designed to estimate the market share that a new
product, or a particular marketing program would achieve in the marketplace.

Exhibit 4.4   The ASSESSOR Laboratory

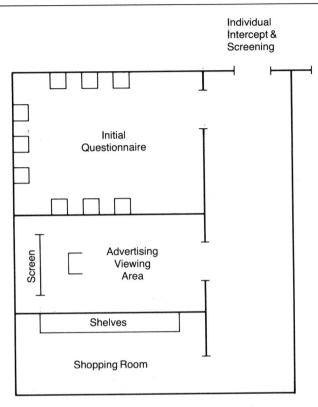

ASSESSOR consists of two separate models, each of which forecasts market share based on different data and according to a different conceptual model. The structure of the ASSESSOR model is shown in Exhibit 4.3.

ASSESSOR predicts market share with two different models: one relates product preference measurements to purchase probability to compute market share; the other estimates market share from actual purchase and repeat purchase measurements. The two models are similar in structure but are calibrated in different ways.

The data collection in ASSESSOR is done in two phases: a laboratory, and a callback phase. During the *laboratory phase*, potential consumers (usually found in shopping malls) are asked to participate in a test market. Those who are willing to participate and belong to the target segment are invited into a testing facility (see Exhibit 4.4), where a five-step testing procedure is used.

1. *An initial questionnaire* is used to determine the brands about which the respondent can provide meaningful information. This list of brands is called the respondent's "evoked set," and includes brands used recently or ever, and

brands that would, or would not, be considered on the next purchase occasion.

2. *The preference questionnaire* is customized for each respondent to include only those brands in her evoked set. The respondent is asked to allocate 11 imaginary chips between each pair of brands in her evoked set. These allocations are used to calculate the respondent's strength of preference for each brand in her evoked set.

3. *Advertising recall* is measured after the respondent is shown commercials for the test product as well as advertisements for other brands.

4. *Laboratory purchasing* takes place in a simulated store where the respondent is given a certificate. If she wants to buy more than the value of the certificate in merchandise, she is asked to pay the difference. In order to estimate the effectiveness of sampling, respondents who did not purchase the test product are given a sample package as a gift. A limited number of those who do not purchase the test product are asked a few additional questions probing their impressions of it and reasons for not purchasing it.

5. *Brand ratings* are done by respondents, who are asked to rate several of their evoked brands on how well they perform on various product attributes. The test product is also rated on these attributes. These ratings, since the respondent had not used the test product, are based on perceptions created through advertising, price, and packaging. A seven-point rating scale is used.

In the *callback phase*, those respondents who indicated they had used the test product are asked about brand preference and purchase intentions. The repeat purchase rate of both laboratory triers and sample triers are computed, along with other information concerning product performance. Callback interviews were conducted by telephone about four weeks after the laboratory interview.

The measurements made in these various steps were used to compute the parameters in the two market share models and to provide diagnostic information on product and marketing plan performance. An overview of measurements and experimental conditions in the ASSESSOR laboratory test is found in Exhibit 4.5.

Each of these two measurement techniques are used to arrive at an "ideal" market share prediction that assumes consumer awareness and product availability. Using these ideal market share predictions as a starting point, a new market share prediction is made that recognizes a target level of advertising awareness and product availability, usually a level that can be achieved approximately one year after introduction. The trial-and-repeat purchase levels in the simulated store are used to make the trial-and-repeat market share prediction. The preference model market share prediction is made from estimates of brand preference calculated from the respondents' perception of, and preference for, the attributes of the test product and the existing brands. Additional qualitative and quantita-

Exhibit 4.5 ASSESSOR Research Design and Measurement

Design	Procedure	Measurement
0_1	Respondent Screening and Recruitment (personal interview)	Criteria for Target Group Identification (e.g., product class usage)
0_2	Premeasurement for Established Brands (self-administered questionnaire)	Composition of "Relevant Set" of Established Brands, Attribute Weights and Ratings, and Preferences
X_1	Exposure to Advertising for Established Brands *and* New Brand	
$[0_3]$	Measurement of Reactions to the Advertising Materials (self-administered questionnaire)	Optional, e.g., Likability and Believability Ratings of Advertising Materials
X_2	Simulated Shopping Trip and Exposure to Display of New and Established Brands	
0_4	Purchase Opportunity (choice recorded by research personnel)	Brand(s) Purchased
X_3	Home Use/Consumption of New Brand	
0_5	Post-Usage Measurement (telephone interview)	New Brand Usage Rate, Satisfaction Ratings, and Repeat Purchase Propensity; Attribute Ratings and Preferences for "Relevant Set" of Established Brands Plus the New Brand

0 = Measurement
X = Advertising or product exposure

Source: Silk and Urban (1978), p. 174, Table 1

tive information gathered during the course of the test are used for product attribute and marketing plan diagnostics. Regardless of which model is used to provide the inputs, the mathematical structure of the forecast is the same.

$$M = TS \tag{4.1}$$

where:

M = market share

T = the ultimate cumulative trial rate (penetration or trial)

S = the ultimate repeat purchase rate among those buyers who have ever made a trial purchase of the brand (retention)

Retention (S) is a function of the initial repeat purchase rate and the rate at which previous triers return to the test product after buying another product (called *switchback*). Since the measurements are all made in a laboratory situation in

Exhibit 4.6   The Retention Process

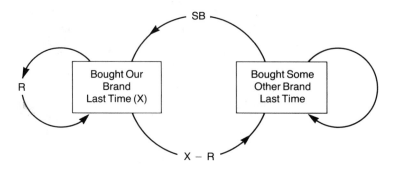

which there is both 100 percent awareness and distribution, there are actually two estimation steps:

1. Forecast the market share that the test product would achieve under the laboratory conditions.
2. Adjust the market share forecast for anticipated market conditions.

It will be easier to understand what happens in the ASSESSOR test if we study the "laboratory condition" forecast fully before dealing with anticipated market conditions.

Trial-and-Repeat Model

The trial-and-repeat model forecasts the market share that a brand will attain by observing the trial-and-repeat purchase behavior of respondents in the simulated store environment. After viewing commercials for various competing products as well as the tested brand, the respondents have the opportunity to buy tested category products in the simulated store. The observed laboratory trial rate is used to estimate the proportion of those potential consumers who are aware of the product and will try it (T in formula 4.1).

Estimation of retention is somewhat more difficult since repeated interviewing over a considerable period of time would be necessary to directly measure the ongoing share of a consumer's purchases that will be devoted to the new brand. This would be both too expensive and too time consuming. The ASSESSOR model estimates retention—the brand's long-term share of the consumers' category needs—as a mathematical function of *repeat purchase* and *switchback* as follows:

Exhibit 4.7 Purchase Rates for Repeat = 81% and Switchback = 20%

Purchase Cycle	Buy Test Product (R + SB)(%)	Buy Other Brands (%)
1	81.0	19.0
2	69.4	30.6
3	62.3	37.7
4	58.0	42.0
5	54.4	44.6
6	53.8	46.2
7	52.8	47.2

At any given time, t, the purchasers of the test brand can be segmented into two groups—those who bought it the last time they purchased in the product category and those who didn't. What could happen at time $t + 1$ is illustrated in Exhibit 4.6. Of those who bought the test brand (x) at time t, some will also buy it at time $t + 1$, their next purchase occasion (R); whereas others will buy a competitive brand ($X - R$). At time $t + 1$ some of those who had bought the test brand *before* time t, but didn't buy it at time t, will repurchase the test brand. This is called *switchback* (SB). Others will continue to purchase a competing brand.

The customers who repeat plus those who don't repeat must equal 100 percent of those who bought the test product at their last purchase occasion. Similarly, switchback plus nonswitchback must equal 100 percent of those who bought the test brand at some time in the past, but not on the last purchase occasion.

Assume 100 consumers have tried the test brand. If the repeat rate is 81 percent and the switchback rate 20 percent, then on successive purchase occasions we would expect to observe the rates shown in Exhibit 4.7.

Notice how the percentage of buyers who will repurchase the test product on a given occasion differs less and less from the previous period as the number of purchase occasions increases. In fact, if we continued this sequence indefinitely, we would finally arrive at 51.3 percent, and this value would be called the retention rate (S). The value at which this process finally stabilizes is determined completely by the repeat rate (R) and the switchback (SB) rate. This illustration is an example of what is called a *two-stage Markov process*. To understand ASSESSOR, all you need to know about a two-stage Markov process is the formula for the final retention rate*:

$$S = \frac{SB}{1 + SB - R} \tag{4.2}$$

We can compute retention quite simply by using this equation. We might also note that, in our example, after only seven purchase occasions we were getting quite close to 51.3 percent.

---

*SB and R are expected to be decimal fractions; that is, .3 instead of 30 percent.

Preference Model

The first step in developing the preference model involves determining the relevant set of alternatives from which the respondent will choose. Urban and Hauser (1980) define the relevant set as

> that subset of the available brands which are familiar to the respondent regardless of whether they are judged favorably or unfavorably as choice alternatives. [p.413]

Once this set of alternatives is identified, three types of data are obtained:

1. Belief/perception data on the extent to which a respondent judges that the brands in his or her relevant set possess attributes

2. Attribute importance ratings

3. Preference data that expresses the respondent's preference for one brand over another

Preference Data. The most interesting of these three types of data are the preference data. Preferences are obtained through a technique called *constant sum, paired comparison*. This technique requires a respondent to allocate 11 chips between each pair of brands, according to the degree to which one brand is preferred over the other. For example:

Choice #	Brand	Chips	Brand	Chips
1	A	8	B	3
2	B	6	C	5
3	A	9	C	2

The derivation of the procedure's name is easy to understand: *constant sum*—11 chips are allocated in each choice; *paired comparison*—the chips are allocated across pairs of brands.

The motivation of the procedure is simple to understand, even though the mathematics of transforming the data into market share forecasts is quite sophisticated. If a respondent were simply asked to rank brands in order of her preference for them, we wouldn't have any feeling for how strongly one brand is preferred over another. Suppose we had asked the respondent only to provide a ranking of the three brands above, and we had learned that A > B > C. We wouldn't know anything about the strength of preference. But since we have the scores above, we know that alternative III in Exhibit 4.8 is the best description of the preferences of the consumer whose choices are given above.

Each of these three preference structures, if representative of the market, would lead to very different market share forecasts for the brands. The important

Exhibit 4.8 Possible Strength of Preference Rating

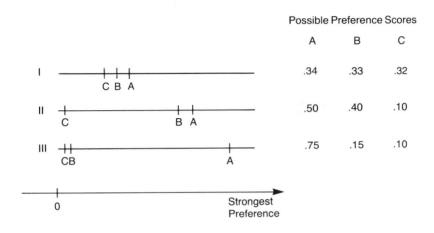

thing about the constant-sum paired-comparison procedure is that as the number of such paired comparison choices is increased, the possible values for the preference for each brand become more tightly defined. The mathematical technique for obtaining these preference scores, called $V(j)$ in the discussion below, is beyond the scope of this book, but understanding the process is not too difficult. Once the preference scores are computed, a brand's market share is estimated as a function of its share-of-preference scores. This is first done for the existing brands in the market to calibrate the model, then the process is repeated with the new brand included in the relevant set. The formulas used in these two estimates are as follows:

Analysis of Existing Brands

1. From a respondent's chip allocations, a preference score $V(j)$ is computed for each brand (j). These preference scores are computed using a technique borrowed from mathematical psychology.

2. The next step is to use these estimated brand-preference scores to compute the probability of a brand j being purchased by a respondent, $P(j)$. The conversion formula is:

$$P(j) = \frac{V(j)^\beta}{\Sigma_k [V(k)]^\beta} \tag{4.3}$$

where the summation is over the k brands in the respondent's evoked set.

These steps are taken to estimate the probability of purchase for the brands that existed in the market before the test product was introduced. In this formulation, β is an estimate of the degree of brand loyalty in the market.

Analysis of the New Brand

3. The chip allocation procedure is repeated during the callback phase of the ASSESSOR process. β is assumed to remain unchanged with the introduction and trial of the test brand, so the following equation estimates the probability that a consumer would choose the test brand after having tried it.

$$L(i) = \frac{A(i)^\beta}{A(i)^\beta + \Sigma_k (A(k))^\beta} \tag{4.4}$$

where:

$A(i)$ = estimated preference of the consumer for the test product after having tried it

$A(k)$ = estimated preference of the consumer for brand k after having tried the test product

Summation is over k, the brands in the consumer's evoked set.

These predicted brand preferences are computed for each consumer separately and are conditional on the evoked set of the consumer. Expected market shares are computed for the brands by aggregating the individual brand preferences and multiplying by the proportion of consumers who include the test product in their evoked sets.

$$M(j) = E(j) \frac{\Sigma_{k=1}^{N} L_k(j)}{N} \tag{4.5}$$

where:

$M(j)$ = expected market share for brand j.

$E(j)$ = proportion of consumers for whom brand j will be in their evoked set.

$L_k(j)$ = predicted probability of purchase of brand j by consumer k.

N = number of consumers.

Forecasting Market Share

The use of two independent market share models provides a validity check on the ASSESSOR procedure in any particular application.

Both models represent market share as the product of two conceptually similar quantities but the sub-models and measures used to estimate the components of each are distinct. Generating two forecasts by alternative plausible methods allows a meaningful check for convergence and the applications experience accumulated over time has served to emphasize that this is an advantageous feature of the system. Finding that the two models yield forecasts that agree strengthens confidence in the prediction. On the other hand, divergent forecasts trigger an investigation of possible sources of error that might account for the discrepancy. Such analyses are guided by systematic consideration of the assumptions underlying each model and its inputs which draw attention to the conditions under which equivalent or dissimilar results are to be expected. Clearly judgment must be exercised in reconciling differences in forecasts but that process is greatly facilitated by an understanding of the structural comparability of the two models. [Urban et al. 1983, p.44]

Once the laboratory share forecast is finalized, the tasks of translating the lab share forecast into a market share and volume forecast remain. This process involves:

1. Estimating the size of the target market.
2. Estimating the awareness level that could be generated through advertising.
3. Making sure that the new brand will be available (distribution level).
4. Estimating the response to sampling if it were to be used.

An overview of the adjustment process is shown in Exhibit 4.9.

The ASSESSOR laboratory trial value is measured when advertising awareness and product availability are both assured, so it has to be modified by the levels of awareness and distribution that will exist at the time targeted by management as the long-term goal. ASSESSOR is a static model (one point in time) as opposed to a dynamic model (a sequence of time periods). The long-term awareness and distribution levels are managerial judgment estimates. The expected level of trial in the marketplace is then estimated as the product of the ASSESSOR trial, advertising awareness, and distribution.

Estimating Sampling-Based Trial

The probable sales response to brand sampling is also tested in the ASSESSOR procedure. At the conclusion of the laboratory test, respondents that had not purchased the test brand in the simulated store are given a sample of the test brand as a gift. A subsequent follow-up interview determines the level of the sample use and the intention to repurchase the test brand.

The ASSESSOR model views the role of sampling to be one of generating incremental trial above that which would be achieved through advertising, since some of the trial generated through sampling would have occurred through advertising anyway. If all sample trial were considered to be incremental, some double counting would occur. Sample-based trial is assumed to be the product

Exhibit 4.9   Translation of ASSESSOR Laboratory Share into Market Share

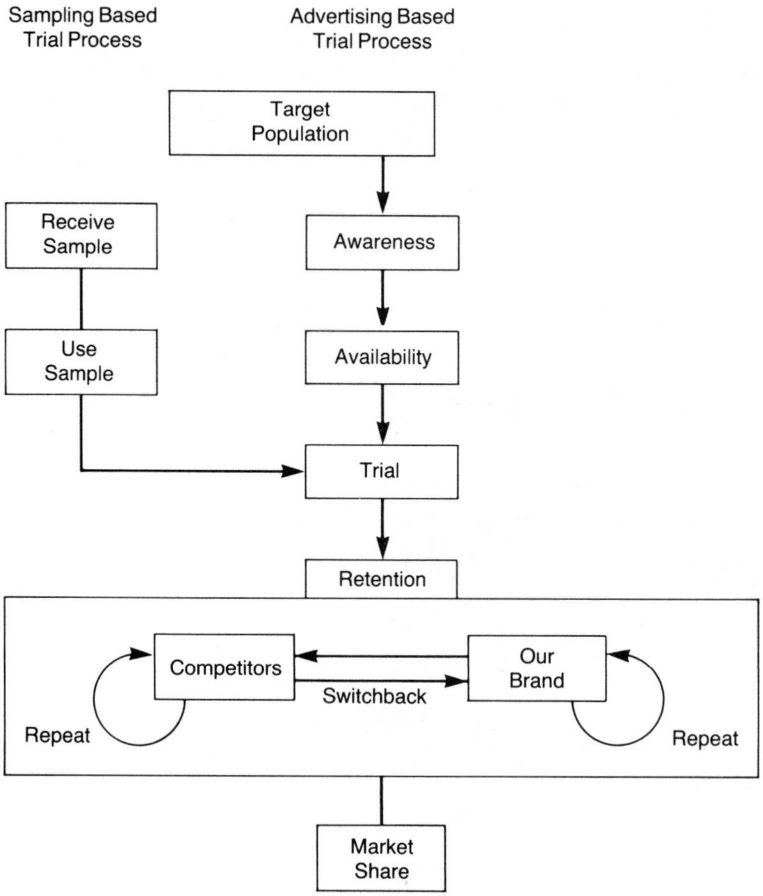

of the size of the target population, the proportion of the target population receiving samples, and the proportion of those receiving samples that will use
them and make a subsequent purchase of the new brand. The formula for trial
used in the ASSESSOR model incorporates these various factors as well as accounting for double counting of advertising and sample-based trial (overlap).

Total Trial = Advertising-Based Trial + Sampling-Based Trial − Overlap

$$T = FKD + CU - (FKD) \times (CU) \tag{4.6}$$

where:

F = the trial rate in the ASSESSOR test—the trial rate that would ultimately occur if all consumers were aware of the advertising and the product were available

K = the long-run probability that a consumer will become aware of the new brand

D = the proportion of retail outlets that will ultimately carry the new brand

C = the proportion of the target market that receives samples

U = the proportion of those receiving samples that will make a first purchase of the new brand

Market share is then estimated as before:

M = trial $\times$ retention

The final step in the ASSESSOR procedure is to develop sales-volume estimates by multiplying the forecasted share by a forecast of category volume.

Accuracy of the ASSESSOR New Product Forecasts

How well ASSESSOR or any other new product forecasting model works is a surprisingly complex question. There are a number of confounding factors that conspire to make the investigation of the question much more complicated than a comparison of the ASSESSOR forecast with the new brands' actual share one year after introduction. In the first place, 40 percent of the ASSESSOR tests discourage introduction of the product, so if ASSESSOR's recommendation is followed, there is no actual share to compare with the forecast.

Among those products that are introduced, an important issue is whether the difference between actual share and forecast share is due to the methodology of the ASSESSOR test, inaccuracy of managerial judgments, changes in the product and marketing plan as a result of what was learned in the ASSESSOR test (for better or for worse), or change in the market itself. A very interesting study on the accuracy of ASSESSOR may be found in Urban and Katz [1983]. The detail of this treatment is again well beyond the scope of this book, but an indication of how well ASSESSOR worked in 44 instances is found in Exhibit 4.10.

A further diagnostic aid available to managers using ASSESSOR is a distribution of trial-and-repeat measures from other ASSESSOR tests in the same product category. See Exhibit 4.11.

Diagnostic Information Produced by ASSESSOR

The ASSESSOR questionnaire yields a great deal of information on advertising awareness, copy point recall, customer demographics, and so on. Most of this

Exhibit 4.10   Plot of Observed vs. Predicted Market Shares for 44 Cases

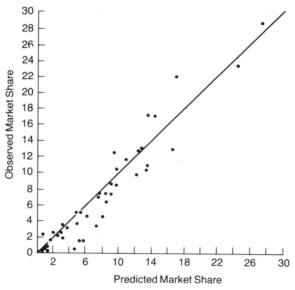

Source: Urban and Katz, 1983.

information requires only a basic statistical background. The product maps produced by ASSESSOR, however, provide an illustration of the power of more advanced statistical methodology in summarizing large bodies of data. The product maps are produced through two multivariate statistical methodologies: *factor analysis* and *preference regression*.

Factor Analysis.   Perhaps the most unusual feature of the ASSESSOR diagnostic material is the graphic representation of the locations of brands relative to one another in a "product map" such as those in Exhibit 4.21 of Johnson Wax I. Many managers have found product maps of this type to be very useful for developing an intuitive, consumer's-eye view of the marketplace. Exhibit 4.21 is a graphic representation of the relative location of existing brands and "ideal direction," developed using factor analysis and preference regression. An intuitive idea of what factor analysis does and how these maps are created is presented in the remainder of this section.

   Data about consumers' perceptions of the attributes of instant hair conditioners is gathered by asking a large number of questions similar to those in Exhibit 4.12, which relates to Enhance, the product whose pre–test market test you will study in the Johnson Wax cases later in this chapter.

Exhibit 4.11   Distribution of ASSESSOR Trial and Repeat Measurements

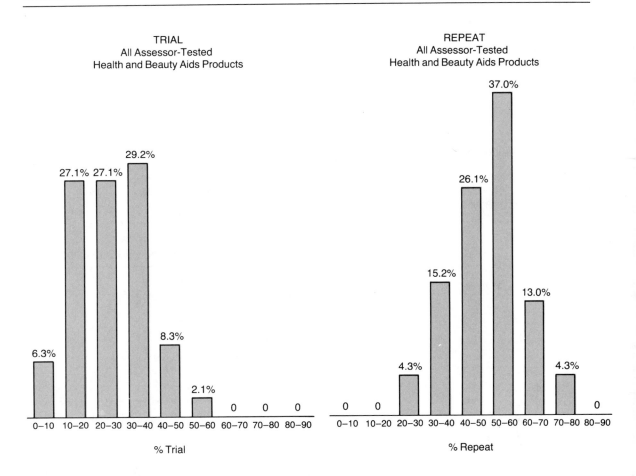

Since there are so many of these kinds of questions, we would like to reduce the number of factors we must consider. We could do this by combining questions that seem to be related and to which there are consistent patterns of response. For example, questions 1 and 5 both seem to have something to do with moisture, so we might expect a respondent to rate a brand similarly on both questions. The degree to which questions are answered similarly is measured by a number called the *correlation coefficient*.

The correlation coefficient simply measures the extent to which a respondent's responses to two questions are both above or both below the average respondent's response. If the respondent gave higher than average responses to both of the questions, the correlation coefficient for those two questions would

Exhibit 4.12 Questionnaire to Determine Consumers' Perceptions

Please rate brand X of creme rinse, hair conditioner, or balsam conditioning product on each of the items below. The *best possible* rating you can give is a 7, the *poorest possible* rating is a 1. Circle *one* number for each item listed. Even if you have never used the product yourself, we would like your impression of what it is like based on what you have seen or heard.

	Best Possible Rating						Poorest Possible Rating
1. Nourishes dry hair	7	6	5	4	3	2	1
2. Leaves hair free of residue, film, and flakes	7	6	5	4	3	2	1
3. Gives hair body and fullness	7	6	5	4	3	2	1
4. Rinses out easily/completely	7	6	5	4	3	2	1
5. Restores moisture	7	6	5	4	3	2	1
6. Keeps control of split ends	7	6	5	4	3	2	1
7. Leaves hair feeling soft and silky	7	6	5	4	3	2	1

Exhibit 4.13 Hypothetical Correlation Between Responses to Selected Questions

Question #	1	2	3	4	5	6	7
1	1.0						
2	0.2	1.0					
3	0.1	−0.1	1.0				
4	−0.3	0.9	−0.1	1.0			
5	0.8	−0.2	0.2	−0.2	1.0		
6	0.7	−0.1	0.1	−0.1	0.9	1.0	
7	0.2	−0.1	0.8	0.2	0.1	0.3	1.0

be close to 1. If the respondent's answer to one question was higher than the average response while her answer to the other question was always lower than the average, the correlation coefficient for the two questions would be close to −1. Correlation coefficients are always between these two extreme values. A correlation coefficient of 0 would mean that there was no consistent pattern of response for the two questions.

Suppose that after questioning a number of respondents we calculated the correlation coefficients for each pair of the seven questions presented above and obtained the results shown in Exhibit 4.13.

The responses to the seven questions do seem to be related—that is, responses to questions 1, 5, and 6 seem to go together, as do 2 and 4, and 3 and 7. Let's rewrite this table by grouping these sets of questions together as shown in Exhibit 4.14.

Notice how the rearrangement has produced three new groups of questions and nine blocks of correlation coefficients. The three blocks above the diagonal

Exhibit 4.14 Rearranged Correlations Between Selected Questions

	Question #	f_1 1	f_1 5	f_1 6	f_2 2	f_2 4	f_3 3	f_3 7
f_1	1	1.0						
	5	0.8	1.0					
	6	0.7	0.9	1.0				
f_2	2	0.2	−0.2	−0.1	1.0			
	4	−0.3	−0.2	−0.1	0.9	1.0		
f_3	3	0.1	0.2	0.1	−0.1	−0.1	1.0	
	7	0.2	0.1	0.3	−0.1	0.2	0.8	1.0

are symmetric with the three below the diagonal blocks. In each of the three diagonal blocks, the correlations between responses to the questions are high, while the correlations between responses to questions in different blocks are low. Now let's consider each of the groups of questions to be a measurement of some underlying factor that generated the responses to the questions we asked. This new set of variables, or *factors*, would have a low correlation with one another. (The off-diagonal blocks have low correlation.) Ideally we would like our new factors to be a set of three uncorrelated variables, with a correlation array that would look like this:

$$
\begin{array}{ccc}
1. & & \\
0 & 1. & \\
0 & 0 & 1.
\end{array}
$$

Exhibit 4.14 looks like this, if we look at the blocks and not the individual questions. If each block represents a variable, or factor, we have a new set of factors: factor 1 would be described by questions 1, 5, and 6; factor 2 would be described by questions 2 and 4; and factor 3 would be described by questions 3 and 7.

What are these new variables? We have to name them ourselves from the common property that defines each set. In the Johnson Wax I case, factor 1 was called "conditioning"; factor 2, "cleaning"; and factor 3, "manageability/effects."

This illustration is simplistic—the groupings are clear from the start. This isn't always the case because many questions are asked to explore consumers' perceptions of products, and the underlying dimensions of the market are by no means obvious. Or perhaps a manager would just like to see whether his or her percep-

Exhibit 4.15   Average Scores for Questions Related to Conditioning and Cleaning

	Average Score	Factor Loadings	
		Conditions	Cleans
1. Nourishes	4.5	0.75	0
5. Restores moisture	5.0	0.6	0
6. Keeps control	3.8	0.5	0
2. Free of residue	3.5	0.0	.85
4. Rinses completely	3.1	0.0	.80
Factor Score (Coordinates)		8.275	5.455

tion of the market is consistent with objective measurement. In either of these situations, factor analysis is very helpful.

Finding these factors is not nearly so obvious when there are lots of observations and lots of questions. A statistical procedure called *factor analysis* had been developed to find the best subgrouping of a large set of variables. In this subgrouping the original variables will be formed into subgroups in which the variables of a subgroup will be highly correlated with the other variables in the subgroup and uncorrelated with the variables in the other subgroup.

Perceptual Maps and Preference Regression.   We have thus seen how a large number of attributes can be reduced to a smaller set of underlying factors. These factors become the coordinate axes in the product map. Each of the original questions (variables) has a coefficient, a_i, (called a *factor loading*) that relates it to the factor to which it belongs, much like a regression coefficient. So we can write:

$$f_i = a_{i0} + a_{i1}v_1 + \ldots + a_{ik}v_k$$

If we take the mean score attributed to each question for a given brand, we can use this equation to compute what is called the factor score, f_i, for that brand. If we have three factors, we can compute three factor scores for each brand. Using these three factor scores, we can locate the brand in a three-dimensional space where each factor represents a dimension.

For example, let's locate Enhance on the "conditioning" and "cleaning" axes from our example. This will involve the questions 1, 5, 6, and 2, 4. Suppose Enhance's average score for each of these questions is as shown in Exhibit 4.15.

Another feature of the perceptual map is the development of an "ideal" vector that defines the combination of attributes that the respondents seem to want. In Exhibit 4.21 of the Johnson Wax I case it appears that consumers seem to want about an even mix of the product attributes "conditions" and "cleans," since the ideal vector is a 45 percent line in the first quadrant. The ideal vector (see Exhibit

Exhibit 4.16   Derivation of the Ideal Vector

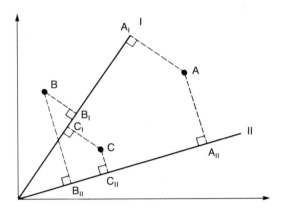

4.16) is derived using a methodology called *preference regression*, which finds a line upon which consumers' stated preferences are best related to the various brands' projections along that line.

Suppose A is preferred to B is preferred to C by some consumer. Line I in Exhibit 4.16 is a better candidate for the ideal vector than line II because the order of the projections of the brands' positions on line I is in the same order as the consumers preference, A, B, C; whereas the projections of the brands' positions on line II are A, C, B. Preference regression finds the single direction that best predicts the brand preferences of the respondents.

CASE: Johnson Wax I

Johnson Wax I describes the pre–test market testing program undertaken for Enhance instant hair conditioner, a product line extension by a major manufacturer. The pre–test market testing procedure used, ASSESSOR, provides market share forecasts and diagnostic information for evaluating marketing plans. Enhance is less "new" than the products in the previous chapter, the market is better understood, and the marketing research approach is more sophisticated.

The case illustrates marketing research at a later stage in the new product development process than the previous cases, as well as the contribution that a very simple preliminary decision model can make to the value of research data.

John Sherman, product development manager for S. C. Johnson & Company, was facing a decision on the future of Enhance, a new instant hair conditioner designed as a companion product to Agree, the company's first hair-care product. Development of Enhance had begun soon after Agree's success appeared assured, and by April 1979 had been under way for about a year and a half.

During the development process, Enhance had been tested against the leading existing products through blind comparisons and had undergone a pre–test market testing procedure called ASSESSOR. The results of these tests would need to play a significant role in Sherman's recommendations, because previous experience had convinced top management that such research was valuable. In fact, the company had performed a number of AS-SESSOR or similar analyses in the past, and top management had on occasion seemed anxious to skip the test market and push for introduction when the ASSESSOR results were favorable.

John Sherman's task was to recommend the next steps for Enhance. While his experience and intuitive judgment would be valued, he knew the managerial climate at S. C. Johnson would require marketing research substantiation for his recommendations.

Company Background

S. C. Johnson & Company, headquartered in Racine, Wisconsin, was founded in 1886 as a manufacturer of parquet flooring. It was incorporated as S. C. Johnson & Son, Inc. and was familiarly known throughout the world as "Johnson Wax." A privately held corporation, Johnson Wax did not publicly report sales or earnings. Still, it was recognized as one of the world's leading manufacturers of products for home, auto, personal care, recreation and leisure-time activities. Johnson Wax and its subsidiaries employed more than 13,000 people worldwide.

The Johnson Wax consumer product line consisted of some of the best-known brands in household, automobile, and personal-care products: Brite, Future, Glo-Coat, and Klear floor waxes; Jubilee and Pledge furniture polish; Rain Barrel Fabric Softener; Shout Stain Remover; Glory Carpet Cleaner; Glade Air Freshener; J-Wax auto care products; Raid insecticide; and Off insect repellent. The U.S. consumer products were distributed to supermarkets and drug, discount, and variety outlets through the company's own national sales force.

New-Product Development at Johnson Wax

Development of numerous product lines over the years had given Johnson Wax considerable experience in new-product evaluation and introduction. New product ideas came from laboratory research,

This case was prepared by Darral G. Clarke.

Copyright (©) 1982 By the President and Fellows of Harvard College Harvard Business School case 9-583-046.

marketing research, and customer contact. The product development process at Johnson Wax was fairly standard: ideas went through various commercial feasibility studies, performance tests against competitive products, and test markets before national introduction or rollout. In recent years developing a new consumer product had become so expensive that Johnson Wax, like other manufacturers, had looked for ways to reduce the cost by including a pre–test market test in their new product development process.

The Hair Conditioning Market

During the 1970s, both the variety and the number of hair-care products and brands had increased drastically. Shampoos to combat dandruff were introduced; others were custom-formulated for use on dry, normal, or oily hair. During the same period, new products were introduced that would "condition" hair as well as clean it. According to one manufacturer:

A good creme rinse conditioner can help combat many hair problems. Hair can be easily damaged when it is combed following a shampoo, since hair is weakest when wet. Washing and towel-drying hair tend to tangle it, making it susceptible to breakage during combing. A creme rinse conditioner helps prevent this type of damage because it helps prevent tangles and makes for easy wet-combing. Creme rinse and conditioners also make hair feel softer; add to its bounce, shine, and body; and help prevent the buildup of static electricity that causes hair to be "flyaway."

There were two types of hair conditioners:

Instant conditioners, which were usually left on the hair for one to five minutes before being rinsed off

Therapeutic conditioners, which generally remained on the hair from five to twenty minutes before rinsing

The term *creme rinse* was still used occasionally for conditioners that stressed easier combing and manageability. Gradually, the term was being replaced by *instant conditioner*. Hair conditioner

Exhibit 4.17   Manufacturers' Sales ($ millions)

Year	Total Conditioner	Instant Conditioner
1975	$132	$116
1976	160	141
1977	200	176
1978	230	202

sales had grown dramatically during the 1970s, spurred by new-product introductions and increased use, especially among young women.

The major instant hair conditioner brands and their 1978 shampoo market shares were Flex (13.4%), Clairol Conditioner (9.9%), Sassoon (5.8%), Tame (5.4%), and Wella Balsam (4.7%).

Manufacturers' sales were as shown in Exhibit 4.17.

Instant conditioners were sold in a variety of packages, but generally in either clear or opaque plastic bottles, often with nozzle tops. Popular sizes were 8-, 12-, and 16-ounce bottles. Retail margins generally ranged between 30% and 38%.

Agree

In June 1977, Johnson Wax entered the hair-care market with Agree creme rinse and conditioner, soon followed by Agree shampoo. At that time some creme rinses and conditioners included oil in their formulation. Agree's selling proposition was that the addition of this oil, especially for people with oily hair, caused hair to look oily, greasy, and limp soon after shampooing. A technological breakthrough by Johnson Wax enabled it to produce a virtually oil-free product (Agree) which helped "stop the greasies." According to Johnson Wax promotional material:

Agree has exceptional detangling properties making the hair easier to wet-comb. It is pleasantly scented and leaves the hair feeling clean, with healthy shine, bounce, and body. Agree contains no harsh or harmful ingredients and is pH balanced to be compatible with the natural pH of hair and scalp.

Exhibit 4.18   Blind Use Test Results

Incidence of Problems

	All Women	25–29	30–34	35 or Older
Dry/Damage Problems	.53	.55	.53	.46
Split ends	.34	.42	.35	.29
Dryness	.32	.29	.35	.31
Brittle/breaking	.12	.13	.17	.09
Damaged hair	.1	.10	.18	.11
Dull/Limp Problems	.65	.64	.68	.58
Hard to manage	.38	.32	.42	.39
Dull/no shine	.24	.16	.21	.30
Fine/limp hair	.44	.45	.39	.46

Each respondent was screened for the presence of any of these seven hair problems. The seven problems, in turn, were subjectively grouped into those to do with "Dry/Damage" and those to do with "Dull/Limp."

Overall Preference

	(Base)	Prefer Enhance	Prefer Flex	No Difference
All Users	(320)	.48	.44	.08
By Age				
Under 35	(166)	.46	.47	.07
35 or over	(154)	.50	.40	.10
By Hair Type				
Oily	(94)	.51	.45	.04
Normal	(154)	.44	.47	.09
Dry	(72)	.53*	.35	.12
By Hair Quality				
Dry/damaged (net)	(168)	.50*	.40	.10
Fine/limp (net)	(208)	.49*	.43	.08

*Significant at 90% confidence level.

Agree had fared well in product comparison tests and an ASSESSOR pre–test market test. By 1978, Agree had a 4.5% share of the shampoo and 15.2% share of the conditioner market.

Enhance Product Development

Agree's early success created optimism and euphoria at Johnson Wax. Gaining a foothold in the attractive conditioner market offered an opportunity to expand the conditioner product line and subsequently make greater inroads on the even larger shampoo market. Management felt Agree was successful largely because it solved a specific hair problem for a segment of the market and that it would be desirable to offer another personal-care product line. Enhance was conceived as an instant hair conditioner targeted toward women 25–45 years old with dry hair, and was formulated to appeal to that audience.

Exhibit 4.19   Blind Use Test Results—Preference on Specific Attributes

	Prefer Enhance	Prefer Flex	No Difference
Fragrance			
In bottle	.27	.32	.41
While using	.34	.37	.29
After dry	.28	.28	.44
Feels Cleaner			
While using	.18	.17	.65
When dry	.26*	.19	.55
Next day	.26	.22	.52
Conditioning			
Conditioning	.28	.24	.48
Softer	.31	.26	.43
Body	.31	.32	.37
More manageable	.32	.30	.38
Better shine	.14	.16	.70
Relieves dryness	.22†	.15	.63
Combing			
Easy to comb	.22	.20	.58
Tangle-free	.16	.16	.68
Use/Application			
Applies evenly	.30†	.14	.56
Penetrates better	.28†	.18	.54
Rinses out more easily	.22	.21	.57
Product			
Better color	.04	.06	.90
Better consistency	.27	.29	.44

BASE: 320 users

*Significant at 90% confidence level.
†Significant at 95% confidence level.

Blind Comparison Test Results

John Sherman and Neil Ford, of the marketing research department, designed a blind use test to determine the preference levels for Enhance, both overall and on specific performance attributes, versus those of Flex, the leading instant hair conditioner. A panel of 400 hair conditioner users was preselected by telephone. Each received both Enhance and Flex, blind-labeled and in identical nonidentifiable packages and, following proper rotations, used first one for three weeks, then the other for an identical period. At the end of the six-week usage period, respondents were interviewed regarding their preferences and behavior regarding the test products. A key part of the analysis was to determine preferences of women with specific hair care problems relevant to Enhance strategy and positioning. A digest of the results appears in Exhibits 4.18 and 4.19. Conclusions drawn by Ford in his August 1978 report to Sherman were that:

Exhibit 4.20   Four Perceptual Factors for Hair Conditioners

Factor	Relative Importance*	Attributes Combined to Form the Factor
Conditioning	33%	Nourishes dry hair Restores moisture Keeps control of split ends Makes dry hair healthy looking Conditions hair Helps keep hair from breaking Penetrates hair
Clean	27%	Leaves hair free of residue/flakes Leaves hair grease- and oil-free Leaves hair clean looking Rinses out easily/completely
Manageability/effects	23%	Makes hair more manageable Leaves hair shiny/lustrous Leaves hair soft and silky Gives hair body and fullness
Fragrance	17%	Has pleasant fragrance while using Leaves hair with nice fragrance

*Share of explained variance.

Differences between the two products are not great, but where they exist, they tend to be focused on the problems Enhance wishes to address and on the women to whom the brand will be targeted. While work should continue to improve the product, it is suitable for use in ASSESSOR in its current state and, if needs be, for use in test-market introduction.

The ASSESSOR Pre–Test Market Test

Following the blind comparison tests, further work on product formulation, product positioning, packaging, and advertising copy produced an introductory marketing plan. Advertising copy presented Enhance as a solution to the dry and damaged hair problem. Enhance samples were produced in "regular" and "extra conditioning" formulas.

When the marketing plan was agreed upon and samples were available, an ASSESSOR pre–test market test was arranged. The primary objectives were to estimate the ongoing market share of En-

hance and determine consumer reaction to the product. The field research for the ASSESSOR test was conducted in three markets—Atlanta, Chicago, and Denver—beginning September 25, 1978, with callback interviews approximately four weeks later. A total of 387 interviews was conducted with users of creme rinse/conditioning products. Respondents included 120 users of Agree creme rinse, a disproportionate number, in order to better determine Enhance's effect on Agree.

ASSESSOR Pre–Test Market Results

ASSESSOR provided results in a number of areas of interest: market structure, advertising recall, trial, repeat purchase, product acceptance, market-share prediction, sampling response, and cannibalization.

Market Structure.   During the laboratory phase of the fieldwork, respondents were asked to rate several of their evoked brands as well as their "ideal"

Exhibit 4.21   ASSESSOR Results—Product Maps

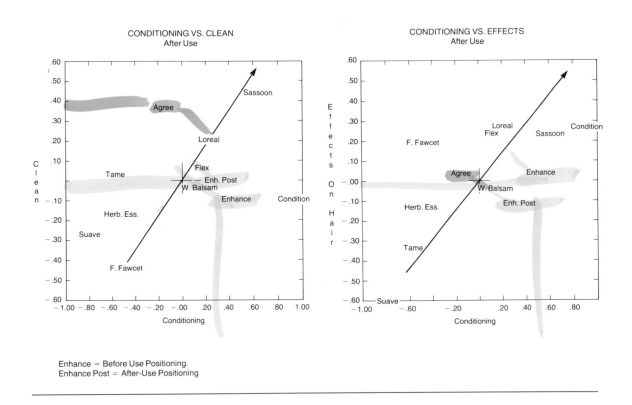

Enhance = Before Use Positioning.
Enhance Post = After-Use Positioning

brand on 22 attributes. These brand ratings were used as inputs to factor analysis, a data-reduction technique used for grouping similar attributes into underlying factors or dimensions. From this analysis, four basic perceptual dimensions, or factors, emerged (see Exhibit 4.20).

Besides identifying the possible factors underlying the instant conditioner market, factor analysis provided a graphic representation of the customer's positioning of the brands in a perceptual map. This was done by using pairs of factors as axes and assigning each brand a factor score that served as a coordinate on each axis. Using these coordinates, a brand was assigned a position on the perceptual map. Although MDS produced perceptual maps for a number of market segments only the maps for the total market are shown in

Exhibit 4.21. (Maps including the fragrance factor are not presented.)

MDS's report concluded that, in terms of market structure,

The fact that all four dimensions are important to all consumers' segments considered in the study suggests that being strongly positioned on only one dimension may not be sufficient to capture a significant portion of the market.

Agree and Breck Creme Rinse have achieved the "clean" position, while Clairol Condition has succeeded in differentiating itself as the "conditioning" brand. Wella Balsam, based on these maps, appears to have virtually no image, and thus might be vulnerable to a new entry. Sas-

Exhibit 4.22   ASSESSOR Results—Copy Point Recall

	Overall (%)	Buyers (%)	Nonbuyers (%)
For Dry Hair			
Good for dry hair	46.8	50.0	46.1
Nourishes hair	33.1	37.9	32.0
Prevents dry hair	5.4	1.7	6.2
Doesn't leave hair dry	.7	0.0	.8
Conditions	20.4	27.6	18.7
Conditions hair	8.0	17.2	5.8
Good for damaged hair	5.4	5.2	5.4
Repairs hair	4.0	6.9	3.3
For brittle hair	3.3	1.7	3.7
Protects from heat damage	.7	0.0	.8
Mends split ends	.7	0.0	.8
Penetrates	19.7	31.0	17.0
Penetrates hair	19.7	31.0	17.0
Doesn't just coat hair	3.3	8.6	2.1
Manageability	11.4	17.2	10.0
Makes hair more manageable	7.7	12.1	6.6
Good for limp hair	3.3	3.4	3.3
Eliminates tangles	.7	1.7	.4
Texture of Hair	6.4	5.2	6.6
Gives hair more body/bounce	4.3	1.7	5.0
Leaves hair soft	2.0	3.4	1.7
BASE:	(299)	(58)	(241)

soon, a relatively new brand, appears to be enjoying a very strong positive image.

Advertising Recall. Unaided advertising recall provided a measure of how well an ad broke through the clutter of competitive advertising. Total unaided recall for Enhance was 76%, about average for ASSESSOR-tested products, but somewhat lower than for other Johnson Wax products subjected to ASSESSOR tests. Unaided recall did not differ by hair type. Among those who recalled the Enhance ad, almost 50% recalled that Enhance was "for dry hair." "Conditions" and "penetrates" received somewhat lower playback. Exhibit 4.22 summarizes the copy-point recall results.

Trial Estimation. Store setups had been designed to reflect local conditions and simulate the antici-

pated competitive environment. Enhance was available in two sizes for both regular and extra conditioning formulations. Enhance had one facing for each size and formulation, and was featured in the middle of the middle shelf. In all, 24 shampoos and conditioners were represented in 60 facings. The 8-ounce Enhance price was $1.31, the same as the 8-ounce Agree; 12-ounce Agree was priced at $1.67; and 16-ounce Enhance was priced at $1.94, the same as the 16-ounce Flex. On a per-ounce basis, this price difference was about twice as great as that between JWC's prices on the large and small sizes of Agree, but was about the same as those of Breck, Wella Balsam, and Tame. Flex was sold only in a 16-ounce size.

Trial was measured as a percentage of total laboratory purchasing. Of the 387 respondents, 307 (80%) made a purchase in the store. The Enhance trial rate was 15.7% among Agree users and 22.2% among users of all other brands. Weighting by current market shares in the instant conditioner market resulted in an overall trial rate of 23%. Agree had achieved an overall trial rate of 32% in its ASSESSOR test. Trial rates for other ASSESSOR-tested products in the health and beauty aids category are found in Exhibit 4.11.

Repeat Purchase Estimation. Repeat purchase and product acceptance were determined through telephone callback interviews four weeks after the laboratory interviews. Since all respondents who had not purchased Enhance were given samples, after-use data were potentially available for all respondents. Those who had not used Enhance were not asked to complete the phone interview. Telephone callbacks were completed with 215 respondents (55% of all laboratory respondents). This was lower than most ASSESSOR callback completion rates. Of those people with whom callback interviews were *not* completed, 23% (42 people) indicated they had not used Enhance because it was specifically formulated for dry hair.

During the callback interviews, respondents were again asked to compare Enhance with other brands in their evoked sets and this information was used to see whether use altered Enhance's position in the market structure.

Respondents were given the opportunity to purchase another bottle of Enhance at the same prices found in the laboratory store. Those who decided to repurchase, plus those who said without prompting that their next conditioner purchase would be Enhance, were classified as repeaters. Repeat rates were as shown in Exhibit 4.23.

The repeat purchase rates of other ASSESSOR-tested products are found in Figure 4.11.

Product Acceptance. During the callback interview the respondent was asked what she liked best about Enhance. Surprisingly, manageability, not conditioning, was mentioned most frequently, even though it was not considered a main copy point. Those who made a repeat purchase were even more likely than nonrepeaters to mention manageability. Open-ended likes and dislikes for Enhance are found in Exhibit 4.24. Exhibit 4.25 presents

Exhibit 4.23 Repeat Rates for Enhance

	Enhance (%)	Agree (%)
Repeat among buyers	60	78
Repeat among nonbuyers	43	63
Repurchased 16-ounce size	64	NA
Repurchased "extra conditioning formula"	72	NA

after-use preferences and comparisons with users' favorite brands.

Market Share. Market share was estimated separately with a trial-and-repeat model and a preference model. The trial-and-repeat model forecast used the purchase information gathered during laboratory shopping and follow-up interview repeat measurements. Since Enhance had obtained a laboratory trial note of 23%, a repeat rate of 60%, and a switchback rate of 16%, retention was calculated to be 28.6%. The market share estimates for Enhance depended not only on data obtained from the ASSESSOR test, but also on John Sherman's estimates of what advertising awareness and distribution levels would be realized for Enhance. Sherman had decided to use initially the advertising awareness and distribution levels realized for Agree:

awareness   70%

distribution   85%

Using these values, and ignoring sampling for the moment, market share at the end of the first year after introduction was predicted by the trial/repeat model at 3.9%. MDS's estimated market shares for Enhance and Agree are found in Exhibit 4.26.

The preference model market share prediction was based on the respondents' answers to the questions about product attributes and the degree to which they perceived these attributes to be present in competing brands. The preference model predicted that Enhance would attain a 27.5% share of those consumers in whose evoked sets it appeared. Using the penetration rate found in the trial

Exhibit 4.24   ASSESSOR Results—Open-Ended Likes and Dislikes for Enhance (multiple mention)

Open-Ended Likes

	Overall (%)	Repeaters (%)	Nonrepeaters (%)
Manageability	42	48	37
Fragrance	21	14	27
Conditioning	11	12	10
Consistency	7	7	6
Application/Ease of use	7	6	7
Penetrates	6	5	7
Clean	5	7	4
Base	(215)	(102)	(113)

Open-Ended Dislikes

	Overall (%)	Repeaters (%)	Nonrepeaters (%)
Manageability	24	9	38
Fragrance	16	7	25
Conditioning	11	8	13
Consistency	1	3	0
Application/ease of use	1	1	1
Nothing Disliked	59	74	46
Base	(215)	(102)	(113)

Exhibit 4.25   ASSESSOR Results—After-Use Preferences

% Prefer Enhance

	Ist	2nd	3rd	4th	(Base)
Dry Hair	38	32	17	7	(93)
Oily Hair	22	34	20	15	(41)
Normal	23	34	19	12	(69)
Total Sample	28	33	19	11	(215)
Total Sample (Agree)	54	26	12	2	(279)

Comparison to Regular Brand

	Among Triers		Among Nontriers	
	Enhance (%)	Agree (%)	Enhance (%)	Agree (%)
Much better	30	44	14	35
A little better	24	25	21	22
About the same	26	13	37	21
A little poorer	14	12	16	13
Much poorer	6	5	12	8
(Base)	(50)	(76)	(165)	(203)

Exhibit 4.26 ASSESSOR Market Share Prediction

Trial/Repeat Model

	Enhance	Agree
1. Trial	.23	.32
2. Awareness from advertising	.70	.70
3. Distribution	.85	.85
4. Net cum trial (#1 × #2 × #3)	.137	.190
5. Repeat	.60	.78
6. Switchback	.16	.16
7. Share of triers' choices (retention)[#6 ÷ (1 + #6 − #5)]	.286	.420
8. Base share (#4 × #7)	.039	.08

Preference Model

	Enhance	Agree
9. Share for Enhance if everyone evokes it	.275	.420
10. Estimated penetration	.14	.20
11. Base share (#9 × #10)	.038	.084

phase of the ASSESSOR study (14%), and the same awareness and distribution estimates resulted in a base market share estimate of 3.8% (see Exhibit 4.26).

Cannibalization. An estimate of Enhance's cannibalization of Agree's share was obtained by computing Enhance's share among Agree users. This analysis demonstrated that Enhance would draw less than proportionately from Agree, with a share of 2.4% among Agree users and 3.0% among all others. Weighting by Agree's current market share indicated that Agree would lose half a share point to Enhance.

Additional analysis indicated that Enhance would draw more than proportionately from Wella Balsam, proportionately from Flex and Sassoon, and less than proportionately from Agree, L'Oreal, and Clairol Condition.

Incremental Share from Sampling. The incremental share that might be expected from sampling could be estimated since those respondents who had not chosen Enhance had been given a sample of the product at the end of the initial ASSESSOR interview. Their use and acceptance levels were determined during the callback interview. The effects of sampling were evaluated by first determining the incremental trial rate that would result from sampling. Of those using samples, a certain percentage (equal to net cumulative trial) would have tried the product anyway, but the remainder were new triers due to sampling. After making a first purchase, these triers were assumed to follow the normal switching process, and their long-run share potential could be estimated in the same way as for the triers. These calculations, and those obtained for Agree, are found in Exhibit 4.27. When the effect of sampling was included, market share was estimated at 5.8% by the preference model and 5.9% by the trial/repeat model.

Volume Projections. Mr. Sherman was also interested in the revenue that would result from the

Exhibit 4.27   ASSESSOR Prediction of Incremental Share from Sampling

	ASSESSOR Test Results	National Projection
1. Number of samples delivered	5MM	35MM
2. % Delivered	90%	90%
3. % hitting target group	70%	80%
4. % used	75%	60%
5. Number of samples used (#1 × #2 × #3 × #4)	2.36MM	15.12MM
6. Percent using samples*	7.5%	25%
7. Overlap	.01	.03
8. Net incremental trial	.034	.218
9. First repeat (repeat among nonbuyers)†	.45	.43
10. Share of triers' choices (retention)	.225	.219
11. Incremental share from sampling (#8 × #10)	.003	.020

*Assumes 60MM households in the U.S. target market.
†Using the switchback estimate from Exhibit 4.26.

Exhibit 4.28   Forecast of Enhance Revenue

	Trial/Repeat Model	Preference Model
Manufacturer's Category Volume	$250MM	$250MM
Unit Share	3.9%	3.8%
Dollar Share	3.8%	3.7%
Enhance Revenue	$9.5MM	$9.3MM
Additional Sales From Promotion		
Promotion Unit Share	2.0%	
Promotion Dollar Share	1.96%	
Enhance Revenue	4.9MM	$4.9MM
Total Revenue	$14.4MM	$14.2MM

Exhibit 4.29 Approximate Health and Beauty Aid Industry Cost Structures* (Indexed to SRP)

Suggested Retail Price	$1.00
Expected Shelf Price (Large, 16 oz.)	$ .83
(Small, 8 oz.)	$ .73
Manufacturer's Selling Price	$ .56
Cost of Goods Sold	21%

*These data are not supplied by the Johnson Wax Company, and are not known to be indicative of its actual costs. They are thought to reflect the average market cost structure closely enough to be helpful in the case discussion.

market share forecasts. Based on expected price and frequency-of-use estimates in comparison with category averages, it was determined that Enhance's dollar share would be 98% of the unit share forecasted by ASSESSOR. 1979 hair conditioner sales were forecast at $250 million. Using these data, Enhance revenue was forecast as shown in Exhibit 4.28.

Recommendations

MDS was not encouraging about Enhance's prospects in general, and stated that it also thought sampling would not be successful for Enhance. Johnson Wax management had set a target market share of 10%. John Sherman knew, however, that the final recommendation was his to make. He could recommend that Enhance be abandoned, reformulated, retested, or that a national rollout begin.

Preparation Questions

1. What is the nature of the shampoo/hair conditioning market?

2. What are the important managerial considerations that must be considered regarding the further new product development of Enhance?

3. Outline the research program that has been followed by JWC. How well has it addressed the issues you identified above?

4. What was learned from the marketing research?

5. What would you recommend as the next steps to take with Enhance?

6. Predict the results of your marketing plan.

Johnson Wax I Decision Model

The decision model for the Johnson Wax I case is intended to allow you to see how sensitive market share and contribution to profit are to the various elements of the marketing plan as well as to the ASSESSOR estimates. In other words, you can put in different values for trial, repeat, retention, distribution, awareness, price, and so on, and see how share, sales, and contribution to profit are affected. This allows you to compare various strategies and determine what would have to be done to reach the managerial goals.

This spreadsheet is a decision model in the sense that was discussed in Chapter 2—ASSESSOR's conceptual response function and parameter estimates are imbedded in a financial spreadsheet that allows consideration of market share, unit sales, revenue, and contribution to profit as deci-

Exhibit 4.30   Spreadsheet for Johnson Wax I

```
              Johnson Wax (I) Decision Model
                  Alternative Evaluation
------------------------------------------------------------
Common Inputs:     Switchback                        16%
                   Target market size (MM)           60
```

	ASSESSOR Based Model Alternatives			
	- 1 -	- 2 -	- 3 -	- 4 -
Distribution	85.0%	85.0%	85.0%	85.0%

Advertising based share

	- 1 -	- 2 -	- 3 -	- 4 -
Awareness	70.0%	70.0%	63.0%	63.0%
Trial	23.0%	32.0%	17.0%	17.0%
Repeat rate	60.0%	72.0%	70.6%	70.6%
Retention	28.6%	36.4%	35.2%	35.2%
Share from advertising	3.9%	6.9%	3.2%	3.2%

Sampling based share   - 1 -   - 2 -   - 3 -   - 4 -

	- 1 -	- 2 -	- 3 -	- 4 -
Number of samples (MM)	30	35	30	30
%Samples delivered	90.0%	90.0%	90.0%	90.0%
%Samples hitting target	80.0%	80.0%	80.0%	80.0%
%Samples used	60.0%	60.0%	60.0%	60.0%
Samples used (MM)	13.0	15.1	13.0	13.0
Incremental trial	18.6%	20.4%	19.6%	19.6%
Repeat rate	42.7%	42.7%	42.7%	42.7%
Retention	21.8%	21.8%	21.8%	21.8%
Incremental share	1.7%	1.9%	1.8%	1.8%

Combined advertising and sampling based trial and share

Net cumulative trial	29.5%	36.4%	25.8%	25.8%
Volume market share	5.6%	8.8%	5.0%	5.0%

(continued)

sion criteria. The sales and contribution to profit estimates are further broken out according to advertising and sampling.

This decision model is intended for comparison of a number of static marketing plans rather than to facilitate the development of pro forma marketing plans over time. (Each of the columns of the spreadsheet is independent of the others.) The spreadsheet, displayed in Exhibit 4.30, consists of four main sections:

The *Advertising Section* is used to compute the market share that will result from advertising. Distribution and awareness are judgmental in-

Exhibit 4.30 (continued)   Spreadsheet for Johnson Wax I

Revenue and contribution calculations

Revenue	- 1 -	- 2 -	- 3 -	- 4 -
Volume market share	5.6%	8.8%	5.0%	5.0%
Unit-dollar adjustment	0.94	0.94	0.94	0.94
Manufacturers' sales	$301	$301	$301	$301
JWC factory sales	$15.9	$24.9	$14.2	$14.2
Contribution				
8 oz. sales share	40.0%	40.0%	40.0%	40.0%
Cost of samples	$0.10	$0.15	$0.20	$0.20
Exp. retail price - 8oz	$1.31	$1.31	$1.31	$1.31
Factory price - 8oz	$1.00	$1.00	$1.00	$1.00
Cost of goods ($0.46)	$0.46	$0.46	$0.46	$0.46
Unit contribution	$0.55	$0.55	$0.55	$0.55
Unit margin (%)	54.5%	54.5%	54.5%	54.5%
Exp. retail price - 16oz	$1.94	$1.94	$1.94	$1.94
Factory price - 16oz	$1.31	$1.31	$1.31	$1.31
Cost of goods ($0.60)	$0.60	$0.60	$0.60	$0.60
Unit contribution	$0.71	$0.71	$0.71	$0.71
Unit margin (%)	53.9%	53.9%	53.9%	53.9%
Wtd avg unit margin (%)	54.1%	54.1%	54.1%	54.1%
Gross contribution	$8.61	$13.45	$7.68	$7.68

Financial Summary ($MM)

	- 1 -	- 2 -	- 3 -	- 4 -
Gross contribution	$8.61	$13.45	$7.68	$7.68
Less				
Advertising expense	$4.50	$4.50	$4.50	$4.50
Sampling cost	$3.00	$5.25	$6.00	$6.00
Net contribution	$1.11	$3.70	($2.82)	($2.82)
From advertising	$1.46	$6.06	$0.39	$0.39
From sampling	($0.35)	($2.35)	($3.21)	($3.21)
ROS	6.98%	14.90%	-19.86%	-19.86%

puts, while trial, repeat rate, and switchback are all measured in the ASSESSOR test. Retention and share from advertising are both calculated using the formulas explained early in the chapter in formula (4.2) and in Exhibit 4.26.

The *Sampling Section* is used to compute the market share that will result from a sampling program. The definitions used in this section are explained early in the chapter under "Estimating Sampling-Based Trial" and in Exhibit 4.27. The number of samples, percent of samples delivered and hitting the target market are used to compute the number of samples used. According to the ASSESSOR model, some of this sample use would have occurred due to advertising anyway and should be deducted to arrive at the incremental trial rate. The repeat rate for sampling triers is measured separately in ASSESSOR, which results in a different retention rate for sampling-based trial. Finally, incremental share resulting from sampling is computed.

The *Prediction Section* is used to convert the market share forecast into a revenue forecast. The volume market share value comes from summing the advertising-based share and the incremental share due to sampling. To convert this share of volume into revenue it must be adjusted to a revenue share and multiplied by the manufacturers' sales for the hair conditioner category. Since Enhance is sold in two sizes and you might want to adjust the product line pricing, you can judgmentally determine the distribution of Enhance sales by product size. Since the factory price is an input value, the unit contribution margin will vary with your price. The cost of samples is also input in this section.

The *Financial Summary* is the final section of the decision model. It is used to display the gross contribution to profit and to compute the net contribution to profit after advertising and sampling costs. Your advertising cost is the only input in this section of the decision model. The net contribution from advertising and sampling are calculated by computing revenues separately from the advertising and sampling sections and subtracting the costs of the respective programs. The final entry in the decision model is ROS, the return on sales.

The spreadsheet follows the same format as all of the other spreadsheets: there is a menu (reached by typing [Alt]M to help you find the sections if you need a menu) and the spreadsheet can be printed by typing [Alt]P. Most of the definitions are just as their names would imply, and the only entries in which the row definitions are not obvious are the retention, share from advertising, and incremental trial rows, and even these are defined as they are in the case. Placing the cursor over a cell that you don't understand will enable you to read the definition of the cell in the upper left corner of the screen. Tracing the cell addresses referred to in the formula will allow you to reconstruct the definition.

Remember that there is no connection between the columns in this decision model since it is intended to let you compare scenarios rather than do pro forma analysis over a period of years. The Johnson Wax I decision model is deliberately very simple in structure and can be easily modified. The only thing to watch out for in modifying the spreadsheet is that you might foul up the macros. That won't hurt anything, except that the menu might not take you to the right place anymore—all calculations should still be fine, assuming you don't make a mistake in defining the cells.

The spreadsheet is written with the global protection option enabled so that you won't accidentally wipe out an equation. One consequence of this protection feature is that if you try to put an entry into a protected cell you'll hear a beep. This is reminder to tell you that you're trying to write to a protected cell. If you want to change the spreadsheet, you'll need to disable the global protection first with /WGPD[Return].

The Johnson Wax I decision model is intended to allow you to quickly do sensitivity analysis on the variables that affect market share and contribution to profit using the ASSESSOR model's logic. If you want to see what share would result if you could increase advertising-based trial, just plug in a new trial figure. You'll find it easy to do, a great time saver, and hopefully, not very constraining to either your creativity or analysis.

CASE: Johnson Wax II

This case takes place about nine months after the introduction of Enhance and finds Enhance not doing nearly as well as was predicted by a second ASSESSOR test prior to the introduction. The ASSESSOR model and other aspects of the marketing research program, when integrated, provide an unusual opportunity to determine and quantify the magnitude of the reasons for Enhance's disappointing performance. A somewhat more sophisticated decision model that is intended to support business planning at an annual pro forma level accompanies the case.

Katherine Thompson had been the Enhance product manager at Johnson Wax (JW) for about three months in January 1982. Enhance, an instant hair conditioner, wasn't doing as well as had been expected. September/October 1981 market share was only 4.2% and, although it had been increasing slowly, it was far below the projected 8.8%.

In the fall of 1978, an ASSESSOR test of Enhance had resulted in a share prediction of 5.9%, much lower than the 10% in the marketing plan.* Targeting Enhance to women with dry hair problems had restricted both trial-and-repeat purchases. Using the results of this ASSESSOR test, a new product position had been developed to appeal to a broader segment of instant conditioner users. Concurrent with efforts to develop a broader product position, R & D had modified the formula to improve its fragrance and increase its conditioning effect.

Enhance had been subjected to a second ASSESSOR test during January 1980. The result of this test was a projected market share of 8.8%, of which 1.9% would result from a 35 million-unit sampling program. Since the 8.8% share projection was a substantial improvement over the initial projection and close to the original target of 10%, the decision was made to skip the test market that normally would have been the next step.

Enhance went national in September 1980, but by mid-May 1981 results were lagging far behind projections. Tracking studies done three and six months after the introduction showed disappointing awareness, trial, and use figures.

Katherine Thompson faced the problem of getting Enhance on track or making a very convincing statement recommending the product be dropped.

Product Modification

The forecast trial, repeat, and market share for Enhance in the initial ASSESSOR had been substantially lower than those attained by Agree, Johnson Wax's successful hair shampoo and conditioner product line. It was these results that led Johnson Wax to reformulate the product and broaden the target market. Katherine Thompson explained the new Enhance product position as follows:

> Women want to look nice—but they start at different places. Some women have oily hair and need more powerful cleaning from a product— Agree was designed for them. Other women have dry hair and need a different kind of product—Enhance was supposed to be for them. The original positioning for Enhance may have been too therapeutic. With the new positioning for Enhance we've tried to serve up the dam-

---

* See Johnson Wax I.

This case was prepared by Darral G. Clarke.

Copyright (©) 1983 By the President and Fellows of Harvard College Harvard Business School case 9-584-009.

Exhibit 4.31   Results of Second Blind Use Test

	Original Formula vs. New Formula	Flex vs. New Formula	Flex vs. New Formula Mineral Oil
Base	318	303	307
Prefer Enhance	53%	52%	57%
Prefer Other	46%	47%	42%
No Preference	1%	1%	1%

aged hair problem in a more palatable way and stress the benefits more than the problem. Our new product position is stated on the label: "Hair can become overworked—overworked from blow dryers, hot rollers, curling irons, perms and even brushing. It can lose its natural moisturizers. Enhance actually puts moisturizers back to leave your hair *full of body* and *manageable* again. Enhance normal formula is specially formulated to penetrate your hair. It makes hair *soft, smooth, shiny* and *healthy looking*. And because Enhance is 98.75% oil-free, your hair is left with a *clean feeling*."

New advertisements had been produced as the product position was developed and the new product formulations were completed.

Blind Comparisons

Two new formulas were produced in addition to the original Enhance: the first differed only in fragrance, while the second included the new fragrance and a small amount of mineral oil. These three formulations were then tested in a blind use test similar to the one done prior to the first ASSESSOR. The results are shown in Exhibit 4.31.

The new Enhance formula without mineral oil was found to be equal to the original formula and Flex regular in overall preference, as well as on the key attributes of clean feel, fragrance, and penetration. Enhance was weakly, but still signifi-

cantly preferred over Flex overall. It was also significantly preferred over Flex on the key attributes of fragrance, clean feel when dry, softness, and rinsing out.

On the basis of these results, a decision was made to further modify the product and produce Enhance formulations for normal, dry, and oily hair, and to test them using ASSESSOR.

The Second Enhance ASSESSOR Test

The second Enhance ASSESSOR test began in Atlanta and Chicago on January 30, 1980, and continued for about four weeks. During the laboratory phase of the test, 301 women, aged 18–44, who were hair-conditioner users with no prior ASSESSOR participation or connection with the Johnson Wax Company, took part in the study. Enhance was priced at $1.59 for the 8-ounce and $2.39 for the 16-ounce size, roughly the same as Silkience, Gillette's new conditioner. The procedure for the new Enhance ASSESSOR test was the same as had been used in the initial Enhance test and for Agree:

1. An initial screening interview to determine category use and demographics, and to provide a measurement of brand knowledge and perceptions before the ASSESSOR test began

2. Exposure to advertising for established brands, as well as Enhance

3. Measurement of reactions to advertising

Exhibit 4.32   ASSESSOR Results—Copy Point Recall

	Overall (%)	Buyer (%)	Nonbuyer (%)
Conditions	**47.6**	**59.9**	**42.3**
For overworked/over processed hair	15.0	22.8	11.5
Conditions damaged hair	8.0	8.8	7.7
Repairs damaged hair	7.5	12.3	5.4
Helps damaged hair from dryer	5.9	5.3	6.2
Helps damaged hair from rollers	5.3	5.3	5.4
Helps damaged hair from perms	5.3	5.3	6.2
Helps damaged hair from coloring	3.2	1.8	3.8
Restores dried-out hair	2.7	1.8	3.1
Protects hair against damage	2.7	0.0	3.8
Abuse can damage hair/ for abused hair	2.7	5.3	1.5
Conditions (unspecified)	2.1	5.3	.8
Other effects on hair	**17.6**	**19.3**	**16.9**
Makes hair shine	6.4	8.8	5.4
Beautiful hair-glamour-natural beauty	4.3	3.5	2.3
Enhances hair	2.7	3.5	2.3
For dry hair	**16.6**	**17.5**	**16.2**
Designed to restore moisture/moisturizer	13.9	14.0	13.8
Fights dry hair	2.7	3.5	2.3
Texture of hair	**13.9**	**12.3**	**14.6**
Gives hair body-fuller-bounce	10.7	10.5	10.8
Makes hair soft	3.7	1.8	4.6
Manageability	**7.0**	**7.0**	**6.9**
Makes hair more manageable	4.8	3.5	5.4
Miscellaneous			
Don't remember	5.9	1.8	7.7
Nothing	5.3	5.3	5.4
Clean feel—not oily/greasy	2.7	3.5	2.3
New product	2.1	2.5	1.5
Ad was interesting	2.1	1.8	2.3
Base:	(187)	(57)	(130)

4. Shopping in a simulated store environment for instant hair conditioner

5. Home use of the new brand

6. Post-usage telephone interview and repeat purchase opportunity

Using the data gathered in these various steps, Management Decision Systems (MDS) supplied Johnson Wax with information and analysis relevant to advertising and brand awareness, trial, repeat, market-share prediction, and response to sampling programs. Market share was estimated by two procedures:

1. One market-share prediction was made from the observed shopping behavior and the repeat

Exhibit 4.33   ASSESSOR Results—Perceptual Dimensions

Factor	Buyer	Importance to Non-buyer	Attributes Combined to Form Factor
Cleans	35%	36%	Leaves hair free of residue Rinses out easily, completely Leaves hair grease- and oil-free Leaves hair clean-looking
Conditions	29%	34%	Makes hair more manageable Conditions hair Gives hair body and fullness Penetrates hair Restores moisture Moisturizes hair Leaves hair feeling soft and silky Leaves hair shiny, lustrous
Protects	28%	18%	Keeps hair from breaking Helps eliminate flyaway/static Helps control split ends Moisturizes hair Restores moisture
Fragrance	17%	11%	Leaves hair with pleasant fragrance Has a pleasant fragrance while using

Exhibit 4.34   ASSESSOR Results—Perceptual Maps

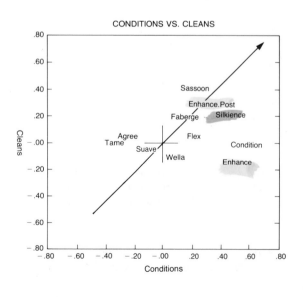

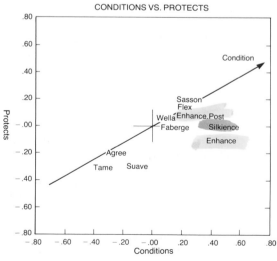

Exhibit 4.35 ASSESSOR Results—Source of Trial

Type Purchased on Trial

Overall Trial	32%
Type	**% Purchased on Trial**
Normal	52
Oily	24
Dry	24
(Base)	(83)

Size Purchased on Trial

Size	**% Purchased on Trial**
8-ounce	48
16-ounce	52

Source of Trial

Brand Last Purchased	**Buyer (%)**	**Nonbuyer (%)**
Agree	18.1	11.5
Silkience	18.1	9.6
Wella Balsam	6.0	13.8
Flex		
Instant	8.4	9.6
Rinse	1.2	1.4
Sassoon	4.8	8.3
Condition II	4.8	6.4
Fabergé Organic	6.0	4.1
Tame	4.8	4.1
Condition	2.4	4.6
Instant Condition	3.6	2.8
Suave	6.0	1.4
L'Oreal	2.4	2.8
(Base)	(83)	(218)

purchase level measured during the callback interviews. This share estimate was called the *trial/repeat* share.

2. A second market-share prediction was made by measuring the attributes consumers indicated were important and their perceptions of the degree to which various brands exhibited those attributes. This share estimate was called the *preference share*.

The results of the ASSESSOR test are found in Exhibits 4.32–4.40. A report to Katherine Thompson from the marketing research department included these quantitative results:

Advertising Recall (see Exhibit 4.32)

Advertising recall indicated a less therapeutic brand image, increased stress on conditioning and a reduction of the "for dry hair" image.

Market Structure (See Exhibits 4.33 and 4.34)

Factor analysis indicated four basic dimensions of consumer perception—cleans, conditions, protects, and fragrance. The cleans and conditions dimensions are relatively more important to the consumer. After exposure to Enhance advertising but before use, respondents gave Enhance a strong conditions perception, average protects perception, weak cleans perception, and virtually no fragrance perception.

Trial (See Exhibit 4.35)

Enhance's overall trial rate was somewhat above average—32% compared with the initial ASSESSOR level of 23%. Trial was split evenly between the 8-ounce and the 16-ounce sizes, but was not skewed toward the dry formula, despite the positioning.

Repeat (see Exhibits 4.36, 4.37, and 4.38)

The repeat rate for Enhance among triers was an above-average 72% compared with the initial ASSESSOR's 60% repeat rate. The repeat rate among nontriers was only 43%, identical to the initial ASSESSOR result.

"Comparison to regular brand" and "Intent to repurchase" were not improved over the levels measured in the first ASSESSOR.

Share Prediction (See Exhibit 4.39)

Based on the assumptions of 70% brand awareness and 85% ACV* distribution at end of the first year, Enhance is expected to obtain a 6.9%

---

*ACV = All-Category Volume, a distribution coverage measure.

Exhibit 4.36   ASSESSOR Results—Repeat Rates

	Among Buyers	Among Nonbuyers
Enhance (Final ASSESSOR)	72%	43%
Enhance (Initial ASSESSOR)	60%	43%
Agree	78%	63%

	Brand Last Purchased (Repeaters vs. Nonrepeaters)	
	Repeaters	Nonrepeaters
Agree	17.4	14.7
Silkience	9.8	25.3
Wella Balsam	7.6	8.0
Flex		
Instant	8.7	8.0
Rinse	—	1.3
Sassoon	8.7	12.0
Condition II	6.5	5.3
Fabergé Organic	6.5	5.3
Tame	5.4	4.0
Condition	3.3	1.3
Instant Condition	3.3	—
Suave	6.5	—
L'Oreal	2.2	2.7
(Base)	(92)	(75)

unit share from advertising. The identical result was obtained from both the preference and the trial/repeat models.

The Decision to Go National

Combining the unit market-share forecast of 6.9% from advertising with the 1.6% market share response from a 30 million–unit sample drop resulted in a unit market share forecast of 8.5% and factory sales of $25.0 million (see Exhibit 4.40). This forecast was close enough to the original market share target of 10% that, when it became available in June 1980, the decision was made to skip the test market and introduce Enhance nationally. Major factors in this decision were:

1. The laboratory people thought they had done as much to the basic formulation as they could, and the Enhance ASSESSOR test showed that the reformulation of the product and the revised product position had increased the share prediction by more than 50%. Management thought that, all things considered, Enhance was about as good as it could be.

2. Management doubted that much more would be learned in a test market.

3. Management had confidence that the marketing organization could implement the marketing plan and make the product successful.

4. Gillette's introduction of Silkience and Agree's slipping share made it appear that entry would only become more difficult as time passed.

5. Management was concerned that if a test market were run, the product positioning could be stolen. Soon after Agree had been introduced, four other brands for oily hair had been introduced.

Exhibit 4.37   ASSESSOR Results—Comparison to Regular Brand

Among Buyers

	Final ASSESSOR (%)	Initial ASSESSOR (%)	Agree (%)
Much better	25	30	44
A little better	31	24	25
About the same	24	26	13
A little poorer	15	14	12
Somewhat poorer	6	6	5
(Base)	(68)	(50)	(76)

Among Nonbuyers

	Final ASSESSOR (%)	Initial ASSESSOR (%)	Agree (%)
Much better	15	14	35
A little better	19	21	22
About the same	34	37	21
A little poorer	19	16	13
Somewhat poorer	12	12	8
(Base)	(99)	(165)	(203)

After-Use Preferences

After-Use Preference for Test Brand	Final ASSESSOR (%)	Initial ASSESSOR(%)	Agree (%)
First	31	28	54
Second	35	33	26
Third	16	19	12
Fourth	9	11	2

6. The cost of a nine-month test in two markets was estimated to be $1 million.

Store audits	$350,000
Product costs	150,000
Media costs	150,000
Commercial production	100,000
Attitude studies	50,000
Consumer research	120,000
Samples, sample study	80,000
Total	$1,000,000

Expenses for the second ASSESSOR study had been about $250,000, including $200,000 for producing commercials, supplying product and packaging, and $50,000 paid to MDS. The regional introduction of a new product like Enhance would generally cost between $5 million and $8 million, and a national introduction was often a $35 million commitment. Product sales would reduce the net outlay for the regional and national introduction and, to some extent, for the test market, but introducing a new consumer product was a major undertaking for any company.

Exhibit 4.38   ASSESSOR Results—Intent to Repurchase

Among Buyers

	Final ASSESSOR (%)	Initial ASSESSOR (%)	Agree (%)
Definitely	38	46	53
Probably	44	32	28
Might	7	10	9
Probably not	7	8	5
Definitely not	3	4	5
(Base)	(68)	(50)	(76)

Among Nonbuyers

	Final ASSESSOR (%)	Initial ASSESSOR (%)	Agree (%)
Definitely	15	19	40
Probably	43	37	32
Might	23	20	16
Probably not	8	13	2
Definitely not	10	10	9
(Base)	(99)	(165)	(203)

Exhibit 4.39   Base Share Projection—Comparison with Past Studies

	Final ASSESSOR (%)	Initial ASSESSOR (%)	Agree (%)
Laboratory trial	32	23	33
Awareness*	70	85	70
Distribution*	85	85	85
Net cum. trial	18.9	13.7	19.6
Retention (Share of trier's choices)	36.4	28.6	42.1
Base share	6.9	3.9	8.3

*Managerial estimates.

Exhibit 4.40 1981 Dollar Volume Prediction

	Number of Samples			
	No Sampling	10 MM	20 MM	30 MM
Base share from advertising	6.9%	6.9%	6.9%	6.9%
Incremental share from sampling	—	0.5%	1.1%	1.6%
Market share	6.9%	7.4%	8.0%	8.5%
Price/usage adjustment	0.98	0.98	0.98	0.98
Category volume	$313.0MM	$313.0MM	$313.0MM	$313.0MM
Factory sales	$ 20.2MM	$ 21.7MM	$ 23.4MM	$ 25.0MM

Enhance Introduction

Enhance Instant Conditioner was shipped for national distribution during the summer of 1980. Advertising began the first week of September—$2.72 million in 1980, and $4.5 million planned for 1981—and a 30 million-unit sample drop ($\frac{3}{4}$-ounce pouch in a Donnelley co-op mailing) took place the week of October 13, 1980. The market into which Enhance was launched was dynamic. Twenty-one new brands—including Gillette's Silkience, a substantial competitor backed by $6 million in media advertising in 1979—had been introduced since the initial ASSESSOR test. The shares of the established brands had declined, and the brands included in the second ASSESSOR test accounted for only 75% of category sales in 1980. Dollar sales and market shares of the leading brands in 1980 were estimated by one national service as shown in Exhibit 4.41.

The market was forecast to reach $397 million in 1980 dollars by 1985, a real growth rate of 6% per year. Instant hair conditioners were estimated by JW to be used in a majority of U.S. households, and penetration was growing slowly. Advertising expenditures in 1979 had been $33.8 million, and would surpass $38 million in 1980 (based on expenditure levels in the first nine months). See Exhibit 4.42.

Retail share data on the instant conditioner market were incomplete, but indicated considerable turmoil. See Exhibit 4.43.

Exhibit 4.41 Sales of Leading Brands in 1980

Brand	Company	$ (Million)
Instant Conditioners		
Flex	Revlon	$ 42
Silkience	Gillette	29
Agree	Johnson Wax	27
Sassoon	Vidal Sassoon	19
Clairol Condition	Bristol-Myers	13
Tame	Gillette	12
All other		153
Total		295

Sampling Effectiveness Study

A separate study to measure the effect of the 30 million-unit sample drop was performed by National Family Opinion (NFO), one of the largest survey houses in the United States.

Telephone interviews with 2,000 women who had used a creme rinse/ conditioner during the past four weeks were conducted October 3–10, 1980, to determine the brand last purchased and which other brands had been purchased during the previous six months. Half of these women received samples during the last three weeks of October. The

Exhibit 4.42   Advertising Expenditures in 1979 and 1980

Brand	1980 (9 mos.) $ (thousands)	1979 (12 mos.) $ (thousands)
Silkience	$ 4,830	$ 6,063
Revlon Flex	3,372	3,008
Vidal Sassoon	3,127	2,876
Clairol Condition Beauty Pack	2,917	1,850
Alberto VO5 Hot Oil	2,880	3,112
Agree	2,798	4,036
Wella Balsam	2,503	3,079
Condition II	955	512
Clairol Small Miracle	856	—
Others	4,290	9,249
	$28,528	$33,785

Exhibit 4.43   Hair Conditioner Market Shares

	1972	1973	1974	1975	1976	1977	1978	1979	1980
Long & Silky	3.7	3.6	3.7	4.0	3.4	2.1	1.4	NA	NA
Clairol Condition	13.0	14.7	15.5	15.2	15.2	14.3	9.9	10.2	9.5
Herbal Essence	NA	3.2	4.5	4.6	2.9	1.9	NA	NA	NA
Wella Balsam	NA	NA	4.8	5.1	5.5	4.9	4.7	4.0	3.5
Flex	NA	NA	NA	16.1	10.5	11.0	13.4	12.0	10.2
Tame	NA	NA	NA	12.3	10.2	6.7	5.4	5.1	3.9
Breck	NA	NA	NA	7.1	10.6	7.0	5.4	NA	NA
Agree	NA	NA	NA	NA	NA	NA	15.2	11.9	8.4
Enhance	NA	NA	NA	NA	NA	NA	NA	NA	2.7*

NA = Not available, either because the product was not marketed or because there were no clients for the data.
* 6 months only.

Exhibit 4.44   Repeat Interviews to Determine Brand Use

	Test		Control		Net
	Number	%	Number	%	
Interviewed	510	100.0	506	100.0	—
Received Sample	158	31.0	40	7.9	23.1
Used Sample	63	12.4	16	3.2	9.2
Purchased Enhance	31	6.1	10	2.0	4.1

Exhibit 4.45 Enhance Sampling Effectiveness*

Assumptions	ASSESSOR	Sample Effective-ness Study	Revised Best Estimate
Sample Size	2 oz.	$\frac{3}{4}$ oz.	$\frac{3}{4}$ oz.
Method of Delivery	Assumed direct mail	Co-op mailing	
Number of Samples	35MM	30MM	30MM
Delivered	.90		
Hitting target group	.80		
Received	.72	.23	
Used/received	.60	.40	
Percent of Samples Used	.43	.092	.22
Number of Samples Used	15.1MM	2.8MM	6.6MM
Percent of Category Users Using Samples	.252	.046	.11
Incremental Trial	.204	.039	.092
First repeat	.430	.480	.450
Retention	.219	.235	.225
Incremental Share	.019	.004	.009
Base Share	.069	.069	.069
Share Prediction	.088	.073	.078

* Assuming 60MM households and 16% switchback.

other half was a control group that did not receive a sample. About eight weeks later, repeat interviews were conducted to determine brand use. The results of this test are shown in Exhibit 4.44.

The net difference in Enhance use due to sampling was significant at the 90% confidence level, but the number of households surveyed that remembered receiving the sample, and those receiving a sample that had used it, were lower that the managerial assumptions in the ASSESSOR test. Incremental share from sampling in the Enhance ASSESSOR had been predicted to be 1.9%, but the findings of the sampling effectiveness study indicated only a 0.4% incremental share. A revised best estimate based on the results of both studies indicated an incremental share from sampling of 0.9% (see Exhibit 4.45).

Enhance Tracking Studies

The progress of Enhance was monitored through a continuing series of tracking studies to measure advertising and brand awareness and trial-and-repeat rates. Each study consisted of telephone interviews within a national probability sample of 1,000 women, at least 14 years old, who had used a creme rinse/conditioner during the past four weeks. The sample included a quota of 145 Enhance buyers. Interviews were conducted throughout the day to obtain interviews with both working and non-working women. Exhibits 4.46 and 4.47 summarize the results of this test. At the end of six months, Enhance had not yet achieved the same level of trial (17%) as Agree had achieved at four months (18%). Conversion (ever used/brand awareness) had not

Exhibit 4.46   Tracking Studies Results

Enhance - Key Measures

	Agree 4 Months 6/77		Enhance 3 Months 12/80		Enhance 6 Months 3/81		Silkience 9 Months 11/79
Base	(800)		(1006)		(752)		(1003)
Brand Awareness	.60	——s*——	.51	——s——	.63		.64
Unaided	NA		.09		.07	——s——	.10
Aided	NA		.42	——s——	.55		.54
Conversion (Ever Used/							
Brand Awareness)	.30		.28		.27	——s——	.30
Ever Used	.18	——s——	.14		.17		.19
Used Last	NA		.04		.04		.05
Past 4 Week Use	NA		.09		.07		.09
Past 4 Week Use/							
Ever Used	NA		.63	——s——	.39		.47
Advertising Awareness	NA		.23	——s——	.30	——s——	.44†

* s = significantly different than Enhance (six months national) at 95% confidence level.

† Silkience advertising awareness had been measured at 72% in 12/80 and 73% in 3/81.

Exhibit 4.47   Tracking Studies Results, March 1981

	Brand Awareness	Ever Used	Past Four-Week Use
Enhance	.63	.17	.07
Agree	.92	.52	.11
Breck	.96	.54	.04
Condition	.92	.58	.18
Flex	.87	.53	.15
Jhirmack	.56	.15	.05
Sassoon	.83	.32	.11
Silkience	.91	.50	.19
Tame	.91	.58	.08
Wella Balsam	.97	.56	.13
Base	(752)		

increased in the three months between the December and March studies. "Recent use" divided by "ever used" dropped from 63% to 39%.

The Current Situation

The arrival of the most recent market share reports showed that Enhance's share for September/October 1981 was 4.2%. The July/August 1981 share, the end of its first year, was only 3.7%, compared with the ASSESSOR forecast of 8.8%. The March/April share had been only 3.2%. The same retail audits estimated that at least one size of Enhance was available in 62.5% and 63.1% of retail outlets. The news prompted Katherine Thompson to review her marketing program yet again:

The problem facing me now is to determine and correct what is keeping Enhance's share low. There is a big temptation in this market, with so many brands appealing to so many different segments, to throw your hands in the air and say, "It's just too complicated to understand." But I don't think it really is. Most women want their hair to look nice, but have one or two problems they need to overcome.

When I look at our sales force reports and other data, I see some problems. Our sales force is stretched very thin. There are 400 good people in that sales force, but they were primarily trained in the supermarket class of trade. Since a large percentage of hair-care products are sold by drug and mass merchandisers, when Agree came along they had to start visiting a whole new class of trade in addition to the old

one they knew. Unless we were terribly overstaffed before, this increase in the number of calls has to hurt somewhere. And it would be a miracle if they were as good in the new class of trade as they were in the old one, even with the good training we gave them.

With both Enhance and Agree, maybe we've stretched them a bit too far. I'm not sure we have all sizes in each store we cover, or that our shelf space is ideal, or whether we get our share of end-aisle displays. Some reports imply that some retailers may be "making margin" on us by pricing Enhance higher than our competition. Our advertising hasn't been nearly as effective as we had planned and, as a result, awareness and trial are low. I'm sure that Enhance is sound! It's just our execution of the marketing plan that is keeping us from reaching our targets!

Preparation Questions

In preparing the Johnson Wax II case assume that A. C. Nielsen retail audit data indicates the following levels of distribution:

Nov–Dec	66%
Jan–Feb	70%
Mar–Apr	73%

1. How well did the changes made in the initial marketing program work out? For example: target market, product modifications, product position, and advertising copy et al.?

2. Why is the ASSESSOR market share forecast so much higher than the market share measured by Nielsen? What does this say about the validity of the ASSESSOR model?

3. Evaluate the effectiveness of the components of the marketing plan. You will find the summary of the Johnson Wax research results in JWAX_R, and the JWAX_I decision model helpful for this analysis. This is a difficult but rewarding preparation.

4. What should be done with Enhance now? Justify your recommendations with a five-year plan. Use model JWAX_II.

5. What do the two decision models add to the usefulness of the ASSESSOR results?

6. What further research and model development steps would you undertake, if any?

Johnson Wax II Pro Forma Decision Model

The Johnson Wax II pro forma decision model (Exhibit 4.48) is intended to perform the calculations necessary in developing a marketing strategy for Enhance over a five-year time horizon. The structure of this decision model is very similar to that of the Johnson Wax I decision model. Since most of the variable definitions in this model are the same as in the Johnson Wax I decision model only the major differences will be discussed; these include the following:

The Johnson Wax II model is a *pro forma* model; the columns represent successive time periods and so the values in one column are related to the values in the previous column.

An explicit response function linking advertising expenditures to awareness has been included.

An adjustment has been made to compensate for changes in the competitive situation since the ASSESSOR test.

This decision model follows the same conventions as all of the other spreadsheet models: there is a menu that can be reached by typing [Alt]M to help

Exhibit 4.48   Johnson Wax II Pro Forma Decision Model

```
                        JOHNSON WAX (II)
                     Proforma Planning Model
------------------------------------------------------------------------
        Switchback            16%        Max. awareness         81.0%
        Target market (MM)    60         Min. awareness         23.0%
                                         Aware. @ 1300 GRPs     61.0%
                                         Cost/GRP               $3,250
```

	1980	1981	1982	1983	1984
Distribution	73.0%	78.0%	80.0%	80.0%	75.0%
Adv exp (MM,$2.72 in 1980)	$2.720	$4.000	$4.000	$4.000	$4.000
GRP's	837	1,231	1,231	1,231	1,231
Cum GRP's	837	2,068	3,298	4,529	5,760
Awareness	51.78%	70.33%	77.11%	79.58%	80.48%
Trial if aware	32.00%	32.00%	30.00%	27.00%	25.00%
Inc trial from adv.	12.1%	4.6%	1.6%	0.5%	0.2%
Cumulative trial	12.1%	16.7%	18.4%	18.9%	19.1%
Retention	36.4%	35.0%	25.0%	20.0%	15.0%
Share from advertising	1.7%	3.2%	2.8%	2.4%	1.7%

Sampling based values	1980	1981	1982	1983	1984
Number of samples(MM)	30	35	0	0	0
Cost of samples	$0.10	$0.25	$0.00	$0.00	$0.00
% Samples used	22.0%	40.0%	0.0%	0.0%	0.0%
Samples used (MM)	6.6	14.0	0.0	0.0	0.0
Incremental sample trial	9.7%	17.2%	0.0%	0.0%	0.0%
First repeat rate	40.0%	43.0%	0.0%	0.0%	0.0%
Cumulative trial	3.9%	11.3%	11.3%	11.3%	11.3%
Retention	22.0%	22.0%	20.0%	15.0%	10.0%
Share from sampling	0.9%	2.5%	2.3%	1.7%	1.1%

Forecasts					
Cumulative trial	16.0%	28.0%	29.6%	30.1%	30.3%
Tested mkt share	2.5%	5.7%	5.1%	4.1%	2.9%

(continued)

Exhibit 4.48 (continued)   Johnson Wax II Pro Forma Decision Model

ASSESSOR Prediction Summary
(millions)

	1980	1981	1982	1983	1984	Total
Tested mkt share	2.5%	5.7%	5.1%	4.1%	2.9%	
Tested mkt/real mk	0.75	0.70	0.65	0.60	0.60	
Real mkt share	1.9%	4.0%	3.3%	2.5%	1.7%	2.6%
Unit-dollar adjust	0.94	0.94	0.94	0.94	0.94	
Real dollar share	1.8%	3.7%	3.1%	2.3%	1.6%	
Manufacturer sales	$81	$341	$361	$383	$406	$1,572
JWC factory sales	$1.4	$12.7	$11.2	$8.8	$6.5	$40.6

Enhance Unit Contribution Analysis

	1980	1981	1982	1983	1984
8 oz. sales share	48.0%	40.0%	35.0%	35.0%	30.0%
Exp. retail price - 8oz	$1.59	$1.59	$1.59	$1.59	$1.59
Factory price - 8oz	$1.22	$1.22	$1.22	$1.22	$1.22
Cost of goods	$0.46	$0.46	$0.46	$0.46	$0.46
Unit contribution	$0.76	$0.76	$0.76	$0.76	$0.76
Unit margin (%)	62.5%	62.5%	62.5%	62.5%	62.5%
Exp. retail price - 16oz	$2.39	$2.39	$2.39	$2.39	$2.39
Factory price - 16oz	$1.61	$1.61	$1.61	$1.61	$1.61
Cost of goods	$0.60	$0.60	$0.60	$0.60	$0.60
Unit contribution	$1.01	$1.01	$1.01	$1.01	$1.01
Unit margin (%)	62.6%	62.6%	62.6%	62.6%	62.6%
Wtd average unit margin (%)	62.5%	62.5%	62.5%	62.5%	62.5%

Financial Summary ($MM)

	1980	1981	1982	1983	1984	Total
Gross contribution	$0.89	$7.95	$6.99	$5.51	$4.07	$25.4
Less						
Advertising exp.	$2.72	$2.72	$4.00	$4.00	$4.00	$17.4
Sampling cost	$3.00	$8.75	$0.00	$0.00	$0.00	$11.8
Net contribution	($4.83)	($3.52)	$2.99	$1.51	$0.07	($3.79)
From advertising	($2.13)	$1.77	($0.11)	($0.76)	($1.54)	($2.78)
From sampling	($2.70)	($5.29)	$3.10	$2.27	$1.61	($1.02)
ROS	-339.95%	-27.73%	26.74%	17.11%	1.02%	-9.34%

you find your way around the spreadsheet and the spreadsheet, can be printed by typing [Alt]P.

The linkages between the time periods make this a pro forma decision model that is dynamic across time, rather than a model for the comparison of static alternatives as in the Johnson Wax I decision model. It should be noticed that ASSESSOR is a static model—providing only forecasts at some particular time period that occurs when certain awareness and distribution levels are attained rather than a number of months—it does not provide insight into the dynamics of how market share behaves until those levels are reached. In order to have a pro forma model of how the market will develop, we need to make some assumptions about how distribution and awareness levels will grow over time as a result of the marketing program. Having made these assumptions we can then use the ASSESSOR conceptual model—that is, that share is a function of awareness, distribution, trial, and retention—to compute market share in a particular time period. The conceptualization used to do this in this model is very simple, but provides a reasonable approximation to the more complex models that exist for this same purpose. In particular, Management Decision Systems, the developers of ASSESSOR, have a model called SPRINTER [Urban 1970] that is a much more sophisticated method of converting ASSESSOR results into a dynamic, multi-year forecast.

The dynamics of this model are found in the advertising and sampling sections of the spreadsheet only. The other sections are the same as in the Johnson Wax I decision model. The computation of awareness will be discussed in the following section, but assuming that we have awareness for a particular time period t, we compute the incremental trial resulting from advertising in time period t as the product of distribution, trial, and change in awareness:

$$\text{Distribution}_t * \text{Trial(if Aware)}_t$$
$$* (\text{Awareness}_t - \text{Awareness}_{t-1}) \qquad (4.7)$$

The treatment of sampling is similar. If more than one sampling program is used, care must be taken that the incremental trial from it is correctly computed. This involves excluding the advertising-based trial as before but also the trial resulting from previous sampling programs.

Awareness Model

One of the frustrations you probably felt in using the Johnson Wax I decision model was in determining advertising budgets that were consistent with the awareness levels that you assumed in your various scenarios. Since the ASSESSOR model was concerned primarily with determining a market share forecast and did not include any consideration of contribution to profit, no emphasis was placed on the cost of the marketing programs. When the ASSESSOR model is imbedded in a financial spreadsheet in order to produce a decision model, however, the cost of marketing programs is relevant and a relationship between the cost of marketing programs and their effect is necessary.

An extensive study of the relationship between cumulative gross rating points (GRPs) and brand awareness has been undertaken by the Leo Burnett Company, a major advertising agency, that resulted in the graph that appears in Exhibit 4.49. Although it is apparent that a nonlinear relationship between cumulative GRPs and awareness exists, it is also clear that a lot of variability exists. The heavy solid line through the middle of this swarm is a regression line that is the best approximation to the assembled experience represented in the data, but the equation of this line is not available to us. Using ELS (eyeball least squares), I have estimated the equation of this line to be:

$$A = A_0 + (A_m - A_0)$$
$$* (1 - \exp(-0.00089 * CGRP)) \qquad (4.8)$$

where:

A	is awareness
A_0	is the minimum awareness level
A_m	is the maximum awareness level
exp	represents e, the Naperian logarithm
CGRP	is the cumulative gross rating points

This response function is modified to our specific use in the decision model by choosing three points on the line and estimating the cost per GRP. These values are entered into the decision model at the upper right of the advertising section. The values in the decision model at present come pretty close to estimating the solid line in Exhibit

Exhibit 4.49   Advertising Weight vs. Awareness Created for Selected Products

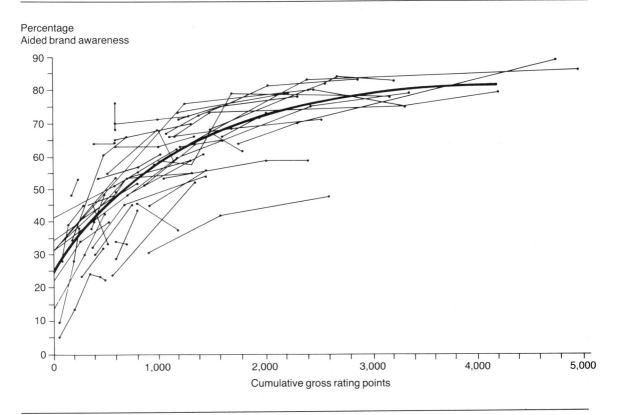

Percentage
Aided brand awareness

Cumulative gross rating points

Source: David Olson, unpublished working paper, Leo Burnett Company.

4.49. If you felt that you wanted to choose a response function that had a higher response than this average function, you could:

1. Increase the maximum awareness level, which would increase the range of response available from advertising.
2. Increase the "Awareness @ 1300 GRPs," which would increase the slope of the response function, so that the maximum level would be approached more rapidly.
3. Decrease the "Cost/GRP," which would leave the shape of the response function unchanged but provide more GRPs for each dollar spent, thus moving you further out the curve for the same amount of money. If you wanted to make judgments about the relative effectiveness of Enhance advertising rather than the shape of the response, this would be the place to do it.

Through the adjustment of the response function with these input values you have a great deal of flexibility in determining the awareness response to your advertising expenditures. The steps that the decision model follows are to determine the number of GRPs that your advertising expenditure will purchase, add those new GRPs to the cumulative sum of the prior GRPs, and then use the response function in formula (4.8) to compute awareness. The conversion of awareness into market share was discussed in the previous section.

Competitive Situation Adjustment

The ASSESSOR forecasts the market share that Enhance would attain against a specific set of competitors. Since the time of the test the hair conditioner market has changed. In particular the brands against which Enhance was tested account for only about 75% of hair conditioner sales. Depending how you feel about what ASSESSOR measured and how conservative you are about the share that Enhance will attain against the new competition, you might want to adjust the ASSESSOR forecast for current market conditions. The values in this line at present are very conservative. They are based on the assumption that Enhance will gain no share against the new brands and that the share of the market that the old brands currently hold will decline over time. These values are just guesses to illustrate a hypothesis. You should feel free to change them to suit your own concept of the market. If you don't think that it matters at all, then just put 1.0 into this row and it will have no effect at all.

Modification of the Decision Model

Even though this model is a bit more complicated than the Johnson Wax I decision model it is still quite simply structured and it can be easily modified if you wish to do so. The global protection feature is enabled to keep you from inadvertently writing over an expression. If you want to change the model, first disable the protection feature with /WGPD [Return].

Concept Testing and Market Planning

The discussion of the new product development process in the introduction to this chapter indicated that the cost and time required for new product development for consumer durable and industrial products are very different from that needed for frequently purchased, low-priced consumer goods. The cost of new product introduction and test marketing dominate the allocation of resources for developing new consumer products, but earlier stages of new product development—applied research, determining product specifications, and prototype development—require very sizeable resources for durable and industrial products. For example, prototype/pilot plant development costs account for 54 percent of new product development cost in the chemical industry (See Exhibit 4.50). Since the cost of developing a prototype model of a new industrial or durable product is so great, many industrial product companies have looked for ways in which to explore customer acceptance of new products and estimate economic feasibility *prior* to the development of the physical product itself.

The term *concept testing* has been applied to this type of research. In concept testing a verbal description, model, or mock-up of a product is presented to potential customers to determine their acceptance of the concept. Concept testing plays the same role for industrial and durable goods as pre–test market testing does for consumer products: it attempts to eliminate questionable new products at a low cost.

Exhibit 4.50   Cost of Industrial Product Innovation in the Chemical Industry

Phase	Average Investment ($000s)	% of Total Development and Intro. Investment	Estimated Range (+ or − one standard deviation)
Applied research	$ 380	17	0–770
Specifications	290	13	0–680
Prototype/pilot plant	290	13	110–470
Total	$ 960	43%	
Tooling and manufacturing facilities	$930	41	270–1580
Manufacturing start-up	180	8	0–360
Marketing start-up	160	7	0–430
Total	$1,270	57%	
Total Development and Introduction Investment	$2,230	100%	

Source: Urban and Hauser (1980), p. 47; adapted from Mansfield and Rapaport (1975), p. 1382.

Trade-Off Analysis

Dr. Richard Johnson developed the methodology called *trade-off analysis* (Johnson 1974) in response to a request by a frustrated marketing research director in a high technology durable goods business. The research director explained to Johnson that in his company it was standard practice to run a concept test whenever a new or modified product was seriously contemplated:

> The product manager tells me that, "We're going to put two handles on it, it's going to produce 20 units a minute, it will weigh 30 pounds and be green." I arrange a test of that concept and in a few weeks when I present him with the results, he invariably says, "Sorry I didn't have time to tell you about this, but instead of two handles it's only going to have one, and instead of 20 units a minute it will produce 22 units a minute, and it's going to be red. Can you test that one in the next three weeks?"
>
> I never have the time to do the concept tests that are required in order to really affect the product design cycle. What I need is a way to test *all* future product modifications *at once*. I want to be able to say to the product manager, "Oh, you say it's going to have two handles, produce 22 units a minute, weigh 30 pounds and be red? Well, the answer to that is 17 share points." [Johnson 1980, p.2]

Johnson's response to the research director's request was to devise a conceptual model in which a product was considered to be a collection of separate attri-

Exhibit 4.51 Attribute Levels for Clark Trade-off
Analysis

Transmission	Performance	Price
Standard	Same as present	$17,000
Automatic	Forklift truck	17,500
	25% better than present truck	18,000

butes, each available at specific levels. The potential buyer was conceptualized as having a hypothetical value for each attribute level (called a *utility*), and the value a buyer might place on the product as a whole could be computed from his values for the individual attribute levels. A number of assumptions are required for the procedure to work:

It must make sense to view the product as a bundle of attribute levels—the product can be decomposed into separate features for which utilities can be computed.

The utility of the product is some simple function of the utilities of the product's attribute levels.

A respondent will buy the product for which he has the highest utility. It isn't necessary to assume that this happens at every purchase occasion; it may be just a purchase probability; but there is an assumption that utilities are translated into real preference behavior.

The attributes in the questionnaire are both relevant and adequately describe the product.

There isn't any redundancy; that is, that nothing gets counted twice.

We must assume that, in real product buying decisions, people act as they behave in the interview.

None of these assumptions are probably completely valid in any particular application of the trade-off model, but according to Johnson they are all assumptions that in the last decade have characterized most of the marketing research that attempted to predict individual choice behavior.

The main problem in obtaining information about the value potential buyers place on attributes is that, given a choice, a rational buyer would choose the most attractive level of each attribute and the lowest available price. Thus a series of simple questions about desired attribute levels would not yield useful results. Trade-off analysis gets around this problem by requiring a respondent to give up (or trade off) a level of one attribute in order to gain a level for another attribute.

Exhibit 4.52   Trade-off Choice Situations—Alternative Forklift Trucks

Choice #	Left	Right	Respondent's Choice
I	Automatic transmission $18,000	Standard transmission $17,000	right
II	Automatic transmission 25% better performance	Standard transmission Same performance	left
III	Automatic transmission 25% better performance	Standard transmission 25% better performance	left
IV	Standard transmission 25% better performance $17,000	Automatic transmission Same performance $17,500	right

The application of trade-off analysis in the Clark Equipment case series that follows is concerned with the design of forklift trucks for Brazil. In order to illustrate how trade-off analysis works, let's consider a simplified problem in designing forklift trucks that considers only three attributes: price, performance, and type of transmission. The attribute levels available in this example are shown in Exhibit 4.51.

A respondent in the survey would be offered a series of choices between descriptions of forklift trucks similar to the choice situations in Exhibit 4.52.

It isn't readily apparent how much information is contained in this series of choices between alternative forklift trucks or how that information could be translated into the respondent's utility for a forklift truck. The computation of the utilities is performed by a computer-based estimation technique*, the details of which are beyond the scope of this book, but it isn't too difficult to understand the process intuitively.

There are so many possible combinations of product attributes that a respondent would tire before judging all of them. The trick is to mathematically deter-

---

* The actual technique used by the John Morton Company for Clark Equipment is more complex than that illustrated here. In particular: (1) JMC's model is multiplicative in the utilities, while this example is a linear model; (2) only the forklift truck chosen is used here (1 or 0), while the JMC model incorporates a "strength of choice" dimension. The simplifications, used here were made to illustrate the concept rather than to describe the actual algorithm used in the case.

Exhibit 4.53 Design Grid with One Respondent's Choices

Choice Number	Alternative	Transmission Stan.	Auto.	Performance Same	+25%	Price $17,000	$17,500	$18,000	Choice
I	left	0	1	0	0	0	0	1	0
	right	1	0	0	0	1	0	0	1
II	left	0	1	0	1	0	0	0	1
	right	1	0	1	0	0	0	0	0
III	left	0	1	0	1	0	0	1	1
	right	1	0	0	1	0	1	0	0
IV	left	1	0	0	1	1	0	0	0
	right	0	1	1	0	0	1	0	1
Level weights		w_1	w_2	w_3	w_4	w_5	w_6	w_7	

mine a balanced way to give a limited set to the respondents. This is a job for an expert, whose first job is to create a *design grid*, which organizes the questioning process so we can see what is being asked and how much information is being gathered about the various factor levels.

Exhibit 4.52 shows the design grid for Exhibit 5.52. The design grid has a row for each forklift truck model used in a choice situation and columns for each factor level. If a factor level is present in a forklift truck model, a 1 is put in the appropriate cell of the grid. Otherwise a 0 is put in the cell. The last column shows which forklift truck was chosen (1 if chosen and a 0 if not). The bottom row contains a weight (w_i) for each factor level. When properly determined, these weights become estimates of the respondent's utilities for the various factor levels.

Although our four choice situations are not enough to get good estimates of the utilities, they are enough to illustrate how a respondent's choices are translated into estimates of his utility for various attribute levels.

The collection of alternative choices between forklift trucks in the design grid demonstrates the methodology used to assure that each factor level is represented in enough tests, and compared with enough other factors.

Consider choice situation I. The right alternative was chosen, so the respondent's utility for a standard transmission at $17,000 is more than his utility for an automatic transmission at $18,000. This means (reading from the first two rows of the design grid):

$w_1 + w_5$ is greater than (>) $w_2 + w_7$

It is easy to find four numbers to use for weights to satisfy this condition. For example:

$$w_1 = 2$$
$$w_2 = 1$$
$$w_5 = 3$$
$$w_7 = 1$$

Where did these numbers come from? Out of the air, but they satisfy the relationship, since:

$$2 + 3 > 1 + 1$$

Many other sets of numbers also satisfy this relationship, but as choice situations are added, the acceptable values for the weights become sharply limited.

Choice situation II gives us the inequality

$$w_2 + w_4 > w_1 + w_3$$

Since we already have values for w_1 and w_2 it follows that:

$$w_4 > w_3 + 1$$

Our previous choice of values for w_1 and w_2 restricts the values that w_3 and w_4 can have to form a consistent set. Further choice situations would make it more difficult to find a consistent set of weights. Since weights w_5, w_6, and w_7 all deal with price, this should mean that, all other things being equal, $w_5 > w_6 > w_7$. The set of conditions that must be satisfied with just these four choice situations is therefore:

I. $w_1 + w_5 > w_2 + w_7$
II. $w_2 + w_4 > w_1 + w_3$
III. $w_2 + w_4 + w_7 > w_1 + w_4 + w_6$
IV. $w_1 + w_4 + w_5 > w_2 + w_3 + w_6$
$$w_5 > w_6 > w_7 > 0 \quad \text{(price weights should decline)}$$

A set of weights that works is:

$w_1 = .5$	$w_5 = 2.5$
$w_2 = 1.6$	$w_6 = 2.0$
$w_3 = .5$	$w_7 = 1.0$
$w_4 = 1.0$	

There isn't very much room to change any one of these weights and still satisfy all the conditions. For example, w_5, the weight that goes with the lowest price, can't be as large as 3, nor can it be as small as 2. If $w_2 = 1.5$ instead of 1.6, this set won't work. This is not the only set of weights that would satisfy all of the conditions derived from these four choice situations. We could multiply each

Exhibit 4.54   Factor Utilities for Forklift Trucks

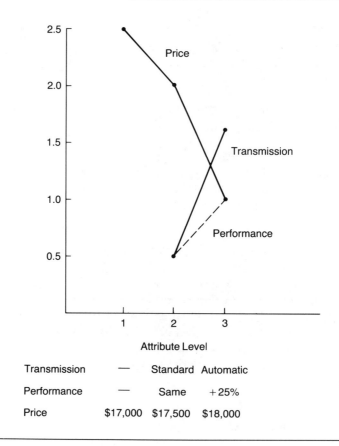

	Attribute Level		
Transmission	—	Standard	Automatic
Performance	—	Same	+25%
Price	$17,000	$17,500	$18,000

of the w's in our revised set by the same positive number and this new set of w's would still work. Thus, only the relative magnitudes of the weights are important.

If, as is commonly the case, there were a broader range of factor levels, resulting in 55 such choice situations, the relative values of a consistent set of weights would be very tightly constrained. It should also be clear that this would be an impossible task to perform by hand, but that a computer algorithm can find the best possible solutions by using a procedure that begins with an initial guess at the set of weights and then adjusts the individual weights to improve the estimates.

This example demonstrates a number of things about how this respondent values the various factor levels. Price is most important, since the range of price

Exhibit 4.55 Forklift Truck Alternatives

	A		B		C	
	Attribute Levels	Utility	Attribute Levels	Utility	Attribute Levels	Utility
Transmission	Std	0.5	Std	0.5	Auto	1.6
Performance	Same	0.5	+25%	1.0	Same	0.5
Price	$17,000	2.5	$17,500	2.0	$18,000	1.0
Total Utility		3.5		3.5		3.1

utilities ($w_5 - w_7 = 1.5$) is greater than the difference between the highest and lowest utility for either of the other two attributes. Transmission is more important than the difference in performance levels.

It is important to realize that the utilities are consistent across product attributes. In our example, the most important product attribute is the $17,000 price ($w_5 = 2.5$) and the least important attributes are the standard transmission and the same level of performance as the respondent's current forklift truck. And the $17,000 price is five times as important to the respondent as these other two attribute levels. See Exhibit 4.54.

Determining Utilities for a Product.   Trade-off analysis assumes that the respondent's utility for a given forklift truck is a function of the utilities for the product's attribute levels. In our forklift truck example, let us assume that the total utility is the sum of the attribute utilities. We can compute our respondent's utility for each of three hypothetical forklift truck models as shown in Exhibit 4.55.

In this example we see that the respondent would be indifferent between forklift trucks A and B, but would prefer either to C. If the price of forklift truck C could be reduced to $17,500, the respondent's utility for it would be 4.1 and it would be preferred over both A and B.

In our example we used additive utilities—we added attribute utilities to obtain a product utility. In the Clark Equipment case series itself, the utilities are multiplicative—they are multiplied to obtain the utility for a particular forklift truck.* Price is treated somewhat differently than the other factors in the trade-off questionnaire in the Clark Equipment cases. In the JMC study, the effect of price is continuous and is expressed in terms of the price difference (d, measured in units of $100s) from a base price of $17,000. See Exhibit 4.56.

---

* Whether the utility model is additive or multiplicative doesn't make much difference—the additive utilities can be thought of as the logs of multiplicative utilities.

Exhibit 4.56   Continuous Price Utility

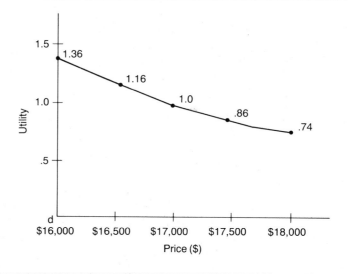

Exhibit 4.57   Current Market Simulation

I. Model Structure

Total Sample: 170 Truck Buyers   This Simulation: 170 Truck Buyers
Total Available Market 1,400 Trucks   This Market: 1,400 Trucks

Market Factors Distinct Levels Measured	Relative Impact On Share	Scale for Distinct Levels	Assigned Competitor Levels			
			Clark	Hyster	Yale	Madal
1 Brand			1.00	2.00	3.00	4.00
1 Clark	1.14	1.00				
2 Hyster	1.22	2.00				
3 Yale	1.16	3.00				
4 Madal	.49	4.00				
2 Performance			2.08	2.01	2.10	2.29
1 25% more performance	1.64	1.00				
2 same performance	.91	2.00				
3 25% less performance	.45	3.00				
3 Reliability			2.06	2.00	2.06	2.24
1 25% less downtime	1.66	1.00				
2 same downtime	.94	2.00				
3 25% more downtime	.40	3.00				
4. Durability			2.09	2.04	2.10	2.30
1 25% longer life	1.63	1.00				
2 same life	1.01	2.00				
3 25% shorter life	.35	3.00				

Exhibit 4.57 (continued)   Current Market Simulation

			2.00	2.00	2.00	2.00
5 Transmission						
1 automatic transmission	1.04	1.00				
2 standard transmission	1.17	2.00				
3 standard B transmission	.80	3.00				
			2.06	2.05	2.09	2.27
6 Parts Availability						
1 25% better availability	1.55	1.00				
2 same parts availability	1.04	2.00				
3 25% worse availability	.41	3.00				
			170.	171.	171.	160.
7 Price						
1 cost in $100	.97	1.00				

II. Predicted Performance

	Share of Choices (%)	Sales–Trucks
1 Clk Clark	27	384
2 Hys Hyster	37	519
3 Yle Yale	27	381
4 Mdl Madal	8	116
	100	1,400

III. Share by Fleet Size (%)

	Small	Medium	Large
Clark	35	33	20
Hyster	30	33	43
Yale	25	25	29
Madal	9	8	8

Estimating Market Share

Market share is estimated from a market simulation model based on the utilities of each individual respondent. The respondent's utility for each forklift truck in the simulation is computed and his choice is assumed to be the forklift truck with his highest utility. These choices, when aggregated across the respondents and divided by the number of respondents, provide the market share estimates for each forklift truck. Exhibit 4.57 displays the results of the market simulation of the Brazilian forklift truck market and Exhibit 4.58 provides a graph of the average factor utilities for "transmission" and "parts availability" across respondents. In this report, attributes are referred to as *factors*. Notice that there are more levels for each factor than there were in our earlier, simplified example. The entries in the report and their relationship to the graphs are as follows:

Exhibit 4.58   Average Factor Utilities for "Transmission" and "Parts Availability"

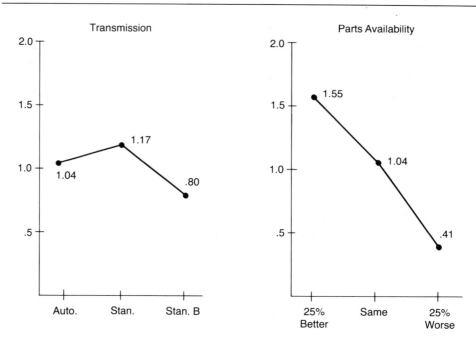

1. *Relative impact on share.*   The numbers in this column give the average utility for each factor. These values provide the y coordinate in the graphs.

2. *Scale for distinct levels.*   This column gives the numerical codes for each factor. These are the x coordinates in the graphs.

3. *Assigned competitor levels.*   These columns give the perceived level for each brand on each attribute. These values were derived from the survey and provide an x-axis coordinate for the brand. For example, in the current market simulation, Clark's performance was perceived as 2.08, which is slightly worse than Hyster's 2.01. The utilities associated with these levels are found by linear interpolation between the levels measured in the survey. In the simulation, these values define the market's product offerings.

4. *Predicted performance.*   These columns present the tabulation of the share of respondent choices allocated to each product and the associated 90% confidence intervals. In other words, the statistical properties of these share estimates would lead one to expect that Clark's market share will be estimated between 25% and 30% nine out of ten times, with the most likely share 27%.

5. *Resulting sales volume.*   These columns project the market simulation into the actual marketplace. Clark's 27% share of the simulation would represent a 27% share of the market, or 384 forklift trucks.

6. *Share by fleet size.*   This table shows the market share in small, medium, and large fleet sizes.

The average utilities, despite their title as "Relative Impact on Share," play no direct role in estimating market share. The factor utilities for individual respondents are used to compute that respondent's total utility for each of the products, and then share is computed by allocating the respondent to the brand for which he had the highest utility and dividing by the number of respondents.

Recent Developments in Trade-off and Conjoint Analysis

At the same time Johnson was developing trade-off analysis, Paul Green and his associates at The Wharton School were developing a similar marketing application based on a method called *Conjoint Measurement* in the psychometric literature. According to Johnson:

> Green was able to see the applicability of this to a whole collection of marketing problems, and for several years there was vigorous activity among Green and his associates, essentially parallel to that in which I've been involved. It has often seemed that our two approaches were quite dissimilar and competitive with one another. [1980, p.7]

Johnson then points out some initial differences in methodology, the most important of which was related to Green's use of "full-profile" choices—all attributes available in every choice—versus Johnson's trade-off of attributes two at a time. He then comments that in recent years both of the approaches have converged somewhat. Green uses some pair-wise (or less than full-profile choices) to arrive at a smaller set of attributes, which are then used in "full-profile" form in subsequent choices; he calls his approach *hybrid conjoint analysis*. Johnson, on the other hand, has relaxed the requirement that the attributes must be independent of the context in which they occur (all-other-things-equal) by including choices that include more than two attributes.

Computerized Questionnaires.   A very important recent development has been the improvement of interviewing results through the use of "smart questionnaires" on personal computers. Using the personal computer, the questionnaire is structured with a mathematical logic capability that allows the computer to customize the questionnaire for each respondent as the interview progresses. According to MacBride and Johnson "the computer continually evaluates new data (each trade-off response) and presents the respondent with a challenging new trade-off decision to make." Thus, two respondents taking the same questionnaire would answer different, and uniquely challenging to them, sets of questions. Advantages of personal computer–administered questionnaires according to MacBride and Johnson are as follows:

> Increased internal consistency—the utilities were more consistent with each other for a greater number of respondents.

> Increased predictive ability—more respondent's choices were predictable using the attributes 20–29%.

> Respondent reactions to "ease of participation" in the study and "interest in the task" were increased.

> Time required for the interview was decreased.

> Several data processing tasks were eliminated, thereby reducing the cost of the interview.

Use of Trade-off and Conjoint Analysis.   A survey by Cattin and Wittink (1981) reported that 698 studies using conjoint analysis or trade-off analysis had been undertaken since 1971 by the seventeen consulting firms that responded to their survey. They also reported that 160 studies had been done during 1980 alone and that 60 percent of the studies had been done for consumer goods, 20 percent for industrial goods, and the rest for transportation, financial services, government, and other industries. Seventy-two percent of the studies involved new product-concept evaluation, 61 percent pricing, 48 percent market segmentation, and 39 percent advertising. The full-profile method of comparisons were used in 56 percent of the studies, two-by-two trade-offs in 27 percent, and a combination of the two in 14 percent. Recent developments would imply that the combination applications were probably dominant by 1985. The sample sizes involved in the studies varied from a high of 1,200 respondents to a low of 100–150. The median sample size was 500 respondents.

Comparison with ASSESSOR.   Both ASSESSOR and the trade-off analysis application presented in this chapter are concerned with estimating market share for new products within an existing product category and market. They both make market-share estimates based on responses to questionnaires designed to obtain meaningful answers to product preference questions. In the ASSESSOR this is done using constant-sum paired comparison questions where a fixed number of chips must be allocated between existing products or existing products and a new product. This is similar in spirit to the methodology of trade-off analysis and conjoint analysis, which forces respondents to make choices between attribute levels. The ASSESSOR preference model does not produce utilities for product attributes but computes share directly from the paired comparison chip allocations. Market share must be derived from the conjoint or trade-off analysis that yields individual utilities for factor attributes by aggregation across individuals.

The ASSESSOR procedure described in the Johnson Wax series is confined to a consumer product for which the development of the physical product prototype and trial purchase by the consumer are both feasible. A modification of ASSESSOR for durable products has been recently developed and tested by Management Decision Systems.

CASE: Clark Equipment I

This case addresses the decision to offer a new forklift truck model featuring an automatic transmission. It provides an example of concept testing, which plays roughly the same role for industrial products as pre—test market testing does for consumer goods. A recommendation is made by the consultants based on a measurement methodology called *trade-off analysis* and market simulation analysis (MSA). The case illustrates how the presentation of a recommendation, even though developed by excellent research, can cause difficulties and limit the usefulness of the results. This case demonstrates the need for managerial access to decision models incorporating the results of the research.

"We don't need all this scientific mumbo jumbo to decide what features our forklift trucks should have. We can prove our ideas like we always have—by gut feel!" These words of João Santos, the Brazilian marketing manager were still ringing in the ears of David Richards, vice president and general manager of Clark Equipment Company's Material Handling Group—Overseas as he sat down in January 1979 to make his recommendations to top management for Clark's Brazilian product line.

It was his own uneasiness about making important decisions by gut feel that had led Richards to commission a product strategy study with the John Morton Company (JMC) of Chicago, Illinois. He respected the experience of long-time forklift truck specialists like Santos—they were close to the dealers, and could talk to customers and think it out—but he thought a more systematic survey of customer preferences might be helpful, especially when considering something new to the Brazilian market, like a forklift truck equipped with an automatic transmission.

Most of the recommendations in the JMC presentation had been consistent with current practice and evoked little response, but the recommendation to offer two forklift trucks in the "heart of the line" (HOL)* classification had met heated objections from Santos and others, culminating in Santos's strong statement.

JMC had recommended that Clark offer one HOL model with the standard oil bath transmission currently used in Brazil, but slightly lower performance and price and slightly higher reliability and durability than the current model. The second model would sell at a higher price but would offer a "powershift" automatic transmission and better performance, reliability, and durability than the current Clark HOL model.

Richards now had to recommend what the HOL product line should be—the present model, JMC's recommended dual-offering strategy, or something else. It was a big decision, because any change in the product line would require new research and product development programs, production-facility modification, and new marketing programs. It would take time to get the ball rolling, and once under way it would be very difficult to change. In

---

* "Heart of the line" was the term used by Clark Equipment to describe the very important 4000- to 6000-pound capacity forklift trucks that represented about 55% of sales.

This case was prepared by Darral G. Clarke.

Copyright (©) 1981 By the President and Fellows of Harvard College Harvard Business School case 9-581-091.

such a situation the slogan of Clark's engineering department, "Right the first time," was not only appropriate but sobering.

Company Background

Clark Material Handling Group (MHG) was one of four major divisions of the Clark Equipment Company, a large (1978 sales of $1.5 billion), highly integrated manufacturer of capital goods. Clark's operations were international in scope. Roughly one-third of sales and operating profit came from outside the United States. Forklift trucks were a major product line of the Material Handling Group, whose 1978 worldwide sales were $630 million, the highest in their history. Operating profit was $76.9 million, a 36% increase over the previous year.

The U.S. was the group's strongest market in 1978. In Europe, some progress had been made in a highly competitive marketing environment, but the market for material handling equipment in South America had been essentially flat. MHG's distribution network was the largest in the world, with 237 dealers operating in 508 locations in 108 countries. During the previous five years the number of sales outlets had increased more than 20%.

MHG manufacturing took place in 14 facilities in 12 countries. Margins had improved in 1978, primarily because of volume increases and improvements in operating efficiency at the manufacturing plants in Battle Creek, Michigan (group headquarters); Georgetown, Kentucky; and Muhlheim, Germany.

Forklift Trucks

A forklift truck (forklift) is a motorized hydraulic lift used for moving heavy loads from one place to another. Forklifts are used in most manufacturing and warehouse operations where heavy materials need to be handled. Because of their varied uses, the Clark forklift truck line included over 125 numbered models, ranging from a 2000-pound capacity forklift truck with a very tight turning radius, to behemoths with 80,000-pound capacities able to lift and stack 40-foot-long containers three units high at seaport facilities. Custom models were also produced. Forklift trucks could be powered by electricity, gasoline, liquid petroleum gas, or diesel fuel. Hydraulic lift ranges could be as high as forty feet. Tires might be pneumatic or solid rubber. One model, called "Jaws," had a clamp large enough to handle rolls of paper nine feet high and nine feet in diameter. David Richards said:

> Our product line is very long; we joke about being able to put Clark forklift trucks end to end from New York to San Francisco and not have an exact duplicate in the line. It's better than it was. We've cut down by one-half. There is a terrific tendency among dealers to tell a customer, "We'll give you anything you want," even if we don't have it. We've been fighting that very hard. You just can't make money giving everyone exactly what they want. So when you design the product line you start with the 4000- to 6000-pound capacity trucks, which account for about 55% of our sales, and build from there.

The Brazilian Fork Lift Market

Brazil was one of the most rapidly industrializing countries in South America. It was the world's largest producer of coffee, the second largest of soybeans, and the fourth largest of sugar. Its iron-ore deposits were the largest anywhere. Its population of 110 million, the seventh largest in the world, occupied a country with the fifth largest land mass, a coastline longer than the combined east and west coasts of the United States, and the world's biggest network of rivers.

Economic policies in Brazil had generally favored growth at the expense of inflation, and, as a result, Brazil had one of the highest inflation rates in the world. Concern about inflation and the balance of payments prompted the government to begin cooling off the economy in 1976. Various measures were instituted to encourage the use of Brazilian industry and discourage imports.

Clark's forklift trucks, although produced in Brazil, used a high proportion of imported parts,

Exhibit 4.59   Clark's Position in the Brazilian Market

South American Financial Highlights ($ millions)

	1974	1975	1976	1977	1978
Sales to Unaffiliated Customers	89.9	107.6	121.1	126.2	184.1
Operating Profit	13.1	16.6	29.6	18.3	29.2
Identifiable Assets	101.0	105.0	127.6	117.3	123.8

Internal Combustion Forklift Truck Market

	1974	1975	1976	1977	1978
Overseas (Non–U.S. Markets)					
Industry Unit Sales	15,197	14,777	14,867	16,444	17,957
Clark Unit Sales	2,640	2,941	2,252	2,186	2,305
Clark Share	17.4%	19.9%	15.1%	13.3%	12.8%
Brazil					
Industry Unit Sales	1,925	2,348	2,072	1,438	1,825
Clark Unit Sales	422	474	607	384	302
Clark Share	21.9%	20.2%	29.3%	26.7%	16.5%
Hyster Share	33.0%	37.0%	31.0%	34.2%	51.0%
Yale Share	35.0%	32.8%	28.0%	24.0%	25.0%
Madal Share	10.0%	10.0%	11.7%	15.1%	7.0%

and as a result of these measures Clark had sought to decrease the proportion of imported parts in its lift trucks in 1977 by using a Brazilian-produced transmission (standard B in tables). This transmission broke down frequently and rapidly became a major headache for Clark and its distributors. At the same time, Hyster, Clark's major competitor, had improvised a reliable transmission from Brazilian components and gained market share at Clark's expense. Subsequently Clark overcame its transmission difficulties, but it was evident that distributor morale had been badly damaged, and the extent of damage to Clark's image with customers was undetermined.

The Brazilian market for forklift trucks was dominated by three large American firms—Hyster, Clark, and Eaton-Yale—and one Brazilian firm, Madal. Hyster was the most formidable of these competitors, not only in Brazil but worldwide. Hyster's recent competitive strategy had featured expanded product lines* and very aggressive pric-

ing, especially in the lower-capacity lift trucks. Eaton-Yale was losing position in Brazil and in the U.S., where it had dropped from second to fifth in market share. Exhibit 4.59 shows Clark's position in the Brazilian market.

As David Richards considered the Brazilian market after this difficult period, he felt that he needed help on three questions:

What was Clark's image with customers in Brazil?

What factors were important to Brazilian forklift truck buyers?

Should he introduce an automatic transmission forklift truck in Brazil?

---

* In 1978, Hyster's Brazilian product line offered forklift trucks in six weight classes. Clark offered forklift trucks in only two weight classes.

He called Mr. Curtis Jones of JMC, which had previously consulted with another Clark division and outlined the situation. Jones outlined methods of measuring Clark's image and discussed how the product-line decision could be based on information on customer preferences for various lift truck features.

The John Morton Company Study

The John Morton Company (JMC) was a marketing consulting firm founded by Curtis Jones and Richard Johnson, both former officers and directors of Market Facts Inc., a large Chicago-based marketing research company. Jones described JMC as follows:

> We formed John Morton because clients didn't associate the kind of strategic consulting we wanted to do with a market research company. We deal with the same kinds of problems that the best-known strategic consulting firms deal with, but our approach is entirely different. Our strategy recommendations are based on market factors rather than predominantly on cost or other internal company considerations. We also differ from them to the extent that we utilize state-of-the-art mathematical and computer modeling techniques.
>
> Our approach to marketing consulting involves:
>
> Assisting the client in identifying and defining his marketing problems.
>
> Analyzing the market needs, the client's current role in the market, and those of his competitors.
>
> Formulating practical marketing and development strategies and designing criteria for choosing among them.
>
> Conducting research to determine the attitudes and opinions of the buyers in the market.
>
> Recommending marketing strategies based on a quantitative analysis of the market, the client's situation, and his short- and long-term goals.
>
> We call the strategies that result from this process "market-driven" strategies.

The study Jones recommended to Richards involved a survey measuring the perceptions that Brazilian forklift truck owners had of the various forklift truck brands and the value they placed on product features. Market simulations based on the survey results and a mathematical technique known as *trade-off analysis* would then forecast the market share that could be expected for various lift trucks. The trade-off analysis and market simulations would be supervised by Richard Johnson, who had developed these techniques (Johnson 1974). Further meetings between Richards and Jones firmed up the consulting plan and the cost. (The previous text section described this research methodology.)

Project Description

The project began with a two-day strategy meeting in Battle Creek directed by JMC, a meeting that brought together Clark executives, marketers, and engineers with JMC personnel. The agenda focused initially on marketing decisions so that all participants would understand and be attuned to the market-driven strategy concept. Subsequent discussions covered a number of other topics: alternative strategies, market conditions, and the identification of product factors (the criteria by which buyers were thought to select among alternative lift trucks). The factors and the different "levels" in which the factors would be available were then field tested and eventually finalized as shown in Exhibit 4.60.

Interviewing took place during August and September 1978 in the states of Rio de Janeiro and São Paulo. Companies were sampled randomly from a list of 750 firms prepared by MHG-Brazil. To qualify for an interview, each company needed to have used a 4000- to 6000-pound capacity lift truck in the past five years, or to have plans to use one in the next year. Qualified individual respondents were required to have primary influence on forklift truck-buying decisions. One hundred ninety-one personal interviews were completed by local Portuguese-speaking executive interviewers. These interviews averaged approximately $1\frac{1}{2}$ hours in length. A breakdown of the sample composition is shown in Exhibit 4.61.

Exhibit 4.60   Field Test Factors and Their Levels

Factor	Levels
Performance	25% increased performance over present trucks Same performance 25% reduced performance (*Performance* was defined as a truck's lifting speed, travel speed, turning radius, etc.)
Reliability	25% less downtime than experienced with present truck Same downtime 25% more downtime
Durability	25% longer life than expected from present truck Same life 25% shorter life (*Life* was defined as the total hours or years a truck can be used before it requires a major overhaul)
Parts Availability	25% better parts availability than at present Same parts availability 25% worse parts availability (*Parts Availability* was defined as the time it takes to get parts from a dealer when the truck breaks down)
Transmission	Automatic Standard Standard B with Brazilian parts (*Automatic* was defined as a type of of transmission new to the Brazilian market that had no clutch and required only minimal shifting)
Brand	Clark, Hyster, Eaton-Yale, Madal
Selling Price	From $l5,000 to $20,000 (U.S. dollars, including taxes)

The questionnaire included standard questions about fleet size, type of business, and perceptions of forklift truck companies; but the major section was designed to discover what value the respondent placed on the various lift truck factors and factor levels. Using this input, the respondent's preference for each lift truck available in the market and the market share for each lift truck could be computed. This approach was computerized by JMC in a simulation model it called *market simulation analysis.*

The market simulation analysis developed by JMC for the Brazilian forklift truck market was based on the responses for 170 of the original 191 survey respondents. Twenty-one of the respondents were excluded because their consistency in answering trade-off questions was judged to be unacceptable.* This respondent rejection rate was consistent with JMC's previous experience.

Project Results.   After the initial intensive involvement with JMC personnel at the outset of the study, there followed a six-month period of very little contact. In December 1978, David Richards received a telephone call from Curtis Jones informing him that the study had been completed, and a date was set for a presentation at JMC's offices in Chicago.

---

* If at least 85% of the choices made by a respondent were not predicted correctly by the model, the model was not felt to explain that respondent's preferences well enough to include that respondent in the market simulation. The information available from these respondents was considered in a more traditional analysis.

Exhibit 4.61 Summary of Survey Composition (N = 191)

	Most Recent Brand Purchased (%)	Primary Brand* (%)	Percent of Trucks (%)
Clark	37	42†	23‡
Hyster	33	28	38
Yale	25	26	32
Other	5	4	7

Fleet Size		Percent of Users	Percent of Trucks
Small (1–2)		40	10
Medium (3–6)		35	25
Large (7 +)		25	65
		100	100

Industry		Percent of Users	Percent of Trucks
Manufacturing		43	36
Transport/Warehousing		16	21
Chemicals		11	13
Food		8	8
Paper		8	7
Other		14	15
		100	100

*If more than one brand is owned, the brand that represents the largest number of forklift trucks owned.

†Forty-two percent of the respondents owned more Clark trucks than other brands.

‡Of all the forklift trucks owned by the survey respondents, 23% were Clark.

The presentation, which was attended by Richards, João Santos, and other Clark personnel, began with an executive summary and recommendations. JMC recommended that Clark should:

1. Target Hyster's market because it was the largest and most vulnerable to the proposed Clark HOL product line.

2. Increase marketing activity generally: promotion, advertising, and selling.

3. Maintain parts availability at present levels but promote it more.

4. Expand the services offered by the dealerships.

5. Most importantly, replace the present HOL model with a "dual offering strategy" featuring two HOL models with characteristics relative to the present HOL truck, as shown in Exhibit 4.62.

The JMC study forecast an 18% share for each of the two HOL forklift trucks. This combined 36% share would represent a nine-point increase over the predicted share for Clark's present model. João Santos disagreed at once with this recommended strategy, but was persuaded to listen to an explanation of the analysis and its support for the recommendations.

Curtis Jones then displayed survey results on buyer perceptions of forklift trucks that did not require an understanding of the market simulation. These results (see Exhibits 4.63 through 4.65) caused little controversy. Clark, Hyster, and Eaton-

Exhibit 4.62   Proposed Dual Offering Strategy

	Present Clark HOL	Dual Offering HOL	
	Lift Truck	Product Modification	New Model
Transmission	Stan.	Stan.	Auto.
Performance	100	90	103
Reliability	100	105	110
Durability	100	105	110
Parts availability	100	100	100
Price	100	95	110
Predicted market share	27%	18%	18%

Yale were viewed by customers to be very similar. There was an indication that the Brazilian transmission problem had done some damage since: Clark owners were less likely to rate their lift truck better than competitors' than were Hyster and Eaton-Yale owners, but the damage to Clark's reputation seemed concentrated in present owners and less severe than Santos and Richards had feared.

The questionnaire had also been administered to some Clark dealers and personnel, who rated Clark much less favorably than the customers did. Richards said:

> The market was willing to give us a 27% share according to the simulation based on the survey, whereas a simulation based on Clark's associated people only gave us 16%. Our actual share at the time had risen to 24%. This indicated to us that the customers in the survey saw us more favorably than we saw ourselves. It also indicated a morale problem and a defeatist attitude among some of our people.

Jones then returned to a discussion of the recommended strategy and the results upon which it was based. He pointed out that a substantial 34% of the forklift truck owners interviewed stated a preference for automatic transmission (Exhibit 4.65) and presented the summary of the relative impact of changes in the factor levels that is found in Exhibit 4.66. He pointed out that the results shown in Exhibit 4.66 were only estimates of market re-

sponse to changes in each factor considered separately and that the full impact of a change in any factor could be evaluated only by considering the total configuration of the Clark product offering and the products offered by competitors.

At this point, João Santos stressed the importance of the price factor, pointing out that a decrease in price would have a greater effect on market share than anything else. He had been advocating a lower-priced HOL model, and felt this result justified his recommendation. Jones cautioned Santos about drawing too strong a conclusion from the single factor results. He pointed out that a lower-priced model with lower performance and reliability than the present Clark model had been considered in one of the simulations, and the estimated market share for such a product had only been 26%. Santos was visibly disturbed by this statement and made the by-now-famous "gut feel" remark. The formal meeting broke up soon afterward.

The Problem

Following the meeting David Richards assembled the information that seemed relevant to making a decision on a Brazilian HOL product-line strategy. He asked engineering for cost estimates on each of the forklift truck models that had been considered and combined them with a summary of the JMC forecasts (see Exhibit 4.67). Although he realized that they played no direct role in the computation of

Exhibit 4.63   How Users Compare Their Brand With Others

Primary Brand	Reliability (%)	Durability (%)	Performance (%)	Parts Available (%)
Clark is:				
better than Hyster	18	30	25	22
same as Hyster	58	48	53	57
worse than Hyster	24	22	22	21
better than Yale	28	29	29	32
same as Yale	55	58	56	55
worse than Yale	17	13	15	13
better than Madal	52	51	52	41
same as Madal	40	43	47	51
worse than Madal	8	6	1	8
Hyster is:				
better than Clark	32	44	40	23
same as Clark	53	45	51	56
worse than Clark	15	11	9	21
better than Yale	39	47	53	54
same as Yale	51	47	41	34
worse than Yale	10	6	6	8
better than Madal	54	61	63	56
same as Madal	33	33	31	36
worse than Madal	13	6	6	8
Yale is:				
better than Clark	35	43	47	41
same as Clark	43	47	41	47
worse than Clark	12	10	12	12
better than Hyster	27	35	33	54
same as Hyster	52	50	48	38
worse than Hyster	21	15	19	8
better than Madal	57	69	67	65
same as Madal	28	24	26	28
worse than Madal	15	7	7	7

Exhibit 4.64   Average Truck Specifications as Perceived by the Market (Clark = 100)

	Clark	Hyster	Yale	Madal
Transmission	Stan.	Stan.	Stan.	Stan.
Performance	100	103	99	90
Reliability	100	103	100	91
Durability	100	102	100	90
Parts Availability	100	100	98	90
Price	100	101	101	94

Exhibit 4.65   Transmission Preferences

		Percent Preferring	
		Standard	**Automatic**
Total Sample:		66%	34%
By Fleet Size:	Large (7 +)	80%	20%
	Medium (3–6)	62%	38%
	Small (1–2)	61%	39%
By Intensity of Use:	High	71%	29%
	Medium	71%	29%
	Low	59%	41%

Exhibit 4.66   Changes in Share Points Induced by 25% Improvement* in Clark (one factor at a time)

		Estimated Change in Share Points for These Brands		
If Clark improves the following by 25%	**Clark**	**Hyster**	**Yale**	**Madal**
Performance	+10	−5	−4	−1
Reliability	+12	−6	−4	−2
Durability	+13	−6	−5	−2
Parts Availability	+11	−6	−4	−1
Price Reduction	+17	−8	−7	−2

*In this case, "25% improvement" refers to increasing the Clark level on each factor from 12.5% below the current truck to 12.5% above.

market share, he graphed the average utility functions for the factors (see Exhibit 4.58 and 4.68) to get an idea of factor importance in general. Finally, he obtained the market simulation analysis runs for the current market situation (see Exhibit 4.57) and JMC's dual-option recommendation (see Exhibits 4.69). Only the utility levels for brand and transmission seemed to differ across market segments (Exhibit 4.70).

Having assembled this information, he sat down to make his own recommendations about an HOL strategy.

Exhibit 4.67   Cost Estimates with JMC Forecasts

Clark Specifications

	Current	Low-Priced	Dual Clark Offering Modified Current Transmission	Automatic Transmission
Transmission	Stan.	Stan.	Stan.	Auto.
Performance	100	95	90	103
Reliability	100	95	105	110
Durability	100	95	105	110
Parts Availability	100	100	100	100
Price	$17,000	$14,500	$16,150	$18,700
Estimated Unit Cost*	$11,613	$ 9,475	$11,757	$12,840

Share Forecasts (%)

Clark	27	26	18	36	18
Hyster	37	38		32	
Yale	27	28		24	
Madal	8	8		7	

*These costs included very rough allocations of investment needed for producing the new models.

Preparation Questions

1. Be sure you understand how market simulation analysis works. In particular:

   a. How are the market factors and factor levels determined?

   b. How do the choices between alternative lift trucks get translated into utility measures?

   c. How are attribute utilities converted to product utilities?

   d. How is market share predicted?

2. What are the major managerial issues facing Mr. Richards in developing a marketing strategy?

3. What were the major steps in the research process? How well did they address the managerial issues you identified?

4. What did you learn from the research?

5. Evaluate the John Morton Company recommendation. Why was Sr. Santos so upset?

6. How would access to the model be beneficial to Mr. Richards and/or Sr. Santos?

Exhibit 4.68   Utility Functions

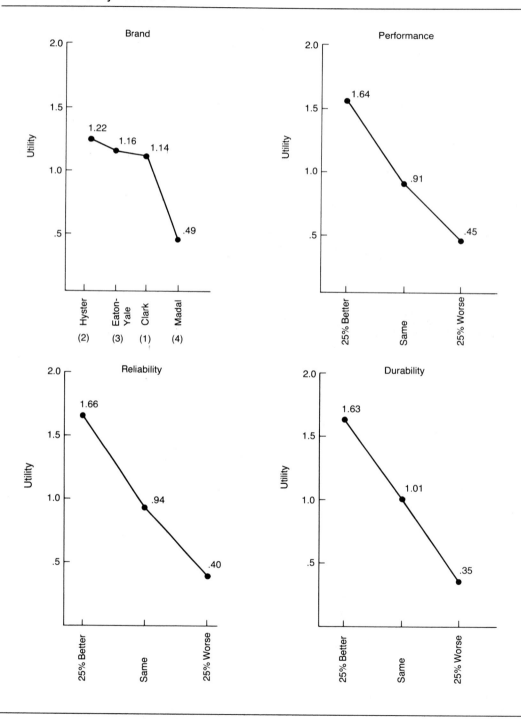

Exhibit 4.69 Dual-Offering Strategy Simulation

I. Model Structure

Total Sample: 170 Truck Buyers

Total Available Market: 1,400 Trucks

This Simulation: 170 Truck Buyers

This Market: 1,400 Trucks

Market Factors Distinct Levels Measured	Relative Impact On Share	Scale for Distinct Levels	Assigned Competitor Levels				
			Clk	Cka	Hys	Yle	Mdl
1 Brand			1.00	1.00	2.00	3.00	4.00
1 Clark	1.14	1.00					
2 Hyster	1.22	2.00					
3 Yale	1.16	3.00					
4 Madal	.49	4.00					
2 Performance			2.48*	1.96*	2.01	2.10	2.29
1 25% more performance	1.64	1.00					
2 same performance	.91	2.00					
3 25% less performance	.45	3.00					
3 Reliability			1.86*	1.66*	2.00	2.06	2.24
1 25% less downtime	1.66	1.00					
2 same downtime	.94	2.00					
3 25% more downtime	.40	3.00					
4. Durability			1.89*	1.69*	2.04	2.10	2.30
1 25% longer life	1.63	1.00					
2 same life	1.01	2.00					
3 25% shorter life	.35	3.00					
5 Transmission			2.00	1.00*	2.00	2.00	2.00
1 automatic	1.04	1.00					
2 standard	1.17	2.00					
3 standard B†	.80	3.00					
6 Parts Availability			2.06	2.06	2.05	2.09	2.27
1 25% better availability	1.55	1.00					
2 same parts availability	1.04	2.00					
3 25% worse availability	.41	3.00					
7 Price			161.*	187.*	171.	171.	160
1 cost in $100	.97	1.00					

II. Predicted Performance

	Share of Choices	Sales–Trucks
1 Clk Clark	18	255
2 Cka Clark Automatic	18	251
3 Hys Hyster	32	454
4 Yle Yale	24	340
5 Mdl Madal	7	100
	100	1,400

(continued)

Exhibit 4.69 (continued)   Dual-Offering Strategy Simulation

III. Share by Fleet Size (%)

	Small	Medium	Large
Clark	19	19	12
Clark Automatic	24	22	14
Hyster	27	30	39
Yale	22	22	28
Madal	8	7	7

*Indicates change from initial level
† Brazilian transmission that had problems.

Exhibit 4.70   Utilities by Segment

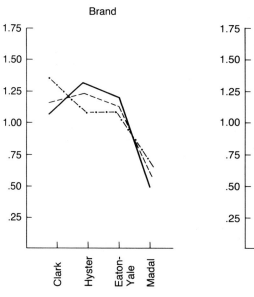
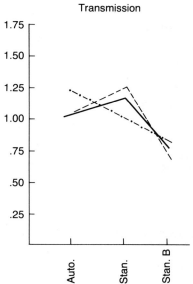

Key:

Large-fleet owners: ———

Medium-fleet owners: — — — —

Small-fleet owners: •—•—•—•

Other factors are quite similar across segments.

CASE: Clark Equipment II

This case is an extension of Clark I; it provides the results of a number of simulations using the Market Simulations Analysis (MSA) model. These simulations were undertaken to address different competitive situations than that considered in the first case. The case illustrates the importance of access to the models used by the consultants to develop their recommendation. Ideally, the MSA model itself would be available to the student, but it won't fit on the PC. The analysis illustrates the use of scenario analysis for analyzing competitive response to Clark's marketing plan.

David Richards, vice president and general manager of Clark Material Handling Group–Overseas, was in the process of making recommendations for the heart-of-the-line (HOL) product for Clark's Brazilian line. He was faced with something of a dilemma. The John Morton Company (JMC), the consultants Richards had hired to analyze Clark's Brazilian product line, had recommended that Clark offer two HOL models:

1. A forklift truck much like the present Clark HOL offering

2. A forklift truck with an automatic transmission

João Santos, Clark's Brazilian marketing manager, did not agree with this recommendation and favored offering a lower-priced lift truck as the HOL. Santos had been an effective manager and was very close to the Brazilian market. JMC, although not familiar with the Brazilian market, nevertheless had produced a number of insights into the market that had not been fully recognized by either Santos or Richards—for example, the difference in the strength of Clark's position with small- and large-fleet customers. Richards was also impressed by the research JMC had done. The approaches Santos and JMC had taken to reach their conclusions obviously differed—the former relied on experience and intuition; the latter, on consumer measurement and market simulation.

Richards did not favor modifying the current forklift truck as JMC recommended, but he did favor the dual-line recommendation if the Brazilian marketplace were to remain unchanged. He was concerned, however, whether that strategy would be best if market conditions changed.

Competition

The competitive environment had been a source of concern for Clark for quite some time. Previous studies included a Boston Consulting Group (BCG) analysis in 1972, which Richards summarized as follows:

BCG did their analysis of the world lift truck market and, in a presentation featuring boxes and balls, identified the biggest threats to our market as Caterpillar and Fiat. They didn't pick Toyota, in particular, or the Japanese in general. In the last five years, however, Toyota has focused on a few select markets and has been pricing so low that it could only be considered as dumping. Everyone has lost share to them.

Clark's markets varied in number of competitors, even though competition was strong in each of them. In the U.S., Clark faced five major competitors and maybe 15 other, more narrowly fo-

This case was prepared by Darral G. Clarke.

Copyright (©) 1981 By the President and Fellows of Harvard College Harvard Business School case 9-581-140.

cused competitors. In Europe there were 90 competitors. Japan itself had ten very formidable competing firms. "Considering all our overseas markets," said Richards, "we have nearly a hundred competitors!"

Santos was concerned about the possible entry of the Japanese into Brazil and had spoken to Richards about the problems that would present. He was sure a Japanese forklift truck would be introduced relatively soon, and that it would be a good quality machine priced below current market levels. He thought the only way to compete against such an entry was to trim manufacturing costs as much as possible and lower the selling price.

Clark's product-line strategy in the past had always been to offer the best lift truck possible—the latest developments and best quality parts were used in its product designs. At the same time, management had been disturbed to see Clark's worldwide share drop from 40% to about 11% over the past 40 years. The growth in the number and strength of competitors accounted for a great deal of that drop, but David Richards wondered whether the product-line policy wasn't also a contributing cause.

> Nobody would think it reasonable for an automobile manufacturer to decide to be simultaneously the volume leader *and* produce Mercedes Benz–type automobiles. As competition has increased and our markets have become more diversified, perhaps our product-line policy and volume goals have become just as inconsistent. Maybe we should consider another dual-option strategy equivalent to making a Cadillac and a Volkswagen.

Richards was concerned not only about Japanese competition, but also about Hyster's response if Clark offered an automatic transmission forklift truck. JMC's dual-offering strategy recommendation had been based on the assumption that no other new lift truck models would be available. What if Hyster also offered an automatic transmission or responded to the Japanese entry with a low-priced model of its own?

Richards decided to call Curtis Jones at JMC to see whether anything could be done to analyze

Clark product-line strategies in different competitive situations.

Strategy Analysis in a Changing Competitive Environment

Curtis Jones's response to Richards's question was that market simulation analysis (MSA) could be used to predict the market's response to other combinations of lift truck offerings than the ones considered in JMC's report. The big difference between analyzing hypothetical markets and the current market lay in making subjective estimates of the factor levels of hypothetical lift trucks rather than measuring the consumer perceptions of existing lift trucks. Such estimates had already been made for the Clark automatic transmission lift truck and for the modifications JMC recommended to the existing lift truck.

Jones felt that the quality of MSA in hypothetical situations depended on:

1. The quality of the managerial estimates of the hypothetical lift truck factor levels

2. The applicability of the customers' preference function estimates in new situations

The first step in extending the market simulation analysis was to determine the array of lift trucks that might be offered and define their factor levels. Richards felt that a Japanese lift truck would provide better factor levels than those of Madal and would be priced at $14,500, about $1,500 less than Madal and $2,500 less than Clark's current model. He thought that if Hyster produced an automatic transmission and a low-priced model, they would have slightly better factor levels than comparable Clark models, and the automatic would be priced $100 more than Clark's automatic while the low priced model would be priced $200 less than Clark's low-priced model (see Exhibit 4.71).

Having estimated the factor levels of the potential market entrants, Richard next faced the task of defining reasonable competitive situations Clark might face. He began with a number of assumptions:

Exhibit 4.71   Simulation Analysis Lift Truck Descriptions and Utilities

Factor Levels

Feasible Lift Truck Models	Brand	Performance	Reliability	Durability	Transmission	Parts Availability	Price ($)	Cost ($)
1 Clark (c)	1.00	2.08	2.06	2.00	2.00	2.06	17,000	11,600
2 Clark (j)	1.00	2.15	2.10	2.15	2.00	2.06	15,000	9,500
3 Clark (a)	1.00	1.96	1.66	1.69	1.00	2.06	18,700	12,800
4 Hyster (c)	2.00	2.01	2.00	2.04	2.00	2.05	17,100	11,650
5 Hyster (j)	2.00	2.15	2.05	2.10	2.00	2.05	14,800	9,200
6 Hyster (a)	2.00	1.89	1.60	1.64	1.00	2.05	18,800	12,700
7 Yale	3.00	2.10	2.06	2.10	2.00	2.09	17,100	11,800
8 Madal	4.00	2.29	2.24	2.30	2.00	2.27	16,000	10,500
9 Japan	3.10	2.15	2.15	2.25	2.00	2.20	14,500	8,900

Utilities by Fleet Size

Market Factors	Scale for Distinct Levels	Relative Impact on Share by Fleet Size		
		Small	Medium	Large
1 Brand				
1 Clark	1.00	1.33	1.13	1.06
2 Hyster	2.00	1.06	1.22	1.28
3 Yale	3.00	1.08	1.13	1.20
4 Madal	4.00	.53	.51	.46
2 Performance				
1 25% more performance	1.00	1.60	1.67	1.64
2 Same peformance	2.00	.95	.89	.90
3 25% less performance	3.00	.44	.44	.46
3 Reliability				
1 25% less downtime	1.00	1.59	1.69	1.68
2 Same downtime	2.00	1.01	1.00	1.03
3 25% more downtime	3.00	.40	.38	.41
4 Durability				
1 25% longer life	1.00	1.62	1.66	1.62
2 Same life	2.00	1.01	1.00	1.03
3 25% shorter life	3.00	.37	.34	.35
5 Transmission				
1 Automatic	1.00	1.17	1.01	1.00
2 Standard	2.00	1.01	1.24	1.18
3 Standard B	3.00	.82	.75	.82
6 Parts Availability				
1 25% better availability	1.00	1.53	1.60	1.52
2 Same parts availability	2.00	1.10	1.01	1.04
3 25% worse availability	3.00	.38	.39	.43
7 Price				
1 cost in $100	1.00	.98	.98	.97

Exhibit 4.72 MSA Summary: Market Share (Revenue) (%)

No Japanese Competition

	Clark's HOL Product Line	
Hyster's HOL Product Line	**Current**	**Current & Automatic**
Current	24.9	32.6
Current & Automatic	22.3	28.2

Japanese Competition

	Clark's HOL Product Line			
Hyster's HOL Product Line	**Current**	**Current & Low Price**	**Current & Automatic**	**Low Price & Automatic**
Current	20.1	24.2	27.6	30.3
Current & Low Price	19.0	22.4	26.8	28.5
Current & Automatic	18.3	21.8	24.6	26.4
Low Price & Automatic	17.5	20.8	24.4	25.5

Neither Eaton-Yale nor Madal was likely to respond to a Japanese entry or the introduction of an automatic transmission lift truck by offering new models.

Neither Hyster nor Clark would offer an HOL product line consisting of only a Japanese-competitive low-priced model.

Neither Clark nor Hyster would be interested in offering an HOL product line that consisted of all three models—current, automatic, and low-priced.

Neither Clark nor Hyster would offer a low-priced lift truck before the Japanese entered the market.

Japanese entry into the Brazilian market would occur within the next two years.

Neither Clark nor Hyster would be interested in an HOL product line that consisted solely of an automatic transmission lift truck.

Japanese entry would increase the size of the market from 1,400 to 1,700 lift trucks per year.

The more Richards considered the HOL decision, the more complex it seemed to become. Santos's advocacy of a lower price for the current model or a new lower-cost lift truck had assumed substitution for the current model. Once the idea of

a dual-option HOL was considered, however, the choices expanded considerably. Richards listed four HOL product lines that deserved consideration:

The current model only

The current model and a new low-priced model

The current model and an automatic transmission model

A new low-priced model and an automatic transmission model

Richards felt Hyster would also find each of these HOL strategies feasible and he reasoned that the attractiveness of any of the four product lines would be affected by the strategy Hyster chose. Furthermore, whether or not the Japanese were in the market would affect them both. If neither Clark nor Hyster offered a low-priced model before the Japanese entered (and he doubted that either Clark or Hyster could offer a low-priced model in less than two years), the number of feasible competitive situations could be reduced to twenty. These twenty MSA simulations were performed and the results were summarized in Exhibits 4.71, 4.72, and 4.73. Exhibit 4.71 presents the descriptions and utilities common to all of the simulations, and Exhibit 4.72 presents the forecast market share

Exhibit 4.73 MSA Simulation Analysis Summary—Contribution to Profit

No Japanese Competition

| | Clark's HOL Product Line ($ millions) | |
Hyster's HOL Product Line	Current	Current & Automatic
Current	1.87	2.50
Current & Automatic	1.77	2.19

Japanese Competition

| | Clark's HOL Product Line ($ millions) | | | |
Hyster's HOL Product Line	Current	Current & Low Price	Current & Automatic	Low Price & Automatic
Current	1.79	2.36	2.54	2.90
Current & Low Price	1.63	2.12	2.34	2.60
Current & Automatic	1.66	2.18	2.25	2.55
Low Price & Automatic	1.52	2.01	2.17	2.40

Exhibit 4.74 Size of Brazilian Lift Truck Market

Fleet Size	No Japanese Competition	Japanese Competition
Small	140	340
Medium	350	450
Large	910	910
Total	1,400	1,700

(based on revenue) in each competitive situation. Exhibit 4.73 presents the contribution to profit and fixed costs. In calculating these values, Richards assumed that the size of Brazilian lift truck market would be as shown in Exhibit 4.74.

Market share, revenue, and contribution to profit by lift truck model for Clark, Hyster, Yale, Madal, and a Japanese competitor are found in the appendix.

In examining Exhibits 4.72 and 4.73 David Richards observed that if the Japanese were in the market, Clark's largest market share and contribution to profit would occur if Clark offered an HOL product line consisting of the low-priced and automatic transmission lift trucks, no matter what Hyster's HOL product line might be. He also observed, however, that the return for this alternative varied with Hyster's HOL product line from $2.40 million to $2.90 million, which caused him to wonder what Hyster would do if the Japanese entered the market or if Clark introduced an automatic transmission lift truck.

Preparation Questions

1. How will Hyster, Yale, and Madal respond to the possible changes in Clark's product line policy?

2. What effect will a Japanese entry into the market have on the attractiveness of the Morton recommendation?

3. What product line strategy would you recommend for Clark?

Exhibit 4.75   Clark Equipment II Spreadsheet

```
                    CLARK EQUIPMENT (II)


Price and Cost Data:
                 Price       Cost
  Clark
    Current      $17,000   $11,600
    Automatic    $18,700   $12,800
    Low Price    $15,000    $9,500

  Hyster
    Current      $17,100   $11,650
    Automatic    $18,800   $12,700
    Low Price    $14,800    $9,200

  Yale           $17,100   $11,800
  Madal          $16,000   $10,500
  Japanese       $14,500    $8,900
```

Mkt. Segment Units:	Large	Medium	Small	Total	MSA #	1
	910	350	140	1400		

```
                    UNIT SHARE FORECASTS
```

	Large	Medium	Small	Units	Revenue	Share	Ctbn
Clark					$5.89	24.9%	$1.87
Current	20%	33%	35%	347	$5.89	24.9%	$1.87
Automatic	0%	0%	0%	0	$0.00	0.0%	$0.00
Low Price	0%	0%	0%	0	$0.00	0.0%	$0.00
Hyster					$9.38	39.6%	$2.99
Current	43%	33%	30%	549	$9.38	39.6%	$2.99
Automatic	0%	0%	0%	0	$0.00	0.0%	$0.00
Low Price	0%	0%	0%	0	$0.00	0.0%	$0.00
Yale	29%	25%	25%	386	$6.61	27.9%	$2.05
Madal	8%	8%	9%	113	$1.81	7.7%	$0.62
Japanese	0%	0%	0%	0	$0.00	0.0%	$0.00
Total					$23.70		

Clark Equipment II Spreadsheet

The Clark Equipment II spreadsheet (Exhibit 4.75) isn't a decision model, but rather just a worksheet that makes some calculations from the results of the MSA model that would be tedious to do by hand.

The Appendix of the Clark Equipment II case provides the market share estimates that resulted from a series of simulations that Mr. Richards requested. The MSA model, however, is too large to be accommodated on the programs diskette so we have to be content with just some results from simulations done on the bigger model.

The worksheet was used to derive the sales and contribution to profit calculations that appear in the appendix. It is available in case you would like to change some of the assumptions that were used. In particular, if you felt that the market size would be different or that it would be distributed differently across the fleet size segments, you could make the changes you felt were appropriate and compute new sales and contribution to profit values. You could also make different assumptions about costs for either Clark or its competitors. You could also change the prices, but you would have to think hard about whether that would change the share forecasts.

As simple as this spreadsheet is, it still provides a number of useful services, including the ability to correct the sample for biases you think are important, develop a number of tables comparing the contribution to profit for both Clark and its competitors in the same competitive situation, and so on. It is also an example of a very simple use of the personal computer that adds greatly to the value of research.

There is no menu associated with this model since it is so small. The cost estimates are off the screen to the right if you need them. As usual, the worksheet will be printed if you type [Alt]P.

Case Appendix: MSA Simulations

Index of Simulations

No Japanese Competition

	Clark's HOL Product Line	
Hyster's HOL Product Line	**Current**	**Current & Automatic**
Current	1	3
Current & Automatic	2	4

Japanese Competition

		Clark's HOL Product Line		
Hyster's HOL Product Line	**Current**	**Current & Low Price**	**Current & Automatic**	**Low Price & Automatic**
Current	5	9	13	17
Current & Low Price	6	10	14	18
Current & Automatic	7	11	15	19
Low Price & Automatic	8	12	16	20

MSA Simulations

UNIT SHARE FORECASTS

MSA #1	Large	Medium	Small	Units	Revenue	Share	Ctbn
Clark					$5.89	24.9%	$1.87
Current	20%	33%	35%	347	$5.89	24.9%	$1.87
Hyster					$9.38	39.6%	$2.99
Current	43%	33%	30%	549	$9.38	39.6%	$2.99
Yale	29%	25%	25%	386	$6.61	27.9%	$2.05
Madal	8%	8%	9%	113	$1.81	7.7%	$0.62
Total					$23.70		

MSA #2	Large	Medium	Small	Units	Revenue	Share	Ctbn
Clark					$5.39	22.7%	$1.71
Current	18%	31%	32%	317	$5.39	22.7%	$1.71
Hyster					$10.78	45.5%	$3.46
Current	31%	24%	13%	384	$6.57	27.7%	$2.09
Automatic	15%	15%	25%	224	$4.21	17.8%	$1.37
Yale	28%	23%	22%	366	$6.26	26.4%	$1.94
Madal	8%	7%	8%	109	$1.74	7.3%	$0.60
Total					$24.17		

MSA #3	Large	Medium	Small	Units	Revenue	Share	Ctbn
Clark					$7.89	33.3%	$2.50
Current	12%	19%	19%	202	$3.44	14.5%	$1.09
Automatic	14%	22%	24%	238	$4.45	18.8%	$1.40
Hyster					$8.51	35.9%	$2.71
Current	39%	30%	27%	498	$8.51	35.9%	$2.71
Yale	28%	22%	22%	363	$6.20	26.2%	$1.92
Madal	7%	7%	8%	99	$1.59	6.7%	$0.55
Total					$24.19		

MSA #4	Large	Medium	Small	Units	Revenue	Share	Ctbn
Clark					$6.91	29.2%	$2.19
Current	12%	19%	19%	202	$3.44	14.5%	$1.09
Automatic	10%	19%	20%	186	$3.47	14.6%	$1.09
Hyster					$10.14	42.8%	$3.25
Current	31%	23%	13%	381	$6.51	27.5%	$2.08
Automatic	13%	13%	21%	193	$3.63	15.3%	$1.18
Yale	27%	21%	20%	347	$5.94	25.1%	$1.84
Madal	7%	6%	7%	95	$1.51	6.4%	$0.52
Total					$24.50		

MSA Simulations (continued)

MSA #5	Large	Medium	Small	Units	Revenue	Share	Ctbn
Clark					$5.64	20.1%	$1.79
Current	15%	23%	27%	332	$5.64	20.1%	$1.79
Hyster					$9.13	32.6%	$2.91
Current	36%	27%	25%	534	$9.13	32.6%	$2.91
Yale	24%	20%	20%	376	$6.44	23.0%	$1.99
Madal	6%	7%	8%	113	$1.81	6.5%	$0.62
Japanese	19%	23%	20%	344	$4.99	17.8%	$1.93
Total					$28.02		

MSA #6	Large	Medium	Small	Units	Revenue	Share	Ctbn
Clark					$5.14	18.3%	$1.63
Current	13%	22%	25%	302	$5.14	18.3%	$1.63
Hyster					$10.11	36.1%	$3.73
Current	7%	4%	5%	99	$1.69	6.0%	$0.54
Low Price	39%	28%	26%	569	$8.43	30.1%	$3.19
Yale	21%	19%	18%	338	$5.78	20.6%	$1.79
Madal	5%	6%	7%	96	$1.54	5.5%	$0.53
Japanese	16%	21%	19%	305	$4.42	15.8%	$1.71
Total					$26.99		

MSA #7	Large	Medium	Small	Units	Revenue	Share	Ctbn
Clark					$5.24	18.7%	$1.66
Current	14%	22%	24%	308	$5.24	18.7%	$1.66
Hyster					$11.07	39.5%	$3.56
Current	26%	20%	10%	361	$6.17	22.0%	$1.97
Automatic	14%	13%	22%	261	$4.90	17.5%	$1.59
Yale	23%	18%	17%	348	$5.95	21.2%	$1.84
Madal	6%	6%	7%	105	$1.69	6.0%	$0.58
Japanese	18%	21%	19%	323	$4.68	16.7%	$1.81
Total					$28.62		

MSA #8	Large	Medium	Small	Units	Revenue	Share	Ctbn
Clark					$4.79	17.1%	$1.52
Current	12%	21%	23%	282	$4.79	17.1%	$1.52
Hyster					$11.45	40.9%	$4.10
Automatic	12%	12%	20%	231	$4.35	15.5%	$1.41
Low Price	34%	25%	17%	480	$7.10	25.3%	$2.69
Yale	21%	17%	16%	322	$5.51	19.7%	$1.71
Madal	5%	5%	6%	88	$1.41	5.0%	$0.49
Japanese	15%	20%	18%	288	$4.17	14.9%	$1.61
Total					$27.33		

MSA Simulations (continued)

MSA #9	Large	Medium	Small	Units	Revenue	Share	Ctbn
Clark					$6.56	24.2%	$2.36
Current	1%	4%	8%	54	$0.92	3.4%	$0.29
Low Price	20%	25%	24%	376	$5.64	20.8%	$2.07
Hyster					$8.69	32.0%	$2.77
Current	34%	26%	24%	508	$8.69	32.0%	$2.77
Yale	22%	19%	18%	347	$5.93	21.8%	$1.84
Madal	5%	6%	7%	96	$1.54	5.7%	$0.53
Japanese	17%	20%	18%	306	$4.44	16.3%	$1.71
Total					$27.16		

MSA #10	Large	Medium	Small	Units	Revenue	Share	Ctbn
Clark					$5.92	21.8%	$2.12
Current	1%	4%	8%	54	$0.92	3.4%	$0.29
Low Price	17%	23%	22%	333	$5.00	18.4%	$1.83
Hyster					$9.48	34.9%	$3.48
Current	7%	4%	5%	99	$1.69	6.2%	$0.54
Low Price	36%	26%	24%	526	$7.79	28.7%	$2.95
Yale	20%	18%	17%	321	$5.49	20.2%	$1.70
Madal	6%	6%	7%	105	$1.69	6.2%	$0.58
Japanese	14%	18%	17%	266	$3.86	14.2%	$1.49
Total					$26.43		

MSA #11	Large	Medium	Small	Units	Revenue	Share	Ctbn
Clark					$6.06	22.3%	$2.18
Current	1%	4%	7%	51	$0.87	3.2%	$0.27
Low Price	18%	24%	22%	347	$5.20	19.1%	$1.91
Hyster					$10.58	39.0%	$3.40
Current	25%	19%	10%	347	$5.93	21.8%	$1.89
Automatic	13%	12%	22%	247	$4.65	17.1%	$1.51
Yale	22%	17%	16%	331	$5.66	20.8%	$1.75
Madal	5%	5%	6%	88	$1.41	5.2%	$0.49
Japanese	16%	18%	17%	284	$4.12	15.2%	$1.59
Total					$27.84		

(continued)

MSA Simulations (continued)

MSA #12	Large	Medium	Small	Units	Revenue	Share	Ctbn
Clark					$5.61	20.6%	$2.01
Current	1%	4%	7%	51	$0.87	3.2%	$0.27
Low Price	16%	22%	21%	316	$4.74	17.5%	$1.74
Hyster					$10.94	40.3%	$3.91
Automatic	12%	12%	20%	231	$4.35	16.0%	$1.41
Low Price	32%	23%	15%	446	$6.60	24.3%	$2.50
Yale	20%	17%	15%	310	$5.29	19.5%	$1.64
Madal	5%	5%	6%	88	$1.41	5.2%	$0.49
Japanese	15%	17%	16%	267	$3.88	14.3%	$1.50
Total					$27.13		

MSA #13	Large	Medium	Small	Units	Revenue	Share	Ctbn
Clark					$8.02	27.6%	$2.54
Current	9%	13%	14%	188	$3.20	11.0%	$1.02
Automatic	12%	18%	20%	258	$4.83	16.6%	$1.52
Hyster					$8.34	28.6%	$2.66
Current	33%	25%	22%	488	$8.34	28.6%	$2.66
Yale	23%	18%	17%	348	$5.95	20.4%	$1.84
Madal	6%	6%	7%	105	$1.69	5.8%	$0.58
Japanese	18%	20%	29%	352	$5.11	17.6%	$1.97
Total					$29.11		

MSA #14	Large	Medium	Small	Units	Revenue	Share	Ctbn
Clark					$7.40	25.4%	$2.34
Current	8%	12%	13%	171	$2.91	10.0%	$0.92
Automatic	10%	18%	20%	240	$4.49	15.4%	$1.42
Hyster					$9.18	33.2%	$3.39
Current	6%	3%	4%	82	$1.40	4.8%	$0.45
Low Price	36%	26%	24%	526	$7.79	28.2%	$2.95
Yale	20%	17%	20%	327	$5.58	19.2%	$1.73
Madal	5%	5%	6%	88	$1.41	4.9%	$0.49
Japanese	15%	19%	17%	280	$4.06	13.9%	$1.57
Total					$27.63		

(continued)

MSA Simulations (continued)

MSA #15	Large	Medium	Small	Units	Revenue	Share	Ctbn
Clark					$7.10	24.6%	$2.25
Current	9%	13%	13%	185	$3.14	10.8%	$1.00
Automatic	14%	9%	16%	212	$3.96	1370.0%	$1.25
Hyster					$10.12	34.8%	$3.25
Current	26%	19%	10%	356	$6.09	20.9%	$1.94
Automatic	11%	11%	19%	214	$4.03	13.8%	$1.31
Yale	22%	17%	16%	331	$5.66	19.4%	$1.75
Madal	6%	5%	6%	98	$1.56	5.4%	$0.54
Japanese	17%	19%	18%	301	$4.37	15.0%	$1.69
Total					$28.81		

MSA #16	Large	Medium	Small	Units	Revenue	Share	Ctbn
Clark					$6.87	23.6%	$2.17
Current	8%	12%	13%	171	$2.91	10.0%	$0.92
Automatic	9%	16%	17%	212	$3.96	13.6%	$1.25
Hyster					$10.63	36.5%	$3.82
Automatic	10%	10%	17%	194	$3.64	12.5%	$1.18
Low Price	34%	24%	16%	472	$6.98	24.0%	$2.64
Yale	20%	16%	15%	305	$5.22	17.9%	$1.62
Madal	5%	5%	6%	88	$1.41	5.0%	$0.49
Japanese	15%	18%	17%	275	$3.99	13.7%	$1.54
Total					$28.11		

MSA #17	Large	Medium	Small	Units	Revenue	Share	Ctbn
Clark					$8.47	30.3%	$2.90
Automatic	9%	16%	19%	219	$4.09	14.6%	$1.29
Low Price	16%	19%	18%	292	$4.38	15.7%	$1.61
Hyster					$8.11	29.0%	$2.58
Current	32%	24%	22%	474	$8.11	29.0%	$2.58
Yale	22%	17%	17%	335	$5.72	20.5%	$1.77
Madal	5%	6%	7%	96	$1.54	5.5%	$0.53
Japanese	16%	18%	17%	284	$4.12	14.7%	$1.59
Total					$27.96		

(continued)

MSA Simulations (continued)

```
MSA #18     Large Medium  Small  Units Revenue Share   Ctbn
  Clark                                 $7.61   27.2% $2.60
 *Automatic    7%    16%    18%    197  $3.68   13.2% $1.16
  Low Price   14%    17%    17%    262  $3.93   14.0% $1.44

  Hyster                                $8.75   31.3% $3.23
  Current      6%     3%     4%     82  $1.40    5.0% $0.45
  Low Price   34%    25%    22%    497  $7.35   26.3% $2.78

  Yale        20%    16%    15%    305  $5.22   18.7% $1.62
  Madal        5%     5%     6%     88  $1.41    5.1% $0.49
  Japanese    14%    17%    16%    258  $3.75   13.4% $1.45
  Total                                $26.73

MSA #19     Large Medium  Small  Units Revenue Share   Ctbn
  Clark                                 $7.40   26.5% $2.55
  Automatic    6%    14%    16%    172  $3.22   11.5% $1.01
  Low Price   15%    18%    18%    279  $4.18   15.0% $1.53

  Hyster                                $9.83   35.1% $3.15
  Current     25%    18%     9%    339  $5.80   20.7% $1.85
  Automatic   11%    11%    19%    214  $4.03   14.4% $1.31

  Yale        21%    16%    15%    314  $5.37   19.2% $1.66
  Madal        5%     5%     6%     88  $1.41    5.1% $0.49
  Japanese    16%    17%    16%    277  $4.01   14.3% $1.55
  Total                                $28.02

MSA #20     Large Medium  Small  Units Revenue Share   Ctbn
  Clark                                 $7.01   25.1% $2.40
  Automatic    6%    14%    16%    172  $3.22   11.5% $1.01
  Low Price   13%    17%    17%    253  $3.79   13.6% $1.39

  Hyster                               $10.24   36.6% $3.68
  Automatic   10%    10%    17%    194  $3.64   13.0% $1.18
  Low Price   32%    23%    15%    446  $6.60   23.6% $2.50

  Yale        20%    16%    14%    302  $5.16   18.4% $1.60
  Madal        5%     5%     5%     85  $1.36    4.9% $0.47
  Japanese    14%    16%    16%    254  $3.68   13.2% $1.42
  Total                                $27.44
```

CASE: Clark Equipment III

This small case describes how the MSA model was used to develop a decision model to determine a five-year plan in which price, product line, and competitive response were all considered. The resulting decision model uses separate demand functions for different competitive situations. Pro forma business planning would have been far too tedious using the consultant's model.

David Richards felt that once the factor levels for a particular forklift truck model had been determined, they would probably remain unchanged for a time. The competitive situation in the next few years, however, would probably be a dynamic one in which Clark and its major competitors could be expected to introduce new models, for which timing and price would depend heavily on competitive actions. Richards could conceive of dozens of reasonable new-model introduction scenarios, even if only product line, price, and competitive environment were to be considered. The MSA model, which featured full analysis of all product factor levels, proved to be too cumbersome for scenario analysis, so a modification of it was designed for a personal computer.

Developing the MSA Model for Personal Computers

The first step in modifying the MSA model for use on a personal computer was to decide which factors could remain fixed at one level during scenario analysis and which would need to be varied. Richards was reasonably comfortable with the design of the current Clark standard transmission model, the Clark automatic transmission model, and a low-priced Clark model to compete with a Japanese forklift truck as described in Clark II. His major remaining uncertainties were:

1. Which HOL models to offer

2. When to introduce new models and/or drop old ones

3. How to price the HOL product line

4. The effect of competitive product lines and prices on Clark's profitability

5. The interaction of competitors' strategies

Although there were still many alternatives, restricting attention to these issues vastly decreased the information required from the MSA model. In a given competitive environment, only price needed to be varied, and the MSA model could be used to develop market-share forecasts from which a demand function for each Clark model in each competitive environment could be computed. Using these demand functions, scenario analysis could be performed by designating the prices of the forklift truck models offered by Clark and its competitors each year of the planning period and computing the resulting market shares.

The first step in developing the demand functions was to compute a utility value for each respondent for each lift truck to be considered in the analysis. Since every variable except price—performance, service level, reliability, and so on—would not change, the composite utility of these factors for a given respondent would be a single, constant value. The total utility for a brand could then be computed by multiplying this value by the price utility.

The next step was to define the product lines and competitive environments that might be en-

This case was prepared by Darral G. Clarke.

Copyright (©) 1983 By the President and Fellows of Harvard College Harvard Business School case 9-584-055.

Exhibit 4.76   Prices Used for Market Share Simulation

	Clark	Hyster	Japanese	Yale	Madal
Current	$17,000	$17,100		$17,100	$16,000
Automatic	$18,700	$18,800			
Low priced	$15,000	$14,800	$14,500		

Note: Prices are drawn from a uniform distribution ± 10% centered on the listed prices from Clark Equipment II.

countered. The four product line alternatives and five competitive environments used in Clark II define 20 possible market situations, 18 of which are reasonable by Richards's criteria.

Market Share Simulation.   The market share simulation was performed in each reasonable competitive situation* as follows:

1. Generate prices for each forklift truck model (both Clark and competitors) by choosing a price at random within +10% of the prices listed in Exhibit 4.76.

2. Using the prices generated in step 1, the total utility for each forklift truck is computed for each survey respondent and the market share is computed as was done in Clark I. This is repeated 100 times in each competitive situation.

Demand Function Estimation.   A multiple regression analysis was then performed for each Clark forklift truck that expressed its market share as a function of its price relative to the prices of other lift trucks in the market. The form of the market share function is a constant elasticity model in relative price. For example, in the current market:

Share = 0.17(Clark Price/Hyster Price)$^{-2.72}$

This simple equation shows that if in the current market Clark and Hyster were the same price, the current Clark forklift truck would have a 17% market share. For each 1% the ratio of Clark's price to Hys-

ter's could be decreased, Clark's share would increase by 2.72%.*

In the other competitive situations the market share response models are more complicated as a result of having more than one forklift truck in Clark's product line and the more extensive list of competitors' products. The price of a particular Clark truck needs to be considered in relation to the other Clark trucks as well as to competitors' trucks. The response model for each Clark forklift truck in each competitive situation was guided by the following conceptual framework:

1. The effect of the price of the other Clark forklift truck was assumed to be the same as the effect of competitors' lift trucks of the same type.

2. Yale and Madal were assumed not to be interested in introducing other lift trucks in addition to their current offerings. Yale's price would continue to be the same as Hyster's. Madal's price would not change.

3. The prices of lift trucks of the same type (low-priced, current, automatic) were averaged, but each type was separately represented.

The price elasticities for each Clark forklift truck in the various competitive situations are listed in Exhibit 4.77. The explanatory power of the regressions from which these elasticities were abstracted was generally quite high—more than 80% of the observed variance in forecast market share was explained. These elasticities were then incorporated into a 1-2-3 personal computer spreadsheet model designed to perform scenario analysis.

---

* This factor is the market share elasticity with respect to the price ratio and is equal to the exponent of the price ratio.

* Reasonable competitive situations were those that Richards would want to consider. Those chosen are listed in Exhibit 4.78.

Exhibit 4.77   Price Elasticities for Clark Forklift Trucks

	Competitive Environment	Product Line	Other Clark Current	Low	Auto	Competition Current	Low	Auto	Intercept
Current	1	1				−2.72			−1.77
Clark	1	3			−1.88	−3.51			−2.51
Model	2	1				−2.67	−0.42		−2.02
	2	2		−0.754		−2.40	−0.544		−2.22
	2	3			−1.62	−2.75	−0.60		−2.64
	3	1				−3.41		−1.59	−2.18
	3	3			−2.16 *	−3.62		−2.16*	−2.61
	4	1				−2.84	−0.37	−1.22	−2.35
	4	2		−1.12		−3.08	−0.43	−0.90	−2.52
	4	3			−1.79 *	−2.65	−0.55	−1.79*	−2.73
	5	1				−2.20	−0.75	−0.80	−2.59
	5	2				−2.54	−1.17	−1.07	−2.69
	5	3			−1.37 *	−2.07	−1.32	−1.37*	−2.80
Clark	1	4			−0.922	−1.73			−2.36
Low-Priced	2	2	−2.06*			−2.06*	−1.33		−2.16
Model	2	4			−1.55	−1.40	−1.02		−2.65
	3	4			−1.69 *	−0.95		−1.69*	−2.47
	4	2	−1.82*			−1.82*	−1.01	−0.61	−2.30
	4	4			−1.69 *	−0.86	−1.27	−1.69*	−2.64
	5	2	−1.51*			−1.51*	−4.64	−0.13	−2.56
	5	4			−0.54 *	−0.37	−1.18	−0.54*	−2.62
Clark	1	3	−1.84*			−1.84*			−1.18
Automatic	1	4		−0.64		−0.96			−1.24
Model	2	3	−1.77*			−1.77*	−0.07		−1.22
	2	4		−0.65		−0.85	−0.60		−1.28
	3	3	−1.75*			−1.75*		−0.01	−1.23
	3	4		−0.70		−0.91		−0.06	−1.27
	4	3	−1.65*			−1.65*	−0.20		−1.27
	4	4		−0.47		−0.99	−0.50	−0.08	−1.38
	5	3		NS		−1.16	−0.86	−0.20	−1.67
	5	4				−0.60	−0.42	−0.14	−1.64

*Clark aggregated with competitors.
NS = not significant.

Preparation Questions

1. How were the response functions derived from simulation runs of the original research model?

2. Develop a five-year plan for Clark.

3. How does the Clark III model differ from the John Morton MSA model described in Clark I? What accounts for the differences?

4. What are the product, market, and marketing strategy characteristics that would lead you to favor trade-off analysis based concept testing over an ASSESSOR pre–test market?

Clark Equipment III Spreadsheet

The Clark Equipment III decision model is intended to allow you to develop a five-year plan in which the HOLS product line, pricing, and competitive environment are considered. The spreadsheet is obtained through the main diskette menu by choosing first **chpt__4** and **clark__3**. Using the spreadsheet requires that market volume, competitive environment, prices, and costs be specified for each year. Once this has been done, the decision model chooses the appropriate response function from Exhibit 4.77, and uses it to compute market share, revenue, and contribution to profit for each Clark forklift truck.

When the spreadsheet appears on the screen, you will see the strategy summary (see Exhibit 4.78), accompanied by the main Clark III spreadsheet menu. The menu choices are *strategy* and *prices, calculate, marketing, financial,* and *quit.* Only the first two choices (*strategy* and *prices*) are used to enter data into the decision model. *Do not enter data into the marketing or financial portions of the spreadsheet,* because you can enter numbers on top of formulas and lose them. The menu choices are quite clear:

Strategy. Use the strategy screen to enter the market size, Clark product line, and competitive environment according to the codes at the bottom of the screen. See Exhibit 4.78. You will encounter a second menu that asks if you wish to *modify* or *print* the strategy screen. *Quit* takes you back to the main menu.

Prices. There are five price screens (see Exhibit

Exhibit 4.78   Clark Equipment III Strategy Summary

	YEAR 1	YEAR 2	YEAR 3	YEAR 4	YEAR 5
Market Volume	1400	1500	1700	1900	2100
Clark product policy*	1	3	3	4	4
Competitive environment**	1	3	4	4	5

* 1-current model only 2-current and low price model 3-current and automatic model 4-low price and automatic model

** 1-Hyster current model 2-Hyster current and Japanese 3-Hyster current and Hyster automatic 4-Hyster current, Hyster automatic and Japanese 5-Hyster low price, Hyster automatic and Japanese

Exhibit 4.79   Clark Equipment III Costs Screen

```
                      Product Prices and Costs     Year 1
                      ***********************************

          Clark Cur   Clark Low    Clark Auto
          ---------   ---------    ----------
Price      $17,000     $15,500      $18,700
Cost       $11,613      $9,475      $12,800

          Hys Cur     Hys Auto     Hys Low      Japan        Yale
          ---------   ---------    ---------    ---------    ---------
Price      $17,100     $18,800      $15,600     $14,500      $17,100
```

Exhibit 4.80   Clark Equipment III Planning Summary

	Year 1	Year 2	Year 3	Year 4	Year 5
Market vol	1,400	1,500	1,700	1,900	2,100
CLARK CUR *					
Price	$17,000	$17,000	$17,000	NA	NA
Mkt share	17.307%	9.282%	7.233%	0.000%	0.000%
Volume	242	139	123	0	0
Sales	$4,119,117	$2,366,821	$2,090,250	NA	NA
CLARK LOW *					
Price	NA	NA	NA	$15,500	$15,500
Mkt share	0.000%	0.000%	0.000%	9.842%	8.081%
Volume	0	0	0	187	170
Sales	NA	NA	NA	$2,898,458	$2,630,441
CLARK AUTO *					
Price	NA	$18,700	$18,700	$18,700	$18,700
Mkt share	0.000%	24.911%	22.954%	18.572%	16.534%
Volume	0	374	390	353	347
Sales	NA	$6,987,479	$7,297,070	$6,598,582	$6,492,860
1					

4.79), one for each year. You are first asked to supply the year, and then you encounter the *modify, print,* or *quit* menu. To change the prices and costs, choose *modify* and make the changes desired. [Enter] will raise the menu again. Choose *quit* to return to the main menu.

Calculate. This recalculates the spreadsheet with the data currently entered. Be sure your scenario is correctly defined before you choose this, because the calculations take a few minutes. Pressing [F9]

will not correctly recalculate this spreadsheet.

Marketing. The marketing summary provides market share, volume, and revenue forecasts for your strategy (see Exhibit 4.80). Your choices here are *scan* (no modification), *print*, and *quit*.

Financial. The financial summary provides forecasts of unit sales, revenue, costs, contribution to profit, and return on sales (see Exhibit 4.81). Menu choices are the same as for *marketing*.

Exhibit 4.81   Clark Equipment III Financial Summary

	Year 1	Year 2	Year 3	Year 4	Year 5
Market vol	1,400	1,500	1,700	1,900	2,100
CLARK CUR *					
Unit sales	242	139	123	0	0
Sales	$4,119,117	$2,366,821	$2,090,250	$0	$0
Cost	$2,813,841	$1,616,817	$1,427,886	$0	$0
Contribution	$1,305,275	$750,004	$662,363	$0	$0
ROS	31.69%	31.69%	31.69%	ERR	ERR
CLARK LOW *					
Unit sales	0	0	0	187	170
Sales	$0	$0	$0	$2,898,458	$2,630,441
Cost	$0	$0	$0	$1,771,799	$1,607,963
Contribution	$0	$0	$0	$1,126,659	$1,022,478
ROS	ERR	ERR	ERR	38.87%	38.87%
CLARK AUTO *					
Unit sales	0	374	390	353	347
Sales	$0	$6,987,479	$7,297,070	$6,598,582	$6,492,860
Cost	$0	$4,782,873	$4,994,786	$4,516,676	$4,444,310
Contribution	$0	$2,204,606	$2,302,284	$2,081,906	$2,048,549
ROS	ERR	31.55%	31.55%	31.55%	31.55%
TOTALS BY YEAR					
Sales	$4,119,117	$9,354,300	$9,387,320	$9,497,040	$9,123,300
Cost	$2,813,841	$6,399,691	$6,422,673	$6,288,476	$6,052,273
Contribution	$1,305,275	$2,954,610	$2,964,647	$3,208,564	$3,071,027
ROS	31.69%	31.59%	31.58%	33.78%	33.66%

TOTALS BY MODEL	CLARK CUR	CLARK LOW	CLARK AUTO	TOTAL
Unit sales	504	357	1,464	2,325
Sales	$8,576,188	5,528,898	27,375,991	41,481,077
Cost	$5,858,545	3,379,762	18,738,646	27,976,953
Contribution	$2,717,642	2,149,136	8,637,345	13,504,123
ROS	31.69%	38.87%	31.55%	32.55%

References and Background Readings

Cattin, Phillipe, and Dick R.Wittink. "Commercial Use of Conjoint Analysis: A Survey." Stanford University working paper #596, May 1981.

Green, Paul, and Yoram Wind. "New Way to Measure Consumer's Judgments." *Harvard Business Review*, July–August 1975, pp.107–117

Johnson, Richard M. "Trade-off Analysis of Consumer Values." *Journal of Marketing Research*, Vol.XI (May 1974), pp.121–27.

——————. "Trade-off Analysis: The First Ten Years." Address to the American Marketing Association, Atlanta, June 1980.

MacBride, J. N., and R. M. Johnson. "Respondent Reaction to Computer-Interactive Interviewing Techniques." Unpublished document of the John Morton Company.

Robinson, Patrick J. "Comparison of Pre–Test Market New Product Forecasting Models." in Wind, Mahajan, and Cardozo (eds.), *New Product Forecasting*. Lexington, MA: Lexington Books, 1981, pp.181–204.

Silk, Alvin J., and Glen L. Urban. "Pre–Test Market Evaluation of New Packaged Goods: A Model and Measurement Methodology." *Journal of Marketing Research*, Vol.15, No. 2 (May 1978), pp.171–191.

Urban, Glen L. "SPRINTER Mod III: A Model for the Analysis of New Frequently Purchased Consumer Products." *Operations Research*, Vol. 18, No. 5 (September–October 1970), pp. 805–853.

Urban, Glen L., and John R. Hauser. *Design and Marketing of New Products*. Englewood cliffs, NJ: Prentice-Hall, 1980.

Urban, Glen L., and Gerald M. Katz. "Pre–Test Market Models: Validation and Managerial Implications." *Journal of Marketing Research*, Vol.20, No. 3, (August 1983), pp. 221–234.

Urban, Glen L., Gerald M. Katz, Thomas E. Hatch, and Alvin J. Silk. "The ASSESSOR Pre–Test Market Evaluation System." *Interfaces*, Vol. 13, No. 6 (December 1983), pp.38–39.

Wind, Yoram, Vijay Mahajan, and Richard M. Cardozo, eds. *New Product Forecasting*. Lexington, MA: Lexington Books, 1981.

5

Test Marketing

(continued)

Because the introduction of a new product involves a substantial investment of time, human resources, and money, most companies have instituted a staged new product development process similar to the one introduced in Chapter 2. In this chapter we will deal with test marketing—the last research step before the product is actually introduced and the company's last chance to make sure that the new product and its marketing program are properly conceived. Even if the new product introduction takes the form of a limited geographic rollout, as opposed to a simultaneous national introduction, the commitment of resources and company prestige is so substantial that research designed to reduce the risk of this final step is commonly undertaken.

Test marketing is probably the most expensive research undertaken for consumer products, and considerable study and research often precedes a commitment to this final stage, usually in the form of more limited testing as we described in chapter 4.

Test marketing for consumer products is quite different from that done for industrial products. The high cost of developing prototype industrial products usually limits test marketing activities to a limited geographic rollout preceded by some form of concept testing such as that described in Chapter 4. Test marketing for frequently purchased, low-priced consumer products consists of a small-scale execution of all, or of some significant part, of a marketing program in a limited geographic area. The test marketing of consumer products has evolved over the last few years into a very sophisticated and powerful tool for advanced marketing analysis. This chapter deals with the managerial use of test marketing for low-priced consumer products.

New Product Test Markets

According to the data that we considered in Chapter 2, the introduction of a new, low-priced consumer product in the early 1980s required an average investment of more than $5 million and had less than a 20% chance of success.

A further risk to the company is that the cost of a new product failure extends far beyond the money and the time invested. For example, a company that had only one successful new product for every five products it brought to market would soon be unable to interest distribution channels in carrying its new products—the competition for supermarket shelf space is very intense because there are more than five products available for every space. If distributors lose confidence in the company's ability to design and market new products, the company will be unable to gain distribution for future new products. Considering what is at stake, it is not surprising that test marketing is so widely utilized.

Test markets provide a more broadly based observation of how a marketing program will work than can be obtained through the pre–test market testing procedures discussed in the previous chapter. Because a broader geographic area may be considered, the conditions of the test market more closely resemble those that will be encountered in the introduction itself, and the increase in the number of customers involved usually dictates that the level of detail in the data gathered is sharply reduced from that found in earlier market tests. Also inherent in the concept of a test market is the close observation of those marketing program factors and environmental conditions that are considered to be critical in forecasting the new product's performance in the marketplace. The investment of more than a million dollars for a test market, however, is no guarantee that useful results or an accurate forecast will occur. A test market is not a uniform, generic process appropriate for any situation. The diverse nature of the market situations that need to be evaluated requires a test that is custom designed to accomplish management's objectives, and the decision maker must be involved in the test's design.

Test markets are generally more successful if relatively few alternatives are tested. It is difficult to isolate the effects of many alternative marketing mix elements because market conditions cannot be completely controlled and it's hard to obtain data that directly measure the effect of specific factors. Another problem with testing a number of alternatives is that it's difficult to find several markets with similar characteristics in which to make controlled comparisons. Thus every effort should be made to reduce the number of factors that require measurement in the test market.

One of the prime benefits of pre–test market testing is that it can reduce the number of factors about which uncertainty remains. In particular, questions about consumer perception and acceptance of a new product formulation should be resolved prior to the test market. Consumer product test marketing is much more effective in estimating the level of product acceptance (market share or sales per capita) than it is in determining which product formulation will be more successful, or which of a number of product positions will find the best market acceptance.

Test marketing is also used to determine the most effective form or level of some marketing activity such as advertising expenditure and/or copy, price, promotion, or package design, etc. Test markets vary considerably depending on the marketing variables being tested, the importance of the decision, the degree of experimentation necessary, and the kinds of data gathered.

The ideal test market—one that provides the opportunity to see how the marketing program will work in the marketplace—is seldom achieved in practice because of the constraints imposed on the test market design by managerial, financial, and research considerations. The design of an effective test market requires balancing the managerial and financial considerations against research requirements in order to produce the best feasible research design. The manager who must interpret test market results must be sensitive to the implications of the compromises and choices that were made at the deisgn stage, because these compromises affect both the quality of the data generated during the test market and the conclusions that can safely be inferred from them.

The best rules of thumb for determining the scope of a test market are that: (1) if there is any other way to answer a question, use it, and (2) one should feel confident in all but one or two elements in the marketing plan before a test market is undertaken.

The cases in this chapter provide an interesting history of test market development over the last twenty years as well as an intensive look at test market data and analysis. At the time each case was written, the test marketing methodologies used were typical of the current state of the art. Each successive case uses a more recent test market methodology, the development of which was motivated by the desire to improve the accuracy of test markets and strengthen the conclusions that could be drawn from them. Studying the cases in their historical order provides an unusual opportunity to develop an understanding of how to evaluate the quality, information content, and bias of test market data as well as an appreciation for the importance of the control of extraneous factors in the test market design.

Another common thread running through the chapter is the focus on the use of marketing research in the management of advertising. The cases in this chapter deal with experimental data, and the two advertising cases in the next chapter provide examples of dealing with cross-sectional data and econometric time series data; together, they provide an extensive look at the opportunities and limitations provided by most of the major types of data available to managers for advertising analysis.

Managerial Test Market Considerations

The most important managerial consideration in the design of a test market is to carefully assess what needs to be learned. This seems obvious, but the discussion of the test market in the CableShop case should have made it clear that the necessary market research data are unlikely to be obtained by good luck in the absence of deliberate premeditation. In a test market it is even more important than at earlier stages to specify precisely what issues are unresolved, what information needs to be obtained to resolve them, and how the information will be used to make a decision. Only a few factors can be tested, and the time and expense involved make it unlikely that a second test market can be undertaken to correct the mistakes and omissions of the first. Before an element of the marketing mix is investigated in a test market, it should be determined what marketing research information is necessary, how it will affect the decision, and whether the information can be obtained in some other, less expensive way.

The most important contribution that a manager can make to the design of a successful test market is a careful analysis of the factors that will affect the marketing strategy for the new product. If this analysis results in a preliminary decision model, a number of useful tasks can be performed. A preliminary economic analysis should reveal which marketing strategies are viable, and a complete specification of marketing strategy alternatives can then be identified. Once that has been done, a sensitivity analysis should be run to determine which are the most important factors and what levels of performance will affect the final decision of whether to go to product rollout and what marketing strategy to use if it is rolled out. If sensitivity analysis is done before the test market is designed, it can be expected to reduce the number of variables that must be considered, define the critical performance levels that must be attained, and provide a framework for interpreting test market results.

Time is another critical factor that is frequently in conflict with the ideal research design. A new product concept that arrives at the test market stage has had the support of a dedicated and enthusiastic manager who pushed it through the prior steps of the new product development process. The twelve- to eighteen-month test markets that are usually suggested by marketing researchers to determine consumer acceptance of the new product and the effectiveness of the marketing program seem unreasonably long to a manager who wants the advantage of being first in the market. The manager's fears are real and need to be considered, but the ability to forecast market performance is severely compromised when it is based on early results alone. In general, market researchers will always want more time for the test market than managers will be willing to tolerate. Balancing these two perfectly valid but conflicting needs is one of the most important and critical decisions made in utilizing marketing research.

The need for market performance forecasts is the impetus for test markets, but counterbalancing this opportunity is the reality that the test market exposes carefully guarded thinking and planning to the competition as well as to prospective consumers. One of the major reasons that pre–test market testing procedures have been widely accepted is the fear of tipping one's hand to the competition through a larger test market.

One final managerial consideration is the cost of doing a test market. Urban and Hauser (1980) estimated the cost of a twelve-month test market in four cities to be more than one million dollars in 1981. Such a test market design would not support more than two experimental levels of a marketing variable in a sound statistical design. The manager trying to design the marketing program for a new product or improving that of an established product seldom has only one variable of interest with only two alternative levels. The marketing researcher will usually want more cities and fewer alternatives to evaluate than the manager will be willing to support. The manager's budget will seldom accommodate a test market design that investigates all of the important managerial issues in a statistically sound test market design that satisfies the market researcher. Another level of compromise will be required and the choices made will strongly affect the quality and reliability of the test market results.

Test Market Research Considerations

There are many technical issues involved in the design, execution, analysis, and interpretation of test markets, and the professional literature on these subjects is extensive. The typical manager cannot hope to find the time to become expert in this area, but with careful attention to detail and personal involvement during design and analysis, a thoughtful manager can adequately evaluate the opportunities and problems inherent in a test market design, be assured that the necessary information will be obtained, comprehend how the results will be used, and have a comfortable understanding of the implications of those results. The previous section noted the importance of sound, intuitive managerial analysis augmented with a preliminary economic analysis as a means of identifying the critical issues to be addressed in a test market. Once the important managerial issues have been identified, they must be operationalized—given precise, quantitative definitions that can be measured—and the test market must be explicitly defined so that the required measurements can be made.

It is critically important for the manager to be involved in the operationalization of the issues in the design of the test market; otherwise, it is very likely that the manager's definitions will not be consistant with the operational definitions used in the test market execution. This leads to two unfavorable consequences: either the research will not directly address the issues identified by the manager, and the test market results are unlikely to be useful; or the manager's interpretation of the results will be based on his or her own definitions rather than those actually used, and the results may be misleading.

The operationalization of the managerial issues in the test market requires that a number of specific choices must be made, such as where the test will take place, how long it will last, and what marketing strategy will be tested; the manager must also be concerned with three major research issues: control, the information content of the data, and the mathematical models that will be used to interpret the data. Numerous technical details are involved, but a manager who knows what to look for, pays attention to detail, uses common sense, and gets a little technical assistance from the researchers can have an adequate understanding of the limitations and value of the information provided by the test market.

Control Considerations in Test Marketing

Sales and market share are influenced by a number of different factors, so it is necessary to control the conditions in the test market as much as possible in order to be sure that the sales and market share movement one sees in the test market are due to the factors that are being tested. Two design factors provide control in a test market: (1) physical control in the design of the test market, and (2) statistical control in the analysis of the data to eliminate the mathematical effects of those factors that have been physically controlled.

A critically important consideration in the analysis of the cases in this chapter is to determine what is and what is not physically and statistically controlled in each situation. This is more difficult than it seems at first, but the difficulty is not technical in nature but rather requires consideration of the details of the test market procedures and what effect they have on the data that are generated. In each of the cases there are important factors that affect the outcome of the test market that are uncontrolled. The effort to control these factors provides the motivation behind much of the development in test market technology over the last decade.

Physical Control

Physical control refers to the way in which the test market is physically structured and executed: availability of the product, its shelf position in test stores, the assurance that the experimental treatments occur as they are planned (stores that should offer certain prices at certain times really do, advertisements are aired as planned, and so on), and that measurements are made as they were designed to be made. Achieving physical control of the test market conditions lies both in the design of the test market itself and in the care with which plans are executed and conditions monitored. Careful attention to operational details can help the manager assess the level of physical control in the test market and its effect on the quality of the resulting data.

Physical control is also highly dependent on technology, particularly in the delivery of advertising and in the measurement of advertising response. The development of new instruments to manipulate and measure has invariably led to increases in both theoretical knowledge and immediate practical applications. Recent advances in our ability to manipulate advertising, price, and other marketing mix variables and to measure consumer response to them promises to be as important for the development of a better understanding of the effects of advertising, promotion, and pricing as were the development of the telescope in astronomy and the microscope in medicine.

The test market described in the UDIA case is typical of state-of-the-art test market methodology used to measure the effects of advertising up until the early 1970s, and in fact the statistical design in this test market is more sophisticated than many of the traditional test markets that are still run today. The design of the UDIA test market recognizes the existence of a number of factors affecting sales other than those that are being tested and tries to eliminate their effects from the study. Most test markets involving the auditing of store-level data in test cities for a period of time do not include a statistical design that tries to eliminate the effects of other factors. The product is placed in the stores for a period of time, advertising is run over local stations, and sales are audited in a number of stores. The marketing program is not varied and only infrequently are category sales monitored in the test cities prior to or after the test, nor are category sales monitored in other cities as a control for the effects of other non-manipulated variables. There are three reasons that may account for not doing this. First, the manager may not understand the need for control in test markets; second, cost considerations; third, the manager may understand the need for control in the test market but may have found it impossible to attain in earlier test markets.

The important developments in computer and communication technology in the last decade have enabled researchers to more closely approach the ideal test market design. The advent of cable television has made it possible to develop test markets in cities using *split-cable television*. In these test markets two samples of households have their TVs permanently connected to one of two cables. This permits the exposure of different households in the same city to different advertising copy or different levels of advertising weight. This provides better control because the differences in the environmental conditions faced by consumers in the control and test groups can be expected to be smaller than those that exist between cities. This test marketing methodology, which appears in the AdTel Ltd. case, is a direct response to problems such as those in the UDIA case.

In split-cable testing, advertising is custom-designed for the test and the consumer's TV is attached to the appropriate cable (consumers in each panel are expected to shop in the same stores); therefore, in the AdTel case, measurement of consumer response to advertising had to be measured at the individual consumer household level. This purchase information was obtained from "diaries" in which the consumer panelists reported their purchases by filling out forms by hand and submitting them to AdTel.

Although this test market methodology exerts a higher level of control than that in the UDIA test market design, there are still a number of important marketing factors that are not controlled, and there are problems with the physical design of the test market and the quality of the data collection process.

In the next case, the development of the BehaviorScan test marketing system by Information Resources Inc. (IRI) increased the level of physical control by applying new technologies in cable television and using electronic scanners and the uniform product code (UPC) to monitor sales at both the store and the consumer panelist level. Consumer households participating in BehaviorScan tests are individually targetable, rather than hard-wired to one half of a split-cable system as they are in the AdTel system. Thus panelists living next door to one another could be members of the same panel for one product and different panels for another, and the control and test groups could be custom designed for test markets for different products. Furthermore, the BehaviorScan system was capable (although not at the time of the G. D. Searle cases) of determining whether or not a panelist's TV had been tuned to the particular channel when a test commercial was aired.

Panelists in the BehaviorScan system are not required to fill out diaries by hand, since their purchases are recorded electronically through scanners as they purchase the products at the supermarket. Store-level data are also collected electronically from nearly every check stand in every supermarket in the test cities. On the average, more than 90 percent of the consumer product purchases in the test cities were collected. Although BehaviorScan is technologically superior to the earlier methods of test marketing, both AdTel and store audit test markets are still commonly done. There are advantages and disadvantages to each of these methods and, depending on the application, there may be reason to favor one of the older methods.

Exhibit 5.1   UDIA Latin Square Design

		City		
Time period	1	2	3	4
1	A	B	C	D
2	B	D	A	C
3	C	A	D	B
4	D	C	B	A

Statistical Control

Test market designers use statistical control to eliminate the effects of physically controlled factors on the measurement of the effects of the marketing mix factors being tested. There are a number of ways in which researchers design controls in their experiments. The simplest and most common form of statistical control in test markets is to compare the results in the *test group*—a group of cities or consumers in which the test conditions are manipulated—with the results in a *control group*—a similar group of cities or consumers in which the marketing conditions are *not* manipulated.

Assuming that the effects of the uncontrolled variables are the same in both the test and the control groups, the difference between the results measured in the two groups will be the effect of the marketing variables being manipulated. This is a very simple concept and there are many refinements that increase statistical control and therefore strengthen the conclusions that can be drawn from the test market.

Control Through Experimental Design

Statisticians have developed a number of experimental designs that are used to eliminate the effects of controlled factors from the analysis of the data. An example is the Latin Square design used in the UDIA case. The research problem addressed in this test market is that of determining which of four advertising levels will provide the highest return. The design of the test market features four matched pairs of similar cities. One of each pair serves as the control (receiving no advertising), and the other receives a different level of advertising in each of four time periods. A fifth time period (which we'll ignore in this discussion) duplicates the fourth period advertising level and is intended to permit the calculation of carryover effect. The schedule of advertising in the test cities is shown in Exhibit 5.1, where A,B,C,and D represent the various advertising levels.

The characteristics of this design are that in each time period each of the advertising levels occurs exactly once, and each city receives each level of advertising exactly once. Anything that happens in a particular time period across all four cities will affect each level of the advertising being tested. Unique city characteristics will affect the measurements of advertising effect at each advertising level. The purpose of this design is to make sure that differences between cities or common occurrences across cities will be averaged out, and it has theoretically accounted for the fact that the time periods are in different seasons, have a different number of shopping days, and so on.

Suppose that consumption differs across the country or that something unusual happens in one time period in just one test city? The Latin Square design couldn't prevent the effects of the geographic differences or that event from distorting the measurement of the effects of the advertising levels. That's why each test city has a control city that is geographically close and demographically similar. Hopefully, unusual events will also affect the nearby control city. The control cities are also intended to compensate for the lack of data before and after the test period.

The statistical theory upon which this test market design is based has been frequently used in the social and physical sciences and is a mainstay of experimentation in those fields. There are many variations of this general idea and an extensive set of statistical tests to interpret the data resulting from similarly designed experiments. A discussion of the statistical models for such analysis is beyond the scope of this book; here we're trying to provide an intuitive understanding of research and an opportunity to learn how to use it. The student interested in a more extensive treatment of these techniques should consider one of a number of excellent texts on analysis of variance, general linear models, or the design of experiments.

Quantifying the Effects of a Controlled Experiment

The importance of physical control in test marketing seems obvious, but quantifying it is very difficult. Poor physical control in a test market compromises the quality of the data in general and does not result in any consistent bias. If the wrong data are measured or the measurements are not correctly done, the data are not reliable. Clearly, errors of this type are so important that responsible research companies take careful steps to avoid them. The best managerial defense against poor physical control is to deal with well-established, reputable companies and to pay careful personal attention to the physical details of the test market procedure.

One research study that dramatizes the importance of physical control was done by Information Resources Inc. to determine the relative accuracy of hand-written panel data as compared to electronic scanner data. IRI found large differences between hand-written consumer purchase diaries and electronically collected purchase histories (see Exhibit 5.2). It appears that the ability of consumers to remember their purchases or take the time to accurately record them is questionable. These errors are at the individual purchase level and would not be reduced by the various other physical control factors in the test market.

The main purpose of physical and statistical controls is to prevent the influence of other, extraneous factors from biasing the measurement of the effects of

---

Exhibit 5.2   Claimed vs. Actual Product Purchase in IRI Study (% of households)

Product	Diaries	Scanner
Prego spaghetti	43%	18%
Betty Crocker cake mix	56%	23%
Heinz ketchup	75%*	23%†
Lean Cuisine	26%	9%
Minute Maid orange juice	45%	18%

*75% of households claimed to have purchased Heinz ketchup.
†23% of households actually bought Heinz ketchup, according to scanner records.

---

the variable being tested. The successful isolation of the effects of the test variables allows the researcher both to assert that the manipulated variables cause the observed results, and to quantify the magnitude of the effect. A further benefit of a carefully controlled experiment is that the statistical errors of estimation are reduced as statistical control is increased.

Another interesting experiment, done by Gerald Eskin of Information Resources Inc., quantified the reduction in statistical error that resulted from the various elements of the BehaviorScan test market system.

The market shares were computed for randomly chosen test and control groups for eight brands in six product categories during time periods in which the marketing strategies of the brands were stable. Since there was no difference in the marketing treatment in the control and the test groups, theoretically there should have been no difference in the market shares computed for them. A difference between the market shares observed in the test and control groups would then be an indication of the amount of statistical error present in the data.

Test and control groups were randomly chosen four times for each brand, for a total of 4 x 6 x 8 = 192 pairs of market shares. The average percent error—the standard error of the difference between the paired market shares divided by the average market share—was computed separately for each element of the BehaviorScan system. The results are listed in Exhibit 5.3. This table provides dramatic evidence of the importance of control in test markets, especially when one considers that the BehaviorScan system is the most sophisticated test market methodology available, and because of its high level of physical control, probably has less measurement error than other test market systems. To extrapolate these results to other test market systems, one should expect the average percent error to be larger than those shown for BehaviorScan and the reduction in error resulting from control elements less.

The importance of attaining a particular level of average percent error is dictated by the sensitivity of the success or failure of the decision to the size of the error. If the expected impact of the variable is less than 10%, then the test market should be very carefully controlled or the percent of error will be larger than that of the impact of the strategy being tested.

Exhibit 5.3   Average Percent Error In BehaviorScan Experiments

Source of Control	% Error	Cumulative Accuracy Gain
One market	17.7%	– –
Two markets	12.5%	29%
Base period	9.5%	44%
Matched panels	7.9%	55%
Covariate analysis	5.2%	71%

Definition, Aggregation, and Information Content of Data

The usefulness of empirical data is dependent upon the operational definition, method of collection, and level of aggregation used to produce them, and one of the most important analytical skills for any manager to develop is a sensitivity to the implications of these three factors on the information content of data. To demonstrate how subtle a factor like method of collection can be, consider the average error in a market share estimate from a BehaviorScan test market shown in Exhibit 5.3. Because we know that BehaviorScan tests are highly controlled, we can say that although a value of 25 percent may be labeled as the market share, we should think of it as 25 percent plus or minus 5 percent.

If the operational definition of a variable is not understood in the same way by the manager and the researcher, serious problems in the estimation of the relationships between variables can develop with the result that inappropriate decisions are made. Consider a very basic example, *price* and *sales*. Obviously the manager and researcher have to agree about what level in the distribution chain is being studied—factory, warehouse, or retail; but beyond this, there are other potential problems. Let's consider retail price and sales. The manager understands these two terms to be the price paid by consumers and the volume sold at retail. But when retail price and volume are operationalized in the generation of data, the manager's definitions are lost. The problem is that although individual consumers pay a specific price and purchase a specific quantity at a particular purchase occasion, these prices and purchase quantities vary from store to store and from day to day.

Some operational rules have to be made in order to summarize the data, and information will necessarily be lost as individual transactions are aggregated across outlets and time periods. How this collection and aggregation is accomplished is an integral part of the operational definition of the data and its information content.

The two most comprehensive sources for retail and wholesale market data are the Nielsen Retail Index and SAMI data respectively. Both of these companies have dedicated considerable technical expertise and financial resources to make their data as good as they can be for their clients' purposes at a cost that they are willing to pay. Nothing contained in this section is intended to be critical of the practices of these companies in producing their data. As in all research, choices have had to be made that affect the operational definition and information content of the data, so the consequences of the choices need to be understood.

Nielsen sales and price measurements for individual stores are determined by a bimonthly audit during which sales are computed from the beginning and ending inventories, and the store's purchases between audits. The price recorded by Nielsen is the price in effect on the day of the audit. Regional sales are obtained by cumulating individual store sales, and regional price is computed as the "sales-weighted average" of the price recorded at the individual store audits.

SAMI sales and price measurements are obtained from reports submitted by cooperating wholesalers and chains. Units shipped by an individual warehouse are obtained from invoices. Dollar sales for a given wholesaler are calculated either directly from the invoices, if available, or by multiplying the unit sales by the price on the last Friday of the four-week period. Unit shipments and the dollar value of shipments are then aggregated across stores. Average selling price is found by dividing the dollar value of shipments by the unit shipments. This also produces a sales-weighted average price. Two consequences result from these aggregation procedures:

1. Loss of precision—sales volume is not matched with the price at which it occurs.

2. Loss of variability—the amount of variation in the aggregated data is less than was present in the unaggregated data.

It is a well-known fact that aggregation reduces the variance of a random variable and that this applies directly to the aggregation of sales and price data across stores and time periods. Even if sales and price were precisely matched at the store level, an aggregated sales-weighted average across stores loses precision and variability.

The effects of the aggregation of data from the store level to the SAMI and Nielsen district levels are graphically illustrated by Clarke and Eubank [1983] in three related sets of data:

1. UPC scanner data from SAMI Kansas City scanner stores. Weekly data from stores that were aggregated across stores and time into four-week and eight-week periods as approximations to SAMI issues and bimonthly Nielsen periods respectively.

2. SAMI warehouse withdrawal data for the Kansas City region.

3. Nielsen retail audit data for the north central region (which includes Kansas City).

Although the time periods are the same, there is no reason to expect that the SAMI and Nielsen data should exactly mirror the scanner data, because of the

Exhibit 5.4   Store-Level Scanner Sales and Price Data

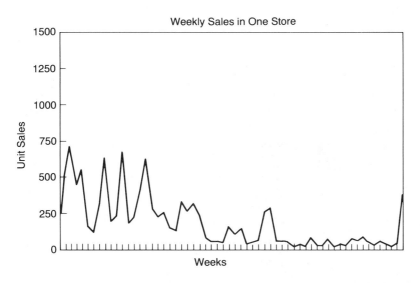

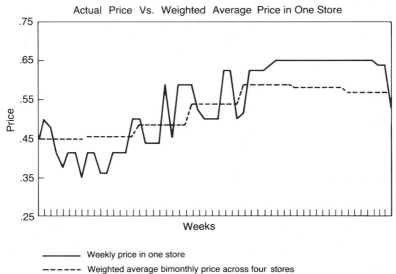

difference in geographic areas. It is also possible that the four scanner stores are atypical of what other stores were doing on any given day.

It is clear in Exhibits 5.4 to 5.6 that the data obtained by aggregating scanner data above the store-week level and the data obtained from the national services are subject to substantial loss of precision and variability.

Exhibit 5.5   Aggregated Scanner Sales and Price Data

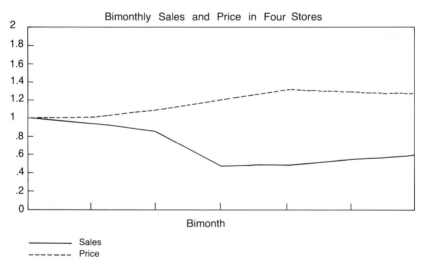

None of these data sets should be considered "true" and the others "false" just because they differ. What is important is that the information content of the various databases varies as does its appropriateness for specific managerial uses. Although the precision and variability of store-level scanner data were much greater than that of the Nielsen and SAMI audits, it should be noted that four stores may not be representative of the stores in the Kansas City area, let alone stores nationally. Nielsen data were collected from a carefully designed national

Exhibit 5.6   SAMI and Nielsen Data

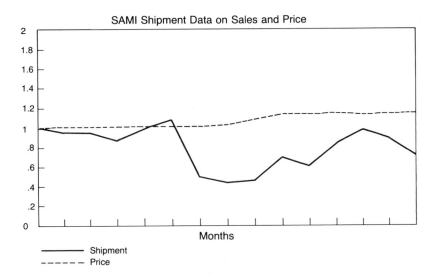

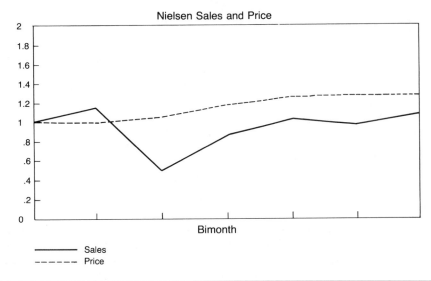

sample of 1,300 food outlets, while SAMI data were collected from 400 supermarket chains and wholesalers in 45 markets.

It should be obvious that if a manager wished to have a measure of market share in Kansas City, the Nielsen and SAMI data would be more reliable. However, if a manager wanted to study the effect of retail price on the consumer's purchase decision, the weekly scanner data provides much more detail.

The problem for the product manager is to determine his or her information needs and then use the appropriate data to meet those needs.

Methodologies Used in the Cases

The issue of control is one of the central themes in the chapter as well as the driving force behind much of the development in commercial test marketing services. A number of data control methods are illustrated in the cases:

The *United Dairy Industries Association* case reflects concern that the effect of advertising on sales will differ across the country, so cities from four different parts of the country are chosen for the test. It is also felt that the difference between cities will be too great to allow a single city to serve as an adequate control group for all of the test cities, so each test city is paired with a control city that is geographically and demographically similar to it.

The possible differences between cities has been eliminated in the *AdTel Ltd.* case by the use of split-cable television and diary panel data, allowing the direct study of the purchase behavior of households in the same city. The panelists whose television sets are attached to one cable are the test group, and the panelists in the same city on the other cable provide the control group. A further level of control is present in the form of panel purchase records prior to the start of the experiment. If a company desired, purchase records could also be gathered after the experiment.

The *Information Resources Inc.* and *G. D. Searle I* cases describe the BehaviorScan system, which provides the test marketer with the capability of matching experimental and control consumer panels for individual products within the same city. Marketing strategies that require different retail store treatments can also be provided across matched test and control cities. The individual panelist purchase histories are readily available and their purchase histories were gathered before any particular test market and will continue to be monitored after the test market period. Thus both prior- and post-test market data could be available for statistical control. The BehaviorScan system greatly increases the level of control over the test market procedures in the first two cases and represents the most tightly controlled experimental system available.

Important issues to consider at the end of this sequence of cases are: (1) What factors are still not controlled in the BehaviorScan system? Would it be desirable or worthwhile to try to control them? (2) Does the high level of control in the BehaviorScan system itself lead to certain biases? (3) Under what conditions would you prefer to use each of the market testing procedures discussed in this chapter?

CASE: United Dairy Industries Association

This case introduces four areas of investigation: test marketing, advertising research, experimental models, and managerial data analysis. The test market involves an experiment performed by a dairy association to determine the best advertising budget to stimulate demand for cheese. Different advertising expenditure levels were carried out across cities according to a predetermined twelve-month plan. The test market procedure in this case is typical of state-of-the-art test markets of ten years ago and many current test markets employ the same methodology. The data evaluation concepts of control, bias, and information content are introduced and form the analytical framework that will be important throughout the chapter.

In August 1973 researchers at the United Dairy Industry Association (UDIA) were evaluating the results of a recent field experiment to test the impact of varying levels of advertising on sales of cheese. The experiment was conducted between May 1972 and July 1973 by the UDIA in cooperation with the Promotion Evaluation Research Group of the United States Department of Agriculture (USDA).

Cheese and the Dairy Industry

The seasonal production patterns of dairy cows result in frequent supply and demand imbalances for fluid milk. Production is generally highest when demand is lowest, and vice versa. Since it is not economically feasible to store fluid milk for prolonged periods, farmers tend to maintain herd sizes to meet peak demand requirements. Excess production of fluid milk is utilized, together with manufacturing-grade milk, in manufactured products such as cheese.

UDIA executives believed that if advertising could stimulate increased demand for cheese, milk prices would be strengthened since cheese plants currently used as much as 19 percent of total milk production. The UDIA was particularly interested in testing the impact of advertising on cheese sales, since among manufactured milk products cheese was absorbing an increasing percentage of milk production. Unlike butter and cream, cheese appeared to be a product with no close substitutes. In addition, attitude surveys available to the UDIA indicated that cheese consumption, in contrast to other milk products, was not adversely affected by consumer concerns regarding weight control or the connection between cholesterol and heart disease.

Design of the Study

The principal objective of the study was to measure retail sales response (in terms of pounds of cheese sold) to varying levels of advertising. In addition, UDIA and USDA researchers were interested in measuring consumer recall of the advertising and changes in consumer attitudes toward cheese associated with the campaign.

Eight markets were selected for the experiment, four of which served as test markets and four as control markets. To facilitate the selection process, data on monthly cheese shipments to retail outlets were obtained for between four and six markets of approximately 600,000 population in each of four geographic regions—the Northeast, Midwest, Southwest, and Southeast. These were the principal regions covered by the American Dairy Association, the advertising and sales promotion arm of the UDIA. Two markets with similar monthly sales patterns were selected within each region in a way that minimized overlap of local television and newspaper coverage. Within each region, the two markets were designated as test or control markets on a random basis, so that a test market and a control market were established in each of the four geographic regions (see Exhibit 5.7).

This case was prepared by John A. Quelch, Harvard Business School, in 1979. Used with permission.

Exhibit 5.7   UDIA Test and Control Markets

Region	Test Market	Control Market
Northeast	Binghamton, NY	Utica-Rome, NY
Midwest	Rockford, IL	Fort Wayne, IN
Southwest	Albuquerque, NM	El Paso, TX
Southeast	Chattanooga, TN	Montgomery, AL

Next, UDIA executives determined the varying levels of advertising that would be tested in the experiment. It was believed that the expenditure levels should be wide enough apart to generate measurable differences in results. At the same time, it was argued that they should represent on a per-capita basis the levels of advertising expenditure at which the industry would be prepared to invest to support a national advertising campaign for cheese. UDIA executives decided to test the impact of four levels of advertising in the test markets—zero cents per capita, three cents, six cents, and nine cents. The six-cent per-capita advertising level represented a national campaign costing approximately $12 million.

Each of the four levels of advertising was implemented in each test market during a three-month period between May 1972 and July 1973. The sequence in which the advertising levels were tested varied from one market to another so that each advertising level was being tested in only one test market during any one time period. During the fifth three-month period (May to July 1973), the levels of advertising implemented in each test market during the fourth period were retained to permit UDIA researchers to subsequently assess the cumulative effects of sustained advertising at each of the four levels. The complete experimental design, technically described as an Extra Period Latin Square, is presented in Exhibit 5.8. By rotating the experimental treatments (in this case, the four levels of advertising) among the four test markets and across time periods, UDIA researchers believed that they would be able to control for the effects of seasonal and other external variables in assessing the results of the study.

The principal medium used in the advertising experiment was television. Approximately $187,000 was spent on TV advertising. Point-of-purchase display material in supermarkets and newspaper advertising together cost $18,500 and were used when the six-cent and nine-cent advertising levels were in effect. A cheese recipe booklet was promoted for sale at 25 cents. Food publicity personnel distributed recipes to newspaper and magazine food editors and appeared on television and radio food programs.

One set of advertisements used in the campaign featured New York chefs preparing cheese dishes. A second set of advertisements featured simpler, home-oriented serving suggestions. The central theme of the campaign was "Cheese—It Gives You Ideas."

Exhibit 5.8   Summary of Experimental Design: Levels of Cheese Promotion by Market and Time Period

	Time Periods	Test Markets				Control Markets			
		Bing-hamton	Rock-ford	Albu-querque	Chatta-nooga	Utica-Rome	Fort Wayne	El Paso	Mont-gomery
1	May–July 1972	A	B	C	D	A	A	A	A
2	Aug–Oct 1972	B	D	A	C	A	A	A	A
3	Nov 1972–Jan 1973	C	A	D	B	A	A	A	A
4	Feb–Apr 1973	D	C	B	A	A	A	A	A
5	May–July 1973	D	C	B	A	A	A	A	A

Note: Letters represent the four levels of advertising applied four in each test market. In terms of investment levels in cents-per-capita annually, A = 0¢, B = 3¢, C = 6¢, and D = 9¢.

Exhibit 5.9 Average Supermarket Cheese Sales (in pounds) During Five Time Periods

Time Period	Binghamton	Rockford	Albuquerque	Chattanooga	Average
1	7,360 (A)	11,258 (B)	11,800 (C)	7,776 (D)	9,548
2	7,364 (B)	13,147 (D)	11,852 (A)	8,501 (C)	10,216
3	8,049 (C)	13,153 (A)	11,450 (D)	7,900 (B)	10,138
4	9,010 (D)	13,880 (C)	12,089 (B)	7,557 (A)	10,634
5	8,909 (D)	14,709 (C)	12,100 (B)	7,658 (A)	10,844
Average	8,138	13,229	11,858	7,878	10,276

Note: Letters in parentheses represent each of four advertising levels for cheese indicated in **Exhibit 5.8.**

Sales Results

Within each market, the UDIA obtained the cooperation of approximately thirty supermarkets in obtaining quarterly audits of cheese sales and supplemental data regarding cheese prices and merchandising. The supermarkets selected represented a cross-section of different areas within each market and together accounted for between 70% and 80% of total food store sales. UDIA studies indicated that approximately 95% of retail cheese sales were made through supermarkets.

Exhibit 5.9 summarizes average cheese sales per store in each test market across the five three-month periods between May 1972 and July 1973. Exhibit 5.10 presents the average cheese sales per store realized at each of the four levels of advertising. Sales at the six- and nine-cents levels were significantly higher than when no advertising was used. Statistical analysis indicated that the incremental sales achieved at these two expenditure levels were equally attributable to direct response during the immediate time period and carryover response from the preceding time period.

The prices of different cheeses and the average display space available to the product category were found not to have varied significantly in relation to the level of advertising. However, the number of retail advertisements for cheese did vary with the level of advertising, because retailers advertised cheese more often when the UDIA was spending at lower levels. When actual cheese sales were statistically adjusted to control for variations in retail advertising, it appeared that the UDIA advertising prompted a 5% sales increase at the three-cent level of investment, 43% at the six-cent level, and

33% at the nine-cent level. UDIA executives were uncertain whether the adjusted or unadjusted sales increases were more likely to represent the results that could be expected from comparable advertising investments nationwide.

Exhibit 5.11 compares sales results in the four test markets to those in the four control markets. In both cases, sales in each of the five time periods were indexed to sales achieved during the May–July 1972 period. Cheese sales were usually subject to seasonal fluctuation in consumer demand, the May–July period being customarily the weakest quarter. A further factor influencing cheese sales during 1972–73 was the rapid increase in meat prices, which prompted recommendations to consumers in the media to substitute lower-priced cheese dishes. Although unable to assess the precise impact of this trend on cheese sales, UDIA and USDA researchers noted that sales in the control markets during May–July 1973 returned to the level of the previous year, while sales in the test markets continued to increase.

Consumer Awareness and Attitude Study

UDIA and USDA researchers were interested in measuring changes in awareness and attitudes as well as changes in sales associated with the advertising campaign. Six waves of telephone interviews were conducted with female heads of households selected from telephone directories on a random probability basis in each of the four test and control markets. Interviewing was carried out just prior to the start of the campaign and at the end of each of

Exhibit 5.10 Average Supermarket Cheese Sales Across Time Periods in Response to Four Levels of Advertising

Treatment	Sales (Lbs.)	Increase (Lbs.)	% Increase
No Advertising (A)	9,454	Base	Base
3¢ Level (B)	9,563	109	1.2%
6¢ Level (C)	11,168	1,714*	18.1%*
9¢ Level (D)	10,920	1,466*	15.5%*

*Difference from base significant at the 0.05 level.

Exhibit 5.11 Index of Cheese Sales by Type of Market and Time Period

Period	Four Test Markets	Four Control Markets
1	100.0	100.0
2	107.0	106.3
3	106.2	104.5
4	111.4	108.0
5	113.6	100.6

the five time periods. In each of the four test markets, four hundred interviews were conducted for each wave of the study. Samples of three hundred consumers were generated in each of the control markets.

Each respondent was first asked: "During the past two or three months, do you remember seeing or hearing any advertising about cheese?" Next, she was asked in which medium she had seen or heard cheese advertising, and, finally, she was asked to recall the content of the advertising. Details of responses along these three dimensions for each wave of the study are presented in Exhibit 5.12. UDIA and USDA researchers noted a tendency among the awareness measures to stabilize in the four test markets after the second period of the campaign.

Average awareness levels across the four test markets were also found to vary with levels of promotion. Awareness of any cheese advertising during the past two or three months was 52% after periods of no advertising in the test markets, 58%

following advertising at the three-cent level, 63% at the six-cent level, and 64% at the nine-cent level. Recall of dishes and recipes mentioned in the campaign occurred among 19% of respondents interviewed after periods of no advertising, 24% at the three-cent level, 34% at the six-cent level, and 37% at the nine-cent level.

In addition to the three awareness measures, respondents were asked to indicate the extent to which they agreed or disagreed on a six-point scale with each of a series of statements about cheese. The average level of agreement with seven of these statements was greater among respondents interviewed following time periods during which some level of advertising occurred than among respondents interviewed following periods of no advertising. These statements were:

American cheddar is a favorite with me.

Cheese adds something special to your daily meals.

Cheese adds the kind of variety I'm looking for in meal planning.

Cheese is a good source of high-quality protein.

Cheese is the product for me.

I (don't) worry about cholesterol from cheese.

Sophisticated people eat more varieties of cheese.

While several of these statements were related to the message strategy of the campaign, those relating to cholesterol and protein were not. In addition, no improvement in levels of agreement could be established for two additional statements ("Cheese can be a part of many recipes" and "I plan to use cheese in recipes more often in the future") that the researchers believed were closely related to the campaign message strategy.

Conclusion

UDIA and USDA researchers were concerned about several issues in evaluating the results of the study. First, they wished to assess the impact of various levels of advertising on cheese sales and, in addition, the carryover and cumulative effects of

Exhibit 5.12 Responses to Awareness Questions, by Interview Wave and Type of Market

	Wave I Before Test	Wave II End Period 1	Wave III End Period 2	Wave IV End Period 3	Wave V End Period 4	Wave VI End Period 5
Saw or heard any advertising for cheese						
Four Test Markets	49%	56%	61%	60%	61%	58%
Four Control Markets	45%	40%	51%	46%	52%	49%
Saw or heard advertising on television						
Four Test Markets	32%	38%	47%	48%	46%	45%
Four Control Markets	31%	25%	34%	31%	29%	29%
Mentioned cheese dishes, recipes, uses						
Four Test Markets	15%	24%	29%	31%	29%	29%
Four Control Markets	13%	12%	15%	11%	18%	14%

advertising at each level. Secondly, they had to assess the evidence of the awareness and attitude study alongside the sales results, and determine whether there were any implications in the results regarding the effectiveness of the message strategy used in the campaign.

Above all, they had to recommend whether or not the UDIA should undertake a national advertising campaign for cheese, and if so, at what level. While some of the researchers believed that the experiment had demonstrated that a short-term, one-shot cheese advertising campaign would generate sufficient incremental sales to justify the expense, others argued that manufacturer advertising of cheese was at such a high level that a comparatively modest UDIA campaign could have little or no additional impact.

To arrive at their recommendation, it was necessary for the researchers to consider the costs and benefits to the dairy farmer associated with national advertising campaigns based upon each of the four advertising levels tested in the experiment. For example, at the six-cents per capita advertising level, supermarket sales of cheese had increased by 1714 pounds on average during a three-month period as indicated in Exhibit 5.10. For the 40,600 supermarkets nationwide that have annual food sales of at least $500,000, an annual increase in cheese sales of 6000 pounds per supermarket would represent an equivalent increase in milk consumption of 2,430,360,000 pounds* worth $195 million to the nation's dairy farmers at current milk prices. In addition, the increased demand for cheese might further benefit the dairy farmer by strengthening or raising fluid milk prices. It was believed unlikely that an expansion in demand would be satisfied by additional cheese imports.

---

*The processing of one pound of cheese utilizes about ten pounds of milk.

Preparation Questions

1. What is the rationale for the pattern of advertising expenditures across cities? To what extent is the objective achieved? Consider the possible effects of city, time sequence, and advertising budget levels on advertising response.

2. The data currently loaded for analysis in the PC statistical model ignore the control cities. What does the ANOVA test of these data tell us about the need for the experimental design?

3. Integrate the data from the control cities into the analysis. What other hypotheses about advertising's effects are reasonable? Test them using the data if possible.

4. What do you conclude from your analysis about the effects of advertising on sales?

5. What advertising budget would you recommend? Optional assignment: Develop a simple decision model to assist you in your deliberations.

6. What improvements in the test market design would you suggest?

UDIA Spreadsheet: Latin Squares Model

The UDIA case describes an experiment attempting to measure which of four advertising levels for cheese will provide the highest return. The experiment is performed using a 4 × 4 Latin Square experimental design. This worksheet is an adaptation of the statistical model that is customarily used to analyze the data generated from this type of experiment. Lotus 1-2-3 isn't really designed to do this sort of thing, so the model used here is quite limited but should still give you the chance to explore a number of hypotheses about the effects of advertising. Unfortunately, the results that one gets with this simplified model don't match those published in the case, even though the input data are the same; the model will give you different averages across city, time period, and advertising level. For purposes of this exercise, try to produce consistent analysis with these data and don't worry about matching the case exhibits.

The basic model of advertising effect in the UDIA case is that the demand for cheese is a linear function consisting of an overall mean (average) supplemented by incremental sales (either positive or negative) due to the three "treatments": city, time period, and advertising level:

$$M_{i,j,k} = C + C_i + T_j + A_k + e_{i,j,k}$$

where

C is a constant

C_i is the effect of city i

T_j is the effect of time period j,

A_k is the effect of the kth level of advertising

$e_{i,j,k}$ is a random disturbance

The goal of this Latin Square experimental design is to be able to compute the effect of the four advertising levels on the demand for cheese by eliminating the effects of the other two treatments (city and time). The UDIA worksheet computes the statistics necessary to test the statistical significance of each of these effects.

The null hypothesis, as is customary, is that there is no effect due to the treatments nor difference between the sales for the different levels in each treatment. For example, the hypothesis concerning the advertising level is that $A_K = A$ (a constant) for all values of k. In other words, the hypothesis is that there is no difference in the sales resulting from the various advertising levels. We hope, of course, to reject this hypothesis so that we can conclude that one advertising level is better than the others. This seems backwards, but there are good statistical reasons for running tests this way.

To test this hypothesis we first have to compute the appropriate test statistic and compare its value with the critical value. If the test statistic that we compute is bigger than the critical value, we reject the hypothesis that there is no difference in the demand for cheese due to the advertising level and conclude that there is an advertising effect. If the test statistic is smaller than the critical value, we conclude that there is no difference in the effect of the different advertising levels and our test fails. Similarly for the other two treatments.

Before going further with the discussion of how the worksheet is used, let's take a look at it (Exhibit 5.13). The model consists of three parts: a data section, a work area, and the statistical results. There is a menu (reached by typing [Alt] M, as usual), which will help you find these areas. The results of your analysis can be printed by typing [Alt] P.

Data Input and Work Area

The data in the spreadsheet are contained in two arrays: the upper array contains the average cheese sales across stores in the test cities; and the lower array contains the average cheese sales across stores in the control cities (see Exhibit 5.9). The work area is composed of a 4 x 4 array (boxed off for emphasis) surrounded by various statistical summaries. The important thing to understand about this worksheet is that all of the computations are based on whatever data are put into the work area. This worksheet is used by developing hypotheses, expressing the hypothesis in terms of the test data, and putting the processed data into the work area. As long as your data fit the Latin Square design criteria, the statistics to test your hypothesis will be computed.

At present the work area contains the raw data for the first four periods in the test cities, so the statistics are computed only for the test cities. This doesn't use the data from the control cities at all, so we would expect trouble with this hypothesis.

Test Results

The test results are found in the section of the spreadsheet labeled "ANOVA table." An explanation of the ANOVA table is as follows: The statistics are computed based on a comparison of the variation between treatment means compared with the amount of variation within treatments around the treatment mean. That sounds like double talk but it's fairly simple. The measure of variation used is the

sum of the squared deviations around the appropriate mean (or average). This is denoted in the ANOVA table as SS for "sum of squares." Consider the method used to compute the sum of squares (SS) associated with the cities treatment (you can follow along on the worksheet):

1. The average cheese sales for each city (for Binghamton it is 7,946) is subtracted from the grand mean (10,134).

2. These differences for each city are then squared.

3. Then these squared differences are added to obtain the sum of squares for cities = 1.983 E + 07 (which is equivalent to 1.983×10 raised to the 7th power).

DF stands for the degrees of freedom associated with the test, which is roughly a way of measuring how many items are being averaged. If you divide the SS by the DF you get the MSS or "mean sum of squares." The MSS is used to compare the size of effects of each of our test considerations. The next-to-last row of the ANOVA table contains the SS and MSS that are due to statistical error in our model. The MSS for the error term is the measurement of how much variation there is between each of the test levels and the means for the test factors—cities, time periods, and advertising levels. Dividing the MSS for each of the factors respectively by the MSS for error we can compare the variation of the treatment means around the grand mean with the amount of variation not due to our model. This ratio is found in the column labeled "F," and this is the test statistic that we've been looking for. We see that the effect of the different cities is very large (80.001) compared with the time and advertising effects.

What we would really like to be able to say, however, is whether or not the amount of variation due to our treatment effects is greater than would be expected just from random variation. In other words, are the differences we observe between the treatments indicative of a real difference between the treatment levels, or could we expect to see similar results due to random variation, even if there was no difference between the treatments? To answer this question we compare the F statistics that we have computed with the critical values listed below the ANOVA table. If our F statistic is bigger than the

Exhibit 5.13   UDIA Spreadsheet

United Diary Industries Association

Raw data section

Cities (Test)

Time		Bing	Rockf.	Albuq	Chatt.
	1	7,360	11,258	11,800	7,776
	2	7,364	13,147	11,852	8,501
	3	8,049	13,153	11,450	7,900
	4	8,959	13,931	12,095	7,608
	5	8,909	14,709	12,100	7,658

Cities (Control)

Time		Utica	Ft. Wayne	El Paso	Mont
	1	7,166	10,970	11,706	7,441
	2	7,489	12,718	11,495	8,250
	3	7,679	12,902	11,753	7,853
	4	8,536	13,826	12,008	7,768
	5	8,563	13,819	11,882	7,714

WORK AREA
Cities

Time								Mean
1	||		7,360	11,258	11,800	7,776	||	9,549
2	||		7,364	13,147	11,852	8,501	||	10,216
3	||		8,049	13,153	11,450	7,900	||	10,138
4	||		8,959	13,931	12,095	7,608	||	10,648
Mean			7,933	12,872	11,799	7,946		10,138

Sum of squares across cities					Total
Dev	(2,205)	2,735	1,662	(2,191)	0
ColSS	4.861E+06	7.478E+06	2.761E+06	4.802E+06	1.990E+07

Sum of squares across advertising treatments

	$0.00	$0.03	$0.06	$0.09
Mean	9,993	9,654	10,570	10,333

(continued)

first of these values F(.05,3,6) = 4.76, then there is only a 5% chance that the results could come from a situation in which there was no difference due to the treatment. The second value, F(.10,3,6) = 3.29, gives the critical value for only a 10% chance that the results came from a situation in which the treatment had no effect.

The ANOVA results based on the raw test data show that there is a significant difference in cheese consumption across the test cities, but that differ-ences observed between the time periods and the advertising levels could well have occurred even if there was no difference in sales due to time periods or advertising treatments.

Changing Hypotheses

We shouldn't be discouraged by this result, be-cause that is exactly what we should have ex-pected—after all, that's why the statisticians hired

Exhibit 5.13 (continued) UDIA Spreadsheet

```
ANOVA Table

Num of cities, M=          4


   Source           SS     DF        MSS           F
   Cities      7.961E+07    3     2.654E+07     84.254
     Time      2.456E+06    3     8.186E+05      2.599
   Advert      1.919E+06    3     6.398E+05      2.031
    Error      1.890E+06    6     3.149E+05
    Total      8.587E+07   15

         F(.05,3,6)=                 4.76
         F(0.1,3,6)=                 3.29

                       Advertising Level (Dollars/capi
                        $0.00      $0.03      $0.06
   Advertising response 9,993      9,654     10,570
   Percent increase over base      96.61%    105.77%
```

by the UDIA went to all the trouble and expense of using control cities in the first place. They anticipated that there would be a big difference between the sales of cheese in the cities and so they tried to match test and control cities as best they could. How well did that work out? Well, that analysis should be your first step in using the model.

You can begin examining this question if you know how to change hypotheses and input them in the work area. The two necessary tasks are: (1) to express the role of the test and control cities as a mathematical expression, and (2) to get the result into the work area.

Testing the hypothesis that advertising has a differential effect on cheese sales using the fact that we have matched control cities is not difficult to conceptualize. The control cities received no advertising, so the cheese sales in those cities will not be affected by advertising. Hopefully, all of the other factors that might affect the sales of cheese in the matched test city will also affect the control city similarly, and therefore if it works, the difference between cheese sales in the test city and cheese sales in the control city will be due to advertising. So what we want to do is subtract the cheese sales in the control city from the cheese sales in the test city.

Now that we know that we want to analyze the difference between the cheese sales in the test and control cities, we can put those sales differences in the work area and the worksheet will compute the appropriate statistics. This can easily be done using the 1-2-3 **copy** command as follows:

Step 1: Move the cursor to the upper left-hand corner of the work area, cell B25. You'll know you're in the right place because the formula at the top of the screen will say "B25: +B7." This tells you that cell B25 gets its value from cell B7, which is the Binghamton sales level in period 1, viz. 7,360. What we want in this cell now is the difference between first period sales in Binghamton and sales in Utica in period 1. We can express that by typing the formula for that difference in cell B25.

Step 2: Enter the formula for the sales difference in cell B25 by typing +**B7** − **B15**[Enter].

Step 3: Copy this formula into all of the other cells in the boxed data section of the work area. This is done in one very easy step. With the cursor still in cell B25, type the following: /C [.] [Enter], then move the cursor to E28, and then hit [Enter]. Your new formula has been copied into all of the cells of the work area.

The statistics that are now computed in the ANOVA table have been computed on the difference between the test and the control cities as we wished. You should now be able to determine what the results tell you about the effectiveness of the test design in isolating the effects of advertising from the effects due to different cities and time periods. There are a number of other reasonable hypotheses that you might also want to test. You can do it by following the three steps above, using the formula that expresses your hypothesis. The tricky part is making sure what advertising hypothesis you've actually tested. The computation of the advertising level averages follows the ABCD checkerboard pattern in the case. You need to make sure that whatever advertising levels get put together by this pattern make sense and *should* be together. This particularly can be a problem in testing cumulative advertising effects; you might need to redefine the definition of the advertising level formulas.

CASE: AdTel, Ltd.

This case describes the AdTel split-cable test market system that was used to determine the best advertising budget for a peanut butter brand in a competitive market. The AdTel test market system utilized an important technological development to eliminate inter-city differences from test marketing. Although the AdTel system represents a great methodological advance over the UDIA case, there were still a number of issues about data quality, control, bias, and information content that affects the results of the experiment. The case continues the test market historical development that began with the UDIA case and provides a powerful argument for the need for additional technology development.

In 1974, the Barrett Foods Company held a 30% national market share of peanut butter sales, and enjoyed a position of market leadership. Its closest and toughest competition came from the Mullen Foods Company, which had a 28% national market share. The balance of the market was fragmented among half a dozen "price" and private-label brands.

Although Barrett's sales volume had grown steadily for the past three years, for several reasons it had not grown as fast as overall peanut butter sales had. For one thing, Mullen Foods had been outspending Barrett on trade deals. This gave Mullen a gross margin advantage with retailers. Mullen had also increased its television advertising expenditures to roughly $2 million, matching Barrett's TV budget. Another factor was that the cost of peanut butter had increased 40% during the previous two years. Predictably, consumers had become more price conscious, and Barrett management believed the increasing shelf price differences between its product and the price and private-label brands had become significant in the consumer's selection decision.

In the face of declining market share, Barrett management had asked AdTel, Ltd. to conduct a "heavy-up" test—one that measures the effect of dramatically increased advertising—to determine the payoff for a $6 million television advertising expenditure versus the current $2 million. Management had decided that a 15% sales increase (on an

equivalent units base) with a minimum 90% confidence level would be required to justify heavy spending nationally.

Company Background

AdTel, Ltd. was founded in 1968 as an outgrowth of a consulting project initiated by the Advertising Research Foundation. Since 1972, it had been a subsidiary of Booz, Allen & Hamilton. The company's expertise was in testing and measuring the sales effectiveness of alternative television advertising consumer promotions, and of introductory campaigns for new products within a single market.

AdTel had developed a minimarket system based on purchase diary panels and split-cable TV that was designed to control all variables except the one being tested. In each of its three unique test markets, AdTel used a dual cable CATV system and two balanced consumer diary panels of 1,000 households each.

The AdTel System

The dual-cable concept employed a unique combination of three elements to determine consumer acceptance of new packaged goods, and to measure the sales effect of television advertising alternatives on new or established brands:

This case was prepared by Claudine B. Malone.

Copyright © 1977 by the President and Fellows of Harvard College Harvard Business School case 9-177-174.

Dual-Cable Television Systems: In each of AdTel's test markets, AdTel has two separate cable circuits. The television sets owned by half the cable subscriber households were wired to the A cable; the sets owned by the other half were wired to the B cable. AdTel could control the signal carried over each of the cables. A push of a button blocked the on-air commercial broadcast by the network or local stations on one side of the cable and simultaneously cut in the desired test commercial, while the other side carried the regular commercial. The ability to test the effect of television advertising alternatives within a single market represented a major cost and control breakthrough in television advertising research.

Large Consumer Diary Panels: In each test market, AdTel maintained a 2,000-family panel (1,000 A- and 1,000 B-cable households). The panels were carefully balanced according to demographic characteristics and store shopping preferences. The panel families recorded their purchases in weekly diaries. AdTel used these consumer sales data to forecast product viability, national market share, and sales volume.

Limited Retail Distribution: The "minimarket" name was derived from the fact that the test brand was stocked in relatively few retail outlets (typically 50 or less) located within the cable household's shopping area.

Because distribution channels overlapped, it was usually impossible for AdTel's packaged goods clients to confine distribution of a test brand to AdTel's cable area. Therefore, AdTel employed the services of another Booz, Allen subsidiary, Market Audits, to warehouse the new product and, through the payment of "cooperation" monies to the major retail factors, to force distribution into the cable area. Market Audits controlled distribution and pricing of the new product throughout the test. The cost benefits derived from this limited distribution were significant. For example:

Pilot-plant or bench-top production could be used, since a relatively few retail outlets carried the product.

Media costs were comparatively small, since minimarket tests were conducted in small markets.

AdTel had carefully avoided publishing the specific locations of its minimarkets, even though their names were open secrets in the marketing community. AdTel considered it to be essential to the validity of the test results that the people in these markets operated under a real-life situation and were not aware of the relationship between their purchase diaries and cable television.

AdTel Testing and Measurement Advantages

Barrett had retained AdTel to measure the sales effects of the spending level test, because management believed there were cost and control advantages inherent in the AdTel dual-cable system. One cost advantage to Barrett resulted from reduced incremental media costs. Fifty thousand dollars in advertising expenditures could be eliminated because the AdTel system allowed one client to cut in test-brand advertising over time owned corporately for other brands in the test category.

Also, AdTel's ability to test television advertising alternatives within a single market was considered a control advantage. In traditional approaches, the sales effects of variables (competitive trade and consumer promotions, retail shelf environments, spot television expenditures, weather, etc.) made it difficult to read tests conducted between supposedly matched markets. Since AdTel's test and control cells were in the same city, the differences between these uncontrolled factors were reduced.

Barrett's Spending Level Test

The basic design of the test was to triple advertising spending on Panel A from a national rate of $2 million per year to a national rate of $6 million. The A panel would receive 60 gross rating points (GRPs) per week and the B panel would recieve 180 GRPs per week for the duration of the 12-month test. During a 6-month pretest period, advertising had been at the 60 GRPs per week level.

To avoid distortions of the trend and repeat data caused by families joining and dropping out of the panel during the test, a static sample was created that included only those families returning at least 80% of their diaries during the 12-month period. As

Exhibit 5.14   Using the AdTel Exhibits

The AdTel case has a number of exhibits that summarize the results of the Barrett's test market. It is sometimes difficult to see what is going on in the test market, because there are so many exhibits and similar data on different brands occur in different exhibits. The graphs are often drawn on a different scale, which further complicates comparison. Unfortunately, the data for the exhibits is not available, so the best that could be done was to approximate the data from the graphs.

Approximate data corresponding to the graphs are found in the file *AdTel* on the diskette. If you know how to use the **graph** option in Lotus 1-2-3, it is quite easy to build the graph you want from this data. A sample of the data is shown below. Data are available for all but Exhibit 5.22.

AdTel Case Data (Estimated)

Periods	Exhibit 5.15 Barrett's Vol/Reporting Family			Exhibit 5.16 Barrett's Share		
	A	B	A-B	A	B	A-B
19	43.0	41.0	2.0	50.0	50.0	0.0
20	22.0	23.0	− 1.0	30.0	30.0	0.0
21	31.0	31.0	0.0	40.0	39.5	0.5
22	17.0	18.0	− 1.0	23.0	24.0	−1.0
23	29.0	25.0	4.0	45.0	44.0	1.0
24	31.0	25.0	6.0	39.0	35.0	4.0
25	22.0	22.0	0.0	20.0	20.0	0.0
26	21.0	23.0	− 2.0	23.0	26.0	− 3.0
27	29.0	25.0	4.0	33.0	30.0	3.0
28	29.0	32.0	− 3.0	27.0	33.0	− 6.0
29	46.0	42.0	4.0	44.0	43.5	0.5
30	40.0	35.0	5.0	32.0	30.0	2.0
31	38.0	29.0	9.0	29.0	27.0	2.0
32	53.0	38.0	15.0	38.0	33.0	5.0
33	47.0	34.0	13.0	41.0	38.0	3.0
34	45.0	26.0	19.0	43.0	34.0	9.0
35	65.0	38.0	27.0	55.0	54.0	1.0
36	40.0	47.0	− 7.0	51.0	57.0	− 6.0
Averages						
Pre-Test	28.8	27.2	1.7	37.8	37.1	0.8
Test	39.6	32.6	7.0	36.3	35.5	0.9
Difference	10.7	5.4	5.3	− 1.5	− 1.6	0.13
Case	10.0	5.0		− 1.7	− 1.1	

The data for each case exhibit are presented by the A and B panels, together with the difference between the A and B panels. The difference is calculated so if you want to revise some estimates, the difference will be recalculated automatically. Average values are computed for both the pre-test and the test periods for each panel, as is the difference between the panels. The row labeled *case* gives the values for the differences between the pre-test and test period averages as they appear in the case. This allows you to see how closely the estimated data fit the case. Graphs drawn from these data should be adequate to explore hypotheses intuitively. If you want to get more exact, you could change a few of the exhibit estimates.

If you have not used the graphics capability of Lotus 1 2 3 but would like to, refer to the Lotus manual. It's very easy to use.

a result, Panel A contained 829 families and Panel B 922. All volume measures in the test were expressed in equivalent units, where one equivalent unit equaled 12.0 ounces.

Volume Trend Test Results

As can be seen in Exhibit 5.15, the Panel A heavy-up strategy resulted in more volume for Barrett

Exhibit 5.15   Barrett's Volume per Reporting Panel Family (Equivalent Units Basis)*

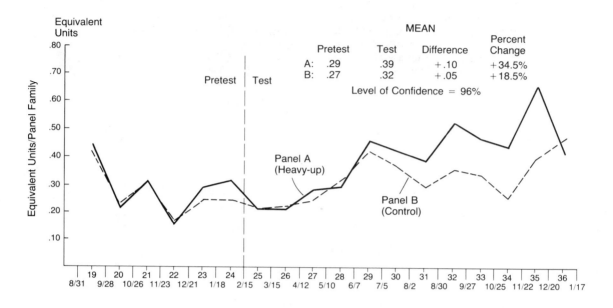

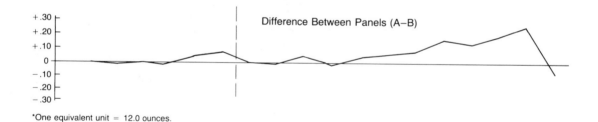

*One equivalent unit = 12.0 ounces.

Exhibit 5.16   Monthly Mean Equivalent Units/Family

	Pretest 19−24	Test 30−35	Difference	Percent Change
A:	.29	.47	.18	+ 62.1
B:	.27	.33	.06	+ 22.2

peanut butter than the Panel B control strategy. On a volume-per-family basis, purchases of Barrett peanut butter increased by 18.5% under the control strategy from the pretest to the test periods. During the same periods, purchases increased by 34.5% under the heavy-up strategy, a difference that was statistically significant at the 96% level.

The difference between the unit volume for the two panels was very small at first, but after five periods began to broaden. The better performance on Panel A came primarily during the latter half of the test. AdTel consultants said this was typical of

Exhibit 5.17 Barrett's Share of the Category (Equivalent Units Basis)*

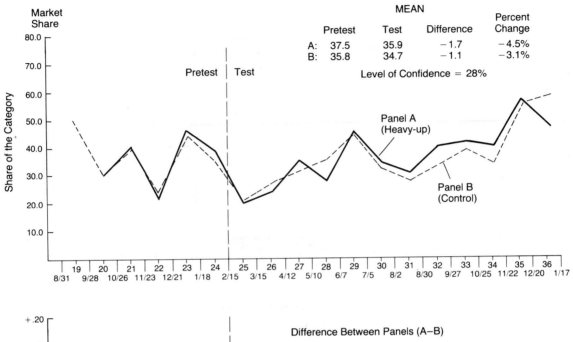

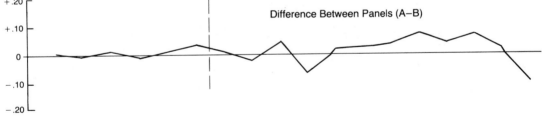

*One equivalent unit = 12.0 ounces.

other AdTel tests and that a three- to six-month lag between the initial advertising heavy-up and the test effects was commonly observed.

When the entire test period was considered, Panel A (heavy-up) did 16% better than Panel B (control), relative to the pretest period. If the volume increase for only the second half of the year (periods 30–35) was considered, the difference was 40% (62.1–22.2). (See Exhibit 5.16.)

AdTel felt that interpreting the results of the test

was a policy decision for the company to make and that it could not go beyond this point in making an economic evaluation.

The last two periods of the test were interesting. The divergence between the panels was greatest during period 35, but there was essentially no difference in period 36. This decrease in volume for the heavy-up panel was statistically significant. Additional brand volume and market-share results are found in Exhibits 5.17 through 5.22.

Exhibit 5.18   Category Volume per Reporting Panel Family (Equivalent Units Basis)*

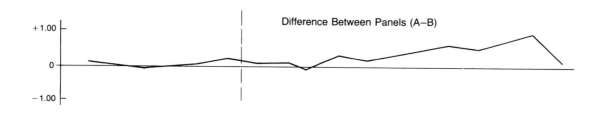

	Pretest	Test	Difference	Percent Change
A:	.77	1.09	+.32	+41.6%
B:	.74	.92	+.18	+24.3%

Level of Confidence = 99%

*One equivalent unit = 12.0 ounces.

Diagnostics

Barrett's management was very interested in what the AdTel test might indicate about why higher Barrett sales resulted from the heavy-up strategy. Theoretically, there were two possible reasons for the better sales performance on the heavy-up panel:

1. An increase in the number of families buying Barrett peanut butter: (a) achieved by attracting users of other brands and/or (b) achieved by attracting previously infrequent or nonusers of Barrett peanut butter.

2. An increase in Barrett peanut butter volume per buying household (a) achieved by increasing the use of the brand and/or the product class, and/or (b) achieved by increasing Barrett peanut butter share among Barrett peanut butter buyers.

Exhibit 5.23 displays the percentage of reporting panel families purchasing Barrett peanut butter per period (penetration), while Exhibit 5.24 charts Barrett peanut butter volume per Barrett peanut butter brand buyer (brand buying rates). Referring to Exhibit 5.23, Barrett peanut butter's mean four-

Exhibit 5.19 Mullen's Volume per Reporting Panel Family (Equivalent Units Basis)*

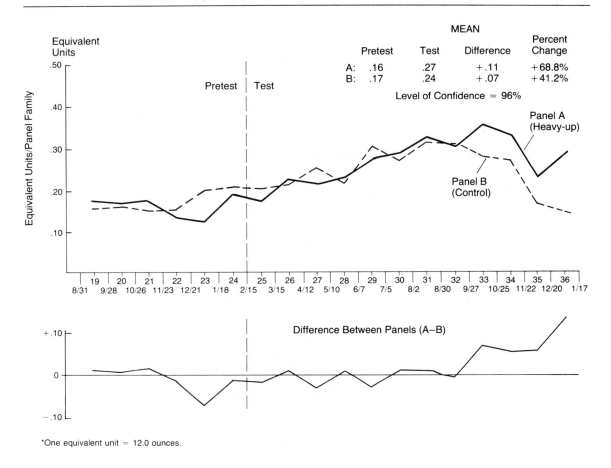

*One equivalent unit = 12.0 ounces.

week penetration increased by 22.0% under the heavy-up strategy and by only 17.9% on the control panel from the pretest to the test period. This better improvement in penetration on the heavy-up panel was significant at a 96% level of confidence. In addition, Exhibit 5.24 shows that buyers exposed to the heavy-up strategy increased their individual volume of Barrett purchases more than the control group did (+9.5% versus +3.9%). Thus, the positive effects of the heavy-up strategy on volume could be traced to both more Barrett peanut butter brand buyers per period, and a heavier Barrett buying rate per period (hypothesis #2, above).

Exhibit 5.25 also indicates that the percentage of reporting panel families purchasing peanut butter increased more for Panel A (+18.9%) than for Panel B (+16.2%) during the test period. This means that Barrett improved its penetration per period under the heavy-up strategy mainly by attracting previous infrequent or nonusers of peanut butter, rather than by attracting users of other brands.

Referring to Exhibit 5.26, while total peanut butter volume per buyer increased by 9.6% in the control panel, the heavy-up panel showed a 19.8% increase.

Exhibit 5.20   Price Brand Volume per Reporting Panel Family (Equivalent Units Basis)*

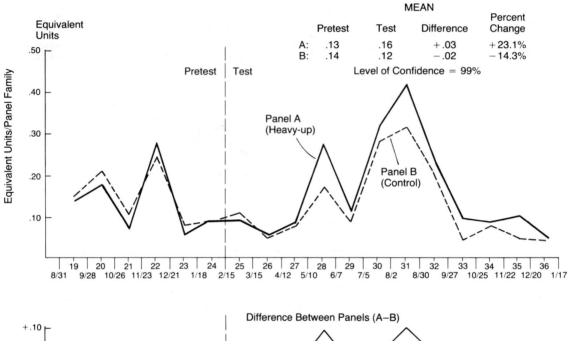

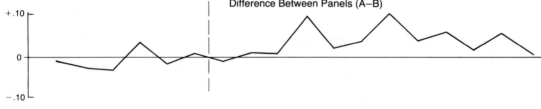

*One equivalent unit = 12.0 ounces.

Changes in Dealing Activity

In an attempt to determine whether any factors other than advertising might have caused the improvements in Barrett peanut butter's volume levels on Panel A, AdTel analyzed changes in Barrett peanut butter and total peanut butter dealing activity from the pretest to the test periods. Exhibit 5.27 displays the percentage of Barrett peanut butter volume purchased on a consumer-recognized deal,* while Exhibit 5.28 presents the same measure for total peanut butter. Referring to Exhibits 5.27 and 5.28, the more favorable volume performance on Panel A for Barrett peanut butter and the product

---

*These are referred to as "consumer-recognized" deals because the consumer was asked to indicate whether the purchase was made on deal, and the answer depended on his or her perceptions of the purchase transaction.

Exhibit 5.21   Private Label Volume per Reporting Panel Family (Equivalent Units Basis)*

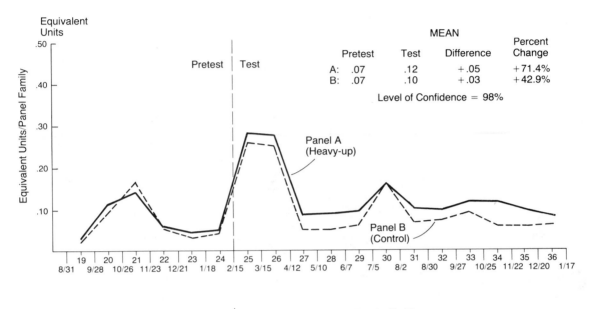

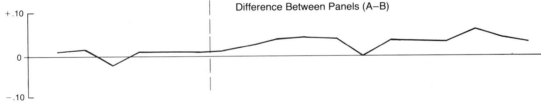

*One equivalent unit = 12.0 ounces.

---

class is not attributable to significantly different levels of dealing between the panels. Dealing was at almost identical levels on both panels during both the pretest and the test periods.

Summary of Test Results

For the one-year test period, Barrett peanut butter volume was 16% greater under the heavy-up ad-

vertising strategy. This just barely met the break-even point for the advertising payout of 15%. Almost half a year elapsed, however, before any differences started to occur. During the last six months, Barrett peanut butter's sales were 40% greater on the heavy-up panel.

Exhibit 5.22   Average Market Share by Brand During the Pretest and Test Period (Equivalent Units Basis)*

	Pretest		Test		Share Point Changes From Pretest to Test		Net Share Point Change (Panel A–Panel B)
	Panel A (Heavy-up)	Panel B (Control)	Panel A (Heavy-up)	Panel B (Control)	Panel A	Panel B	
Barrett	37.5%	35.8%	35.9%	34.7%	−1.7	−1.1	−.6
Mullen	20.8%	23.2%	24.5%	26.4%	+3.7	+3.2	+.5
Price Brand	17.3%	19.5%	14.4%	13.6%	−2.9	−5.9	+3.0
Private Label Brand	9.3%	9.4%	11.3%	10.4%	+2.0	+1.0	+1.0
All Other	15.1%	12.1%	13.9%	14.9%	−1.2	+2.8	−4.0

*One equivalent unit = 12.0 ounces.

Reaction of Barrett Foods' Management

After reviewing the results of the test, Barrett peanut butter's president asked his marketing management group to submit written recommendations regarding the implementation of the $6 million advertising plan and to use the test data to support their decisions. In addition, he asked for recommendations for additional testing, if any, that appeared to be warranted by the results of the business-building test.

Exhibit 5.23 Percent of Reporting Panel Families Purchasing Barrett

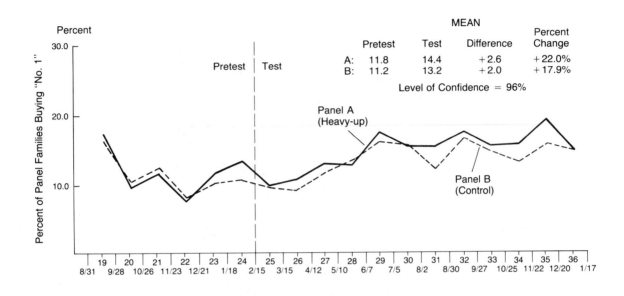

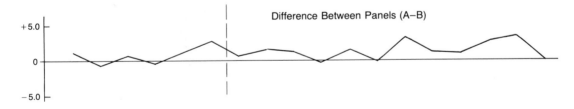

Preparation Questions

1. What are the managerial issues that must be considered in determining the marketing program for Barrett's peanut butter?

2. How well does the research design address these issues?

3. What is going on in period 36?

4. What advertising and marketing strategy do you suggest for Barrett? Optional: Develop a preliminary decision model to analyze the Barrett decision.

5. What improvements would you suggest to the AdTel system? What would it take to implement them?

Exhibit 5.24   Barrett Volume per Barrett Buyer (Equivalent Units Basis)*

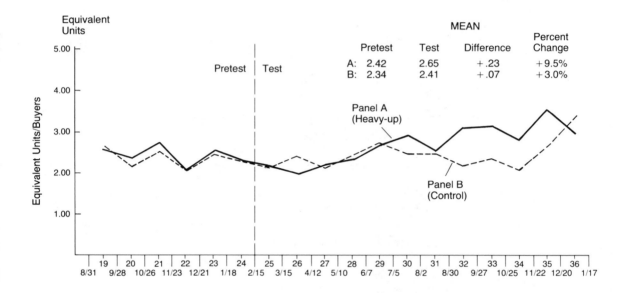

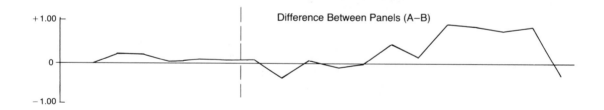

*One equivalent unit = 12.0 ounces.

Exhibit 5.25   Percent of Reporting Panel Families Purchasing Category

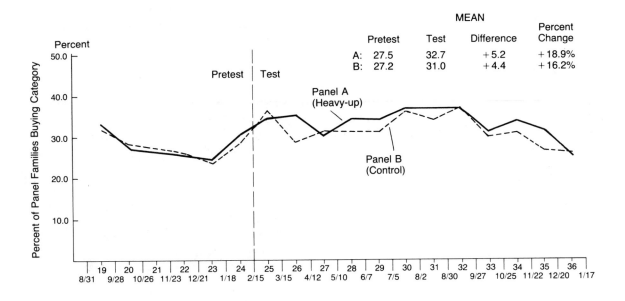

	MEAN			
	Pretest	Test	Difference	Percent Change
A:	27.5	32.7	+5.2	+18.9%
B:	27.2	31.0	+4.4	+16.2%

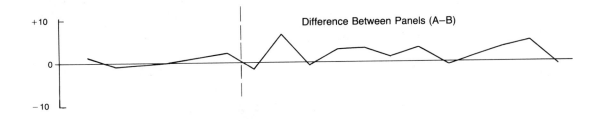

Exhibit 5.26 Total Category Volume per Category Buyer (Equivalent Units Basis)*

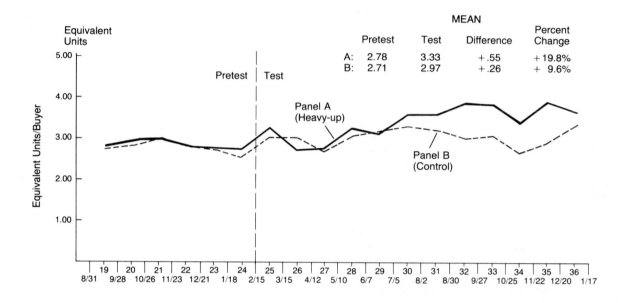

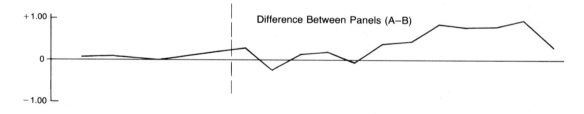

*One equivalent unit = 12.0 ounces.

Exhibit 5.27 Percent of Barrett Volume Purchased on a Consumer-Recognized Deal (Equivalent Units Basis)*

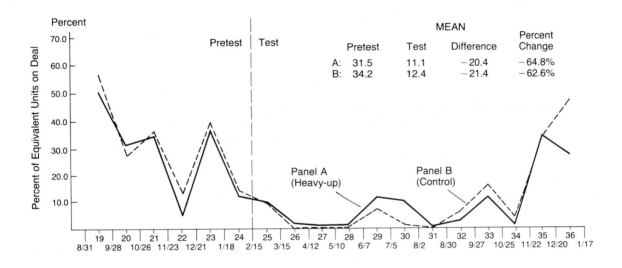

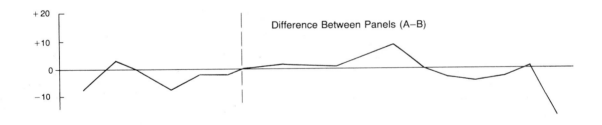

*One equivalent unit = 12.0 ounces.

Exhibit 5.28 Percent of Category Volume Purchased on a Consumer-Recognized Deal (Equivalent Units Basis)*

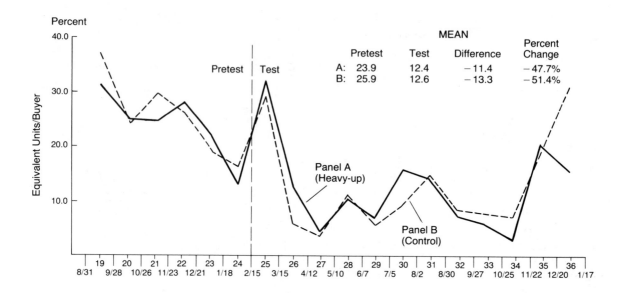

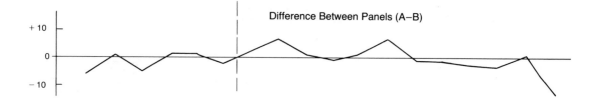

*One equivalent unit = 12.0 ounces.

CASE: Information Resources, Inc.

This case describes how IRI incorporated the latest developments in information technology, computer systems, and experimental design to produce the BehaviorScan test marketing system. BehaviorScan controls most of the factors that we have considered in the other cases in this chapter. The database that is generated in the course of the operation of BehaviorScan is also valuable for other purposes and IRI has developed one alternative use. While the immediate managerial problem is to define a marketing strategy for this new product, the larger managerial problem is to develop a strategic marketing plan for IRI. In terms of model development and managerial data analysis, the BehaviorScan system represents the fulfillment of many of the research dreams we've generated in the other cases. The issues of control, bias, information content, and data quality are continued here, in general, before being addressed specifically in the Searle I case. Don't lose sight of the overall theme of the chapter in preparing this case. It is the same set of problems, except that it is from the research supplier's point of view rather than that of the research buyer.

In a company as young and dynamic as Information Resources, Inc. (IRI), discussions about new product development and marketing strategy seemed to be almost continuous. Nevertheless, the agenda for the June 1982 executive committee meeting was to discuss these topics from a more strategic viewpoint.

Specifically, the agenda included:

1. A review of the company's marketing strategy for BehaviorScan, IRI's oldest and major product, and the *Marketing Fact Book*, the first major new product IRI had brought to market since BehaviorScan was introduced in January 1980

2. Suggestions for further new product developments

The executive committee consisted of John Malec, chairman of the board and cofounder of IRI; Gerald Eskin, vice chairman of the board and cofounder; Gian Fulgoni, president and chief operating officer; and William Walter, director of R&D and vice chairman of the board.

Although IRI was young and quite small, it had generated a great deal of excitement in the marketing research community by its innovative use of modern communication and computer technology to produce a research facility that could only have been dreamed of a decade earlier.

IRI's test market product, BehaviorScan, made it possible for supermarket goods manufacturers to monitor electronically, on a daily basis, the sales of their products* through every checkstand, in every supermarket, in each of four communities. In addition to these data, transmitted daily from the supermarkets to IRI's Chicago, Illinois, headquarters, more detailed data were available on the purchases of 2,500 households in each city. Each of these households had an electronic device attached to its CATV-connected television set that allowed IRI to selectively insert advertisements according to a predetermined schedule and reported whether the TV set was tuned to the channel on which the advertisement would be shown.†

---

*BehaviorScan tracked 130,000 different items and monitored over 95% of the all commodity volume (ACV) in these communities.

†By the end of 1982, 1,000 homes would have this metering feature. All panelists' homes could be individually targeted for advertising inserts.

This case was prepared by Darral G. Clarke.

Copyright © 1982 by the President and Fellows of Harvard College Harvard Business School case 9-583-053.

This extensive and detailed monitoring and control capability had been hailed by some as the ultimate test market and deplored by others as the "Big Brother is watching you" nightmare in George Orwell's novel *1984* come to life.

Company Background

IRI was founded in 1978 by John Malec, a former executive vice president of NPD Research, a research firm specializing in diary panels; and Gerald Eskin, a marketing research consultant and professor at the University of Iowa. Eskin described IRI's development from a concept to a rapidly growing company as follows:

> The company as an entity is less than four years old, but the development project was started about six years ago, primarily by John and myself. John had started the Chicago operation of NPD and built it up to 75% of NPD's business. I was working for NPD as a consultant, primarily doing product forecasting. We learned a lot about what diary panels could do and we also learned more about what they couldn't do and what they did wrong. Conceptually, researchers loved the idea of measuring sales impact at the individual consumer level...the question was how to overcome the problems and measure it accurately. We spent a lot of time talking about how we could fix these problems. There were little fixes and big fixes and it turned out that the big fixes looked much more promising to us than the little fixes.
>
> This led us to the idea of using scanners* to avoid the many biases that exist with diary panel data, the first of which is that the participation rates are only from 2% to 10%. The next problem is the panelist's task itself—filling out reports of purchases. They don't do it, they make mistakes, they get tired of it, and on and on and on.
>
> We basically saw the scanner as a way to collect the data unobtrusively and without the coverage

and error problems of diary panels. We did some surveys on where people shop and we found that people shop in lots of places. The average number of different stores shopped per month was three, and the favorite store was shopped only 65 percent of the time. We felt there was absolutely no way that a good representative measure of consumer purchasing could be obtained using scanners without blanketing the whole market, but people said that was prohibitively expensive. We said, "Why is it prohibitive? Why can't we just do it?" It just took money, and since we didn't have any, that wasn't a problem for us. We solved the measurement problem of the BehaviorScan system with the scanner and full coverage of the market.

> The other issue was how to run experiments. AdTel's split-cable approach was a good first start, but it had bias problems. Some of the problems were measurement problems, but their biggest problems was, and still is, the split cable. Sometimes the panels would be mismatched and sometimes they weren't. The idea of individual household targeting was an easy idea to come up with, although it took awhile before it occurred to us. The hard problem was how to implement it. It was a major electronic problem, but we were encouraged enough to do the research that eventually led to the targeting device. We now have several patents; a systems patent for BehaviorScan as a research system, and a patent on the device itself.
>
> We decided to fix all the problems at the same time because if we didn't, somebody else would come along, sure as shooting, and they'd knock us out of the water. We would be vulnerable.

Having solved the conceptual problems of designing BehaviorScan, Eskin and Malec decided to form their own company to exploit the idea rather than develop it within an existing company. Since neither had major economic resources (or, as John Malec put it, "We didn't have minor economic resources either"), this was a big decision. They estimated that $4 million would be necessary to open two test markets, the smallest number necessary, to run experiments.

Malec by then had resigned from NPD Research and Eskin took a leave of absence from the Univer-

---

*Electronic scanners are devices that read the UPC codes on products (the patterns of black and white bars on packaging) and transmit the identity and price of the product being purchased from the cash registers to the computers in the store.

sity of Iowa. Together they walked the streets looking for someone who would give them $4 million without demanding any ownership.

Gerry Eskin felt that:

> The key to our ability to raise money was our personal reputations and established client relationships. We went to a number of people we thought were opinion leaders in the industry and asked them if they would buy this thing conceptually, if we could get it going. Surprisingly, most of them were interested, and eight companies signed contracts calling for initial payments on projects the day that we could open our doors. The banks still didn't want to loan us money based on these conditional contracts, but we eventually got the hardware supplier National Semiconductor to finance about $2 million worth of scanners for us, and we also obtained a Small Business Administration loan and a further financial investor that got us to the point where we felt we could open our doors.

> Those eight companies that pre-agreed to join up were enough to get the first two markets started in January 1980. So initially, business really took off. Other companies who had initially been reluctant to sign up came around as it became clear that the system was working.

> Even though our sales were rapidly growing, we found that for the next two years, every time we got a new client, we needed just one more client to break even. This was due to our limited capital and our desire to maintain ownership of IRI. All our growth in revenue has gone into expanding capacity to try to keep up with demand.

IRI had sales of $2.8 million in 1980 and $5.85 million in 1981. By June 1982, sales for the year were forecast at $11 million and the debt/equity ratio had been reduced from 12/1 in 1980 to 2/1. Average profitability in the marketing research industry was about 10%. IRI operated at a net loss in 1980 and slightly below the industry average in 1981, and expected to be well above average in 1982. In the fall of 1981, two new towns—Midland, Texas, and Eau Claire, Wisconsin—were set up as test markets in addition to the original markets in Pittsfield, Massachusetts, and Marion, Indiana. In total, there were 33 grocery outlets using IRI's scan-

ners, and scanners were being installed in drugstores in Pittsfield and Marion.

Details of IRI's financial reports are found in Exhibit 5.29. IRI employed approximately 140 people, nearly 100 of whom were involved in the field operations in the four test towns.

BehaviorScan

BehaviorScan is probably best understood by considering it from the client's point of view. Suppose the product manager for a new consumer product had decided on two possible marketing programs, the first involving a high base price, a moderate advertising campaign, and a discount coupon in the newspaper; and the second, a lower base price, a more intensive TV advertising campaign, no discount coupons, and point-of-sale advertisement.

As a BehaviorScan client, the product manager would have two towns at his or her disposal for one year to test these two programs. Since IRI had operated these test markets for about two years, the manager would have two years of sales history about the category into which the new product was to be introduced. These data were available for each of 13 stores and 2500 households in each town. Thus, the new product test could begin immediately, without waiting for measurement of pretest purchasing levels and trends.

The advertising schedule and target audience for the alternative treatments would be fed into a computer, which would then air the predetermined sequence of TV ads to each household. IRI would deliver newspapers that either did or did not contain discount coupons, as predetermined in the test; and monitor the price, shelf placement, and availability of the test product in the supermarket.

Every supermarket in the town would be used to monitor the sales of the new product (as well as other supermarket products), and IRI would extract sales data daily.

The panel households would use their identification cards when they shopped, and their purchases would be stored separately by the computers. This monitoring and recording of store sales and panelists' purchases would continue after the test.

Using IRI's analysis, the product manager would be able to compare sales during the test with the prior history of the category, as well as sales across

Exhibit 5.29   IRI's Financial Reports

Selected Operating Information
(in thousands, except per share amount)

	Year Ended December 31			
	1978	1979	1980	1981
	— (unaudited) —			
Revenue	$ 29	$ 389	$2,769	$5,853
Cost and expenses				
Operating expenses	56	298	2,009	4,617
Selling, general administrative expenses	87	419	634	854
Interest and other expenses	1	33	247	46*
Total cost and expenses	144	750	2,890	5,517
Earnings (loss) before income taxes & extraordinary credit†	(115)	(361)	(121)	336
Net earnings (loss)	(115)	(361)	(121)	336
Earnings (loss) per common share and common share equivalents	$ (.39)	$ (.18)	$ (.03)	$ .08

Selected Balance Sheet Information
(in thousands)

	December 31			
	1978	1979	1980	1981
	— (unaudited) —			
Working capital (deficit)	$ —	$ (736)	$ 882	$(2,073)
Total assets	11	3,236	5,393	8,751
Total long-term obligations, less current maturities	91	2,029	1,790	2,436
Stockholders' equity (deficit)	$ (81)	$ (150)	$ 1,908	$ 2,245

*In 1981 the company entered into a litigation settlement in which it was the plaintiff. The net settlement, which was netted against interest and other expenses, amounted to $446,360 in 1981.

†During the years through 1980, the company paid no income taxes. In 1981 income tax was $147,000. The company had an extraordinary credit of $147,000 in 1981, arising from the tax effect of operating loss carry-forwards, which offset income tax expense in that year.

the test and control groups. Sales after the test could be compared with those during and before the test. Brand shares could be tracked before, during, and after the test to determine from which established products sales of the new product were drawn.

Major differences (other than accuracy) between the store audits used in conventional test markets and BehaviorScan could be found in the pretest sales records. Virtually all the purchases in the test market would be measured electronically and be available almost immediately.

The biggest differences between BehaviorScan and conventional test markets lay in the tracking of sales at the individual household level and in BehaviorScan's ability to target ads to specific households. These targeted households' purchases during the test could be compared with their purchases before, and with purchases of households that had not been exposed to the new product advertisements. IRI studies showed that this led to a dramatic increase in accuracy.

Designing BehaviorScan

Creating this testing facility made stringent demands, not only on technology, but also on the choice of BehaviorScan test towns. A BehaviorScan town had to:

1. Be large enough so that results would be meaningful, yet not so large that providing scanners at every checkstand would be prohibitively expensive. (IRI believed towns of 75,000 to 100,000 population were about right.)

2. Have residents who did at least 95% of their shopping in the town.

3. Have one main newspaper with high penetration to allow monitoring and control of newspaper advertising.

4. Have CATV to allow monitoring and control of television advertising and isolation from the advertising of other cities.

5. Be demographically representative of the United States (population, industrial balance, types of stores, goods sold, etc.).

6. Have clear boundaries.

By mid-1982, IRI had found six towns that satisfied these requirements. Facilities had been set up in four of them, with two more towns to come on-line by year-end. In each supermarket, IRI placed a laser scanner at every checkstand and a minicomputer that collected the data as they were generated. The initial cost of equipping the 13 supermarkets in the first two cities was approximately $4 million. Each night the supermarket minicomputers were called by automatic dialing devices that triggered transmission of the day's data to the main computer. The monthly telephone bill at IRI for the four markets was over $30,000. On average, 95% of the stores reported nightly. The store minicomputers were capable of holding from 4 to 9 days' data, and had an emergency power

supply. The main computer facility at IRI included two IBM 370 computers (models 148 and 158) and a forest of 64 disk packs, each holding 70 megabytes of data. Even with this vast amount of storage space, only data on the categories of current projects were on line. Other data were kept on tape.

Probably the part of the IRI system that gained the most public attention was IRI's ability to control the advertising seen by panel members and monitor the station to which the TV was tuned. Panelists had a device installed on their TVs that not only delivered test ads on a signal from IRI, but also reported the channel to which the set was tuned. IRI's arrangement with the local CATV stations gave IRI's clients the right to purchase advertising time and to have IRI substitute one advertisement for another in what were called "cut-ins." IRI designed a computer-operated system to control the advertisement to each panel household separately. Since any given household could potentially be involved in a number of experiments, controlling which advertisement each of 10,000 households should receive was very complex. To control this operation, IRI had designed a computerized scheduling information system. Gerry Eskin said, "Thanks to this computer system, we are now hitting more than 95 percent of our cut-ins correctly." IRI also had a contract with the local newspaper to place special promotional items in the copies of the paper delivered to panel members and to deliver panelists' newspapers.

Perhaps the biggest surprise to IRI in designing its system was the amount of manpower and training necessary to assure the accuracy and completeness of the data. Cashiers had to be trained extensively to ensure that they obtained full purchase detail. It was necessary for cashiers to scan each item separately. If a consumer bought 20 assorted jars of baby food, for example, the purchase would be recorded as 20 jars of, say, Gerbers beets unless each jar were scanned. IRI maintained a library of more than 130,000 UPC codes that included manufacturer, type of product, size, and flavor information.

About 20% of all supermarket purchases were items that did not have national UPC codes, such as fresh produce. IRI assigned codes for these products that then had to be entered by hand. Other items, such as 50-pound bags of dog food or large sizes of detergents, are difficult to scan, so cashiers had to be trained to hand enter these UPC codes also. Household coupons had to be collected and put into a bag labeled with the panelist's identification number and later entered into the database by IRI personnel to ascertain the price actually paid for a product.

The completeness of the panel data depended not only on the total coverage of the town's supermarkets with IRI scanners, but also on each household using its ID card. In return for participation, the panel households received an annual prize such as a small appliance (for example, a toaster), and participated in monthly prize drawings. Each time a household's card was shown, its number was entered into the drawing. Panelists were guaranteed anonymity and told that the information on their behavior "counted" in the decisions made by manufacturers.

IRI Database

IRI's combination of computer, communication, and scanner technology, and personal attention to potential data problems produced a raw database on consumer purchasing behavior of which John Malec said, "It is simply the best in the world!" The store database included the price, store location, promotion detail, and sales for each of 30,000 items on an hour-by-cash-register basis. These data were usually aggregated and used at a weekly store level. Aggregated in different ways, they could be used to provide sales and share by product, manufacturer, or store, etc., over time.

Additional detail could be obtained on the 2,500 households in each market that were members of the panel. When the panel member showed his or her identification card at the supermarket, each individual product purchased was not only added to the store sales files, but was also entered in a file containing a history of the panel member's purchases. In June 1982, it was possible to examine everything some 5,000 households (soon to be 10,000) had purchased in supermarkets for up to two years. This included size, flavor, price, date purchased, time between purchases, total amount spent on each shopping trip, which stores shopped, and so on.

When the records in the panel database were combined with the store data, it was also possible to see what the panel member had *not* purchased. For each purchase made, there are numerous other choices available. These data on the point-of-sale environment had never been available from conventional diary panels. Using IRI's panel and store data, it was possible to study the effect of price differences on brand choice for various individuals or market segments.

In addition to maintaining these two purchase-related databases, IRI recorded the newspaper and television advertising available to influence consumers' purchase behavior.

When all of these databases were integrated, an amazing amount of data was available about the sale of supermarket products and the people who bought them. For a single transaction—say, the purchase of a 24-oz. package of Ore-Ida frozen hash brown potatoes on May 18, 1982—the IRI database would include:

1. The store where the purchase was made
2. The price paid
3. Whether the purchase was promoted by:
   a. a coupon (amount of discount)
   b. point-of-sale display
   c. in-store price reduction (amount)
4. Location of the product in the store
5. Price and sales volume of competing products
6. Promotion of competing products
7. Ore-Ida newspaper and TV advertising
8. Advertising for other products

If this particular package of hash brown potatoes had been purchased by a panelist, the IRI database could also provide:

1. What other products had been purchased on that shopping trip
2. The income, number and ages of children, etc., of the household
3. Which TV advertisements the household had had the opportunity to see
4. Which newspaper coupons the household had had the opportunity to use

5. The complete history of what the household had bought in the past two years

6. Which stores the household shopped in, etc.

The basic transaction database played the same role in new-product development for IRI as raw petroleum might play for a plastic or chemical manufacturer. Just as petroleum can be fractionated and recombined to produce an almost uncountable variety of products, so the IRI database could be aggregated and cross-linked in various ways to provide different information.

One aggregation could provide an ongoing record of the performance of every UPC-coded product: sales, brand share of category sales, size share of brand sales, and so on. Another aggregation could be used to compare the performance of the product in different stores. Aggregation by households over time could be used to study brand loyalty or the effects of price and advertising on brand switching in different market segments. Aggregation of household data for a new product could shed light on who was buying the product, what products they had bought before, and so on.

The list of possible uses of the data seemed endless, and of course the client who did a BehaviorScan test could study all these things as a response to the marketing program being tested. Before-and-after test comparisons were possible because of the histories maintained in the store, panel, and promotion databases.

BehaviorScan Applications

The use of BehaviorScan by IRI's clients had evolved rapidly, according to Gerry Eskin:

When AdTel first came in about ten years ago, everybody got excited about the possibility of doing weight tests,* but there was subsequently a lot of disillusionment because the sensitivity in control and measurement wasn't adequate to give the budget insights the clients wanted. So everybody turned to copy tests. That seemed

crazy to me because if you can't read a weight test, how in the world could you do a copy test? I figure that the reason was that you can't be embarrassed by a copy test. You don't get the high effect in the low-budget area and the low effect in the high-budget area! So a lot of our initial projects were copy tests. However, as clients have gained confidence in the BehaviorScan system, we are now doing a number of weight tests and most of them turn out reasonably.

What is most encouraging about many of our present projects is that our clients have become so much more sophisticated—they test different marketing strategies now: one price, promotion, and product strategy against another. We can read the effects of each strategy on trial, repeat purchase, and market share—and monitor the results weekly!

Behavior Scan has been used to shed light on the response to many marketing actions. One test measured the effect of couponing a new product at different coupon values.

The advertising and promotion test in Exhibits 5.30 and 5.31 shows the pretest balance between the test and control panels as well as the effect of advertising and promotion during the test. IRI claimed that through their statistical balancing process, it was able to improve dramatically on sensitivity and accuracy in measuring the impact of advertising. Exhibit 5.31 shows that BehaviorScan's measurement of the impact of the higher advertising and promotion budget could be observed on both trial and repeat.

Other IRI studies had included using weekly individual store data to match sales volume with price more closely than was possible with broader-scale audit services such as Nielsen and SAMI (see Exhibit 5.32). Further analysis of IRI data yielded estimates of the effect of displays, features, and price discounts on market share (see Exhibit 5.33). Eskin felt that IRI's ability to provide this kind of detailed data and analysis was unique in the marketing research industry.

BehaviorScan Marketing Strategy

The marketing strategy for BehaviorScan was essentially the same in June 1982 as it had been at its

---

*Weight tests are tests to determine the size of the advertising budget.

Exhibit 5.30   BehaviorScan Test Results: Advertising and Promotion Test

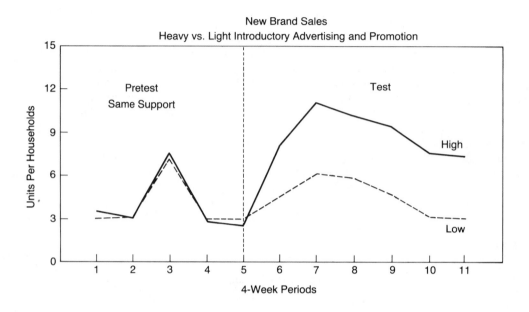

introduction. Initial contacts with clients were usually made by Malec, Eskin, Fulgoni or one of the marketing vice presidents, frequently at the invitation of the prospective client. The prospects had usually heard of BehaviorScan through advertisements or public relations articles, or had heard Malec or Eskin speak at marketing research conferences. Because of its high price, BehaviorScan selling usually included the vice president of marketing level, or higher.

Once the account was sold, it was serviced through an account team supervised by one of IRI's two sales vice presidents.

Gerry Eskin summarized the BehaviorScan product policy as follows:

BehaviorScan is an exclusive sales product. We sell a two-market set in which the client has access to the market for his or her product category for a year, plus the right to do experiments in those markets and the right to *not* have someone else do something in the category in those markets. Each category is sold at the same price, which is contrary to current marketing research practice. We don't know if that's the right policy for the future. We've basically looked at BehaviorScan as selling a big testing unit for a fixed price. It's a high-fixed-cost operation for us, and we make it a relatively high-fixed-cost purchase for the client. The basic contract price is about $150,000, with low incremental costs for additional experiments. These are typically $10–20,000. We charge for stocking product, cut-ins, and so on. If a client has some really complicated treatment or lots of special analysis, we charge for that, but our philosophy has been that the basic contract should cover most of what a client would normally want.

There are some categories that we could sell twenty times if we had the markets, like cereals. Our present clients are, by and large, the most sophisticated marketing researchers in the world—and so are their competitors. Our exclusive category contract severely limits our market

Exhibit 5.31   BehaviorScan Test Results: Advertising and Promotion Effect on Trial and Repeat

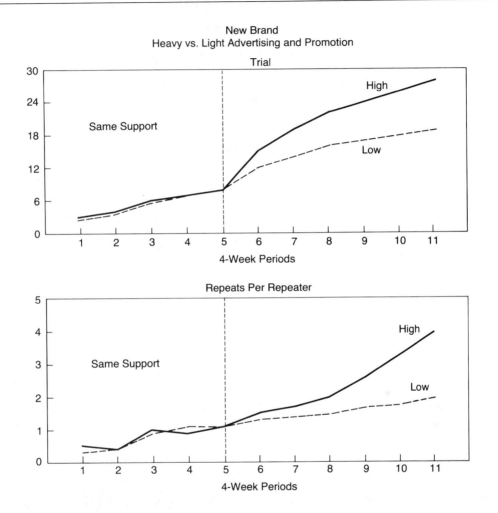

New Brand
Heavy vs. Light Advertising and Promotion

by excluding all but one—or at most two—of the possible clients in each category.

BehaviorScan sales in 1981 were $5.79 million, and by June 1982, about 80 different manufacturers had used BehaviorScan. Of the then-current BehaviorScan projects, 85% were by clients who had done at least one previous project. BehaviorScan had been advertised in various trade sources, and numerous articles about it had appeared in marketing management and research-oriented magazines, journals, and newpapers, as well as in *Time* and *Business Week*.

The Marketing Fact Book

In the second half of 1981, IRI introduced plans for the *Marketing Fact Book* as a way to gain more revenue from the now substantial panel database. The *Fact Book* would be published quarterly and report on all items in the 130,000-item UPC code li-

Exhibit 5.32   IRI Study Matching Sales Volume with Price

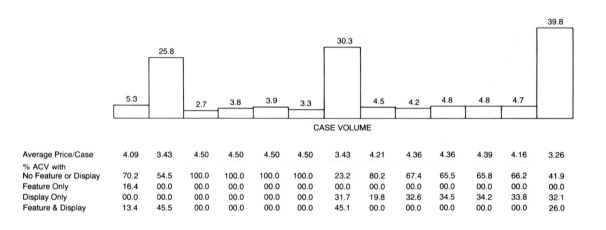

Pittsfield Market
Total Brand X Volume
4/6/81–7/5/81

Week Ending Dates

	4/12	4/19	4/26	5/3	5/10	5/17	5/24	5/31	6/7	6/14	6/21	6/28	7/5
Average Price/Case	4.09	3.43	4.50	4.50	4.50	4.50	3.43	4.21	4.36	4.36	4.39	4.16	3.26
% ACV with													
No Feature or Display	70.2	54.5	100.0	100.0	100.0	100.0	23.2	80.2	67.4	65.5	65.8	66.2	41.9
Feature Only	16.4	00.0	00.0	00.0	00.0	00.0	00.0	00.0	00.0	00.0	00.0	00.0	00.0
Display Only	00.0	00.0	00.0	00.0	00.0	00.0	31.7	19.8	32.6	34.5	34.2	33.8	32.1
Feature & Display	13.4	45.5	00.0	00.0	00.0	00.0	45.1	00.0	00.0	00.0	00.0	00.0	26.0

brary that were purchased by at least 1% of the combined panels. All other items would be collected in a miscellaneous listing for their subtype (including BehaviorScan-tested new products). IRI promotional material described the *Marketing Fact Book* as follows:

> How would you like to cut part of your budget for national audit/warehouse withdrawal services, do away with much of your spending for national diary panel data and virtually eliminate the need for continuous or one-time usage studies?
>
> Would you believe you can do this while at the same time increasing the timeliness, accuracy, and utility of your information?
>
> Brand manager, new product guru, promotional director—all will find the *Fact Book* indispensable.
>
> The *Fact Book* is no pipe dream. You can buy hard copy data on all product categories plus

access rights to the database for follow-up, indepth analyses. You will quite likely find our cost for data on all product categories to be less than half the price of a single national diary panel contract. [Exhibit 5.34 is a sample page.]

The data in the *Fact Book* consists of household-level purchase data with traditional coverage biases removed. This, in turn, is achievable only with the electronic technology used in the very tightly controlled BehaviorScan universe. Not only are purchases collected, but we also collect and code data on all coupons used as well as features, displays, and price activity. The data are accurate and comprehensive. The household-level data have an accuracy heretofore available only at the store level.

Since the BehaviorScan system routinely produced both store audit and panel sales figures, they could be compared on a "sales per 1,000 households" basis as seen in Exhibit 5.35.

Exhibit 5.33 BehaviorScan Test Results: Effects of Price, Display, and Promotion on Share

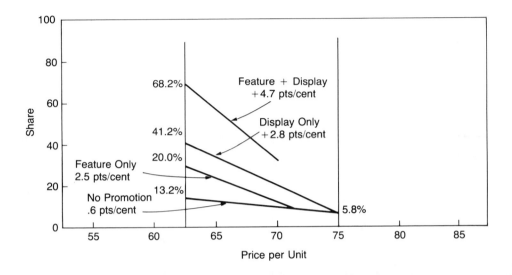

BehaviorScan's mean coverage ratio was 1.0, with only a .03 standard deviation for food and household categories, compared with the .78 coverage ratio published for diary panels.

Although there were only four BehaviorScan markets, IRI contended that they had been selected to cover a wide range of geography; that for use in the *Fact Book*, the BehaviorScan data had been balanced exactly to the U.S. census controls on age, household size, and income; and that the markets had shown themselves to be generally representative across dozens of categories during the past two years of client testing.

Perhaps the most unusual aspect of the *Fact Book* was the opportunity for clients to obtain direct access to the entire database by requesting special analysis from IRI or through timesharing. The entire database on which the *Fact Book* was based was to be maintained on-line or in quick-access, off-line storage. Data would be stored at the individual household level, complete with household demographics at the raw panel record level. On-line, dial-up access directly by the client would allow entry to any portion of the database for any of the following IRI programs:

Market summary (volume, share, households buying, etc.

Brand switching

Source of volume

Trial/repeat

Demographic profile

Promotional effectiveness

Cross-purchasing analysis

These analyses could be specified on-line by the client and the request would be run during the least costly period during the next 48 hours. Report costs varied from $2,000 to $10,000.

The *Marketing Fact Book* was priced at $9,000 for each quarterly report or $24,900 for four quarterly reports plus an annual summary. The five hard-copy reports plus the database access rights were priced at $34,900. Current BehaviorScan clients received a 20% discount. Additional copies of the quarterly reports were $500 each (annual summary $900.) It was estimated that special report fees and time-sharing charges would double the revenue per client. By June 1982, IRI had sold about

Exhibit 5.34   Page from the Marketing Fact Book

THE MARKETING FACT BOOK FROM INFORMATION RESOURCES, INC.

--- DATA REFLECT GROCERY STORE PURCHASES ONLY ---

CATEGORY - FROZEN POTATOES
VOLUME EXPRESSED IN POUNDS
ANNUAL - OCT 1981 TO SEPT 1982

INCLUDING ONLY BRANDS PURCHASED BY 1% OR MORE OF ALL HOUSEHOLDS

	CATEGORY VOLUM SHARE	TYPE % VOLUM SHARE	TYPE % OF HSHLDS BUYING	VOLUM PER PURCH	PCHAS CYCLE (DAYS)	SHARE CTGRY RQMTS	PRICE PER VOLUM	ANY TRADE DEAL	PRINT AD FEATR	IN STORE DISPL	SHELF PRICE REDUC	MIR/ STORE COUPN	AVG % OFF ON PRICE DEALS	SOCIO /ECON CODES
								22%	14%	4%	17%	6%	29%	***
CATEGORY - FROZEN POTATOES	10430.8*	100.0%	76.6%	2.2	56	100%	0.64							
TYPE - HASHBROWN POTATOES	17.6	100.0	33.5	1.8	71	32	0.66	18	8	5	16	3	19	M H M
IDAHO FROZEN FOODS	1.8	10.1	4.5	1.9	75	17	0.66	23	7	9	20	2	18	L L H
RUS-ETTES	1.8	10.1	4.5	1.9	75	17	0.66	23	7	9	20	2	18	L L H
REGULAR HASHBROWNS	1.8	10.1	4.5	1.9	75	17	0.66	23	7	9	20	2	18	L L H
INTERNATIONAL CO-OP	1.4	8.2	4.5	1.7	82	15	0.68	27	5	8	24	2	17	L L L
OKRAYS	1.4	8.2	4.5	1.7	82	15	0.68	27	5	8	24	2	17	L L L
REGULAR HASHBROWNS	1.4	8.2	4.5	1.7	82	15	0.68	27	5	8	24	2	17	L L L
NORTH PACIFIC CAN	0.7	4.0	2.0	2.0	74	16	0.51	11	6	3	11	0	21	L L M
WESTPAC	0.6	3.6	1.8	2.0	71	16	0.52	4	4	0	4	0	23	M L M
REGULAR HASHBROWNS	0.6	3.6	1.8	2.0	71	16	0.52	4	4	0	4	0	23	M L M
ORE-IDA FOODS	10.4	59.0	24.6	1.7	73	25	0.70	15	6	5	14	4	20	M H M
ORE IDA	10.4	59.0	24.6	1.7	73	25	0.70	15	6	5	14	4	20	M L M
REGULAR HASHBROWNS	9.1	52.0	22.5	1.7	72	24	0.68	17	6	6	16	4	19	M M M
ALL OTHER HASHBROWNS	1.2	7.0	3.9	1.7	65	19	0.80	1	1	0	1	2	29	H H L
PRIVATE LABEL	3.0	17.1	8.4	1.8	74	20	0.60	19	14	0	14	4	16	M H H
REGULAR HASHBROWNS	2.9	16.5	8.1	1.8	76	20	0.59	20	14	0	14	4	16	M H H
TYPE - FRENCH FRIED POTATOES	59.9	100.0	58.9	2.2	63	66	0.60	25	18	5	18	7	36	L L H
CARNATION	0.9	1.5	1.6	3.2	91	23	0.41	23	21	21	16	0	50	L L L
LYNDEN FARMS	0.9	1.5	1.6	3.2	91	23	0.41	23	21	21	16	0	50	L L L
FRENCH FRIES	0.6	0.9	1.0	3.5	102	20	0.39	30	30	30	24	0	52	L L H
GENERAL FOODS	0.5	0.9	2.2	1.1	58	15	0.93	18	6	0	17	3	23	M M M
BIRDSEYE	0.5	0.9	2.2	1.1	58	15	0.93	18	6	0	17	3	23	M M M
FRENCH FRIES	0.5	0.8	2.0	1.1	58	15	0.94	19	6	0	19	3	22	M M M
IDAHO FROZEN FOODS	5.3	8.8	6.6	3.5	61	32	0.41	20	16	3	13	0	14	L L L
IDAHO	5.3	8.8	6.6	3.5	61	32	0.41	20	16	3	13	0	14	L L L
CRINKLE CUT FRIES	0.8	1.3	1.9	2.1	67	17	0.46	12	9	0	12	0	16	L L L
FRENCH FRIES	3.4	5.7	3.2	4.7	66	36	0.42	21	18	3	14	0	11	L L L
SHOESTRING FRIES	1.0	1.6	1.2	2.9	44	21	0.31	25	18	2	9	0	19	L L H
MC CAIN FOODS	0.9	1.5	2.9	1.7	60	14	0.69	31	20	0	27	4	16	L M H
MCCAIN	0.9	1.5	2.9	1.7	60	14	0.69	31	20	0	27	4	16	L M H
SHOESTRING FRIES	0.3	0.6	1.5	1.5	58	11	0.74	23	14	0	16	4	13	L M H

* CATEGORY VOLUME PER 1000 SHOPPERS

*** CATEGORY DEMOGRAPHIC INDICES: FEMALE AGE = 96   FAMILY SIZE = 107   INCOME = 101

Exhibit 5.35   BehaviorScan Panel Coverage Across 47 Food and Household Categories

Coverage Ratio*	Product Categories
< .9	3%
.91 − 1.10	91
> 1.10	6

*(Sales volume/1,000 HH measured in the panel only) ÷ (sales volume/1,000 HH measured at the store level)

a dozen *Fact Books* before the first edition was published or the database made accessible.

The major costs involved in producing the *Fact Book* were those incurred in operating BehaviorScan. Substantial programming had been required to produce the first *Fact Book* from the database, but the incremental costs of subsequent editions included only 24 hours of computer time and reproduction costs, so the printed editions of the *Fact Book* were a very high-margin item.

Client Reaction to the Fact Book

One early buyer of the *Marketing Fact Book* was the research director of a major advertising agency. He said that his major reasons for buying it were:

It provides some key market measures, important for advertising decision making in virtually every supermarket category. Since the agency has many clients, having these few key measures on hand may relieve the agency and the client of the need to perform a separate panel analysis costing $100,000 and requiring four to six months to execute. The availability of information on the number of purchases per buyer, the market penetration, and share-of-category requirements for every product in every category is useful in judgmentally planning advertising budgets.

It will also be useful in identifying market gaps for new products and getting some preliminary estimates of the nature of the competition in new markets. How strong are the present brands? How much price-cutting is going on? And so on.

The accuracy of the data should be better than that of panel data, since the IRI panel is stable and the measurement is unobtrusive.

As the director of a group of some 70 professionals, this buyer was especially interested in access to the database, and felt that his group would be a heavy user of the data and time-sharing facilities.

Potential problems with the *Fact Book* as he saw them were:

1. Questions about the representativeness of the data, since the distribution of many products varies considerably from region to region.

2. Distortions due to a marketing push in one of the test cities. The "pushes" would be difficult to identify from the *Fact Book* alone.

He felt these problems would make it difficult and risky to make national projections from the *Fact Book*.

Sentiment within the advertising agency had been that the *Fact Book* had unique potential to provide new insights into the working of its clients' businesses, and that the agency should take advantage of the opportunity to learn from it. They also felt the biases in the database were known, in principle, and that the seriousness of the bias for any particular client could be estimated.

A second early buyer of the *Fact Book* was the manager of consumer and advertising research for a major food product manufacturer that marketed 14 major and 16 smaller brands, which together totaled hundreds of items. The company was an active BehaviorScan client.

The manager felt the *Fact Book* provided:

. . . a valuable resource to provide penetration and share data on a number of smaller product categories that don't have the money to spend on custom research. The large number of categories offered will be valuable in new-product planning and seeing what might be driving sales in our more geographically extensive SAMI reports.

I'm not terribly concerned that IRI's data isn't national in scope. You really can't do better on a national scale, or even in selected market areas with the major panel companies such as MRCA or NPD. The alternative to IRI's detailed data on individual purchase behavior on a regional basis is an absence of data—not good national data. Our most important use of the *Fact Book* will be to learn about customers and products. We have other ways to make national projections of market share.

The head of a relatively small research group, the manager planned to order IRI's special analyses rather than accessing the database himself. If the analyses proved useful, he thought he might add a computer analyst sometime in the future.

Preparation Questions

1. To what extent does the BehaviorScan system overcome the data problems we've discussed in the previous cases?

2. What research needs does the *Marketing Fact Book* satisfy, and is this a compatible companion product for BehaviorScan?

3. What marketing strategy do you suggest for IRI?

4. What problems and opportunities would you anticipate that the BehaviorScan system presents to a manager planning a marketing strategy?

5. Evaluate the BehaviorScan system.

CASE: G.D. Searle I

This case presents the BehaviorScan test market results for Equal* low-calorie sweetener. The problem is, of course, to develop a marketing strategy for Equal. The situation is somewhat unusual, however, since previous tests have convinced Searle management that Equal will enjoy a large market and have a successful introduction. The objective of the test market is to fine-tune the marketing strategy to improve profitability. In terms of the marketing research considerations that have been directing our analysis in this chapter, this case represents the utilization of a test market methodology that fulfills most of our wish list of features.

In July 1981 Phillip Watson, director of sweetener products for G.D. Searle's Consumer Products Division, had agreed to a test market that would delay the market entry of Equal low-calorie sweetener from 6 to 12 months. He explained his decision, which had been a difficult one:

> When you finally get FDA approval for a new product, you are anxious to get the product on the market and start recovering your investment—especially after eight years of waiting, 112 safety tests, and $78 million in product development costs. But when your primary ingredient costs 35 times as much as the leading artificial sweetener and you don't have much production capacity, the amount consumers will pay for the product and the expected demand for it are critically important.

Numerous other marketing research studies had been undertaken during this eight-year period, but until the FDA approved aspartame, Equal's prime ingredient, a test market for the new sweetener had not been possible. Since price and demand were so critical for this product introduction, Norris Frederic, director of marketing research, had recommended that Equal's market introduction plan be tested using BehaviorScan, a new test market concept that had aroused much excitement in the market research community. The BehaviorScan test began on October 26, 1981.

After the April 1982 BehaviorScan interim report, Watson, Frederic, and Susan Tracey, associate manager of marketing research, met together to discuss next steps in the introduction of Equal. The BehaviorScan test market results, although based on only 20 weeks of data, appeared very favorable.

There seemed little question at that time that Equal would be a successful product, but there was considerable ambiguity about the appropriate levels of the marketing variables being tested. Cumulative trial was lower in households that had been exposed to the high level of advertising than in the low-advertising group, and although the first repeat rate was higher in the high advertising group, the additional repeat rate was nearly identical to that of the low advertising households. Cumulative trial was 4.4 points higher in low-priced stores than in high-priced stores. Promotion effectiveness had only been tested with one coupon and one sample mailing.

Phillip Watson, while not encouraged by the advertising results, was very pleased with the trial-and-repeat rates. He felt they indicated that Equal was a viable mass market product despite its high price premium, and decided to proceed with the planned rollout in the southeastern U.S. According to Watson:

---

*Equal® and NutraSweet® are registered trade names.

This case was prepared by Darral G. Clarke from two Harvard cases by the same author.

Copyright © 1984 by the President and Fellows of Harvard College Harvard Business School cases 9-585-010 and 9-585-011.

Our planning for the southeastern market rollout was based on the assumption that the high price level would be acceptable. Since we had to have budgets planned in advance, we were pretty well locked into that price. We had some flexibility in the advertising budget. The test results were near or above the goals in the plan, and since we were only rolling out in the southeast, I felt that if we had capacity problems we could delay going national.

Norris Frederic supported the decision to go ahead with the rollout in spite of the limited data in the test market.

The test market step in new product development is probably the one that has the highest risk associated with making a wrong decision, both for the company and for the individuals doing the research. You can recommend not to do something at any step and, if management follows your recommendation, probably nobody will know if you were right or wrong. When you say, "Here is the forecast, go national," that's when the personal risks escalate; but you have to remember that you also hurt the company if you are too conservative. You look at it both ways and try to balance the risks, but when big decisions and capital commitments are based on my recommendation, I get very nervous.

In January 1983 Norris Frederic received market audit data for the southeast rollout markets, which had been under way since June 1982, and for the rest of the country, where Equal had been on the market since mid-September. Equal had achieved retail dollar sales slightly over $4 million during September, October, and November, which accounted for a 17.2% dollar share of the non-sugar sweetener market. Its case sales for the same period were 171,000, or 4.2%. The results were very good. Equal was one of the most successful new products introduced in a decade.

Company Background

G.D. Searle & Company was founded in 1908 and headquartered in Chicago, Illinois. In 1981, Searle and its subsidiaries had sales of $942.3 million and

aftertax earnings of $130.9 million. The corporation's major divisions included a research and development organization and three major business groupings: pharmaceuticals/consumer products; optical products; and other businesses, which included specialty chemicals and gases. Searle products were sold worldwide through an extensive network of foreign subsidiaries and working arrangements.

The pharmaceuticals/consumer products group manufactured and marketed ethical pharmaceutical drugs and three nonprescription products. The group's 1981 sales were $637.4 million, of which $565.6 million came from ethical drugs and $71.8 million from consumer products. Operating earnings were $168.4 million.

The Sweetener Market

In 1981, granulated sugar retail sales in large supermarkets were $945 million and contributed $62 million to retailers' profit (6.6% of sales). Retail dollar sales for tabletop sugar substitutes were $114.7 million in 1981. Retail margins for these products averaged 25.9%. Retail dollar and unit sales had grown steadily from the 1970 ban on cyclamates until 1978, when sales decreased substantially following negative findings about saccharin's effect on health and the resultant threat that the Food and Drug Administration (FDA) would ban that substance.

Food stores accounted for 83% of the category's 1981 retail sales, while drugstores accounted for 15% and mass merchandisers 2%. Sugar substitute products were marketed in packets, tablets, granulated bulk, and liquids. Packets were the dominant product form, accounting for 61% of unit sales and 58% of dollar sales. Exhibit 5.36 summarizes sales trends for sugar and sugar substitutes.

Since the ban on cyclamates, all artificial sweeteners had been saccharin-based. Products containing saccharin were required to carry a label warning customers that it had been found to cause cancer in laboratory animals. Objective taste tests found that many people noticed a bitter aftertaste from saccharin and felt that it did not live up to their sweetening expectations. Experts believed that the 1981 sales level did not represent the artificial

Exhibit 5.36 Sugar Substitute Market Retail Sales

Dollar Sales ($ millions)	1976	1977	1978	1979	1980	1981
Total market	86.3	99.5	81.2	91.3	104.2	114.7
Growth rate	+10%	+15%	−18%	+12%	+14%	+10%
Unit Sales (billions of equivalent teaspoons)						
Total market	26.3	30.6	22.3	27.2	28.6	29.4
Growth rate	−6%	+16%	−26%	+22%	+5%	+3%
Advertising ($000)						
Artificial sweeteners	2,579	2,379	3,972	3,585	2,748	3,388
Sugar	3,509	4,876	3,114	3,462	4,019	4,636

Source: Compiled by Searle from SAMI, IMS America, and LNA.

sweetener market's full potential because consumers were dissatisfied with current products.

The sugar substitute market was dominated by Sweet 'N Low, which held a 60% market share, and Sugar Twin with a 13% share. Saccharin was about fourteen times as expensive as sugar per pound ($4.00 vs. $0.29/pound), but because it's 300 times sweeter than sugar, it cost only 1.3 cents per pound on a "sugar-equivalent-sweetening basis."

Advertising expenditures for Sweet 'N Low and Sugar Twin were $1.8 million and $1.5 million respectively in 1981, representing 2% and 9% of sales and virtually all category advertising. There were no true national brands of sugar, but Domino, C&H, and Imperial were large regional manufacturers. Advertising for these brands in 1981 totaled $4.6 million, or less than 0.5% of their sales.

NutraSweet™

Aspartame (APM), the sweetening ingredient in Equal, had been discovered by Searle's Pharmaceutical Research and Development Division in 1965. James M. Schlatter, a Searle scientist engaged in peptide research, discovered serendipitously that a compound made of L-aspartic acid and the methylester of L-phenylalanine was surprisingly sweet (neither of these two amino acids is sweet by itself). Two years of extensive research determined the properties of aspartame and resulted in NutraSweet, Searle's registered trademark for aspartame. Aspartame was 200 times sweeter than sugar but cost $90.00 per pound, so on a sugar-equivalent-sweetening basis it costs 45 cents per pound. Aspartame would be protected under its patent until 1992.

In January 1969, Searle began safety testing to obtain data for FDA review, and in January 1974 NutraSweet won approval for use in dry-base foods and beverages. However, special interest groups filed objections that caused the FDA to convene a public board of inquiry and to stay the approval until certain Searle research studies had been validated. By the time NutraSweet finally obtained FDA approval on July 15, 1981, 112 studies had been completed. FDA Commissioner Arthur Hull Hayes, Jr., observed, "Few compounds have withstood such detailed testing and repeated close scrutiny. . . . The process through which aspartame has gone should provide the public with additional confidence in its safety."

The FDA authorized the use of NutraSweet in products such as tabletop sweeteners (packets and tablets), powdered soft drinks, presweetened cereals, chewing gum; dry mixes for products such as gelatins, desserts, and toppings; and presweetened coffees and teas. NutraSweet was not approved for use in soft drinks. By 1982 NutraSweet had also been approved for use in 13 countries.

After all the testing, one health warning remained. One of the amino acids in NutraSweet poses a danger to individuals with the hereditary disease phenylketonuria (PKU), which affects about one in 15,000 infants. Therefore, all products containing NutraSweet had to carry the label statement "Phenylketonurics: Contains Phenylalanine."

Early products containing NutraSweet were Equal, Lipton Presweetened Iced Tea Mix, Sugar-Free Kool-Aid, and Quaker Oats' Halfsies cold cereal. Since NutraSweet lost its sweetness at high cooking temperatures, it could not be used in many prepared foods or as a bulk sweetener for home-baked cakes, breads, and cookies.

In numerous consumer taste tests conducted by Searle and major food manufacturers, most adults could not distinguish beverages and gelatins sweetened with NutraSweet from the same items sweetened with sugar. In one study, 76% of those who tried Equal agreed with the promotional claim that NutraSweet had an "honest-to-sugar taste."

Equal's Proposed Introductory Marketing Plan

The introductory marketing plan tested by BehaviorScan called for positioning Equal as a general-purpose, low-calorie tabletop sweetener. Equal's product benefits, as indicated by the name, were that it was a safe, "nonartificial" sweetener equal in taste to sugar, but with only one-eighth the calories.

Equal would be available in packets (equivalent to two teaspoons of sugar) and tablet form (equivalent to one teaspoon of sugar). An Equal packet would contain NutraSweet, a bulking agent, and an anticaking agent. Equal contained no sucrose or sodium, only one gram of carbohydrate, and four calories. Equal tablets contained no carbohydrates and only 0.1 calorie per tablet. Equal would be packaged in 50- and 100-packet cartons (50s and 100s) and 100-tablet bottles. An introductory trial-size carton of 10 packets was also planned.

Product Position. The decision to market Equal as a general-purpose tabletop sweetener for the full family was a difficult one. The Searle staff and various consultants had suggested a number of different product positions, almost all of which were directed at special-interest markets. Although the mass market position was attractive because of its size, there was serious concern about whether the product's premium price would be acceptable to consumers or to the trade.

Extensive marketing research indicated that consumers of low-calorie sweeteners could be divided into three groups: unconcerned sugar users, concerned sugar users (some of whom had been cyclamate users), and saccharin users. Although the segmentation scheme made sense conceptually, there was some uncertainty about the size of the segments and considerable uncertainty about the intensity of their needs and their acceptance of Equal.

Price. Watson believed that most retailers would follow the same pricing policy they used for Sweet 'N Low, pricing Equal so as to make 25% on packets and 35% on tablets. Because aspartame cost so much more than saccharin, Searle could not attain its normal profit levels unless Equal's retail price was at least $1.99 for a 50-packet carton, about three times the retail price of Sweet 'N Low.

Advertising. Watson planned to announce the introduction of Equal with the most aggressive advertising program in the category's history. His planned advertising level of $3.8 million was more than the combined 1981 advertising expenditures of Sweet 'N Low and Sugar Twin. The advertising objective was to quickly establish a high level of brand awareness in Equal's two target audiences: current sugar substitute users and concerned sugar users. The advertising campaign would consist of both television and print media to obtain the most effective levels of reach against the target audience.

The creative strategy of Equal advertising was to position Equal as a revolutionary new sweetener equivalent to sugar in taste but without the calories—with support focusing on Equal's "natural" sugar taste and the absence of saccharin.

Promotion. Consumer and trade promotions were also intended to provide strong support for the Equal introduction. Trade promotion would include a distribution allowance on all sizes, a display/feature allowance, and co-op advertising. Consumer promotion would include the distribution of samples and store coupons in addition to a self-standing floor display holding 72 10-packet trial-size cartons priced at 39 cents.

Public Relations. A further element of the Equal introductory plan was an extensive public relations campaign, which began with FDA approval in July 1981. By the time the Equal test market program got under way in October, the public relations effort had succeeded in generating numerous newspaper and magazine articles.

Distribution. Searle's distribution strength was concentrated in drugstores and included little or no coverage of either food stores or mass merchandisers, where 83% of the artificial sweetener sales occurred. Searle's 40-person over-the-counter sales force sold a product line that included Dramamine, a travel sickness preventative; Icy Hot, an analgesic balm; and Metamucil, a natural fiber laxative.

A marketing strategy consultant, who was hired to research the grocery trade, reported that Searle, as a company, was unknown to the dry grocery trade; even those who were familiar with Metamucil were unfamiliar with Searle. Watson concluded that it was not feasible to build an in-house sales force and distribution system, and began a search that included 15 companies and culminated in a contract with the Thomas J. Lipton Co. for the distribution of Equal in food stores. In return for a fixed commission rate,* Searle would receive the services of Lipton's 600-person sales force and the physical distribution of Equal.

Marketing Research Activities Before the Test Market

Prior to the beginning of the BehaviorScan test market in October 1981, 48 market research studies of various types were conducted. When FDA approval began to look imminent and as the introductory marketing plan became more complete, the need for more specific market information increased. Research projects designed to test specific elements of the marketing mix during late 1979 included focus groups, name validation tests, price and product concept tests, a market profile study, product taste tests (in countries where aspartame had been approved), and advertising claim tests.

Choosing BehaviorScan

Frederic and Tracey considered a number of test market options including controlled store test audits, AdTel's split-cable facility, and Information Resources, Inc.'s BehaviorScan. Finally, as Tracey explained,

> We decided to go with BehaviorScan because it offered the most flexibility and complete measurement. We traded off the complete coverage in only two cities available through BehaviorScan against the incomplete measurement we would get from a controlled store test in more cities, and chose BehaviorScan.

The key elements of BehaviorScan, according to Frederic, were the ability to measure the source of business and to test individual marketing variables.

> We felt that we were introducing a premium-priced product in an existing category and that Equal had the potential to bring in a lot of new users. Just measuring market share wouldn't have shown us the source of the volume. We needed to see if the business came just from artificial sweetener users or also from sugar users. We needed to understand trial and repeat because we felt we had to base our forecast on household consumption and not just the share of an existing market. We also needed to control price, advertising, sampling, and promotion and be able to separate their effects. None of the other systems could do this for us.

The BehaviorScan* test market began in Pittsfield, Massachusetts, and Marion, Indiana, on October 26, 1981. The cost of planned research activities directly connected to the test market are listed in Exhibit 5.37.

Test Market Design

The Equal test market tested two consumer price levels as well as two levels of media spending. The

---

*For purposes of analysis assume the commission rate was 7% of trade sales.

*See the Information Resources, Inc. case or Sahumer (1983).

Exhibit 5.37 Cost of Equal Test Market

BehaviorScan
Standard services	$140,900	
Additional services	69,100	
(drugstore data,		
price control, stocking)		
		$210,000
Telephone tracking study		
(baseline and two waves)		49,500
Sample/coupon redemption study		17,000
Additional test expenses		
Publicity	110,000	
Advertising media	145,300	
Co-op mailing	5,800	
Displays, product, costs, etc.	17,400	278,500
Total		
		$550,000

two test cities were about the same size, each accounting for about 0.03% of the U.S. population. There were six food stores and six drugstores in Pittsfield, and seven food stores and eight drugstores in Marion. The level of sweetener use was higher in Marion (126 CDI) than in Pittsfield (91 CDI).* A summary of the market design follows:

The test was to run for 13 four-week periods. An initial analysis of Equal's performance would be conducted after five periods of data were available, and a final report would be made in December 1982.

Equal (in 50- and 100-count packet boxes) would be control-stocked in supermarkets and drugstores. BehaviorScan personnel would check two to three times per week to assure adequate stocks and proper facings.

Approximately half of the stores in each market would feature Equal priced at a base level, while the remaining stores would carry Equal priced at a higher level:

*CDI = Category Development Index, which measures the ratio of regional to national per capita consumption. Marion uses 1.26 times as much sweetener per capita as the national average.

Carton Size	Base Level	High Level
50s	$1.59	$1.99
100s	2.99	3.69

Two media weight levels ($3.8 million and $5.7 million) would be tested. BehaviorScan would arrange for "cutting-in" test advertising over Searle's commercial air time for other products. The high- and low-media weight panel members would be as closely matched as possible on (1) predominant shopping patterns (high- and low-priced stores); (2) artificial sweetener and sugar penetration and volume movement; and (3) the demographic variables of income, age, education, and family size.

Approximately one-fourth of the panel members, consistent with the proposed national sampling plan, would receive a co-op mailing including a two-packet sample of Equal and a 30-cent coupon. Sampled households would be drawn equally from each of the four price and media weight cells. A separate sampling/coupon redemption study was also planned.

The Southeastern U.S. Rollout Decision

On April 16, 1982, Watson, Frederic, and Tracey met with consultants from IRI for a presentation of results based on data through the week of March 14, 1982. At this time, 25% of the households had tried Equal, and 34.2% of the triers had repeated at least once. There was no difference between trial in the high and low advertising panels. The IRI consultant began his presentation by warning that this was very little data upon which to base important decisions, especially since the average low-calorie sweetener buyer made only about six purchases per year. Despite these warnings, Frederic supported Watson's decision to begin the southeastern rollout.

Rollout Marketing Plan

The marketing program that Watson recommended for the southeastern rollout established a 1982 retail sales objective of $8 million, 80% of which would come from food stores and 20% from drugstores and mass merchandisers. On June 1, 1982, Searle began shipments to the southeast region in order to "fill the pipeline," and some sales occurred before the advertising campaign began the week of August 15, 1982. Rollout to national markets was scheduled to begin the first week of September, accompanied by a media plan similar to that used in the southeast. A summary of the marketing program follows.

Advertising. Watson's southeastern rollout plan included annual advertising at a level equivalent to $5.2 million, using both television and print media to obtain desired levels of reach. It was estimated that the advertising program would reach 80% of the target audience an average of 3.8 times a week.

Pricing. Equal was priced at $1.99 for 50-packet cartons (50s), the high level tested in the BehaviorScan test market; and $3.89 for 100-packet cartons (100s), $0.20 higher than the test market high level.

Retail Sales Objectives. Watson had developed extensive sales force programs and materials designed to obtain distribution and favorable shelf position for Equal. His goals included 70% distribution within 90 days, 95% distribution within 150 days, 90% of the large accounts stocking two package sizes, and target price achievement in 80% of all outlets. Trade promotion and cooperative advertising allowances were also a part of the initial marketing program.

BehaviorScan Test Market Subsequent to the Rollout Decision. Amid the excitement of the southeastern rollout and planning for the national rollout, the BehaviorScan test market had continued. Since Equal's share in the high- and low-priced stores seemed to differ only slightly, Watson wanted to test an even higher price level. Even though Norris Frederic and the IRI consultants explained that this would represent a disturbance in the test design that would compromise their ability to directly quantify the degree to which observed sales changes could be related to the various prices, Watson directed that the price be increased by the same percentage in both high- and low-priced stores (see Exhibit 5.38).

Promotion. A 40-cent refund-on-purchase (ROP) coupon was tested just before the price increase. A

Exhibit 5.38   Mid-Test Equal Pricing Changes

	Original Pricing (10/26/81-7/4/82)		New Pricing (Effective 7/5/82)	
	Base Level	High Level	Base Level	High Level
50-packet carton	$1.59	$1.99	$1.79	$2.19
100-packet carton	2.99	3.69	3.49	4.29
Tablets (100)	2.09	2.09	2.49	2.49

trial size with a display featuring a 29-cent ROP coupon and a further 25-cent coupon inside the trial package was tested early in September. Several promotion and merchandising programs were planned between the time the rollout decision was made and October 24, 1982, the planned end of the test market.

Twelve-Month BehaviorScan Results

The results of the one-year BehaviorScan test were presented December 11, 1982. Equal's volume per thousand households and the promotion testing schedule are shown in Exhibit 5.39. Since no significant difference in the response to the advertising weight levels was observed throughout the test, most of the analysis done by IRI was based on the entire sample of households, rather than separate analyses for the high- and low-advertising households.

Trial and Repeat. By October 24, 1982, at least one purchase of Equal had been made by 21.0% of panel households. Equal buyers purchased, on average, 380 teaspoon-equivalents during the test (3.8 50s)* and Equal achieved a 23.0% unit share of low-calorie sweetener sales and a 44.3% share of category dollar volume (see Exhibits 5.40 and 5.41). Equal had been tried by 37.3% of low-calorie sweetener buyers and 16.4% of the "nonbuyers" (see Exhibit 5.42). By the end of the 13 periods, the trial rate had leveled off and repeat-purchase volume accounted for 93.9% of total volume (see Exhibit 5.43).

---

*One packet was the equivalent of two teaspoons of sugar; a 50-packet carton contained 100 teaspoon-equivalents.

Exhibit 5.39   Equal Volume per 1000 Households (10/26/81 — 10/24/82)

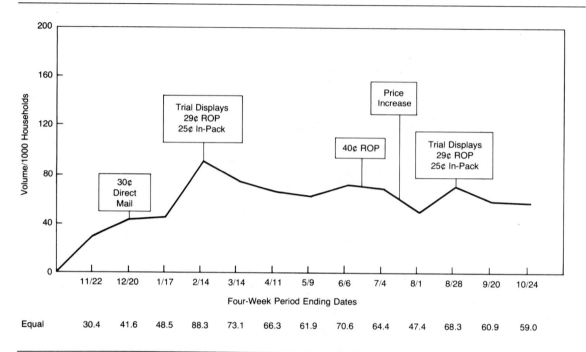

| Equal | 30.4 | 41.6 | 48.5 | 88.3 | 73.1 | 66.3 | 61.9 | 70.6 | 64.4 | 47.4 | 68.3 | 60.9 | 59.0 |

Equal's cumulative trial rate exceeded Sweet 'N Low's first purchase rate after the January 1982 trial-size promotion, but its repeat rate remained slightly less than Sweet 'N Low's (see Exhibit 5.44).

Advertising.   There was no statistically significant difference in cumulative share between the household panels receiving the high and low advertising weights, and no significant difference was found in cumulative trial. The cumulative percentage of triers repeating at least once was 4.0 points higher in the high advertising panel (52.8% vs. 48.8%). Commenting on these results, Watson said:

I don't think that the advertising levels we tested represented a low and a medium advertising level. We tested a very low and a low—even though both expenditure levels were large relative to category spending levels. We had a 50% difference in TV advertising, but the print advertising level and public relations were the same for both panels. Direct mail was the same across both advertising panels. I'm also not convinced that the advertising copy itself was as good as we've now developed. All these things combined make me think there really wasn't much difference in the total Equal-related communications to the two panels.

A telephone survey showed that brand awareness had increased since March, but that advertising awareness had not shown a statistically significant increase (see Exhibit 5.45). The perceptual map derived from the survey results showed that Equal's image had become more like that of Sweet 'N Low, particularly on the "safe to use" dimension (see Exhibit 5.46).

Price.   On July 5, 1982, the first day of period 10, prices were increased in both high- and low-priced stores. By October 24 the difference between Equal's cumulative shares of category volume in the low- and high-priced stores had risen to 23%, up from 9% in the five-period report. Equal rep-

Exhibit 5.40   Equal Purchasing Summary: Total Panel

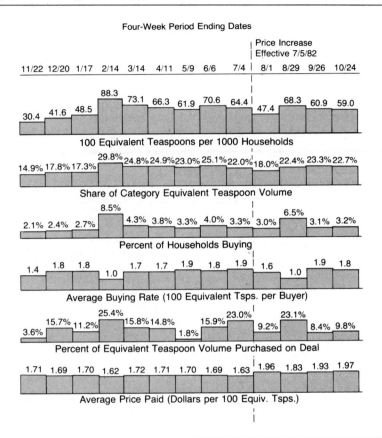

Four-Week Period Ending Dates

Price Increase
Effective 7/5/82

11/22 12/20 1/17 2/14 3/14 4/11 5/9 6/6 7/4 8/1 8/29 9/26 10/24

100 Equivalent Teaspoons per 1000 Households

Share of Category Equivalent Teaspoon Volume

Percent of Households Buying

Average Buying Rate (100 Equivalent Tsps. per Buyer)

Percent of Equivalent Teaspoon Volume Purchased on Deal

Average Price Paid (Dollars per 100 Equiv. Tsps.)

resented 20.6% of the category volume in the low-priced stores and only 16.6% in the high-priced stores (see Exhibit 5.47).

The effects of the price increase and the price level appeared to be quite different for the 50s and the 100s. The price increase had no measurable effect on 50s sales, but the effects were substantial for the 100s (see Exhibit 5.48).

The 100s share of total Equal sales declined in both the high- and low-priced stores after the price increase. Nevertheless, the 100s represented the main source of Equal sales in both high- and low-priced stores (see Exhibit 5.49). The household-level data also shed light on the relationship between package size and trial and repeat. The 50s,

for example, accounted for four times as much trial as the 100s, but the 100s dominated repeat.

Sources of Volume.   A major concern in choosing Equal's product position had been whether it would appeal primarily to current low-calorie sweetener consumers or to "concerned sugar users." BehaviorScan provided the opportunity to study Equal's sources of volume not only at the store level (through comparison of its low-calorie sweetener market shares before and after Equal's introduction), but also at the household level.

At the store level, Equal increased the low-calorie sweetener category volume by 27% and its dollar sales by 132%. Only a relatively small part of

Exhibit 5.41   Total Sugar Substitutes Purchasing Summary (Total Panel)

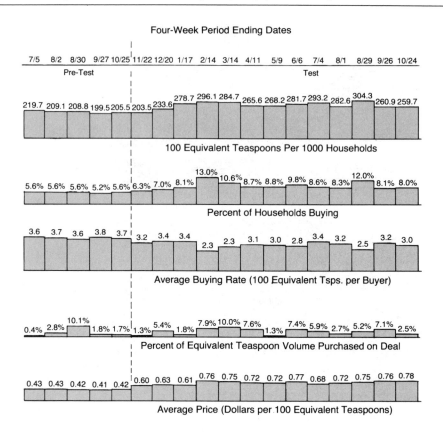

Equal's volume, however, was drawn from existing brands. (See Exhibit 5.50.)

The BehaviorScan source-of-volume analysis examined the change in the share of each household's *total* volume allocated to various brands before and after Equal was tried.* The results obtained from individual households were then aggregated over all households to yield a summary of gains and losses. The technique recognized three possible sources of volume change for a brand from one period to the next:

Gains or losses due to exchange of volume between competitive brands (*brand shifting*)

Gains or losses due to a net volume difference caused by *infrequent category buyers* entering or leaving the market

Gains or losses caused by changes in *category consumption* in households that purchased the category in *both* time periods

To determine whether brand shifting between two brands was greater or less than expected, a brand attraction index was computed by dividing the brand's share of brand shifting by the brand's share of category volume. A brand attraction index

_____

*Triers = Households that tried Equal during the first 24 periods of the test.

Exhibit 5.42 Cumulative Trial Among Pretest Buyers/Nonbuyers* of Sugar Substitutes

Period Ending	Equal		Sugar Substitute	
	Buyers	Nonbuyers	Buyers	Nonbuyers
11/22	5.0	1.3	20.4	2.2
12/20	9.2	2.7	34.8	4.5
1/17	12.8	3.7	44.4	6.6
2/14	20.5	9.0	54.9	12.3
3/14	24.1	10.5	61.6	15.5
4/11	27.4	11.5	65.4	17.2
5/9	29.1	12.2	67.9	18.5
6/8	30.4	12.9	70.5	20.3
7/4	32.7	13.5	72.6	21.7
8/1	33.1	13.9	73.8	22.8
8/29	36.0	15.8	75.7	24.9
9/28	26.9	16.2	76.9	25.7
10/24	37.1	16.4	77.5	26.4

*Buyers and nonbuyers of sugar subsitutes defined over 32-week pretest period (March 16 to October 25, 1981). Buyers accounted for 23% of the panel.

over 100 implied greater than expected brand shifting. Nearly half (49%) of Equal's sales were attributable to households that never or seldom bought sugar substitutes. Another 20% of Equal sales resulted from an increase in sugar substitute consumption among Equal buyers. Only 31% of Equal sales came from shifts from other sugar substitute brands.

Nearly 60% of Equal sales were the result of households' shifting away from regular sugar; shifting from sugar represented 72% of Equal's shifting volume (see Exhibit 5.51).

All households showed a decline in category consumption, but among Equal triers there was a greater decline in sugar purchasing and a corresponding increase in sugar substitute consumption, as shown in Exhibit 5.52.

Forecasting

BehaviorScan forecast Equal sales using a modification of the Fourt-Woodlock model (Fourt and Woodlock 1960), a model based on measurements of trial, first repeat, and additional repeat:

$$\frac{Volume}{100HH} = \frac{Triers}{100HH} * Actual\ Volume$$
$$+ Triers * \frac{First\ Repeat}{Triers} * \frac{Average\ Volume}{First\ Repeat}$$
$$+ First\ Repeaters * \frac{Average\ Repeats}{First\ Repeater}$$
$$* \frac{Average\ Volume}{Additional\ Repeat}$$

Each of these components was computed on a per-1,000-household basis and then combined to obtain a sales/1,000 household projection. This was then multiplied by the size of the target market to yield a potential sales forecast.

On the basis of the test market results, and assuming 83.5 million households in the United States, first-year sales were forecast at 5.52 million cases.* Projecting trial and first repeat rates at 25%

*A case was equivalent to 12 50-packet cartons.

Exhibit 5.43   Total Equal Trial and Repeat Components of Four-Week Period Volume (100 Eq. Tspn. Volume per 1000 Households)

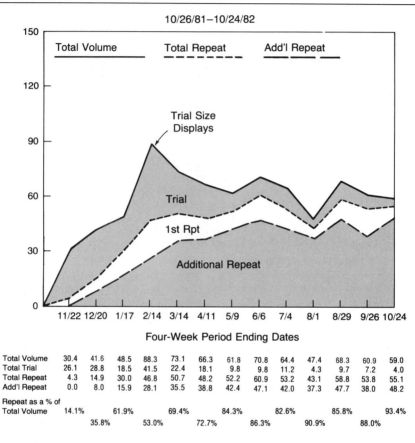

Total Volume	30.4	41.6	48.5	88.3	73.1	66.3	61.8	70.8	64.4	47.4	68.3	60.9	59.0
Total Trial	26.1	28.8	18.5	41.5	22.4	18.1	9.8	9.8	11.2	4.3	9.7	7.2	4.0
Total Repeat	4.3	14.9	30.0	46.8	50.7	48.2	52.2	60.9	53.2	43.1	58.8	53.8	55.1
Add'l Repeat	0.0	8.0	15.9	28.1	35.5	38.8	42.4	47.1	42.0	37.3	47.7	38.0	48.2

Repeat as a % of

Total Volume	14.1%		61.9%		69.4%		84.3%		82.6%		85.8%		93.4%
		35.8%		53.0%		72.7%		86.3%		90.9%		88.0%	

Equal
Percentage of Triers Repeating in Period *N*
10/26/81–5/8/83

Trial Class By Period		Periods After Trial												
	% Trial	Trial	+1	+2	+3	+4	+5	+6	+7	+8	+9	+10	+11	+12
					Percentage Repeating *N* Periods After Trial									
1	2.1	8.6	17.2	27.6	44.8	55.2	56.9	58.6	60.3	62.1	62.1	62.1	65.5	69.0
2	2.0	14.3	35.7	60.7	66.1	67.9	67.9	69.6	69.6	69.6	71.4	73.2	73.2	
3	1.6	11.4	43.2	56.8	59.1	63.6	70.5	70.5	70.5	72.7	72.7	72.7		
4	6.0	7.2	13.3	19.3	21.7	27.1	29.5	30.7	39.2	39.8	43.4			
5	2.0	12.5	25.0	35.7	48.2	51.8	51.8	53.6	55.4	57.1				
6	1.5	4.9	19.5	26.8	34.2	34.2	41.5	41.5	41.5					
7	0.9	8.3	29.2	37.5	50.0	58.3	62.5	62.5						
8	0.8	4.4	21.7	34.8	56.5	60.9	60.9							
9	0.9	4.2	20.8	50.0	50.0	50.0								
10	0.4	0.0	36.4	36.4	36.4									
11	2.2	3.2	11.3	16.1										
12	0.7	11.1	33.3											
13	0.3	0.0												

Exhibit 5.44 Sugar Substitutes Trial and Repeat Purchasing

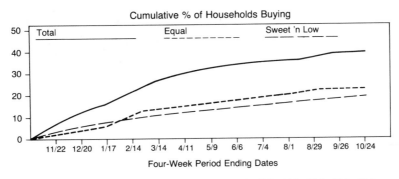

Cumulative % of Households Buying

Four-Week Period Ending Dates

	11/22	12/20	1/17	2/14	3/14	4/11	5/9	6/6	7/4	8/1	8/29	9/26	10/24
Total	8.2	11.1	14.8	21.7	25.7	27.0	29.4	31.3	32.8	34.0	28.1	37.0	37.0
Equal	2.1	4.2	5.7	11.0	13.8	13.0	15.8	10.7	17.7	10.1	20.2	20.8	21.0
Sweet 'n Low	2.8	5.2	7.1	6.5	10.3	11.9	12.1	13.1	13.8	14.7	15.3	19.0	18.7

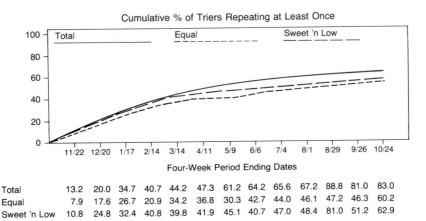

Cumulative % of Triers Repeating at Least Once

Four-Week Period Ending Dates

	11/22	12/20	1/17	2/14	3/14	4/11	5/9	6/6	7/4	8/1	8/29	9/26	10/24
Total	13.2	20.0	34.7	40.7	44.2	47.3	61.2	64.2	65.6	67.2	88.8	81.0	83.0
Equal	7.9	17.6	26.7	20.9	34.2	36.8	30.3	42.7	44.0	46.1	47.2	46.3	60.2
Sweet 'n Low	10.8	24.8	32.4	40.8	39.8	41.9	45.1	40.7	47.0	48.4	81.0	51.2	62.9

Exhibit 5.45 Telephone Survey Results—Test Market and Southeast Rollout Market

	Test Market				Rollout Market	
Sample Size	334	334	333	300	250	250
Date	1/82	3/82	6/82	11/82	6/82	11/82
Total Brand Awareness						
Sugar Substitute Users	46%	60%	64%	66%	3%	57%
Sugar Users	22	32	34	54	4	28
Total Advertising Awareness						
Sugar Substitute Users	39	51	49	44	1	43
Sugar Users	15	23	23	34	0	17
Total Usage	7	10	14	18	0	12
Total Purchase Intention	3	6	10	11	—	8

Exhibit 5.46   Telephone Survey Perceptual Map

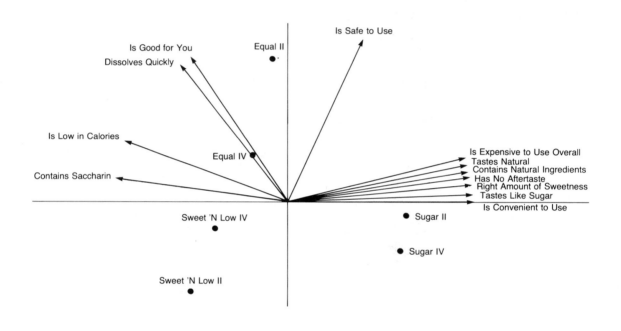

Perception of Key Sweeteners: Equal, Sweet 'n Low, Sugar

Changes from Post-Wave II to Post-Wave IV

and 56% respectively, and assuming 4.75 repeats by each first repeater over two years, a two-year forecast of 9.75 million cases was made.

The final volume forecast was obtained from the potential forecast by adjusting for the distribution and sales force service level expected in the southeastern and national rollouts as shown in Exhibit 5.53.

When the potential forecasts were adjusted to conform to expected market conditions and plans,

Equal's sales during the first year following its introduction were forecast to be 2.95 million cases and $68.0 million at retail. Sales were forecast at 3.66 million cases and retail sales at $84.3 million during the second year. When these forecasts were allocated to the calendar years 1982 and 1983, factory shipments were forecast at .98 million and 3.7 million cases, respectively. Retail sales forecasts were $22.6 million and $84.3 million (see Exhibits 5.54 and 5.55).

Exhibit 5.47   Equal Market Share:* High- vs. Low-Price Stores

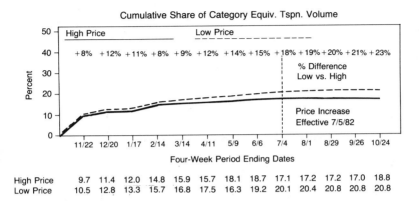

Cumulative Share of Category Equiv. Tspn. Volume

	High Price												
High Price	9.7	11.4	12.0	14.8	15.9	15.7	18.1	18.7	17.1	17.2	17.2	17.0	18.8
Low Price	10.5	12.8	13.3	15.7	16.8	17.5	16.3	19.2	20.1	20.4	20.8	20.8	20.8

+8% +12% +11% +8% +9% +12% +14% +15% +18% +19% +20% +21% +23%
% Difference Low vs. High
Price Increase Effective 7/5/82

Share of Total Category Equiv. Tspn. Volume by Period

	High Price												
High Price	9.7	12.8	13.2	21.3	18.1	17.8	18.2	20.3	18.9	18.4	17.3	15.5	15.0
Low Price	10.5	15.0	14.4	21.4	19.8	22.0	22.7	23.7	26.0	23.2	23.8	21.0	20.8

+8% +17% +9% +1% +8% +24% +25% +17% +38% +26% +38% +35% +37%
% Difference Low vs. High
Price Increase Effective 7/5/82

*Based on 50- and 100-packet Equal only.

Present Situation

Norris Frederic was pleased that Equal had done so well. He was still concerned because the introduction had proceeded so rapidly and decisions had been made in advance of the full test market results.

The basic reason I believed we had to have a test market was to maximize the marketing po-tential for Equal. I believed that we would all have smiles on our faces if we introduced Equal without a test market and that we would see what we'd consider a terrific sales volume. I wasn't af-raid of a disaster. I was concerned then, and I still am, that we aren't achieving the profits we could if we got the marketing plan just right. And considering our cost structure, every little bit of extra margin or increased volume would have a terrific impact on profitability.

Exhibit 5.48 Equal 100-Packet Volume Share: High- vs. Low-Price Stores

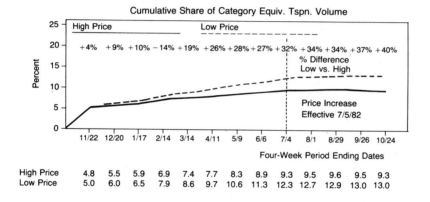

High Price	4.8	5.5	5.9	6.9	7.4	7.7	8.3	8.9	9.3	9.5	9.6	9.5	9.3
Low Price	5.0	6.0	6.5	7.9	8.6	9.7	10.6	11.3	12.3	12.7	12.9	13.0	13.0

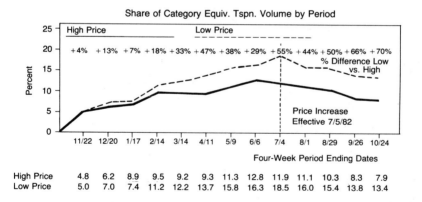

High Price	4.8	6.2	8.9	9.5	9.2	9.3	11.3	12.8	11.9	11.1	10.3	8.3	7.9
Low Price	5.0	7.0	7.4	11.2	12.2	13.7	15.8	16.3	18.5	16.0	15.4	13.8	13.4

Exhibit 5.49   Equal Size Share Summary

| Period | High-Priced Stores | | | Low-Priced Stores | | |
| | Size | | | Size | | |
Ending	50s	100s	Tablets	50s	100s	Tablets
11/22	50.4%	49.6%	0%	52.3%	47.7%	0%
12/20	51.7	48.3	0	53.5	46.5	0%
1/17	47.9	52.1	0	46.6	51.4	0
2/14*	49.0	39.2	4.8	43.4	47.5	4.7
3/14	45.1	48.5	8.5	35.1	58.2	6.7
4/11	42.9	48.1	8.9	35.5	58.5	6.0
5/9	34.4	58.5	9.1	29.4	64.9	5.7
6/6	34.0	55.6	10.5	29.7	65.2	5.1
7/4	34.1	56.0	8.0	27.2	66.9	5.8
Price Increase						
8/1	36.6	55.6	7.8	29.6	65.8	4.8
8/29*	35.4	52.0	7.5	31.6	58.0	4.4
9/26	42.5	48.8	8.9	32.6	61.9	5.4
10/24	42.7	47.5	9.8	33.1	61.0	5.9
Cumulative to Date	40.8	50.8	7.2	34.8	59.4	4.8

*Trial size share

2/14	7.0%	4.3%
8/29	5.1	6.0

Preparation Questions

1. What are the important managerial issues related to the introduction of Equal?

2. Evaluate the research design. How well does it address the managerial issues? How well does it address the research issues we've raised in the other test market cases?

3. Discuss the decision to proceed with the rollout so early in the test market.

4. Watson's decision to change the price midway through the test interfered with the statistical design of the test, but it also provided us with more price points to consider. Determine the best price for Equal using this data. Discuss the effect of the corrupted design on your estimates.

5. What changes, if any, would you make in the marketing strategy for Equal? Forecast the results of your strategy.

6. Compare the test market methodologies used in the three cases in this chapter. Suppose you were the new president of a marketing research company that currently offered each of these methodologies. What would your product line strategy be? Would you offer all of them or terminate one or more of them?

Exhibit 5.50 Sugar Substitutes Purchasing Summary by Brand: Pre- vs. Post-Equal Introduction

(10/27/80–10/24/82)

Metric	Total Sugar Substitutes Yr 1	Yr 2	Equal Yr 1	Yr 2	Sweet 'n Low Yr 1	Yr 2	Sugar Twin Yr 1	Yr 2	Pills, Sweet 10 Yr 1	Yr 2	Private Label Yr 1	Yr 2
100 Equivalent Teaspoons Per 1000 Households	2685	3446	0.0	792.6	1583.9	1479.7	200.1	220.0	333.0	200.5	125.2	122.0
Share of Category Equivalent Teaspoon Volume			0.0%	23.0%	58.4%	42.9%	8.2%	7.5%	12.4%	8.3%	4.7%	3.5%
Percent of Households Buying	26.7%	37.5%	0.0%	21.0%	19.0%	16.7%	4.7%	8.0%	2.4%	1.9%	1.3%	1.3%
Average Buying Rate (100 Equivalent Tsps. Per Buyer)	10.0	9.0	0.0	3.0	8.2	9.9	4.7	4.3	13.7	18.5	10.0	9.3
Percent of Equivalent Teaspoon Volume Purchased on Deal	2.9%	5.5%	0.0%	14.8%	3.7%	3.1%	1.3%	3.2%	2.8%	0.0%	0.0%	1.3%
Purchase Occasions Per Buyer	3.1	3.8	0.0	3.0	2.8	2.9	2.4	2.2	3.3	3.7	1.9	1.7
Average Price Per Volume	$.40	$.73		$1.74	$.43	$.45	$.49	$.50	$.42	$.45	$.15	$.10

Exhibit 5.51 Source of Volume Analysis

Within Sugar Substitute Category

Source of Volume	Equal	Period 2 Gains/Losses from Period 1 (%)	
		Sweet 'N Low	**Sugar Twin**
Infrequent category buyers	49.0	23.2	33.3
Increased category consumption	19.8	38.2	21.4
Brand shifting	31.2	26.6	45.3

Source of Equal Brand Shifting	% from	Attraction Index	Shifting as % of Total
Sweet 'N Low	61.1	111	19.1
Sugar Twin	12.5	212	3.9
Others	22.9	NA	8.2

Sugar Substitutes Plus Sugar (Equal only)

Source of Volume	Equal
Brand shifting	80.9
Increased category consumption	17.0
Infrequent category buyers	2.1

Source of Equal Brand Switching	% Share	Attraction Index	Shifting as % of Total
Sweet 'N Low	17.3	577	14.0
Sugar Twin	3.6	1200	2.9
Other substitutes	7.1	NA	5.8
All substitutes	28.0	518	22.6
Sugar	72	76	58.3

Exhibit 5.52 Volume Change Among Equal Triers and Nontriers

	% Volume Change Among	
	Triers	**Nontriers**
Category consumption	−18%	−18%
Sugar substitutes	+48	+8
Regular sugar	−26	−19

Exhibit 5.53   Forecasted Levels of Distribution

1. First-year distribution levels (% ACV–All Category Volume) were estimated as:

		Month After Introduction							
	Start	1	2	3	4	5	6	7	8+
BehaviorScan	10/81	100%	100%	100%	100%	100%	100%	100%	100%
Southeast									
(33%)	6/1/82	20	60	70	75	85	90	90	95
Balance of U.S.									
U.S. (67%)	9/15/82	20	50	60	75	85	85	90	95

Second-year distribution level was assumed to be 95%.

2. Downward adjustment of 15% to account for quality of distribution. In the BehaviorScan test, IRI personnel visited stores three times a week to maintain shelf presence and stock Equal. This service level could not be maintained nationally with the planned sales force.

3. Equal sales in the national rollout were decreased by 50% from forecast levels during September, October, and November to account for the planned late start of advertising. Some light advertising began in November, and the full program was in place by December.

Exhibit 5.54   Equal Unadjusted Forecasts

Trial Volume	**First Year***	**Second Year†**
Triers per 100 Households	21.01	25.0
100 Equivalent Teaspoon Volume		
per Trier	1.00	1.0
Total Trial Volume	20.92	25.0
First Repeat Volume		
Percent of Triers Repeating	50.16	56.0
First Repeat per 100 Households	10.54	14.0
100 Equivalent Teaspoon Volume per First Repeat	1.38	1.4
Total First Repeat Volume	14.53	19.6
Additional Repeat Volume		
Additional Repeats per Repeater	2.93	4.75
Additional Repeats per 100 Households	30.86	66.5
100 Equivalent Teaspoon Volume		
per Additional Repeat	1.42	1.4
Total Additional Repeat Volume	43.82	93.1
Total 100 Equivalent Teaspoon		
Volume per 100 Households	79.26	137.7
Total Unadjusted U.S. Case Sales		
(millions) - Case 12-50-count cartons	4.09	4.23

*Based on actual test market measurements.
†Based on projection of test market measurements.

Exhibit 5.55 Adjusted Case Forecasts

Price and Cost Structure

Retail Price/50-Packet Carton	$ 1.92
Retail Price/Case	23.04
Factory Price/Case*	16.07
Cost of Goods Sold/Case	10.66
Contribution/Case	5.41

Adjustments

Distribution Level /Build (.86/.96)	4.75	4.06
Later Ad Start (.95/1.00)	4.51	4.06
Distribution Quality (.85/.85)	3.83	3.45
National Rollout (.77/1.06)	2.95	3.66

Adjusted First - and Second-Year Forecasts (millions)

Retail Price	First Year	Second Year
Retail Volume (Cases)	2.95	3.66
Retail Sales	$68.0	$84.3
Factory Sales	47.4	58.8
Contribution	16.0	19.8

Adjusted 1982 and 1983 Forecasts (millions)

Retail Price	1982	1983
Retail Volume (Cases)	.98	3.66
Retail Sales	$22.6	$84.3
Factory Sales	15.8	58.8
Contribution	5.3	19.8

*Assumes retail margins of 25% and distribution cost of 7%.

G. D. Searle I Spreadsheet

The G. D. Searle I spreadsheet duplicates the forecasting method presented in Exhibits 5.54 and 5.55. It isn't a pro forma planning model, but it does consider the time necessary for the marketing program to reach planned levels in making a variety of short-run forecasts. In particular, it provides forecasts for the first and second years of the introduction as well as forecasts for the calendar years of 1982 and 1983. There are a number of marketing program factors that can be varied. Exhibit 5.56 presents the worksheet format. Use of the worksheet is the same as the other worksheets: [Alt]M

gets the menu to help you find your way around if you need it; [Alt]P will print the worksheet.

Variable definitions are self-explanatory, but if there is a question, you can just put the cursor on the cell in question and read the formula. The spreadsheet is intended to be used to test the sensitivity of the forecast to the trial, first repeat, and additional repeat levels as well as certain managerial aspects of the introduction. The columns of the worksheet are independent even though they represent successive twelve-month periods. You will need to assure that your inputs make sense. There are no carry-over effects. The worksheet is intended for a rather elementary two-year pro forma

Exhibit 5.56 G. D. Searle I Spreadsheet

```
                         G. D. Searle & Co. (I)
                         =========================
Assumptions
-----------
Households yr1 (mm)                      83.5
Households yr2 (mm)                      85.0
Retail Price/50 Packet Carton          $1.99
Retail Margin (%)                       25.0%
Wholesale Margin (%)                     7.0%


Price and Cost Structure Per Case
---------------------------------
Retail Price        $23.88    Factory Price        $16.66
Retail Margin        $5.97    Cost of Goods Sold   $10.66
Retail Cost         $17.91    Unit Margin           $6.00
Wholesale Margin     $1.25


                              First Year        Second Year
                              ----------        -----------
Trial Volume
   Triers per 100 HH             21.01             25.00
   100 Equivalent Teaspoon
     Volume per Trier             1.00              1.00
   -------------------------     -----             -----
   Total Trial Volume            21.01             25.00

First Repeat Volume
   Percent of Triers Repeating   50.16%            56.00%
   First Repeat Per 100 HH       10.54             14.00
   100 Equivalent Teaspoon
     Volume per First Repeat      1.38              1.40
   -------------------------      ----              ----
   Total First Repeat Volume     14.54             19.60

Additional Repeat Volume
   Additional Repeats Per Repeater    2.93          4.75
   Additional Repeats Per 100 HH     30.88         66.50
   100 Equivalent Teaspoon
     Volume per Additional Repeat     1.42          1.40
   Total Additional Repeat Volume    43.85         93.10
-------------------------------      -----         -----
Total Volume Per 100 HH              79.40        137.70

National Forecasts - Unadjusted (millions)

   Retail Volume (Cases)             5.52          4.23
   Retail Sales                   $131.94       $100.98
   Factory Sales                   $92.02        $70.44
   Contribution Margin             $33.13        $25.36
```

Exhibit 5.56 (continued)   G.D. Searle I Spreadsheet

```
Forecasts Adjusted for Expected Market Conditions

Expected Market Conditions and Plans
-------------------------------------
                               First Year          Second Year
                               ----------          -----------
Distribution Level/Build          86.0%               96.0%
Later Ad Start                    95.0%              100.0%
Distribution Quality              85.0%               85.0%
National Rollout                  77.0%              106.0%

Adjustments
-----------
Distribution Level/Build           4.75                4.06
Later Ad Start                     4.51                4.06
Distribution Quality               3.84                3.45
National Rollout                   2.95                3.66

Adjusted First- and Second-Year Forecasts (millions)
-----------------------------------------------------
Retail Volume (Cases)              2.95                3.66
Retail Sales                     $70.55              $87.35
Factory Sales                    $49.21              $60.92
Contribution Margin              $17.72              $21.93


Adjusted 1982 and 1983 Forecasts (millions)
-------------------------------------------
                                   1982                1983
                                   ----                ----
Retail Volume (Cases)              0.97                3.32
Retail Sales                     $23.11              $79.38
Factory Sales                    $16.12              $55.37
Contribution Margin               $5.80              $19.93
```

analysis. The first column provides a forecast for the first twelve months following the introduction of Equal in the southeastern region. The second column is intended to be used for the second twelve months.

The approach used to adjust the BehaviorScan estimates for expected market conditions is similar to that used in the ASSESSOR model. An ideal condition forecast is made and then it is adjusted for expected market conditions; in particular, the following adjustments can be made:

Distribution build (the distribution rates that will prevail during the time period)

Advertising start time and awareness build

Distribution quality—the degree to which both sizes are stocked to satisfactory levels

National rollout—the difference between the starting times of the southeast region and the rest of the country

Each of these factors are to be estimated in terms

of the percent of the BehaviorScan situation that will be achieved in the relevant time period. This estimate should be a weighted average of what level is achieved for various periods of time; that is, if we felt that distribution would be at 66.7% for one-fourth of the year and 80% for the rest of the year, then we would enter $(.75 \times .667 + .25 \times .8 = .7)$.

The major part of your analysis of this case will surely be managerial with relatively little emphasis on the use of this model, but the model should be helpful to you in developing a forecast for your alternatives.

References and Background Readings

Clarke, Darral G., and Sandra K. Eubank. "Measuring the Relationship of Price and Brand Share: The Vantage Point Question." Proceedings of the 1st TIMS Marketing Science Conference, Fred S. Zufryden, ed. Los Angeles, CA, May 1983.

Fourt, Lewis A., and Joseph W. Woodlock. "Early Prediction of Market Success for New Grocery Products." *Journal of Marketing* (October 1960), pp. 31–38.

Sahumer, Fern. "The New Magicians of Market Research." *Fortune* (July 25, 1983), pp. 72–74.

Urban, Glen L., and John R. Hauser. *Design and Marketing of New Products.* Englewood Cliffs, NJ: Prentice-Hall, 1980.

6

Marketing Mix Management

(continued)

After a product has attained some stability in the marketplace, the managerial task becomes one of balancing the conflicting pressures arising from the need for further growth or maintaining market position, and of profit generation. The decisions that need to be made are considerably different from those made during the development of a new product. Generally, much more is known about the marketplace in which the product competes. There are frequently more reports and more data than the manager can possibly keep track of, and the emphasis changes from finding out about the competitive situation to deciding which data are important and what action they indicate. The decision situations earlier in the new product development process were never very far removed from forecasting product acceptance and demand; but the emphasis now changes to using the marketing mix more effectively to manage the product. The manager asks such questions as: Are we advertising at the right level? How large should our sales force be, and how should we allocate their effort across our product line and customers? Should we promote this brand more, or just reduce the price? Is the marketing mix as a whole functioning efficiently to achieve our marketing and financial goals?

The cases in this chapter deal with the use of marketing research and the development of decision models to manage one or more elements of the marketing mix. The issues addressed and research methods employed are more typical of those encountered subsequent to product introduction. One contrast between the cases in this chapter and those of the previous chapter is that, with the exception of G.D. Searle II, the data in the cases are typically generated by the normal operation of the business, rather than through market survey or experiment. These data are uncontrolled, and the manager must be cautious about attributing causality to particular marketing factors, since the effects of the entire marketing strategy are contained in the sales or market share data.

The discussion of the use of advertising research for advertising budgeting purposes in the last chapter is continued in three of the cases in this chapter: General Foods, Convection Corporation, and G. D. Searle II. Sales management is also featured in the Convection case, but it receives top billing in the Syntex Laboratories cases. The G. D. Searle II case adds a strong focus on promotion management, and provides an example of the use of decision models to manage the entire marketing mix for a consumer product.

The cases in this chapter provide a number of interesting contrasts with the cases of Chapter 5. They also provide a further opportunity to address the methodological issues associated with the evaluation of both models and data.

The data used in the first two cases are very different from the experimental data we encountered in Chapter 5, but the consideration of information content and bias are still extremely important. A decision model based on advertising expenditures and sales records is developed in the General Foods case. This type of data is generated by most consumer product companies and it is commonly used to analyze the response of sales and market share to advertising expenditures. The statistical methodology used to analyze these historical data is different from that used in previous cases, and comparison with the experimental models and data in the cases in Chapter 5 will provide a broad overview of these important considerations.

The Convection Corporation case deals with the allocation of marketing effort across advertising and sales force for three industrial products; it provides an important opportunity to observe differences in the role of advertising for industrial as compared to consumer products. Advertising is the dominant communication force in the marketing strategy of the consumer products in the previous cases, whereas one of the problems in this case is to determine the respective roles of both advertising and personal selling for different industrial products. This case also provides an effective bridge from advertising to the emphasis on personal selling in the Syntex Laboratories cases that follow. The last case, G.D. Searle II, deals with the promotion and pricing elements of the marketing mix.

Econometric Models of Advertising Effect in the General Foods Case

The first case, General Foods, presents an example of the use of econometric modeling to develop the advertising response function for an advertising decision model. Econometric analysis of time series data is often used in marketing research to determine an advertising response function. The incorporation of the response function in a decision model, however, is an unusual step, especially at the time this case was written. The philosophy of the econometric research in this case is very straightforward: Since the company has been advertising this product for a number of years, what can be learned from the sales and advertising histories to help market the product more successfully in the future? Even though the approach is straightforward, there are many methodological issues that must be considered. Econometric analysis is used to: (1) account for various trends in the data, (2) measure historical relationships between advertising and sales, and (3) project both trends and relationships in order to forecast the probable results of different advertising programs.

One noted econometrician has likened econometric analysis to trying to drive a car forward while looking in the rear-view mirror. As you analyze the case, you will no doubt discover some of the shortcomings of the approach, but remember that there are no perfect models for predicting the results of future actions in an uncertain marketplace.

Despite the shortcomings of econometric analysis, few of even its most outspoken critics believe so strongly that the past has no bearing on the present or future that they keep no records of their marketing efforts or market results. Econometric analysis is the most powerful methodology available for extracting the information contained in the historical records of the company, and a well-informed manager with the skill to utilize it intelligently has much to gain.

The General Foods case includes two different advertising models that are fairly typical of those developed by marketing researchers and economists. Both are multiple regression models of advertising effect that were developed from the sales and advertising histories of the company. Each model also includes an estimate of the effects of promotion and distribution, but we'll ignore those terms in the following discussion. (Promotion modeling will be discussed more completely in the introduction of the decision model for the G.D. Searle II case.) The General Foods data on orange-flavored Tang include factory shipments, Nielsen retail audit data, and advertising histories in the form of expenditures and GRPs (gross rating points) collected on a quarterly basis. Such data are referred to as *time series data*.

The two models are based on different assumptions about advertising's effects on sales, and as a result the models' recommendations about the optimal level of advertising also differ. A technical description of how the models were estimated is beyond the scope of this book, but even though the statistical properties of the estimates are not presented in the case, it is still possible to do an adequate job of evaluating the two models. The major factors that a manager should consider in evaluating a market response function and decision model are: *specification*—the shape of the response function; *estimation*—the method by which the coefficients in the response function were calculated; and *data evaluation*—the type of data used in the estimation.

Comparison of the two models in the General Foods case provides an excellent opportunity to apply this approach to response function evaluation. The advertising response functions are not described as completely as most statisticians and econometricians would like them to be, and evaluation of the two models needs to be done with common sense. In this case, the only tool available to the technically trained as well as the untrained is evaluation of the hypotheses upon which they are based and the reasonableness of the results produced. This exercise is as rewarding for those with technical skills as for those without them— perhaps more so—because it can become almost automatic to rely on statistical diagnostics alone to evaluate models, but statistical significance by itself does not guarantee that a model is suitable for the managerial purpose. Although in this case there is not much difference between the fit obtained by using a curvilinear model or a linear model over the range of the available district data, the difference in the recommendations of the two models is considerable. It is an important issue to determine which of the models makes the more reasonable recommendations and which, if either, is the more dependable.

A second difficulty is that no details of the decision models are provided other than the description of the response functions and the fact that allocations are made by the agency model according to the economic principles of marginal analysis—additional resources are allocated to the sales district for which the greatest incremental return is forecast. This turns out to be enough information to do a remarkably adequate job of evaluating the two decision models and their recommendations.

A simple regression model and the national data in the case are available for elementary analysis in the form of a Lotus 1-2-3 worksheet. Although these data are not used to estimate either the internal or the agency models (which were based on district-level data), it is adequate to illustrate the factors that need to be considered in choosing between the two model specifications.

CASE: General Foods Corporation

This case illustrates the use of econometric analysis to determine two advertising response functions for planning the advertising budget. The case describes an early application of the decision model concept. The immediate problem is that the two decision models lead to different advertising budget recommendations. Since we don't have the decision models or even the response functions' definitions, we have to infer their nature and decide which is the better representation of the situation solely from the results of simulation studies using the decision models. The case provides one of our best opportunities for managerial model analysis—specification and data foundation play very important roles in the analysis of this case.

Early in September 1973, Richard Jackson, product manager of General Foods' Tang instant breakfast drink,* recognized that Tang would not reach its goal. He needed a new plan for the rest of the year as well as a budget for Tang advertising and promotional activities (cents-off deals, coupons, etc.).† The members of his product group disagreed about Tang's future potential. Some believed that Tang, even after 14 years, could continue to justify investment spending on marketing activities to build future sales, while still meeting satisfactory profitability goals for next year. Others believed that Tang's business had peaked and could not support further long-run marketing investment, and that a strategy concentrating on short-term profits would be more appropriate. Jackson wanted to present a spending plan that would deliver $7 million in net contribution to profit that year and still assure long-run sales volume.

Jackson was considering the results and recommendations generated by two market response models that had been developed to analyze the advertising and promotion spending decision. One

model had been developed by the division's operations research group. The other was developed by Young & Rubicam, Tang's advertising agency. The conclusions of the two models, unfortunately, appeared to conflict.

Company Background

General Foods Corporation (GF) was a leading manufacturer and marketer of grocery products, chiefly convenience foods. Sales for 1973 were expected to be over $2.5 billion and net profit over $100 million for the year. GF marketed 400 products, including 30 of the food industry's best-known brand names such as Maxwell House coffee, Bird's Eye frozen foods, Post cereals, Jell-O desserts, Gaines pet foods, and Tang instant breakfast drink.

GF's marketing organization was based on a product management structure: product managers reported to a group product manager, who in turn reported to a strategic business unit (SBU) manager. An SBU was a group of products and brands that were considered by consumers to be similar, and that could be managed together as strategic markets rather than just as individual products. Tang was included in the Beverage SBU, along with frozen beverage products (frozen orange juice concentrate and Orange Plus), other breakfast beverages (Start and Postum), and refreshment beverages (Kool-Aid products).

---

*Tang, a concentrated, instant beverage that, according to its package label, is "A natural-tasting orange flavor breakfast drink. It contains more Vitamin C and A than like amounts of orange, grapefruit, or tomato juice."

†Dollar, unit figures, and time periods used in this case are disguised.

This case was prepared by H.N. Singer and F.S. DeBruicker.

Copyright © 1974 by the President and Fellows of Harvard College, Harvard Business School case 9-575-063.

Product managers at GF had both marketing and business responsibilities, including

1. Planning and executing all advertising, promotion, pricing, and merchandising strategies for the brand
2. Obtaining and coordinating all of the division's functional resources, technical inputs, marketing research, marketing spending, sales force activities, processing, packaging, etc.
3. Attaining contribution to profit goals
4. Working with GF top management in the development of current year and longer-range objectives

Richard Jackson was assisted by an associate product manager and assistant product manager.

Tang's History

Following its introduction in 1958, Tang volume grew slowly but steadily until it seemed to plateau in 1962. Marketing spending was increased and new copy devised that renewed sales growth through 1968 when another plateau was reached. Marketing efforts were again intensified in 1969: the product was significantly improved, and sampling, advertising, and promotional spending were increased. Tang's media copy program, which tied into America's space exploration program, provided frequent opportunities for media saturation during the televised Apollo flights. Tang sales increased about 30% in both 1969 and 1970, even though the price had been raised. The gains were also due in part to the government's ban on cyclamates and Tang's immediate advertising noting that it used no artificial sweeteners.

In 1971 and 1972, sales growth slowed as competitive powdered breakfast drinks and private label brands with prices 40% less than Tang's appeared. Tang prices were increased to maintain profit margins close to historical levels, and two flavor extensions, Grape and Grapefruit Tang, were introduced using advertising and promotion funds diverted from Orange Tang. Orange Tang sales for fiscal 1972 were up only slightly.

The Current Situation

During the first nine months of 1972, sales in some periods had fallen as much as 13% versus previous year figures, and the product group became increasingly concerned about Tang's strategy, especially advertising copy and marketing spending. Exhibit 6.1 shows Orange Tang sales, estimated price, and marketing spending figures from 1968 through mid-1973, as well as similar data for competing powdered orange beverages. The price difference between Tang and frozen orange juice is also shown.

Richard Jackson was concerned that Tang would not meet the 1973 business plan goal of $7 million contribution to profit after marketing costs (primarily the amounts spent on advertising and promotion). Jackson felt that a further price increase was infeasible and that the primary area of leverage was marketing spending. But the necessary spending levels for advertising and promotion to meet the profit goal *and* assure sustained sales growth were not clear. This was not a new situation for Jackson; in order to meet 1972's financial goals he had been forced to reduce planned advertising spending in the final quarter to an annual rate of just below $3.0 million (from the $4.0 to $4.5 million that had been planned). He had also increased promotional spending by $800,000 to provide an immediate sales impact.

The Planning Models

The two advertising budgeting models were developed to help the product group in decision making by computing the optimal total marketing spending level and the optimal advertising/promotion split. The impetus for developing the models came from the brand's depressed performance and the fact that the group product manager wanted both present diagnostic analysis and future planning to be on a sound quantitative basis. In particular, both he and Jackson wanted the answers to the following questions:

1. How do sales and profits respond to various levels of advertising and promotional spending?

Exhibit 6.1   Orange Tang National Data

Period		Tang Sales (1000s)*	Adv. ($1,000)	Prom. ($1,000)	Est. Retail Price*	Competitive Sales (1000s)*	Competition Estimated Price*	Price Difference: FOJC–Tang†	Competitive Adv. ($1,000)
Year	Quarter								
1968	1	530	365	289		0		−0.5	
	2	511	435	338		0		0.1	
	3	514	303	330		0		1.4	
	4	545	188	190		0		2.2	
	Total	2,100	1,291	1,147	$8.41	0			
1969	1	579	437	1,006		0		3.3	
	2	615	331	51		0		3.8	
	3	664	570	129		0		4.7	
	4	850	1,176	471		0		6.0	
	Total	2,708	2,514	1,657	$8.38	0			
1970	1	801	992	254		0		6.3	
	2	853	771	356		0		5.1	
	3	872	802	128		0		4.8	
	4	1,029	988	448		0		4.0	
	Total	3,555	3,553	1,186	$8.71	0			
1971	1	1,019	1,400	710		0		3.4	
	2	1,002	806	549		0		3.2	
	3	1,024	843	1,011		0		2.5	
	4	1,197	1,110	684		0		2.1	
	Total	4,242	4,159	2,954	$8.70	0			
1972	1	1,088	883	339		0		3.4	
	2	1,070	769	1,070		22		4.8	
	3	1,052	864	1,006		50		5.1	
	4	1,142	430	763		89		·8.0	
	Total	4,352	2,946	3,718	$9.03	161	7.49		59
1973	1	1,044	884	576		200		7.9	
	2	965	363	851		271	7.53	7.9	630
			(est.) 520	(est.) 490	$9.08				

*Per 10 1/2 pound units. 1973 COGS/10 1/2 lb. units $5.93.

†Cents per 24 ounces. FOJC = Frozen Orange Juice Concentrate

2. Given a particular budget level, what advertising/promotion split would be most efficient?

3. What is the most efficient geographic allocation of TV advertising dollars? What mix of national network TV and spot TV should be used?

4. How should advertising and promotion be allocated to districts?

Jackson decided to support two separate modeling efforts. Mike Goldberg, an operations research specialist assigned to work with the Tang product group, would develop an in-house model. Goldberg was a recent MBA graduate who had joined the company late that spring. The Tang model would be his first major assignment as a member of the marketing research staff. The second model would be developed by the management science group of Tang's advertising agency, Young & Rubicam. Although Jackson had full confidence in the in-house effort, he also wanted the agency to participate in the study so that they would be tied into at least some of the conclusions and thus work better with the product group to implement those conclusions. The cost of each model was minimal—the in-house model was charged to Tang's existing research budget, and the agency model cost less than $15,000. Jackson welcomed alternative viewpoints and felt that the backing of two models to justify his recommendations would carry more weight.

Data sources for the two studies included factory shipments, advertising and promotional spending, Nielsen store-audit data, and network and spot TV cost data for each sales district. Because TV delivery costs differed in different areas, advertising expenditures were converted to gross rating points or GRPs.* Consumer and trade promotion dollars in past years were also compiled. A database aggregated at the quarterly level was developed at both national and district levels. The national data are found in Exhibit 6.1. Once the databases were completed, the agency and in-house model building efforts proceeded independently.

---

*One GRP equals one impression per TV household per time period.

The In-House Model

The response model developed by Goldberg assumed that Tang sales were driven by advertising, promotion, and distribution. Goldberg also hypothesized that the effects of advertising persisted, but with decreasing effectiveness, subsequent to the period in which the advertisement occurred (see Exhibit 6.2). He therefore defined a variable he called *effective advertising*:

$$A^*_{i,t} = \sum_{m=0}^{M} R^m A_{i,t-m} \qquad (6.1)$$

where

$A^*_{i,t}$ is the "effective advertising" in district i during period t.

R is the advertising retention rate. R is a number between 0 and 1 that designates what proportion of the advertising in one period is still effective one period later.

$A_{i,t}$ is the number of GRPs in district i during period t.

M is the number of periods advertising's effects were assumed to persist.

From the results of previous studies, Goldberg assumed that $R = 0.8$ and $M = 12$. This implied that 80% of the advertising in a given period would still be operative in the next period. Using the effective advertising measurements, Goldberg estimated a separate response function for each district (i):

$$S_{i,t} = a_{0,i} + a_{1,i} A^*_{i,t} + a_{2,i} P_{i,t} + a_{3,i} D_{i,t} \qquad (6.2)$$

where

$S_{i,t}$ is the estimated sales in the ith territory during period t.

$A^*_{i,t}$ is the effective number of GRPs impacting in territory i during period t.

$P_{i,t}$ is the promotion expenditure during period t, determined by the amount of trade allowances off-invoice.

$D_{i,t}$ is the percentage of retail outlets stocking Orange Tang in all package sizes in territory i in time period t.

Exhibit 6.2   In-House Model Showing Declining Effects of Advertising Over Time

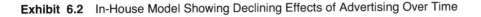

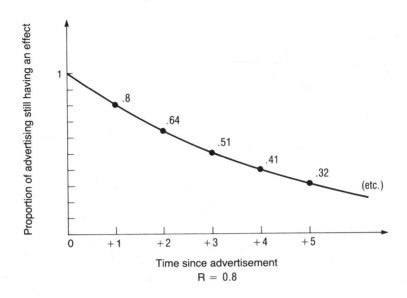

a_0, i, $a_{1,i}$, $a_{3,i}$ are response coefficients estimated by the regression analysis.

Goldberg included the distribution variable, $D_{i,t}$, because he found it improved the equation's "fit" with the data.

The response function coefficients $A_{i,t}$, if positive, described an upwardly sloping straight line such that sales increased $a_{i,t}$ units for each additional unit of effective advertising no matter how high advertising expenditures already were. Even though he believed this to be unrealistic, this *linear function* fit the data better than any of the curvilinear functions that he had tried. In order to limit the incremental response of sales to advertising to reasonable levels for both high and low GRP levels, Goldberg asked the product group to judgmentally determine the GRP level above which increased spending would produce no further sales increase, and a threshold or minimum spending level that had to be attained before any effect on sales would occur. Exhibit 6.3 illustrates the advertising response function relationship between sales and advertising used in the in-house model.

The market response function coefficients and judgmental estimates were estimated separately for each territory using 12 quarterly observations. As a test of the model, which integrated the 26 territory response functions, the 1973 spending plan for each of the 26 territories was used to predict 1973 sales. The model forecast 4.5 million units; the brand group's best estimate was 4.3 million units.

The Agency Model

The agency's advertising response function differed from the in-house model in a number of respects. It hypothesized diminishing returns to incremental advertising and used regression analysis to estimate a *curvilinear response* to advertising and promotion rather than relying on managerial judgment to estimate an upper bound on response. Exhibit 6.4 shows the agency model contrasted with the in-house model. The agency model had no threshold level, and the agency response function was a single equation for the entire country rather than treating each sales territory independently. Regional differences were accounted for by a

Exhibit 6.3   Judgmental Adjustment of the Linear Advertising Response Model

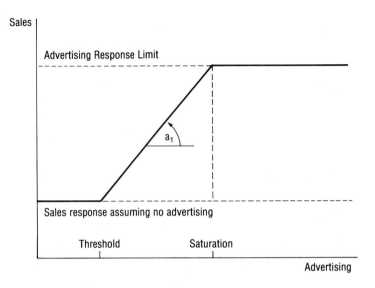

Exhibit 6.4   General Foods' Two Advertising Models*

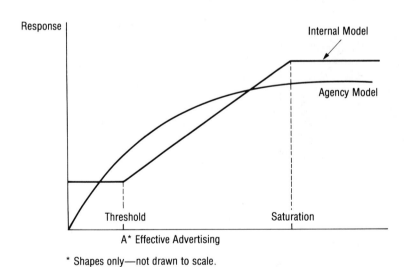

* Shapes only—not drawn to scale.

Exhibit 6.5 Agency Model's Advertising Response Function

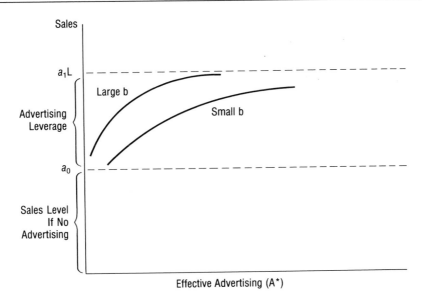

special district variable. Since the data were available for each of 26 territories, there were 312 observations available for estimating the response functions in the in-house model. The estimation process for the agency model involved a number of steps (which won't be described here). The final form of the agency response model was:

$$S_{i,t} = a_0 + a_1 L_i(1 - \exp(-bA^*_{i,t})) + a_2 P^*_{i,t} + a_3 S_{i,t-1} \quad (6.3)$$

where

$S_{i,t}$ is the sales of district i at time t.

$A^*_{i,t}$ is effective advertising in district i at time t.

$P^*_{i,t}$ is effective promotion spending in district i.

L_i is a measure of the potential sales in district t.

$S_{i,t-1}$ is the sales in the previous period $(t-1)$.

a_0, a_1, a_2, a_3, and b are the coefficients to be estimated.

The general form of the sales response to effective advertising according to the agency's model is shown in Exhibit 6.5. The sales volume that could be attained through advertising in a district was called *advertising leverage*, and it depended on both the district's market potential and the coefficient of advertising, which was assumed to be the same across districts.

The potential, L_i, was defined as:

$$L_i = D_i^c M_i^{c2} S_i^{c3} \quad (6.4)$$

where

D_i is a measure of the distribution level in district i.

M_i is a demographic measure of the population in district i.

Exhibit 6.6   Estimated Orange Tang Sales Under Different Levels of Distribution and Advertising Spending

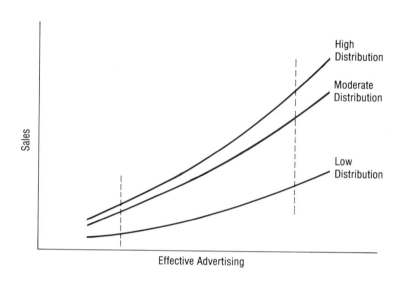

S_i is a measure of the existing sales level.

c_1, c_2, and c_3 were coefficients found by analysis.

The sales response to advertising in the agency model was a function of both advertising and district characteristics. According to the agency, the addition of L_i to the response function was an important factor, because its inclusion increased the statistical significance of the advertising coefficient. Exhibit 6.6 shows the joint effect of advertising and distribution on sales.

No significant effects of seasonality, package size, promotion, and competitive price differential were found. The range of L_i across sales territories was 0.8 to 1.5 times the national average.

The agency model also hypothesized that advertising and promotion had cumulative effects on sales. The agency model assumed the relationship between effective advertising A^* (accumulated advertising) and advertising A (advertising in a given time period) was:

$$A_t^* = A_t + A_{t-1} + \ldots + A_{t-n} \tag{6.5}$$

where n was the number of preceding periods for which the estimated cumulative advertising effects were desired.

A similar hypothesis about promotional effects was assumed:

$$P_t^* = P_t + P_{t-1} + \ldots + P_{t-n} \tag{6.6}$$

Using equations (6.5) and (6.6), long-term carryover effects of both advertising and promotion for up to n time periods could be computed. The agency believed that the carry-over effects for promotion expenditures were substantially lower than for advertising.

From the response functions, the agency developed an allocation model that allowed Tang sales and profit projections to be based on assumed competitive sales levels. This model assumed that 40% of competitive sales would come from market expansion, while the rest would be cannabalized Tang sales. The in-house model made no explicit adjustment for anticipated competitive sales.

Allocating Marketing Resources

Similar decision support models for evaluating alternative spending strategies were developed by both the in-house and the agency groups. Allocation between sales territories and between advertising and promotion was based on a comparison of marginal cost and marginal revenue for the territories. For example, assuming a fixed media budget and two sales territories with different sales response curves, the agency's allocation procedure divided funds between the territories by holding the total budget constant and setting each territory's budget at that point on the sales response curve where the respective slopes were equal.

The in-house model allocated funds only up to a judgmentally determined saturation level of 2250 GRPs. Both models could be used either to allocate a fixed budget, or to compute an optimal advertising and promotion budget at the district level. Furthermore, each model could be used for either a long-run or short-run planning horizon by using estimated carry-over effects.

In-House Model Recommendations

1. A minimum of $4 million per year in advertising expenditure is necessary to maintain volume at current levels. Maximum long-term sales growth and profitability require advertising levels in excess of $6 to $7 million per year.

2. Promotion spending does not affect long-term growth, but does affect short-term sales volume. However, some minimal level of promotion is probably a "cost of the business."

3. Approximately 20% of media expenditures goes to spot TV in selected districts despite its 60% price premium.

The model's proposed allocations of several budgets are found in Exhibit 6.7.

Agency Recommendations

The agency used their model to develop both short- and long-term implications. The agency model recommended higher advertising spending levels under the long-term assumption than it did when a one-year time frame was assumed.

1. A sustained media spending level of $6.9 million would be the most profitable over either a four-year or a six-year time horizon.

2. If a one-year time frame were assumed, a media spending level of $4.0 million would maintain current sales volume but would not sustain long-term sales volume.

3. No spot TV, except for the Denver territory where spot TV was relatively low-cost, or for other territories if competing products exhibit rapid growth.

The agency model's one-year forecasts for ten alternative advertising and promotion budgets are found in Exhibit 6.8. Long-term forecasts for sales and profits at the end of two, four, and six years are found in Exhibit 6.9.

As Richard Jackson prepared his 1974 annual business plan, he summarized his analysis as shown in Exhibit 6.10.

Jackson was concerned about making his recommendations. The long-term recommendation of each model was to increase advertising spending from the present annual rate of about $4 million to about $7 million, and reduce promotion from $3.5 million to less than $2 million. He wondered whether this was the time to initiate a major change in advertising and promotion strategy for Tang. He was also concerned about what to recommend for the rest of 1973. If Tang missed its targets in 1973 by too much, the question of how to justify a long-term, volume-building marketing plan would probably be academic.

Exhibit 6.7 Recommended Allocations Based on the In-House Model

Yearly Budget	Advertising/ Promotion Split	First Year Volume (units)	First Year* Net Contribution	Years to Peak†	Peak Year Volume (units)	Peak Year Net Contribution
$7,000,000	$5,000,000 Ad 2,000,000 Promo	4,763,000	$8.0 million	3	5,152,000	$ 9.2 million
7,000,000	4,000,000 Ad 3,000,000 Promo	4,502,000	7.2 million	1	4,502,000	7.2 million
7,000,000	3,000,000 Ad 4,000,000 Promo	4,291,000	6.5 million	0	Will not Sustain Current Vol.	—
7,000,000	6,500,000 Ad 500,000 Promo	4,806,000	8.1 million	4	5,381,000	9.9 million
8,000,000	7,000,000 Ad 1,000,000 Promo	5,409,000	9.0 million	3	5,790,000	10.2 million
5,000,000	4,750,000 Ad 250,000 Promo	4,203,000	8.2 million	4	4,500,000	9.2 million
10,000,000	8,000,000 Ad 2,000,000 Promo	5,816,000	8.3 million	2	6,092,000	9.2 million

*Net Contribution = Sales in units x Variable Gross Profit of $3.15 per unit — Ad and Promo Costs.

†Peak year is the year in which Tang volume fails to grow significantly (starting with the given budget level and repeating it each year thereafter).

Preparation Questions

1. What are the managerial issues that must be considered in determining an advertising strategy for Tang?

2. How well does the research address these issues?

3. The general form of the market response function in the in-house decision model that generated the results in Exhibit 6.7 is shown in Exhibit 6.3. What is the advertising budget level that corresponds to the saturation points?

4. Evaluate the use of the in-house model in determining the optimal advertising budget.

5. The data in the statistical model described in the spreadsheet notes that follow are taken from Exhibit 6.6. The agency model was estimated with more data than this, of course, but it probably had similar properties. Discuss the estimation of a diminishing returns to advertising specification using this data. In particular, how would you decide between a linear (as in the in-house model) and a diminishing returns model (as in the agency model) using this data?

6. What advertising budget do you recommend?

Exhibit 6.8   Tang One-Year Forecasts Estimated by Agency Model*

Yearly Budget ($ million)	Ad/Promotion Split ($ million)	If Competition Sells 1.0 Million Units		If Competition Sells 1.5 Million Units		If Competition Sells 2.0 Million Units	
		Sales (million units)	Net † ($ million)	Sales (million units)	Net† ($ million)	Sales (million units)	Net† ($ million)
$ 5.0	$2.50A 2.50P	3.68	$6.60	3.46	$5.90	3.23	$5.18
5.5	2.50A 3.00P	3.72	6.22	3.50	5.52	3.27	4.79
6.25	3.75A 2.50P	4.28	7.23	4.06	6.54	3.83	5.81
6.5	3.75A 2.75P	4.31	7.07	4.08	6.35	3.86	5.65
7.0	4.50A 2.50P	4.39	6.61	4.17	6.13	3.94	5.41
7.5	4.50A 3.00P	4.42	6.42	4.20	5.73	3.97	5.01
8.0	5.50A 2.50P	4.48	6.11	4.25	5.23	4.03	4.69
8.5	5.50A 3.00P	4.50	5.67	4.27	4.95	4.05	4.26
9.5	7.00A 2.50P	4.57	4.89	4.34	4.17	4.12	3.47
10.0	7.00A 3.00P	4.59	4.45	4.36	3.73	4.14	3.04

*Assumes 40% of competitive sales come from market expansion, 60% from Tang's franchise.

†Net = unit sales x unit contribution of $3.15 − advertising and promotion costs.

Exhibit 6.9   Tang Long-Term Forecasts Estimated by Agency Model*

Yearly Budget ($ millions)	Ad/Promotion Split ($ millions)	Year 2		Year 3		Year 6	
		Sales (million units)	Net† ($ millions)	Sales (million units)	Net† ($ millions)	Sales (million units)	Net† ($ millions)
6.5	4.5 Ad 2.0 Promo	5.58	11.1	5.68	11.4	5.71	11.5
7.0	4.5 Ad 2.5 Promo	5.63	10.7	5.76	11.1	5.79	11.2
7.5	4.5 Ad 3.0 Promo	5.70	10.5	5.83	10.9	5.85	10.9
8.0	6.0 Ad 2.0 Promo	5.75	10.1	6.48	12.4	6.55	12.6
8.5	6.0 Ad 2.5 Promo	5.83	9.9	6.56	12.2	6.62	12.3
9.0	6.0 Ad 3.0 Promo	5.89	9.6	6.62	11.9	6.69	12.1
9.5	7.5 Ad 2.0 Promo	5.86	8.9	6.91	12.3	7.00	12.6
10.0	7.5 Ad 2.5 Promo	5.94	8.7	6.99	12.0	7.08	12.3
10.5	7.5 Ad 3.0 Promo	6.01	8.4	7.06	11.7	7.15	12.1

*Assumes competitive sales increases of 500,000 units per year and 75% of competitive sales come from market expansion, 25% from Tang's franchise.

†Net = unit sales × unit contribution of $3.15 − advertising and promotion costs.

Exhibit 6.10   1974 Annual Business Plan (In $ millions)

	Original Plan	Mgmt. Revision	In-House	Agency*
Advertising	4.0	4.0	4.0	4.5
Promotion	3.0	3.5	3.0	2.5
Total Marketing	7.0	7.5	7.0	7.0
Units	4.400	4.625	4.500	4.390
Net Contribution	7.00	7.27	7.20	6.61

*Assumes competitive volume of 1 million units.

General Foods Regression Spreadsheet

The General Foods case presents the problem of determining which, if either, of two decision models is providing reliable insight into an advertising budgeting problem. The key is to understand why the two decision models provide such different advertising recommendations. This little spreadsheet is designed to help you investigate the two market response functions. Remember that the three major considerations in evaluating a market response function are *specification*, *estimation*, and *data*.

The worksheet consists of two components:

1. A simple regression program that you can use to estimate the coefficients of both a linear and curvilinear specification.

2. A series of graphs that allow you to investigate visually the inputs to the regression model and the "fit" of the forecasts made by your regression with the data.

Using the Regression Model

To use the regression model, copy the data that you want to analyze into the dependent and independent variable columns in the worksheet. (See Exhibit 6.11.) The data in the first two columns are the sales and advertising values found in Exhibit 6.1. If you want to compute the regression of sales on advertising, just copy these values into the dependent and independent columns using the 1-2-3 **copy** command as you did on the UDIA worksheet. There are two other columns that can be used to

Exhibit 6.11   General Foods Regression Model

```
Simple Regression Program
      N=        22
           ---------Input Dat----------        Adjusted data
           Sales      Adv    ID log(sls) log(adv) Dep. var Ind. var
Obs        ================================================================
  1        530.0     $365    A1    2.724    2.562    530.00   365.00
  2        511.0     $435    A2    2.708    2.638    511.00   435.00
  3        514.0     $303    A3    2.711    2.481    514.00   303.00
  4        545.0     $188    A4    2.736    2.274    545.00   188.00
  5        579.0     $437    B1    2.763    2.640    579.00   437.00
  6        615.0     $331    B2    2.789    2.520    615.00   331.00
  7        664.0     $570    B3    2.822    2.756    664.00   570.00
  8        850.0   $1,176    B4    2.929    3.070    850.00  1176.00
  9        801.0     $992    C1    2.904    2.997    801.00   992.00
 10        853.0     $771    C2    2.931    2.887    853.00   771.00
 11        872.0     $802    C3    2.941    2.904    872.00   802.00
 12      1,029.0     $988    C4    3.012    2.995   1029.00   988.00
 13      1,019.0   $1,400    D1    3.008    3.146   1019.00  1400.00
 14      1,002.0     $806    D2    3.001    2.906   1002.00   806.00
 15      1,024.0     $843    D3    3.010    2.926   1024.00   843.00
 16      1,197.0   1,110.0   D4    3.078    3.045   1197.00  1110.00
 17      1,088.0    883.0    E1    3.037    2.946   1088.00   883.00
 18      1,070.0    769.0    E2    3.029    2.886   1070.00   769.00
 19      1,052.0    864.0    E3    3.022    2.937   1052.00   864.00
 20      1,142.0    430.0    E4    3.058    2.633   1142.00   430.00
 21      1,044.0    884.0    F1    3.019    2.946   1044.00   884.00
 22        965.0    363.0    F2    2.985    2.560    965.00   363.00
           ================================================================
Sums     18966.0  15710.0          64.2     61.7   18966.0  15710.0
Means                                               862.1    714.1
```

Exhibit 6.12   Output from General Foods Regression Model

Regression Results		Actual	Estimate	Error
Slope=	0.460762	530	701.2	-171.24
T statistic=	2.716703	511	733.5	-222.50
Intercept=	533.0645	514	672.7	-158.68
Std Err coef=	0.169603	545	619.7	-74.69
Std Err Est=	178.0874	579	734.4	-155.42
R-square=	0.424692	615	685.6	-70.58
		664	795.7	-131.70
		850	1074.9	-224.92
		801	990.1	-189.14
		853	888.3	-35.31
		872	902.6	-30.60
		1029	988.3	40.70
		1019	1178.1	-159.13
		1002	904.4	97.56
		1024	921.5	102.51
		1197	1044.5	152.49
		1088	939.9	148.08
		1070	887.4	182.61
		1052	931.2	120.84
		1142	731.2	410.81
		1044	940.4	103.62
		965	700.3	264.68
		18966.0	18966.0	.0

compute intermediate values if you need them, which could then be transferred, or further transformed into the dependent and independent variable columns. At present these columns contain the logarithms of sales and advertising. A regression between these two sets of data would yield a curvilinear specification somewhat similar to the agency model. You can, of course, develop the data to test the specification of the agency model. You would have to estimate the advertising leverage visually from the input data.

The regression output is found with the menu or to the right of the work area. An example is shown in Exhibit 6.12. The meaning of these statistical results is as follows:

Slope is the coefficient of advertising

T statistic is the statistic used to test the hypothesis that the slope is zero. If the T statistic is greater than 2, there is less that a 5% chance that there is no relationship between sales and advertising; that is, Slope = 0.

Intercept is the sales value if advertising is zero.

Std. Err coef is the standard error of the slope coefficient.

Std. Err Est is the standard error of the forecast estimate.

R-square is the coefficient of determination. It is the measure of the amount of variation explained by the regression equation. The current R-square value (0.424692) indicates that the regression equation explains 42+% of the variation of sales around its mean value.

Using the Graphs

The graphs are accessed through the graph menu or by typing [Alt] G. In either case you find yourself with the 1-2-3 menu choice at the top of the screen. There are four graphs from which to choose:

SCIN is a scatter plot (SC) of the input data (IN) that is used to compute the regression. The data used in this graph are the data that are in the independent and dependent variable columns. An important feature of this plot is that the data points are identified by year and quarter. The point labeled "A2" is the data from the second quarter (2) of the first year (A).

TSIN is a time series (TS) plot of the input data. As above, the data for the plot are drawn from the independent and dependent variable columns of the work area.

SCAE is a scatter plot of the actual data versus the regression estimate.

TSAE is a time series plot of the actual versus the regression estimate.

When you are finished with the worksheet and want to print out the regression result, type [Alt] P. The graphs, however, are not printed out this way; if you want to print the graphs, the procedure is explained in the 1-2-3 manual.

A Cross-Sectional Model of the Industrial Communication Mix

Providing analytical insight for budgeting marketing effort for industrial products is much more difficult than it is for consumer products. The purchase process for many industrial products is more complex, and advertising and sales effort play multiple and diverse roles in influencing the purchase process. A fairly common model of industrial communication mix roles includes:

Finding: Locating a potential customer

Intrusion: Getting the customer's attention

Qualification: Determining interest in and ability to buy the product

Informing: Teaching about the product

Problem solving: Overcoming application problems related to product use

Closing: Obtaining the sale

Advertising may increase the likelihood that a sales rep will be received by a potential customer, or that a particular product will be considered, but it is seldom useful in problem solving or closing the deal. Sales force effort may be utilized in informing, problem solving, and developing relationships for many months before a sale is made. The nature of the selling task for industrial products makes research and analysis complex for at least four reasons:

1. *Variation in the input measures.*   Aspects of the selling task are difficult to measure and the variation of performance in what is defined similarly can be very great. While an advertising exposure for a network TV advertisement may differ from one situation to another, the message at least is the same. It is obvious that the variation in sales calls from one sales rep to another, and even from one sales call to the next by the same sales rep, is much greater.

2. *Matching effort and results.*   Since the purchase decision for many industrial products can take a considerable period of time and require many sales calls before a purchase is made, the historical data of the company will not provide a matching of effort and result at a low level of aggregation—i.e., weekly or monthly. This reduces the value of time series data for analytical purposes because it precludes the use of econometric models as a means of summarizing the experience. Correlations may indeed be found at higher levels of aggregation, say annual data, but the use of aggregate data increases the number of other factors that are also affecting sales. If the only variables in the response function are sales force effort and advertising, the effects of these other variables will be attributed to sales force and advertising.

3. *Tautological relationships.*   A tautology is a relationship that is true by definition rather than by a relationship between phenomena. For example, suppose that advertising is budgeted as a percent of sales and sales reps are paid by

commission. If a regression model is used to measure a relationship between sales, advertising expenditures, and sales force expense, a strong statistical relationship will be found, but it doesn't tell us anything about the response of sales to advertising and sales force effort, it merely reproduces the budgeting process.

4. *Lack of industry data.*   One of the factors that makes the analysis of marketing effort for consumer products much easier than it is for industrial products is the existence of industry data sources such as Nielsen and SAMI that make comparison with other competitors much easier and more accurate. Determining market share, or even defining the market, is much more difficult for most industrial products.

The ADVISOR project, which developed the ADVISOR model used in the next case, was instituted in direct response to many of the problems listed above. A number of major industrial firms agreed to cooperate in the development of a joint database and its analysis in the hope of obtaining better insight into the factors that determine an effective allocation of the advertising and sales force effort for industrial products.

The biggest difference between the ADVISOR model and the other decision models encountered in this book is that the other models were developed from data that are specific to the particular product for which decision support is desired, while the data from which the ADVISOR model was developed come from numerous products in diverse industry situations. The data used to estimate the response function in the ADVISOR model are called *cross-sectional data*, and the ADVISOR model is called, not surprisingly, a *cross-sectional model*. The ADVISOR cross-sectional model seeks to extend our knowledge about the communication mix in a particular situation by determining the factors that determine the communication mix in various situations. That seems rather vague; let's try an example:

At Normal University, grade point average is computed for a student across all of the courses he or she has taken during college and, based on the final GPA and the number of courses taken, a degree is awarded. At Cross-Section University, things are done a bit differently. Having studied the performance of a number of students in the past, the faculty has determined that the final GPA of the students can be predicted from their performance in the basic freshman classes and a few personality characteristics. While Cross-Section U. sounds like a great deal, if you happen to have the right personality scores and do well in your freshman classes, we would all be very nervous in paying our tuition up front. If we failed the test, we'd have a lot of very good reasons why the general results shouldn't apply to our particular situation.

On the other hand, few of us would dispute the fact that studying the experience of its students could provide a university with some insight about how to make a student's educational experience more successful. It could even help an entering freshman to set priorities and plan a more productive college career. So the value of cross-sectional data would appear to lie primarily in the insight that it provides, particularly in new situations, rather than in a definitive statement of what should be done in any particular situation. For this reason, the results of cross-sectional studies are often presented as *norms* or *par reports* rather than strategy recommendations.

The difference between a norm and a recommendation is frequently overlooked, both by model builders and decision makers. A norm provides an estimate of what the average marketing strategy would be in a situation described by the input variables for a particular situation. Since the data used by the response model do not fully describe the situation and the response model is an average that doesn't describe any particular situation, it doesn't make much sense to consider the norms that result as a prescription for what should be done. The conversation between the various managers in the Convection case highlights some of the commonly encountered conceptions and misconceptions about the use of cross-sectional models.

The ADVISOR Model

The ADVISOR model is a cross-sectional model of the communication mixes of nearly 200 industrial products supplied by nearly 30 participating companies. Two basic hypotheses form the philosophical basis of the ADVISOR study: (1) successful industrial product managers have learned to make good decisions about the appropriate levels of advertising, personal selling, and other communication methods for the products they manage, and (2) if the characteristics that define similar industrial communication situations could be discovered, then similar communication mix allocations would be appropriate. In order to define similar advertising situations, data on 19 factors that were felt to affect the communication mix were gathered for each of the products, and the data was analyzed using cross-sectional regression techniques. The resulting regression models provided response functions that predict the appropriate expenditure level and communication mix, rather than sales or market share.

The ADVISOR model consists of a number of related response functions, only three of which will be discussed here and presented in the Convection Corporation case: the total marketing budget; the advertising budget; and the advertising share (the share of the marketing budget allocated to advertising). These models are used to provide norms for marketing spending, personal selling and technical service, advertising, change in advertising from previous levels, and distribution.

The advertising/marketing ratio was computed using a special regression formulation called logit analysis, which won't be discussed here, but the interpretation of the coefficients obtained with this technique is the same as for the other two models, so for managerial purposes it doesn't represent anything different.

The research process that was undertaken on the database resulted in the identification of nine important general characteristics of industrial marketing situations that influenced, to a useful degree, the choice of a communication mix. The variables identified were:

1. Current sales level
2. Number of users (customers) for the product
3. Degree of customer concentration (share of purchases accounted for by the largest customers)
4. Fraction of the sales made directly by the manufacturer to the customers rather than through intermediaries.
5. Difference between the attitudes of customers and prospects toward the product
6. Fraction of sales made to fulfill orders
7. Life cycle stage of the product
8. Marketing plans for the product (aggressive, hold share, harvest, etc.)
9. Product complexity

Although there are certainly a number of other variables that, in any particular situation, might prove to be as important as these factors, this particular set exhibited an ability to predict the communication mix of the products in the database that was superior to any other set tested.

The analysis of the database, in addition to identifying important general characteristics, also resulted in the estimation of a mathematical relationship between the factors and the communication mix. The total marketing expense model and the advertising expense models were both exponential specifications as follows:

$$B_t = \beta_0 S_{t-1}^{\beta_1} U^{\beta_2} \prod_i C_{\text{var } i}^{\beta_i} \prod_j \beta_j D_{\text{var } j} \tag{6.7}$$

B^t = Marketing or advertising spending budget

S_{t-1} = Sales dollars (previous year)

U = Number of users of the product

$C_{\text{var } i}$ = Continuous independent variable i

$D_{\text{var } j}$ = Discrete independent variable j

$\beta_0, \beta_i, \beta_j$ = Parameters to be determined

The exponential specification provides a diminishing marginal effect of the variables like that we observed in the Tang agency model. (The response is a curve whose growth rate decreases for higher levels of the input factors.) Such an equation is usually estimated using linear regression analysis of the logarithms of the variables. This is what was done by Gary Lilien, who developed the ADVISOR models, and his results are found in Exhibit 6.13. Observations on the models include the following:

The explanatory power of the advertising and marketing models (as measured by the R^2 in the next to last column), although lower than usually seen in time series analysis, is quite high for a cross-sectional study.

The coefficients in Exhibit 6.13 for which the t-statistics are greater than 1.96 are significant at the 5% level. Those coefficients for which the t-statistics are not significant but are greater than 1 are retained because they increase the explanatory power of the regression.

The sign of the coefficient determines the direction of the effect on the dependent variable. If higher levels of the independent variable are associated with higher levels of the dependent variable, the sign is positive. In the case of the "product plans" and "attitude difference" variables, the relationship is also direct, even though the signs of these variables are negative due to how the variables are defined. If the marketing plans for a product become more aggressive, both the marketing and the advertising expenditures need to be increased. The more the attitude of current customers toward the product is more favorable than that of prospective customers, the lower the marketing expenditure, but the higher the necessary advertising expenditure level.

These models are used to produce norms for marketing, advertising, and personal selling levels for a given communication budgeting situation. The model is intended to provide these norms not only for the situations in the database that were used to estimate the models, but also for products that were not in the database and for new marketing situations for a product. The use of the model is somewhat analogous to the use of the market simulation analysis model described in the Clark Equipment cases to estimate the market share for a product that had not been offered to the market.

The ADVISOR norms have been used by companies in a number of different ways: (1) as a screening device to identify communication plans that are unusual and should be subjected to a second evaluation; (2) as a standard of comparison and as guidelines in budget preparation; (3) to provide insight into the appropriate changes that might be indicated by different marketing scenarios; (4) to estimate the communication budgets of competitors; and (5) to provide justification for communication plans.

The Convection Corporation case provides an ADVISOR analysis for each of three industrial products for use in allocating a limited communication budget across the three products. Unfortunately, the ADVISOR model itself is too large to include on the program diskette (although a personal computer version has been developed), but a number of scenarios for the three products have been run

Exhibit 6.13 Norm-model Results of the ADVISOR Study

Dependent Variable	Continuous Variables							Dichotomous Variables						
	Sales (LSLS)	No. of Users (LUSERS)	Customer Concentration (LCONC)	Fraction of Sales Made to Order (LSPEC)	Prospect/Customer/Product Attitudes Difference (DIFF)	Sales Direct to Users (LDIR-USER)	Stage in Life Cycle (LCYCLE)	Product Plans (PLANS)	Product Complexity (PROD)	Constant	R^2	F	SEE	N
Advertising (LADV)	+0.618 (9.1)	+0.104 (3.6)	−1.881 (3.1)	−1.989 (4.4)	a	a	−0.892 (3.2)	−1.503 (6.0)	a	−0.651	0.59	25.0	1.12	110
A/M [Logit (A/M)]	−0.232 (4.5)	a	a	a	+0.383 (2.0)	−0.255 (2.1)	a	a	−0.230[b] (1.2)	+0.544	0.24	7.5	0.91	100
Marketing (LMKTG)	+0.712 (12.6)	+0.082 (3.1)	−1.633 (3.1)	−0.993 (2.8)	−0.305 (1.7)	−0.194[b] (0.6)	−0.424 (2.0)	−0.809 (3.9)	+0.528 (2.5)	+0.185	0.72	28.2	0.91	110

Note: t statistics in ( ); all equations significant at $\alpha < 0.001$.

[a] Variable insignificant and logically irrelevant.

[b] Variable retained for logical consistency.

Source: Gary L. Lilien, "Advisor 2: Modeling the Marketing Mix for Industrial Products," *Management Science*, Vol 25, No. 2 (February 1979), p. 195. (c)1979, The Institute of Management Sciences, 290 Westminster Street, Providence, R.I. 02903. Used with permission.

Exhibit 6.14   Par Report for Heatcrete

Marketing Spending Analysis		Heatcrete	
Norm Range	100.97	155.34	237.67
Current spending		58.30	

Diagnosis

Marketing Spending Base	170.46
Number of Customers	− 7.11%
Fraction of Special Orders	20.58%
Customer Concentration	− 21.22%
Fraction of Direct Sales	− 0.09%
Plans	41.41%
Customer/Prospect Attitude	6.18%
Product Complexity	− 15.49%
Life Cycle	− 18.53%

and the results are found in the Convection model description at the end of the case. The 1-2-3 spreadsheet described in the same section is a very simple worksheet designed to relieve the computational burden of designing a communication budget for the three products that satisfies (as much as possible) the various pressures on the decision maker.

Interpreting the Output from the ADVISOR Model

The results of the ADVISOR analysis for a particular product are presented in what is called a *par report*. The par report provides not only an indication of the marketing and advertising budget levels that would be consistent with the industry practice as interpreted by the ADVISOR model, but also an indication of the relative importance of each of the nine factors on the par level. Let's take a specific example—the marketing spending analysis for Heatcrete, one of the products in the Convection case. You will notice that the par report in Exhibit 6.14 provides estimates of a number of different values that need definition:

Norm: The norm is the "normal spending amount as predicted by the AD-VISOR model using the data available. (The norm is the middle value in the "norm range" line in Exhibit 6.14.)

Norm Range: Since the norm is a statistical estimate, it has a confidence interval around it. The norm range is so defined that the current spending levels for communication budgeting situations similar to the one defined for the product would be between these two values. In other words, there is approximately a three out of four chance that the current spending level should be within the norm range, and only one chance out of four that it would fall outside it. If the current spending level is outside of the norm range, it should be considered unusual.

Base: The base is the predicted spending level for the average product in the database; in other words, if we find the average value for each of our nine variables and plug those numbers into the ADVISOR model, the result would be the base.

As one might expect, the base and the norm are mathematically related. The norm is equal to the base times an adjustment for each of the nine variables. These adjustment factors, which show how much of the deviation of the norm from the base is due to the individual factors, are shown in Exhibit 6.14.

The spending norm (155.34) is the predicted marketing spending for a product with Heatcrete's ratings on the various factors in the marketing spending model. The marketing spending base (170.46) is the predicted marketing spending for an average product with the same sales level as Heatcrete ($1.2 million). The diagnostic details present the importance of each factor in obtaining the norm from the spending base. The formal relationship between the norm and base levels is:

$$\text{Norm} = \text{Base} (1 + \text{Effect of Customers}/100) \qquad (6.8)$$
$$\times (1 + \text{Effect of Special Order}/100)$$
$$\times (1 + \text{Effect of Life Cycle}/100) \text{ and etc.}$$

A positive percentage for a given factor in the diagnosis increases the spending norm relative to the spending base. Similarly, a negative percentage reduces the norm relative to the base.

An Alternative Model of Industrial Communication

The ADVISOR model presents one empirically based conceptualization of how industrial advertisers determine communication budgets. Another broadly based empirical model of advertising budgeting was developed by Farris and Buzzell on data obtained from the PIMS study undertaken by the Strategic Planning Institute (see Exhibit 6.15). The PIMS database is larger than the ADVISOR database, and includes data on more products for a longer period of time. The model estimated by Farris and Buzzell differs from that of the ADVISOR model and is presented here to provide an alternative viewpoint.

Exhibit 6.15   Farris-Buzzell Advertising Model Results: Regression Analyses of Cross-Sectional Variations in the Logarithm of A and P/S Ratios

Independent Variables	Regression Coefficients	(Estimated Standard Deviation)[a]
Produced to order (dummy variable)($\times$ 10)[b]	-3.59	(0.71)
Number of end users (scale)($\times$ 100)	6.45	(3.07)
Purchase frequency (reverse scale)($\times$ 10)	1.72	(0.26)
Purchase amount (scale)($\times$ 10)	-1.75	(0.26)
Importance of auxiliary services (scale)($\times$ 10)	1.66	(0.46)
Percent of sales direct to end users[c] ($\times$ 1000)	-5.15	(0.93)
Market share[c] ($\times$ 1000)	-7.26	(1.84)
Relative price[c] ($\times$ 100)	1.47	(0.46)
Contribution margin on sales[c] ($\times$ 100)	2.34	(0.27)
Percent capacity utilized[c] ($\times$ 1000)	-7.12	(1.95)
Percent sales from new products ($\times$ 1000)	7.19	(1.69)
Constant	-1.77	(0.56)
$R^2 =$	0.416	
$N =$	791	
$F =$	50.44[d]	

[a]All coefficients significant at the 0.05 level.

[b]For ease of reading the tables, coefficients have been multiplied by the noted numbers: either 10, 100, 1000.

[c]4-yr average.

[d]Significant at the 0.01 level.

CASE: Convection Corporation

This case considers the problem of allocating the communication budget across three industrial products. The Convection Corporation is attempting to develop a corporate communication policy, and the allocation of the budget across these three products will form an important precedent. To assist in the planning effort, CC has decided to participate in the ADVISOR project, a major intercompany research effort studying the determinants of industrial advertising budgeting practices. Comparison of the problems of advertising management and the types of research available for industrial products with those available for consumer products provides a good opportunity to examine the many roles of advertising in the communication mix for different types of products. ADVISOR's use of cross-sectional data provides an important complement to the previous cases' use of experimental and time series audit data.

Paul Warren's new position, group marketing coordinator, had only recently been created at Convection Corporation. The position called for him not only to coordinate the marketing communication expenditures of three product managers, but also to develop a systematic approach to communication budgeting. His new assignment curtailed the independence of the product managers and their relationship with the advertising department. Warren was concerned about developing good working relationships with these people.

Warren was also apprehensive about his upcoming annual budget review. John Smiley, the company's controller, had distributed a budget memo stating that a financial crunch appeared likely and that budget recommendations would have to be supported very carefully and more specifically. Smiley had directed Warren to give serious consideration to cutting his communication budget to $2.1 million, only two-thirds that of the previous year.

Company Background

Convection Corporation (CC) was a midwestern company founded in 1880 to produce steam boilers for use in the nearby northern Indiana steel mills. This initial product provided the experience base and opportunity to develop more general expertise in high-temperature production process machinery and high-pressure hydraulic systems. Over the years, CC had developed a diverse product line that served a wide range of industrial customers.

CC's 1979 operating income before tax was nearly $170 million on sales that exceeded $2 billion, despite increased competition and economic uncertainty. Selling, general, and administrative expenses were 6% of sales. CC had been seeking to establish a more systematic approach to marketing in recent years. The reorganization that had created Paul Warren's position was a part of this effort. In the new organization, marketing was directed by a senior vice president for marketing and three vice presidents, each of whom supervised a number of group marketing coordinators. Roles and responsibilities in the new management structure were still somewhat fluid. As one of the first group marketing coordinators, Warren had been specifically asked to develop guidelines on how marketing communication should be managed under the new organization.

This case was prepared by Gary L. Lilien and Darral G. Clarke.

Copyright © 1982 by the President and Fellow of Harvard College, Harvard Business School case 9-583-045.

Advertising Decision Making at CC

Before the reorganization, all advertising had been planned by the advertising department. Product managers had played an advisory but largely passive role. Proposals had been submitted to the vice president for sales by advertising departments. Support for advertising proposals had been based on response to the advertising campaigns by direct competition, recent sales increases, and the perceived need for high visibility for high-revenue products.

The advertising department had also managed relations with outside advertising agencies, one of which CC had retained for the past 11 years. This agency provided a comprehensive advertising service for its industrial clients that included: contracting annually for space in appropriate technical journals and industry publications and then reselling this space to CC and its other clients, developing advertising copy, and designing ad layouts and commercial art for trade show exhibits, product displays, and so on.

Development of an advertising plan usually began with the advertising department's budget proposal, which included the media schedule for each product, the product's five-year marketing program, and the advertising department's understanding of what the product manager hoped to achieve in the market. The advertising department then contacted the chief sales engineer for the product, who supplied technical information, identified the product's advantages over competitors, and suggested the competitive angle.

It was not clear to Paul Warren exactly what roles he, the advertising department, and product managers should play in decision making in the new organization. He felt that this first budget determination process would set some important precedents.

Paul Warren

Paul Warren had been a field sales manager before he was appointed group marketing coordinator. While a field sales manager he had observed that there wasn't much coordination between sales efforts in the field and the company's promotion support. Sales engineers got lots of printed material when a new product was launched, but had to decide how to use it themselves. There wasn't much coordination across related products, and little effort was made to evaluate the impact of various programs.

Paul Warren's Product Group

Warren's product group consisted of three related products—Heatcrete, the Flowclean sootblower, and the Corlin valve.

Jim Stapleton, the product manager for Heatcrete, had a background that included both field sales experience and a period of time in the controller's office. Stan Bloch, the Flowclean product manager, had been with the company for 22 years. He had done some of the early development work for the Flowclean sootblower. Wayne Collins had been with CC for three years and had an advanced degree in materials science. His first research assignment had been to improve the corrosion resistance of conventional steel alloys, and the first application of his work had been the Corlin valve. After the valve went into production, Collins requested a sales assignment to increase his knowledge of the marketing and management of new products. These three industrial equipment products varied considerably in their age, technical selling requirements, and size of the sale. Paul Warren felt that if he could develop a communications budget allocation system that would work for products as diverse as these, he would have a system that could be applied generally within CC.

Heatcrete

Heatcrete was a castable concrete refractory material used in the construction of high-temperature furnaces, chemical reactors, and other process applications. CC had marketed the product for a number of years. Similar products were offered by all full-time refractory product manufacturers, and three new competitors had entered the refractory supply business during the past year.

Exhibit 6.16 Tentative Heatcrete Budget

Industry Sales	1980 (plan)			1979 (actual)	
Heatcrete sales	$632,000			$601,000	
Marketing share	10%			10%	
Marketing Expenses		**% of Sales**			**% of Sales**
Personal selling	28,000	4.4		$20,000	3.3
Technical service	5,300	0.8		3,900	0.6
Advertising*	25,000	3.2		25,000	3.3

*Advertising included media costs, direct mail, brochures, catalogs, sales promotions, trade shows, and exhibits.

Heatcrete was usually sold with other refractory products. Jim Stapleton estimated that there were approximately 600 Heatcrete customers, who were reached through a direct sales effort or through 100 distributors. Heatcrete sales reps reported that they usually dealt with about three people in a customer company for a given purchase. Industry refractory product demand in 1980 was forecast at $23 million, and growth of about 8% was anticipated. Total industry sales of Heatcrete-type products were forecast to be $6.3 million.

Stapleton was concerned about scattered sales rep reports of customer dissatisfaction with Heatcrete, as well as its low market share. He felt some research into possible product problems should be undertaken, and if no problems existed or if existing problems could be solved, advertising and promotion for Heatcrete could probably reach 5% of sales before it would begin to cut into margins.

Martin Skelly, the new director of the advertising department, in response to a request from Paul Warren, reported that in 1979 ads for Heatcrete had been placed in *Iron Age*, as had been done for a number of years. The ads appeared in a two-page color spread in the "company format." The total 1979 advertising expense for Heatcrete was $25,000, which included Heatcrete's share in the production cost of the *Refractories Catalog*, a CC refractory product catalog, and $7,500 for brochures, catalogs, and direct mail pieces. Skelly recommended the same budget levels to Jim Stapleton for 1980.

Mr. Stapleton submitted a tentative budget for Heatcrete (see Exhibit 6.16).

Flowclean Sootblowers

As a result of environmental pressures and increased fuel costs during the 1970s, sootblowers were expected to be either designed into, or planned to be retrofitted to, virtually every large-scale fossil fuel steam boiler. Sootblowers increased efficiency and reduced the need for cleaning, resulting in less boiler downtime. Because sootblowers extracted airborne heavy particulates from the combustion chamber, they had recently been adapted for pollution control purposes. Convection's current line had been developed 17 years ago and had been modified only slightly since. There were about a thousand corporate customers for this equipment. Sales reps visited about five people at each location and selling a sootblower required working with the system manufacturer as well as the buyer to understand the design parameters of the complete boiler system.

There were three competing manufacturers, of which Convection was the largest. The technical nature of the application was such that only a company with a complete understanding of boiler systems could manufacture sootblowers. Stan Bloch explained the selling situation as follows:

When I was selling sootblowers, everybody knew me and knew that I understood the prod-

Exhibit 6.17   Tentative Flowclean Budget

	1980 (plan)		1979 (actual)	
Sales	$24,160,000		$23,500,000	
Market share	50%		50%	
Marketing Expenses		**% of Sales**		**% of Sales**
Personal selling	2,338,000	9.7	2,166,000	9.2
Technical service	314,000	1.3	304,000	1.3
Advertising	248,000	1.0	338,000*	1.7

*This included $138,000 for production and mailing costs of a new series of brochures.

uct. Sometimes I would talk to final users because the sootblowers would have to work with their existing equipment or special environmental protection procedures. In such cases it was nice to be able to show these people our ads in the key industry publications, to let them know that we were the biggest. It was always good to have some brochures that let people know that Convection was a major firm with an excellent reputation for engineering. Beyond that it was the product specs and applications engineering that sold the product.

In 1979, Flowclean sales were $23.5 million, which represented a 50% market share. Forecasts for 1980 presented a muddled picture. The rate at which utilities, a major market segment, appeared to be adding generating capacity was declining. At the same time, many other facilities were converting from gas to coal. Exactly how these two oppositely directed trends would balance out for sootblower demand was uncertain.

In 1979, a one- or two-page Flowclean spread was run in *Power and Power Engineering* every other month at a total cost of $162,000. Advertising had been budgeted as a fixed percentage of forecast sales. Bloch's tentative budget for Flowclean is shown in Exhibit 6.17.

Corlin Valve

The Corlin valve was made from a special alloy that resulted in higher resistance to corrosion than had previously been possible with stainless steel. The Corlin valve was felt to have a substantial potential market, since it could replace existing corrosion-resistant valves that were much more expensive. Some applications involving highly corrosive substances would still require the existing valves, but for a wide variety of uses, the Corlin valve could offer much better performance per dollar.

It hadn't been easy to convince chemical companies to switch to the Corlin valve. Wayne Collins, the product manager, said:

We need to convince customers that our product can meet their technical performance requirements. A lot of engineers just expect that any valve for corrosives must be titanium-lined. I think we should get some articles in the technical press with some specific test results for Corlin in comparison with other materials. Beyond that, we have to generate some interest in the product so engineers will become interested in the technical details. If we could devise some dramatic exhibit for trade shows, we could refer to it later in print ads. Hopefully, this whole series would generate some inquiries upon which we could build a more successful sales effort.

The market for corrosion-resistant valves was estimated at $23 million in 1979, and was growing at 15% annually. There were nearly 4,000 potential customers. Selling the Corlin valve usually required dealing with about five people.

Most 1979 Corlin ads had been placed in *Oil and Gas Journal*, the most widely read publication

Exhibit 6.18   Tentative Corlin Valve Budget

	1980 (plan)		1979 (actual)	
Sales	$500,000		$100,000	
Market share	1.9%		0.43%	
Marketing Expenses		**% of Sales**		**% of Sales**
Personal selling	$225,000	45	130,000	130
Technical service	30,000	0.6	20,000	20
Advertising	80,000	16	65,000	67

in the field. Plans in 1980 called for placing a series of black-and-white quarter-page ads in three other publications as well. The ads were to appear in at least two publications every other month, at a cost of $40,000. Martin Skelly was dubious, however, about the value of these "backpage" ads. Collins' (Skelly-assisted) tentative budget was as seen in Exhibit 6.18.

Development of an Approach to Advertising Planning

Paul Warren felt that any budgeting method he recommended would need to have a consensus of approval from his product managers. As a first step in achieving this consensus, he scheduled a meeting to discuss the various budgeting methods he had been reading about since being appointed to his new position. The result of that reading was that, although he had found no solid scientific method for budgeting industrial advertising, he had gathered a number of interesting facts about industrial advertising.

Industrial Advertising Budget Planning

Warren found that, until recently, approaches to setting advertising spending levels had seemed to fall into the following categories:

1. *Simple decision rules* such as "all you can afford," "percentage of sales," and "competitive parity." All you can afford seemed to imply covering all product and selling expenses and then determining how much of the remaining margin should be devoted to advertising. This often re-

sulted in a percentage-of-sales rule. When a constant percentage of sales was budgeted, advertising expenses increased or decreased with sales levels. This seemed to be viewed by many managers as a desirable expense control. Competitive parity was based on the premise that all the competitors in an industry couldn't be wrong and that parity stabilized industry advertising expenditures. Another supporting concept for competitive parity was that one should not be at a disadvantage with respect to competitors in advertising or anything else.

2. *Objective setting and task methods* were based on a hierarchy-of-response model of customer purchase behavior. The general hierarchy-of-response model suggested that purchase was not spontaneous, but rather customers moved through stages such as awareness → knowledge → liking → preference → conviction → purchase. Such methods rejected the idea that advertising caused industrial product sales directly, so objectives had to be set in terms of moving customers from one stage to another. As customers moved through the different stages, different elements of the marketing mix might well have to be stressed.

3. *Arbitrary* methods were based on the experience of the manager and involved an intuitive, nonexplicit decision process. The use of this method might result from a "good feel" for the marketing advertising requirements or from frustration with other methods and the need to advertise anyway.

Warren found a survey of 557 subscribers to *Industrial Marketing* that showed that the percentage-of-sales method was used by 24.8%; the task method by 35.6%; and some arbitrary method by 27.7%. Other methods accounted for 11.9%.

The ADVISOR Project

Warren's research also discovered a cross-sectional study of industrial advertising behavior known as the ADVISOR project (Lilien 1980), and he found it interesting enough to attend an ADVISOR seminar. At the seminar, he learned that the ADVISOR project was based on the idea that successful industrial managers have learned to make good communications decisions.

ADVISOR sought to understand and generalize managers' decision experience by identifying product and market characteristics that would affect the marketing and advertising levels for a given product. The data on which the ADVISOR project was based were drawn from 197 industrial products supplied by 27 participating companies. Data were collected on 19 factors thought to affect advertising budget levels, and models were constructed that computed norms, called *par reports*, for marketing spending, advertising spending, and the advertising-to-marketing ratio. *The norms were predicted by multivariate regression models that appeared to Warren to be rather technical, but he found a summary of the direction of the effects of the major factors both interesting and understandable. (See Exhibit 6.19.)

At the conclusion of the seminar some different uses of ADVISOR were presented:

One company uses a comparison grid to guide its use of the model. "When a product's spending level is outside the norm range, that's a signal that a question might be asked, 'Is there a good reason for the product to be so far above or below the norm?'

Some companies include ADVISOR norms in their annual budget plans for comparison purposes and as guides for budget reallocation.

Another company completed five questionnaires for one product, each representing different assumptions about the future of the marketplace. The different ADVISOR norms refined thinking about the impact of market forces on the product.

One participant in the ADVISOR program uses the model to project marketing spending for long-range product plans, thus avoiding plans that rely on constant advertising-to-sales ratios.

Another company uses ADVISOR, along with careful estimates of competitors' visible marketing spending, to estimate competitive personal selling expenses. And another ADVISOR participant, who admits he used to dread delivering his annual report to top management, finds that ADVISOR provides compelling quantitative support for his recommendations. [Lilien 1980, p. 84]

When the seminar was over, Warren had no illusions that ADVISOR would solve all his communication budgeting problems, but he felt the approach was sufficiently interesting to have an ADVISOR analysis performed on each of the three products for which he was responsible. A summary of the results is found in Exhibit 6.20, and detailed reports for each brand are found in Exhibits 6.21–6.23. The product descriptions supplied to the ADVISOR project are found Exhibit 6.24.

The ADVISOR par reports made sense to Warren, but he wasn't sure the product managers would feel the same way. He decided to meet with them to discuss their communication budgets as a group.

Communication Budget Meeting

Warren began the Thursday afternoon budget meeting with the results of his research on industrial advertising budget methods. He discussed the per-

---

*Definitions used in ADVISOR: *Marketing expenditures* include advertising, personal selling and technical service expenditures (direct plus overhead). Sales management expenses are excluded. *Advertising* consists of: (a) impersonal advertising media—space costs, direct mail, brochures, catalogs, TV, and radio costs; and (b) personal advertising media—sales promotion and trade shows.

Exhibit 6.19   ADVISOR Norm Models: Direction of Effect for a Factor Increase

FACTORS	MARKETING	ADVERTISING	ADVERTISING/ MARKETING
Sales	▲	▲	▼
Number of Customers	▲	▲	▬
Customer Concentration	▼	▼	▬
Fraction Special Orders	▼	▼	▬
Life Cycle	▼	▼	▬
Plans*	▲	▲	▬
Product Complexity	▲	▬	▼
Attitude Difference: Customers-Prospects	▼	▬	▲
Fraction of Sales Direct	▲	▬	▼

*If plans for the product become more aggressive.

*If plans for the product become more aggressive.
Source: Gary L. Lilien, "Keeping Up with the Marketing Joneses." *Industrial Marketing*, March 1980, p.81.

centage-of-sales, task, and arbitrary methods and then asked for comments.

Stapleton: I don't see that the three methods commonly used offer much guidance. It doesn't make sense for us to go out and collect lots of additional marketing information like consumer goods companies. I prefer a fixed percent of sales because it's the easiest to use.

Warren: But if we used that or one of the other simple rules, we have no guidance about which rule to use for a given product. What percentage of sales is right? When should we try for parity? And we have to develop support for the budgets or they are sure to be cut.

Bloch: I think Jim is on the right track. It's hard for us to tell what effect our advertising is having. I

Exhibit 6.20   Summary of ADVISOR Par Reports ($000)

	Heatcrete	Flowclean	Corlin
Marketing Spending			
Norm	155	1,813	539
Norm Low	101	1,179	350
Norm High	238	2,774	825
Current Spending	58	2,900	335
Personal Selling/Technical Service			
Norm	108	1,712	368
Norm Low	70	1,113	239
Norm High	165	2,620	563
Current Spending	33	2,652	255
Advertising Spending			
Norm	48	101	171
Norm Low	31	66	111
Norm High	73	155	261
Current Spending	25	248	80

don't think it is that important a component of our selling effort. I'd take an extra sales rep in exchange for $60,000 in advertising any day.

Collins: What you are saying may be applicable to products that have been out for a while. But the Corlin valve is a new, multi-application product. I don't think the accounting approach Jim is suggesting should apply. We should be willing to sell at a loss in the early stages of product introduction to build up the product.

Bloch: It doesn't look like you are going to be able to find a consistent approach for all of these products, Paul. They are in different markets, and are different in terms of manufacturing materials and uses.

Warren then summarized what he had learned about the ADVISOR project and asked for reactions.

Stapleton: I'm no statistician, so I can't understand the models completely, but I can't believe that product margin and number of competitors don't matter.

Collins: Well, maybe you feel that way about engineered materials, Jim. But I think most of the results Paul described are really common sense. For instance, you'd expect a new product to require more marketing. And if it's also a technical product, you would expect to rely on personal selling more than ads.

Bloch: I think you're right, Wayne. But if it is all common sense, why didn't we see it before?

Stapleton: You'll need more than common sense to make any significant budget changes. You'll need hard numbers!

Warren: I am inclined to agree with that, Jim. I thought ADVISOR seemed interesting and that

Exhibit 6.21   ADVISOR Par Report for Heatcrete ($000)

Marketing Spending Analysis:

Norm Range:	$101.0	$155.3	$238.7
Current Spending:		$ 58.3	

Diagnosis:

Marketing Spending Base	$170.5
Number of Customers	−7.1%
Fraction of Special Orders	20.6
Customer Concentration	−21.2
Fraction of Direct Sales	−0.1
Plans	41.4
Customer/Prospect Attitude	6.2
Product Complexity	−15.5
Life Cycle	−18.5

Personal Selling/Technical Service:

Norm Range:	$69.9	$107.6	$164.6
Current Spending:		$ 33.3	

Diagnosis:

Spending Base	$124.5
Number of Customers	−8.9
Fraction of Special Orders	6.8
Customer Concentration	−20.8
Fraction of Direct Sales	−2.9
Plans	63.6
Customer/Prospect Attitude	5.5
Product Complexity	−23.4
Life Cycle	−12.7

Advertising Spending Analysis:

Norm Range:	$ 31.0	$47.8	$73.0
Current Spending:		$25.0	

Diagnosis:

Advertising Spending Base	$ 45.9
Number of Customers	−9.2%
Fraction of Special Orders	49.6
Customer Concentration	−28.5
Plans	81.9
Life Cycle	−41.1

(continued)

Exhibit 6.21 (continued)   ADVISOR Par Report for Heatcrete ($000)

Advertising Change Analysis:

Norm Range:	90.3%	111.5%	137.2%
Actual		100.0	of last yr.

Diagnosis:

Advertising Change Base	106.5%
Change in Plans	0.1
Change in Market Share	1.2
Change in Number of Competitors	5.0
Customer Concentration	− 8.8
Number of Customers	− 1.4
Advertising Spending Level	9.5

Distribution Channel Analysis:

Norm for Percent of Sales Direct to Customers Through Company Sales Force	54.0%
Actual Percent of Sales Direct	59.0

Diagnosis:

Base	48.7%
Size of Firm	0.4%
Average Order Size	2.9
Technical Purchase Complexity	− 10.9
Stage in Life Cycle	12.7
Fraction of Sales Standard	0.2
Purchase Frequency	6.7

was why I collected the required information from reports you'd sent me to see what AD-VISOR would say about our products. I thought that maybe our competitors might know something we don't.

Bloch: But are the companies included in the study really our competitors? Only three companies make sootblowers and they're not in the study! I don't think a sootblower has much similarity with a punch press. I won't feel comfortable with ADVISOR until there is a product in there like mine.

Warren: I'm not sure it matters. The theory is that market and product characteristics are more important than having our exact competitors in the study. I'm more concerned about how we can use the results to justify budget decisions.

Bloch: Are these data up to date? The study began in 1973. The world has changed a lot since then. Frankly, I'm skeptical.

Warren: Do you all feel confident of your proposed budgets? Are you sure they are right? And we've all relied on Skelly pretty heavily. There is one final problem I hate to bring up, but

Exhibit 6.22 ADVISOR Par Report for Flowclean ($000)

Marketing Spending Analysis:

Norm Range:	$1,178.6	$1,813.3	$2,774.3
Current Spending:		$2,900.0	

Diagnosis:

Marketing Spending Base	$2,226.2
Number of Customers	1.7
Fraction of Special Orders	− 27.6
Customer Concentration	− 35.6
Fraction of Direct Sales	− 0.5
Plans	41.4
Customer/Prospect Attitude	− 5.8
Product Complexity	59.1
Life Cycle	− 18.5

Personal Selling/Technical Service:

Norm Range:	$1,112.9	$1,712.2	$2,619.6
Current Spending:		$2,652.0	

Diagnosis:

Spending Base	$1,882.4
Number of Customers	− 0.4%
Fraction of Special Orders	− 25.1
Customer Concentration	− 35.1
Fraction of Direct Sales	− 2.6
Plans	51.5
Customer/Prospect Attitude	− 8.8
Product Complexity	− 66.4
Life Cycle	− 16.2

Advertising Spending Analysis:

Norm Range:	$ 65.7	$ 101.1	$ 154.6
Current Spending:		$ 248.0	

Diagnosis:

Advertising Spending Base:	$343.8
Number of Customers	$ 2.3%
Fraction of Special Orders	− 50.1
Customer Concentration	− 46.2
Plans	81.9
Life Cycle	− 41.1

(continued)

Exhibit 6.22 (continued)   ADVISOR Par Report for Flowclean ($000)

Advertising Change Analysis:

Norm Range:	86.9%	107.3%	132.0%
Actual		73.2	of last yr.

Diagnosis:

Advertising Change Base	106.5%
Change in Plans	31.2
Change in Market Share	0.6
Change in Number of	
Competitors	0.6
Customer Concentration	−16.6
Number of Customers	−0.6
Advertising Spending Level	−8.4

Distribution Channel Analysis:

Norm for Percent of Sales	
Direct to Customers Through	
Company Sales Force	78.7%
Actual Percent of Sales Direct	55.0

Diagnosis:

Base	48.7%
Size of Firm	−2.6%
Average Order Size	2.7
Technical Purchase	
Complexity	16.7
Stage in Life Cycle	41.1
Fraction of Sales Standard	−2.7
Purchase Frequency	0.7

I have a memo from John Smiley, telling me to cut this year's budget to two-thirds of last year's budget because of difficult economic conditions. Here are his current 1980 profit projections for our products:*

These figures represent business or profit-center profits after allocation of all direct and corporate overhead expenses.

Heatcrete	$ 12,640
Flowclean	4,212,000
Corlin Valve	(197,000)

Where do we make the cuts? Or should we just let Skelly do it for us? Do you trust his judgment that much? Can we argue against his proposed cuts?

Following this statement, comments flew so rapidly and heatedly that Mr. Warren decided to call off the meeting:

Warren: I don't think we'll settle this in this meeting. Will you all please meet with me again Monday morning? For that meeting I would like a justification for your present budget. Second, I

Exhibit 6.23   ADVISOR Par Report for Corlin Valve ($000)

Marketing Spending Analysis:

Norm Range:	$350.4	$539.1	$824.8
Current Spending:		$335.0	

Diagnosis:

Marketing Spending Base	$144.5
Number of Customers	14.2%
Fraction of Special Orders	16.2
Customer Concentration	2.3
Fraction of Direct Sales	1.8
Plans	41.4
Customer/Prospect Attitude	6.2
Product Complexity	59.1
Life Cycle	13.0

Personal Selling/Technical Service:

Norm Range:	$239.2	$368.0	$563.1
Current Spending:		$255.0	

Diagnosis:

Spending Base	$104.2
Number of Customers	9.3
Fraction of Special Orders	4.8
Customer Concentration	−0.8
Fraction of Direct Sales	−0.3
Plans	65.1
Customer/Prospect Attitude	5.7
Product Complexity	77.2
Life Cycle	0.9

Advertising Spending Analysis:

Norm Range:	$111.2	$171.1	$261.7
Current Spending:		$80.0	

Diagnosis:

Advertising Spending Base	$40.4
Number of Customers	19.1%
Fraction of Special Orders	38.2
Customer Concentration	3.3
Plans	81.9
Life Cycle	37.0

(continued)

Exhibit 6.23 (continued) ADVISOR Par Report for Corlin Valve ($000)

Advertising Change Analysis:

Norm Range:	75.1%	92.7%	114.1%
Actual:		123.1	of last yr.

Diagnosis:

Advertising Change Base	106.5%
Change in Plans	0.1
Change in Market Share	− 21.7
Change in Number of	
Competitors	0.1
Customer Concentration	0.8
Number of Customers	0.6
Advertising Spending Level	9.5

Distribution Channel Analysis:

Norm for Percent of Sales Direct to Customer Through Company Sales Force	52.0%
Actual Percent of Sales Direct	80.0

Diagnosis:

Base	48.7%
Size of Firm	0.5%
Average Order Size	5.9
Technical Purchase Complexity	− 6.8
Stage in Life Cycle	14.8
Fraction of Sales Standard	0.3
Purchase Frequency	− 6.5

Exhibit 6.24 ADVISOR Product Descriptions

	Heatcrete mature	**Flowclean** mature	**Corlin** growth
1. Stage in product life cycle:			
2. (a) Product sales ($ mil.) to users plus independent retailers			
last year =	0.63	24.1	0.5
year before last =	0.60	23.5	0.1
(b) Industry sales ($ mil.) to users plus independent resellers			
last year =	63.80	48.2	26.5
year before last =	59.20	47.0	23.0

(continued)

Exhibit 6.24 (continued) ADVISOR Product Descriptions

	Heatcrete	Flowclean	Corlin
3. Fraction of product's volume sales			
produced to order =	0.05	1.00	0.10
carried in inventory =	0.95	0.00	0.90
Total =	1.00	1.00	1.00
4. Fraction of industry dollar sales purchased by industry's			
3 largest customers =	0.40	0.63	0.15
5. Usual number of people influencing decision to buy			
in an end users organization =	2	5	5
in a resellers organization =	1	8	2
6. Number of			
industry end users last year =	600	1,000	3,696
independent resellers last year =	113	25	2,000
downstream specifiers last year =	37	24	0
7. Product plans and objectives (1 = positive)			
this year: increase share:	1	0	1
maintain share:	0	1	0
leave unprofitable market:	0	0	0
improve image:	1	1	0
retaliate against competitive action:	0	1	0
more fully utilize capacity:	0	0	1
stimulate distribution channels:	1	0	1
support price:	0	0	0
decrease selling cost:	0	0	0
increase product quality:	0	0	0
last year: increase share:	1	0	1
maintain share:	0	1	0
leave unprofitable market:	0	0	0
improve image:	1	1	0
relaliate against competitive action:	0	0	0
more fully utilize capacity:	0	0	1
stimulate distribution channels:	1	0	1
support price:	0	1	0
decrease selling cost:	0	0	0
increase product quality:	0	0	0
8. Number of major competitors (over 1% market share)			
this year =	28	2	7
last year =	25	2	7
9. (a) Total amount spent on personal selling ($ thousands)			
this year =	28.00	2,338	225
last year =	20.00	2,166	130
(b) Total amount spent on technical service ($ thousands)			
this year =	5.30	314	30
last year =	3.90	304	20

(continued)

Exhibit 6.24 (continued)   ADVISOR Product Descriptions

		Heatcrete	Flowclean	Corlin
10. Product category: (Fabricated material)	=	3	3	3
11. Product quality relative to industry average				
as perceived by current customers =		5	6	6
as perceived by prospective customers =		5	5	6
12. Fraction of sales volume made				
direct to end users =		0.51	0.25	0.80
to users via company owned resellers =		0.08	0.30	0.00
to independent resellers =		0.41	0.45	0.20
Total =		1.00	1.00	1.00
13. Total amount spent on advertising ($ thousands)				
this year =		25.00	248	80
last year =		25.00	330	65
14. Fraction of advertising dollars allocated to personal media				
this year =		0.20	0.40	0.31
last year =		0.20	0.51	0.31
**Fraction of advertising dollars allocated specifically for trade shows and exhibitions:				
this year =		0.00	0.21	0.00
15. Total company (or division) sales ($ millions)				
this year =		62	62	62
16. Importance of technical service				
in this category =		4	7	3
17. Average purchase size (volume, units) of this product by users				
this year =		5,000	1,000	10,000
18. Fraction of your customers who consider the purchase decision				
is routine =		0.60	0.15	0.00
needs some review =		0.35	0.60	0.10
requires close analysis =		0.05	0.25	0.90
19. Fraction of customers who makes a decision to buy				
weekly or more frequently =		0.00	0.00	0.00
once/week − once/month =		0.05	0.15	0.40
once/month − twice year =		0.22	0.17	0.30
yearly =		0.22	0.17	0.30
once/2-9 years =		0.40	0.50	0.00
once/10 years or less frequently =		0.10	0.00	0.00

need a new budget in which your 1980 budget is two-thirds of your 1979 budget, and a discussion of it. You can have the ADVISOR results for your products, if you think it will help. I'm going to consider them because I feel I need all the help I can get.

Preparation Questions

1. What are the pressures that Mr. Warren must balance in determining his communication budget and allocating it to the three products?

2. How should Mr. Warren respond to the controller's directive to cut the budget by one-third?

3. What advertising budget and allocation do you recommend?

4. How should communication policy be determined at the Convection Corporation? What role, if any, should ADVISOR play in the process?

5. Evaluate the usefulness of the ADVISOR model for industrial communication budgeting.

Convention Corporation Allocation Model

If Paul Warren had been faced with his marketing communication budgeting problem in 1984 instead of 1980, he might have approached it somewhat differently. First, he might have made greater demands on the ADVISOR model to compute budget norms under alternative marketing and environmental scenarios. Second, he might have used a personal computer spreadsheet model to ease the computational burden inherent in evaluating budget proposals.

Expanded Use of the ADVISOR Model

The ADVISOR model can be used to compute marketing expense norms that are specific for the product manager's plans for the product. One input to the ADVISOR model is the product manager's marketing plan and its intended effect on market share. The ADVISOR model can provide norms for communication plans intended to increase, decrease, or maintain current market share. Investigation of the effect of other marketing goals on marketing communication norms is also possible.

The ADVISOR norms in Exhibits 6.25 and 6.26 are computed under the assumption that each of the product managers wanted to increase market share. John Smiley's directive to consider decreasing the marketing communication budget to two-thirds of the previous year's budget makes the assumption that the market share of all three brands could be increased highly questionable. Faced with this situation, Warren could have requested additional ADVISOR reports in which the norms were computed for different market-share goals. Exhibit 6.25 contains ADVISOR norms for decreasing, maintaining, and increasing market share for Flowclean sootblowers. The ADVISOR marketing spending norm for decreasing market share for Flowclean is about one-half the norm for increasing it. The effect of the "plans" variable on computing the norm is also presented in the exhibit. The effect of each of the other variables used in computing the norms is unchanged from those in Exhibit 6.24. A similar set of communication budget norms for Heatcrete are presented in Exhibit 6.26. It did not seem necessary to examine each of these alternatives for Corlin valve since it is a new product. Either it should be dropped or the market share should be increased, which was the assumption used to com-

Exhibit 6.25   Flowclean ADVISOR Norms (000s)

| | Market Share Strategy | | |
	Decrease	Maintain	Increase
Marketing Spending			
Current $2,900			
ADVISOR			
High	$1,390	$1,965	$2,779
Norm	908	1,285	1,816
Low	590	835	1,818
"Plans Effect"	− 29.3%	0.0%	+ 41.4%
Personal Selling			
Current $2,650			
ADVISOR			
High	$1,343	$1,880	$2,624
Norm	878	1,229	1,715
Low	571	799	1,115
"Plans Effect"	− 29.4%	+ 4.2%	+ 51.4%
Advertising Spending			
Current $248			
ADVISOR			
High	$ 47	$ 85	$ 115
Norm	31	56	101
Low	20	36	60
"Plans Effect"	− 45.0%	0.0%	− 81.9%

pute the norms found in Exhibit 6.23. The ADVISOR model does not provide norms that depend on the size of the intended market share increase or decrease.

The Convection Corporation Spreadsheet

The 1-2-3 worksheet for the Convection case is designed to ease the computational burden in developing a budget for the three products and to help in comparing it with the previous year's budget, the controller's budget guideline, forecasted sales levels, and ADVISOR norms. There is nothing complicated about making these comparisons, but it is a tedious process to do by hand. The worksheet is shown in Exhibit 6.27. If you input your own budget recommendations for selling/ technical service and advertising, the marketing spending level for each product and the total budget across products will be computed.

The worksheet also provides various comparisons that are useful in assessing the impact of your proposed budget. Comparing your budget with Smiley's directive, as well as comparing your budget as a percent of sales with last year, will give you an idea of his response to it. Comparing your budget with the budgets requested by the product managers ("Asked") will give you an idea of how

Exhibit 6.26   Heatcrete ADVISOR Norms (000s)

| | Market Share Strategy | | |
	Decrease	Maintain	Increase
Marketing Spending			
Current $48.3			
ADVISOR			
High	$119	$168	$238
Norm	78	110	155
Low	51	71	101
"Plans Effect"	−27.6%	+0.0%	+41.4%
Personal Selling			
Current $33.0			
ADVISOR			
High	$97	$128	$165
Norm	63	84	108
Low	41	54	70
"Plans Effect"	−27.6%	+10.6%	+64%
Advertising Spending			
Current $25.0			
ADVISOR			
High	$22	$40	$73
Norm	14	26	48
Low	9	17	31
"Plans Effect"	−45.0%	0.0%	+81.9%

well they will receive it. Finally, comparing your budget with the ADVISOR norms will give you an idea of how your budget compares with the results of a broadly based study of industrial marketing communication expenditures.

The budget norms can also be changed, depending on the market share goals that you decide are appropriate. Again, if you input the norms at the selling/technical service and advertising levels, the spreadsheet computes the aggregates.

There are, of course, lots of other factors that Warren needs to consider in arriving at a final budget, and you should be careful not to ignore the qualitative aspects of the analysis; don't get carried away with the "numbers game" that is so easy to play with this model.

The worksheet follows the same format as the other decision models. [Alt] P will print your results. The worksheet is short, so no menu was created for it.

Exhibit 6.27 Convection Corporation Allocation Model

```
                       CONVECTION CORPORATION
                              Heatcrete Flowcln    Corlin
                              --------  --------  --------
Marketing spending     Low         $50     $835      $350
                       Norm        $77   $1,285      $539
                       High       $119   $1,965      $824
                       Asked       $58   $2,900      $335
                       Budget      $77   $1,936      $539

Selling/Tech service   Low         $41     $799      $239
                       Norm        $63   $1,229      $368
                       High        $97   $1,880      $563
                       Asked       $33   $2,652      $255
                       Budget      $63   $1,880      $368

Advertising            Low          $9      $36      $111
                       Norm        $14      $56      $171
                       High        $22      $85      $261
                       Asked       $25     $248       $80
                       Budget      $14      $56      $171

            1980 Marketing Communication Plan Summary

                       Heatcrete Flowcln    Corlin     Total
                       --------  --------  --------  --------
     Total asked            $58   $2,900      $335    $3,293
     Total budget           $77   $1,936      $539    $2,552
     Budget/Asked        132.8%    66.8%    160.9%     77.5%
     Budget/Norm         100.0%   150.7%    100.0%    134.2%
     Budget/Target                                    121.5%
     Sales forecast        $632  $24,160      $500   $25,292
     Budget/Sales Ratio    12.2%     8.0%    107.8%    10.1%

Controller's target       $2,100

               1979 Marketing Summary Data
                       Heatcrete Flowcln    Corlin     Total
                       --------  --------  --------  --------
     Marketing expense      $49   $2,858      $215    $3,122
     Sales                 $601  $23,500      $100   $24,201
     Marketing/Sales Ratio  8.2%    12.2%    215.0%    12.9%
```

A Sales Force Size and Allocation Model

The sales force strategy model in the Syntex cases is intended to assist a manager in determining the size of the sales force and the allocation of sales effort across products or customers by: (1) predicting the net contribution and sales volume that would result from a particular sales force size and allocation policy; and (2) providing an efficient means of searching over various sales force sizes to find both the optimal sales force size and the optimal allocation policy.

The basic concept of the model is that each additional sales representative should be assigned to visit the product or customer that, considering the current sales force allocation, would provide the highest incremental contribution. Consider the following example. Suppose a company has two products, A and B; three sales reps who sell only A, and two sales reps who sell only B; and the response of products A and B to sales effort are as shown in Exhibit 6.28.

Suppose that the company now wants to add two sales reps. If the first new rep is assigned to sell product A, the result will be $100 of incremental contribution ($500–400). If the first additional rep is assigned to sell B, only $75 of incremental contribution ($375–300) will result. Thus, the first additional sales rep should be assigned to sell A. The company now has four A sales reps, and two B sales reps. If the second additional sales rep is assigned to sell product B, he or she could still generate $75 incremental contribution. But if the second rep is assigned to sell A, now only $50 could be generated, so the second additional sales representative should be assigned to sell B.

Of course this marginal analysis does not necessarily imply that each sales representative should sell only one product; that assumption is only a mathematical convenience. What is implied by our example is that if we have seven sales representatives, the equivalent of four sales representatives should be applied to A and the equivalent of three to B.

The concept of allocating incremental sales effort to the product and/or customer for which the incremental effect will be the greatest is consistent with the principle of marginal analysis in basic economic theory and leads directly to a procedure that can be used for determining both the optimal sales force size and the optimal allocation of sales force effort across products and/or customers. *Marginal analysis* makes optimal size and allocation decisions by comparing incremental response to the last, or incremental, effort.

If the company is not constrained in the number of sales representatives that it can employ, then additional sales effort should be directed toward a product and/or customer until the cost of adding the last sales representative (the *marginal*

---

*The simplified algorithm presented here does not assure an optimal solution for S-shaped response curves. The actual SSM algorithm is the same in spirit as this example but has a refinement to assure an optimal solution for all reasonable response functions.

Exhibit 6.28   Example Sales Force Response Curves

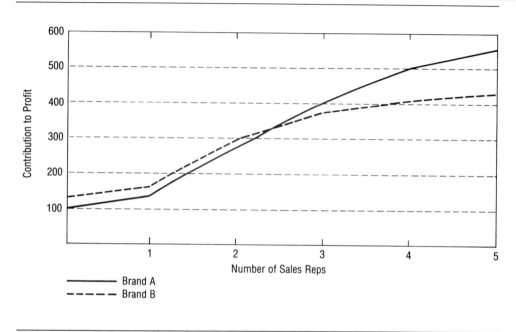

Brand A
Brand B

cost) is the same as the incremental revenue that the last sales representative gen-
erates (*marginal revenue*). The optimal sales force size for the company as a whole
is then the sum of the optimal sales force sizes for the individual products and/or
customers.

If there is a constraint on the total size of the sales force because of the time
required to hire, train, or manage new sales representatives, or because of other
budget restrictions, then profit will be maximized if the marginal revenue from
each product and/or customer is the same. This is easy to see if you think about
it for a minute. If the marginal revenue for one product is higher than that for
another, then reallocating sales effort from the product with the lesser marginal
revenue to one with a higher marginal revenue would increase the overall profit.
You would continue reallocation until the marginal revenue was the same for all
products and/or customers. When the marginal revenue for all of the products
and/or customers was the same, you'd have no reason to reallocate sales
effort and there would be no other allocation of that sales force size that would
provide a higher profit. The operation of both of these principles is easy to see in
the Syntex I Lotus 1-2-3 decision model at the end of the next case.

The optimization model described in the Syntex cases combines the marginal
analysis principle with a powerful optimization program that efficiently decides

Exhibit 6.29 Syntex Laboratories Sales Force Strategy Model Step Report

Step No.	No. of Reps	Chg. in Reps	Sales ($000s)	Chg. in Sales ($000s)	Net Profit ($000s)	Chg. in Net Profit Per Rep ($000s)	Alloc. To:
26	391.8	0.9	367,818	312.4	224,144	185.7	RHEU
27	392.6	0.8	368,119	300.5	224,285	176.0	ENT
28	428.7	36.1	380,052	11,933.4	230,390	169.1	ORS
29	437.0	8.3	382,766	2,713.5	231,752	164.3	GP
30	463.7	26.7	393,586	10,820.2	235,995	158.7	DERM
31	470.9	7.2	395,871	2,285.4	237,133	157.6	FP
32	477.5	6.6	397,911	2,039.6	238,149	155.0	IM
33	480.8	3.3	399,201	1,290.2	238,646	148.7	DERM
34	481.6	0.8	399,463	262.2	238,763	146.3	ENT
35	489.4	7.8	401,814	2,350.5	239,873	142.0	OB/GYN
36	493.0	3.6	402,863	1,049.4	240,385	141.9	ORS
37	493.9	0.9	403,114	251.1	240,505	138.1	RHEU
38	502.2	8.3	405,412	2,297.6	241,586	130.4	GP
39	509.7	7.5	407,603	2,191.4	242,529	125.9	ALLG
40	510.6	0.9	407,874	270.8	242,645	123.9	ALLG
41	517.8	7.2	409,787	1,913.1	243,530	122.7	FP
42	524.4	6.6	411,452	1,665.1	244,291	116.1	IM
43	525.2	0.8	411,659	206.4	244,374	103.0	ENT
44	533.5	8.3	413,610	1,951.8	245,221	102.2	GP
45	534.4	0.9	413,814	203.8	245,309	101.3	RHEU

not only which product or customer should receive the incremental sales effort, but how large that increment should be. This process is much more efficient than adding only one sales rep at a time. Exhibit 6.29 is a portion of the so-called "step report," which shows how many sales reps are allocated to which customer segment for a number of steps in the optimization process. As you can see, some of the steps are quite large, which drastically reduces the number of steps required to find the optimal sales force size (142.6 reps are added in twenty steps).

The optimization process increases the efficiency of finding an optimal sales force size, but it does have some drawbacks. The optimization process only produces allocation reports for sales force sizes that occur as steps in the optimization. If for some reason a manager is interested in an optimal allocation of a sales force size that didn't occur as a step, it is not available. If for some reason a manager wanted to look at a non-optimal allocation, the model in the Syntex case could not provide it. As you will see in the analysis of the Syntex cases, there is often a good rationale for both of these things, and one of the reasons the Lotus

1-2-3 model was developed was to enable a manager to look at arbitrary sales force sizes and allocations that might not be mathematically optimal but that, for managerial reasons, are still of interest.

Development of the Sales Effort Response Functions

The Syntex model and the example in the previous section depend critically upon the response functions that drive the allocation procedure. The response functions can be obtained in a number of different ways, ranging from managerial judgment (as you'll see used in the Syntex cases) to empirical estimation procedures based on statistical analysis of historical data or experimentation. The allocation procedure itself doesn't depend on how the response functions were obtained, only on their specification.

The judgmental method used in the Syntex cases is very simple and requires only four judgments from the managers. The process begins by identifying a base level of sales force effort and the expected response to it. The base levels of effort and response are usually tied to the current levels or to the strategic plan for some future time period. Once the base levels have been identified, the managers are asked to estimate what the market response would be for more and less effort than the base level: What would happen to the sales of the product in the planning period if it received:

1. No sales effort?
2. 50% of the base level of sales effort?
3. 150% of the base level of sales effort?
4. A saturation level of sales effort?

The market response function is then estimated from the base level and these four response levels. The natural question to ask at this point is whether managers can provide these kinds of estimates with acceptable accuracy. The answer is, of course, that it depends on the manager and the situation, and that it would be impossible to generalize. The model used in the Syntex case was developed by Leonard Lodish [1971] and has been applied in a number of different situations. Lodish feels that the managers involved in most of the situations that he's studied were reasonably comfortable in making such estimates, and that in the situations where empirical estimates of the response functions could also be made, were very good at it. The data in the Syntex II case provide an opportunity to evaluate the quality of the judgmental estimates in Syntex I.

There are also a number of things a manager can do to check the reasonableness of the response functions. One can compare the sales effort levels that the model indicates are optimal with the range of the response function. If the model's optimal sales force size is too far out on the extremes of the response function range, one should be cautious. If the model recommendations result in market share estimates that are questionable, it is an indication that the response functions may need attention. Finally, sensitivity and scenario analysis will also usually reveal any problems. As time passes and the sales force plan is implemented, and if adequate records are kept, empirical data will be gathered that could be used to recalculate the response functions.

It should be recognized that a model based on judgmental estimates (such as the one in the Syntex cases) is directed more at defining a sales force strategy that is consistent with the managers' understanding of the marketplace than it is with absolute abstract truth. In a complex situation, a model makes a great contribution if it can help in developing a strategy that is consistent with one's hypotheses about the marketplace.

Perhaps the last comment about the Syntex model that should be considered in evaluating the cases is that this model was developed within one week, and with current computer technology could be done in less time than that. The Syntex model is a good example of an initial attempt at a decision model that:

1. Brought a number of levels of management together and formalized their expertise in the development of a strategy
2. Integrated a number of areas of consideration, such as sales effort, sales response, differences in contribution margins, etc., into a single explicit mathematical model
3. Provided strategic managerial, research, and reporting system directions

In addition, this was accomplished within a very short period of time.

CASE: Syntex Laboratories I

This case describes the efforts of a major pharmaceutical firm to determine its sales force management strategy—optimal sales force size and the optimal allocation of sales effort across the company's products and customers. The methodology used is an example of a normative decision calculus model. The data used to estimate the model's coefficients consists primarily of data gathered from company records and managerial judgments of likely market response. The case is important in the development of our conceptualization of the analytical process because of the normative nature of the decision model, the data acquisition process, and the differences between the research model used by the consultants and the decision model developed for our use.

"What should you do when you obtain research results that indicate that a decision you've made could cost the company about $100 million in sales and over $50 million in contribution to profit?" This was the question facing Robert Nelson, vice president of sales for Syntex Laboratories, as he considered the results of a sales force size and allocation study he had just received. Nelson's 1982 business plan proposed an increase in the number of sales representatives from 433 to 473, and now the corporate budget cycle of which that plan was a part was well under way. The study indicated, however, that sales and contribution to profit for fiscal 1985* at the 473 level would be much less than could be obtained with an optimal sales force size of over 700. Nelson was unsure how fast Syntex Labs could hire and train sales reps, but a sales force growth rate of only 40 reps per year would fall far short of the optimal sales force size and severely limit both present and future profitability. Nelson had decided to arrange for himself and Laurence Lewis, manager of promotion research and Syntex Labs' liaison to the consultants that had done the analysis, to present the results to Stephen Knight, senior vice president of marketing for human phar-

maceuticals. Nelson and Knight then agreed that the results were so dramatic that, if they had confidence in the results, they should attempt to interrupt the corporate planning cycle and request more sales reps.

Company Background

Syntex Corporation began in 1940 when Russell Marker, a steroid chemist, derived a cheap and abundant source of steroid hormones from the black, lumpy root of a vine growing wild in the jungles of the Mexican state of Veracruz. Syntex's first products were oral contraceptives and topical steroid preparations prescribed by gynecologists and dermatologists, respectively. By 1982 Syntex Corporation had become an international life sciences company that developed, manufactured, and marketed a wide range of health and personal care products. Consolidated sales in fiscal 1981 were $710.9 million with $98.6 million net income. Since 1971, Syntex had recorded a 23% compound annual growth rate.

Syntex Laboratories, the U.S. human pharmaceutical sales subsidiary, was the largest Syntex subsidiary. During fiscal 1981, Syntex Laboratories' sales increased 35% to $215.451,000 and grew as a percentage of total pharmaceutical sales to 46%,

---

*Syntex's fiscal year ended on July 1.

This case was prepared by Darral G. Clarke.

Copyright © 1983 by the President and Fellows of Harvard College, Harvard Business School case 9-584-033.

Exhibit 6.30   Recent Sales Trends in Syntex Markets* (000)

Therapeutic Class	Retail Drug Purchases			Total RX			New RX		
	July 80–July 81	81–82	%	80–81	81–82	%	80–81	81–82	%
NSAI (anti-arthritics)									
Market	$477,834	$533,980	+16%	49,759	51,466	+3%	23,829	24,569	+3%
Naprosyn	90,448	114,242	+26%	6,837	7,849	+19%	3,323	3,656	+10%
Syntex Share	18.9%	21.4%		13.7%	15.3%		13.9%	14.9%	
Analgesic (pain killers)									
Market	$315,324	$346,784	+1%	89,774	91,881	+2%	65,976	67,160	+2%
Anaprox	8,119	13,027	+60%	762	1,569	+106%	591	1,040	+76%
Syntex Share	2.5%	3.8%		0.8%	1.7%	0.9%	1.5%		
Oral Contraceptives									
Market (all forms)	$359,942	$442,669	+23%	50,811	53,896	+6%	13,730	13,182	−.4%
Syntex Total	36,925	50,726	+37%	5,636	5,865	+4%	1,620	1,520	−7%
Syntex Share	10.3%	11.4%		11.1%	10.9%		11.8%	11.5%	
Topical Steroids (skin ointments)									
Market	$138,895	148,895	+7%	24,948	24,531	+2%	15,345	15,009	−2%
Syntex Products	31,361	37,768	+20%	5,181	5,241	+1%	3,044	3,103	+2%
Syntex Share	22.6%	25.4%		20.8%	21.4%		19.8%	20.7%	

*Compiled from IMS data.

continuing a recent upward trend. Operating profit in 1981 was 27% of net sales.

Syntex Labs' Product Line

Syntex Labs' product line consisted of seven major products. Naprosyn was by far the largest and most successful, while Norinyl and the topical steroids represented Syntex's early development as a drug manufacturer. Exhibit 6.30 presents retail drug purchases and market shares for Syntex products.

Naprosyn.   Naprosyn was the third largest selling drug in the nonsteroidal anti-inflammatory (NSAI) therapeutic class in the country, behind Clinoril and Motrin. NSAIs were used in the treatment of arthritis. The drug market would soon become even more competitive as other pharmaceutical firms entered the huge and fast-growing market for alternatives to aspirin in treating arthritis. According to one expert, Naprosyn would "weather the storm of increased competition better than any existing agent, although its share will be lower in 1985 than today."

Major selling points for Naprosyn were its dosage flexibility (250, 375, 500 mg tablets), twice daily regimen (less frequent than for competing products), and low incidence of side effects within a wide dosage range. The NSAI market in fiscal 1980 was $478 million. Exhibit 6.31 has details of NSAI market trends.

Anaprox.   Anaprox was launched in the United States early in fiscal 1981. It was initially marketed for analgesic use and for the treatment of menstrual

Exhibit 6.31   Nonsteroidal Anti-Inflammatory Market Trends

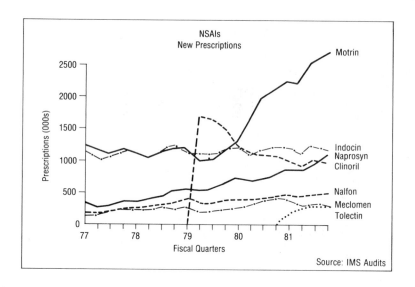

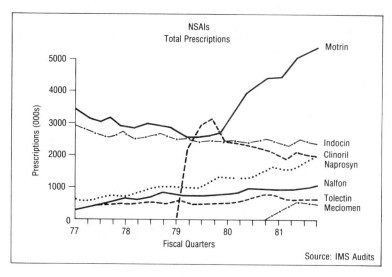

pain. Nearly twice as many prescriptions were written for analgesics as for anti-arthritis in the U.S., making this an important but highly competitive market. Exhibit 6.32 presents details on analgesic market trends. At the end of fiscal 1981, the U.S. Food and Drug Administration approved Anaprox

for the treatment of mild to moderate, acute or chronic, musculoskeletal and soft-tissue inflammation.

Topical Steroids.   Lidex and Synalar were Syntex's topical steroid creams for treating skin inflamma-

Exhibit 6.32 Analgesic (Drug Store Only) Market Trends

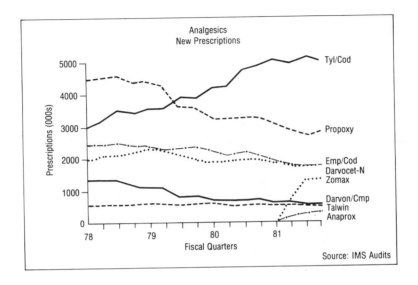

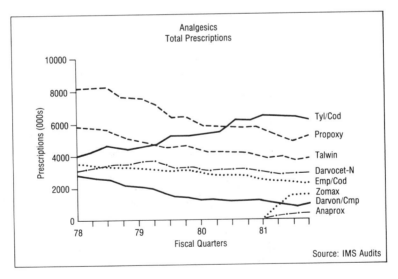

tions. Although the U.S. patents on two of the active ingredients in Lidex and Synalar, had expired during 1981, Syntex still anticipated some continued growth from these two important products and new dermatological products were under development. During fiscal 1980, Syntex was the only established

company to increase total prescription volume in topical steroids, while two new entrants grew from smaller shares. Market shares of new prescriptions and total prescriptions are found in Exhibit 6.33. Syntex had a very strong following among dermatologists—21% of all *new* topical steroid pre-

Exhibit 6.33   Topical Steroid Market Trends

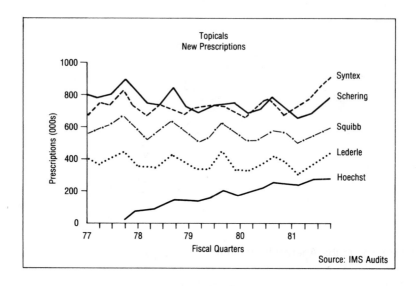

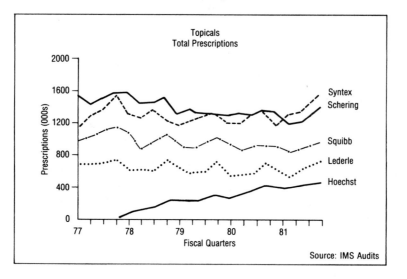

scriptions written by dermatologists were for Syntex products. Topicort, a competitor's brand, had enjoyed 65% growth ($3.66 million to $6.02 million) as a result of successful selling to both dermatologists and general practitioners.

Norinyl. The oral contraceptive (OC) market was extremely competitive, with seven major competitors and dozens of products. Total cycle sales* declined by 3.5%. New prescriptions overall declined 1.5%, while new prescriptions for low-dose oral contraceptives increased by 21%. The low-dose segment was the growth segment of the OC market; 30% of all new prescriptions were for low-dose products. Mid-dose products accounted for 54% of all new prescriptions, and high-dose products, only 16%.

Syntex's oral contraceptive, Norinyl, was available in three dosages that together totaled $37 million, or 10% of the market.

Syntex's fiscal 1981 sales increase was due primarily to larger sales to the Agency for International Development than in the previous year, price increases, and the introduction of low-dose Norinyl, which was approved by the FDA in that year. Exhibit 6.34 contains OC market trends.

Nasalide. Nasalide was a steroid nasal spray for the treatment of hay fever and perennial allergies. It was approved for U.S. marketing early in fiscal 1982.

Sales Management at Syntex Labs

The Sales Rep. The sales rep's job was to visit physicians and encourage them to prescribe Syntex drugs for their patients. This was usually done by providing the physician with samples and information about the appropriate dosage for various medical uses. Performance of this task was complicated by the difficulty of getting appointments with

---

*Oral contraceptive sales were recorded by the amount of the drug used for one menstrual cycle.

busy physicians, obtaining and maintaining credibility as a reliable source of information on drug use, the number of competing sales reps vying for the physician's time, and the difficulty of measuring the results of the detailing effort. The average sales call lasted less than six minutes.

Robert Nelson described the physician visit as follows:

A good sales rep will have a pretty good idea of what the physician's prescribing habits are. For example, most physicians are aware of Naprosyn by now, so our sales rep would try to find out what the physician's usage level is. If the physician was not prescribing Naprosyn, the sales rep would present clinical studies comparing Naprosyn with other drugs, probably stressing Naprosyn's lower incidence of side effects and its twice-a-day regimen and then request the physician to prescribe Naprosyn for their next six rheumatism patients. The same sort of information might be used to persuade a physician to move Naprosyn up from third choice to second or first choice. Physicians already prescribing Naprosyn could be encouraged to increase the dose for severe cases from 750 to 1,000 mg per day, using recent research showing Naprosyn to be safe at those levels. New uses cleared by the FDA could also be explained, or the rep might just reinforce the physician's choice of Naprosyn and counteract competitors' claims for their drugs.

The choice of which physicians to visit, how often to visit them, and what to present were major considerations for the individual sales rep. Though sales management might set quotas and provide guidelines, on a day-to-day basis the final choice was largely the rep's. Laurence Lewis explained:

Sales reps tend to divide the physicians in their territories into two groups: "prescription-productive" physicians and "easy-to-call-on" physicians. Suppose a company sets a minimum daily call average of seven. The sales rep tries

Exhibit 6.34 Oral Contraceptive Market Trends

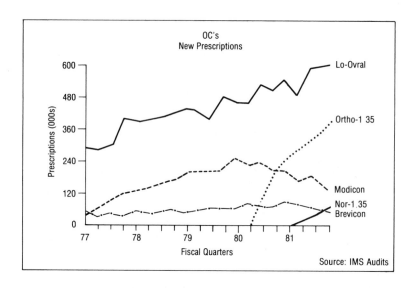

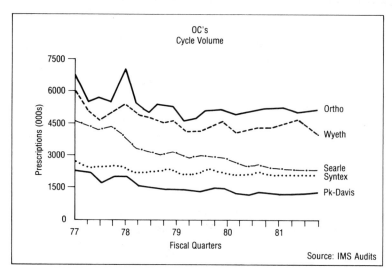

to visit the most productive physicians first; they are busy physicians for the most part, so the rep may have to wait awhile to see them. Later in the day the sales rep gets nervous about making the seven calls, so he fills in with easy-to-call-on physicians that might not be terribly productive. His bonus, however, is based on quota and an-

nual sales increase over the previous year, so he can't be totally unconcerned about the productivity of the physicians he visits.

Nelson felt that once the decision had been made about the number of sales reps, and the sales territories had been defined and assigned, the

Exhibit 6.35   Competitors' Sales Force Size

NSAI		Oral Contraceptives		Topical Steroids	
Upjohn	930	Ortho	330	Schering	615
Merck	955	Wyeth	724	Squibb	761
McNeil	457	Searle	405	Lederle	600
Pfizer	663			Hoechst	379
Lilly	880				
Desta	325				

limits of his organizational authority had about been reached. Decisions he might make about which physician specialties to visit and what drugs to feature would be subject to individual reps' interpretation and preferences. It would be necessary to educate and motivate the reps to act in accordance with the sales plan. If the reps didn't agree with the plan, strict quotas and overly directive policies would be counterproductive.

Organizational Roles.   Robert Nelson had been promoted to vice president of sales from director of marketing research. In his new position, he reported directly to Stephen Knight, the senior vice president of marketing for Syntex Laboratories. Reporting to Nelson through Frank Poole, the national sales manager, were 6 regional managers, 47 district sales managers, and 433 general sales reps. Also reporting to him separately was a group of reps that specialized in hospital sales.

After some consideration, Nelson decided he had a few major decisions to make that were of a relatively strategic nature: The size of the sales force and its geographic allocation were of obvious importance. Call frequency, allocation of sales calls across physician specialties, and product-featuring policies were also important decisions that were relatively difficult to change once implemented.

Sales Force Size.   Data available in 1980 showed that Syntex's sales force* was rather small compared with those of its direct competitors (see Exhibit 6.35.) Since each competitor had a different product line that required calling on a different mix of physician specialties, Nelson didn't think it was at all clear how the size of the Syntex sales force should compare with the others.

Call Frequency.   The 433 sales reps at Syntex had been generally adequate to support a six-week call cycle (each physician was scheduled to be visited once every six weeks) with approximately 70,000 targeted physicians. Indeed, this was how the number of reps had been determined in the first place. Since many of these physicians were visited by other companies with four-week call cycles, Nelson had considered that possibility.

The four-week call cycle seemed attractive for at least two reasons. First, if one believed that the sales force had a positive influence on physicians' prescribing behavior, it seemed reasonable that offering less frequent positive contact than the competition had to hurt. Second, dermatologists and rheumatologists were already visited by Syntex sales reps in almost a four-week cycle, and these were felt to be Syntex's most successful physician specialty groups.

Allocation of Sales Effort Across Products and Physician Specialties.   The Syntex sales policy called for a rep to attempt to make seven sales calls per day, during which presentations would be made for two or three Syntex products. (The average was 2.7 presentations per sales call.) Which products would be featured depended on a number of factors, such as the physicians' specialty, the availability of new information on Syntex

---

*This case deals only with the general sales force and does not include the hospital sales force. For simplicity, *sales force* will be used to mean the general sales force.

product efficacy and/or comparative advantages, and national sales priorities.

Since not all physicians were likely to prescribe all of Syntex's products, the fact that a sales rep could make an average of seven calls and 19 presentations in a day did not necessarily mean that a recommended product-featuring schedule could be followed exactly. For example, if the rep called on four dermatologists and three obstetricians in a particular day, there would be no opportunity to make Naprosyn presentations.

Geographic Allocation of Sales Force. When Robert Nelson became vice president of sales, geographic allocation of the sales force seemed to be the most critical factor, so it had received immediate attention. The problem turned out to be a reasonably tractable one, however, as Laurence Lewis explained:

> Almost everyone deploys their sales reps based on regional physician counts. We made an effort to get away from just physician counts, and looked at market potential. I know other companies have done that. In the end, it all came down to where Lilly, Pfizer, Merck, and ourselves would all have a rep in a given geographical territory. Maybe one of the big companies would have two reps in a particular territory, but regional deployment ended up being almost standard. I don't suppose any of us have any real hope of coming up with good enough data to override that allocation, at least at the territory level.

Sales Force Strategy Model

Nelson and Knight had observed that the rapid growth of Naprosyn was changing the balance in Syntex Laboratories. According to Knight:

> We had always been a specialty-oriented company. We began with a product for dermatologists, then followed that with an oral contraceptive, so we visited OB/GYNs* too, and for

the first 15 years those were the main physicians we visited, along with a limited number of primary-care physicians.† So we've thought of ourselves as a small, specialty-oriented pharmaceutical company. Along came Naprosyn and suddenly we had the ninth largest selling drug in the U.S. and we were growing at over 25% a year. We are being forced to rethink just what kind of a company we are. It was this dynamic change in the nature of Syntex that led us to consider a more sophisticated analysis.

According to Nelson:

> We knew we had some opportunities to expand the sales force. We could see how rapidly Naprosyn was growing and that our detailing penetration with generalist doctors was very low compared to the big anti-arthritis competitors like Upjohn and Merck. They each had 900 sales reps, so we knew we were behind them. But we were trying to make major plans on the back of envelopes! We'd make notes like: If there are 60,000 generalist doctors and we've got this many people, how many calls can we make a year if each of them makes 1,360 calls a year? We then realized we were saying that all the doctors and products respond to sales effort the same way. We all knew that they didn't, but we could never make the differences explicit!

Nelson created the position of manager of promotion research in an effort to find a better way to plan sales force policy. The position was filled by Laurence Lewis, an analyst in the marketing research department who had earlier been a sales rep. Lewis's first task was to identify a method for determining the size of the sales force and allocating sales force effort across products and physician specialties. After studying the marketing research and trade literature and consulting other knowledgeable people, Lewis approached Leonard Lodish, a professor at the Wharton School,

*OB/GYN: obstetrician/gynecologist.

†Primary-care physicians (PCP) included physicians specializing in internal medicine, general practice, and family practice.

whose name had surfaced repeatedly during his research.

Lodish was subsequently invited to visit Syntex and make a presentation on his approach to determining sales force size and sales effort allocation. Two aspects of his approach struck responsive chords with Knight and Nelson. Nelson stated:

> One of the attractive features of the approach was getting our sales and marketing management people together and making explicit what we believed about how each of our products responds to detailing.

Knight felt that:

> Our history had been one of increasing the sales force size in relatively small steps. I'd never been really satisfied that there was any good reason why we were expanding by 30 or 50 representatives in any one year other than that was what we were able to get approved in the budget process. Over the years, I'd become impatient with the process of going to the well for more people every year with no long-term view to it. I felt that if I went to upper management with a more strategic or longer-term viewpoint, it would be a lot easier to then sell the annual increases necessary to get up to a previously established sales force size objective.

Subsequently, a contract was signed with Management Decision Systems (MDS), a Boston-area management consulting firm of which Lodish was a principal, to produce a sales force strategy model for Syntex. Laurence Lewis was appointed liaison with MDS.

Model Development Process

The sales force strategy model (SSM) was designed to help Syntex management deploy the sales force strategically. The model would be used to calculate the optimal allocation of sales effort to Syntex products and physician specialties for a given sales force size. Repeated applications of the model with different numbers of reps could be used to find the optimal sales force size. The technique used in the model combined management science techniques, historical data, and management judgment to calculate the incremental gain in net contribution for each additional amount of sales resource (either product presentations or physician calls). There were two separate but similar versions of the SSM model. One sought to allocate the number of *sales rep visits to physician specialties* to maximize contribution, while the other sought the optimal allocation of *sales presentations to Syntex products*. Each estimated the optimal sales force size independently of the other.

Defining the Model Inputs. The SSM used information from various sources. The average number of presentations per sales call, the number of sales calls per day, the contribution margin for each Syntex product, and the cost per sales representative were estimated from company records and syndicated data sources. The current allocation of sales force effort was a key element in developing the model, since these data provided the background for Syntex managers to use in estimating the response of various Syntex products and physician groups to different levels of sales effort. (See Exhibit 6.36.)

Judgmental estimates of response to sales effort were obtained during a series of special meetings held in conjunction with the annual marketing planning meetings. Leonard Lodish, Stephen Knight, Robert Nelson, Laurence Lewis, Frank Poole, and a few product managers and regional sales managers participated. According to Lewis:

> The meeting began with a short lecture on sales response and an exercise in which we were each asked to come up with an optimal sales plan for a sales rep who had six accounts and four products. Trying to do this led us to understand what the model would try to accomplish and demonstrated the impossibility of trying to plan by hand for more than 400 sales reps selling seven products to 13 different physician specialties.

The main agenda of the meetings was to develop a group consensus on the likely response

Exhibit 6.36:   Basic Model Inputs*

Normal Planned 1985 Calls or Presentations Based on FY 1981

Product (Presentations)		Specialty (Calls)	
Naprosyn	358,000	General practice	124,000
Anaprox	527,000	Family practice	108,000
Norinyl 135	195,000	Internal medicine	98,000
Norinyl 150	89,000	Orthopedic surgeon	54,000
Lidex	101,000	Rheumatologist	13,000
Synalar	110,000	Obstetrician/	
Nasalide	210,000	gynecologist	117,000
Total	159,000	Dermatalogist	50,000
		Allergist	14,000
Avg./rep.	3,677	Ear, nose, throat	12,000
		Total	590,000
		Avg./rep.	1,360

Planned 1985 sales ($000) with present policy

(Syntex 1985 estimates by product, allocated to specialties on FY 1981 product by specialty distribution)

Product		Specialty	
Naprosyn	$214,400	General practice	$92,398
Anaprox	36,500	Family practice	78,083
Norinyl 135	21,200	Internal medicine	79,082
Norinyl 150	37,200	Orthopedic surgeon	19,671
Lidex	38,000	Rheumatologist	16,961
Synalar	14,600	Obstetrician/	
Nasalide	11,200	gynecologist	51,312
Total	$373,100	Dermatologist	26,598
		Allergist	3,434
		Ear, nose, throat	5,561
		Total	$373,100

Contribution as % of Factory Selling Price

Product		Specialty	
Naprosyn	70	General practice	67.6
Anaprox	55	Family practice	67.8
Norinyl 135	72	Internal medicine	68.1
Norinyl 150	72	Orthopedic surgeon	68.4
Lidex	62	Rheumatologist	67.5
Synalar	53	Obstretician/	
Nasalide	52	gynecologist	66.2
		Dermatologist	55.3
		Allergist	62.5
		Ear, nose, throat	62.2

Estimated 1985 average cost per representative (excluding samples) $57,000

Estimated 1985 fixed selling overhead (present organization) $2,800,000

*1985 plans have been disguised.

Exhibit 6.37 Product and Specialty Response Functions

Product Response Functions

	No Calls	One-Half	Present	50% More	Saturation
Naprosyn	47	68	100	126	152
Anaprox	15	48	100	120	135
Norinyl 135	31	63	100	115	125
Norinyl 150	45	70	100	105	110
Lidex	56	80	100	111	120
Synalar	59	76	100	107	111
Nasalide	15	61	100	146	176

Specialty Response Functions

	No Calls	One-Half	Present	50% More	Saturation
General practice	29	62	100	120	136
Family practice	31	62	100	124	140
Internal medicine	43	69	100	111	120
Orthopedic surgeon	34	64	100	116	130
Rheumatologist	41	70	100	107	112
Obstetrician/ gynecologist	31	70	100	110	116
Dermatologist	48	75	100	107	110
Allergist	17	60	100	114	122
Ear, nose, throat	20	59	100	117	125

of each Syntex product and physician specialty to sales rep effort. During the first meeting, worksheets were distributed to the participants on which they were asked to estimate the change in sales for each of seven product and nine physician specialties that would result from changing the sales effort it received: "According to the strategic plan, if the current level of sales force effort is maintained from 1982 to 1985, sales of Naprosyn (Anaprox, etc.) would be the planned level. What would happen to Naprosyn's (Anaprox, etc.) 1985 sales (compared with present levels) if during this same time period it received:

1. No sales effort?

2. One half the current effort?

3. Fifty percent greater sales effort?

4. A saturation level of sales effort?

After a summary of the participants' answers had been presented to the group and discussed, new worksheets were passed out and the process repeated. When a reasonable consensus had been obtained, the meeting was recessed.

Following this meeting, a preliminary version of the model was produced. When the group reconvened a few days later, a preliminary analysis was presented and the results were discussed. The initial analysis appeared generally reasonable to the participants, and after a final discussion and some later fine-tuning, resulted in the response estimates that appear in Exhibit 6.37. Commenting on the process, Knight explained:

Of course, we knew that the responses we estimated were unlikely to be the "true responses" in some absolute knowledge sense, but we got the most knowledgeable people in the company

Exhibit 6.38   Optimal Sales Force Sizes

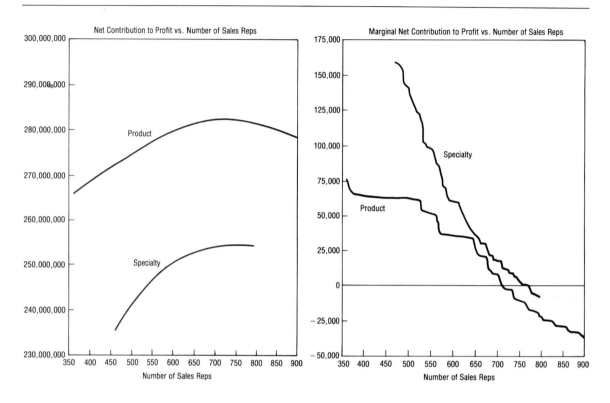

together in what seemed to me to be a very thorough discussion and the estimates represented the best we could do at the time. We respect the model results, but we utilized them with cautious skepticism.

Results of the SSM Analysis

Although the recommended optimal sales force sizes computed on the basis of physician specialty and products were reasonably close together (768 and 708, respectively), the models differed considerably in incremental net contribution per sales rep at levels between the current sales force size and 600 reps. (See Exhibit 6.38.)

Not only did both SSM analyses indicate that the current Syntex sales force was too small (433), it also showed that current allocation across products and specialties was suboptimal. According to the specialty-based analysis, FY 1985 net contribution at the present sales force size would be $7.2 million less than could be obtained with an optimal deployment policy. (See Exhibit 6.39.)

A direct comparison of present and optimal deployment according to the product-based analysis was somewhat more difficult, since the SSM indicated that Anaprox should either receive no sales attention or 130 sales reps. (See Exhibit 6.40.) Nothing in between was optimal. This resulted in reported optimal sales force sizes of 369 and 499

Exhibit 6.39   Comparison of Existing Policy with Recommended Policy at Current Sales Force Levels (1985)*

Present Policy

Allocation to	Number of Reps	Sales Calls	Sales ($000)	Gross Profit ($000s)	Net Profit ($000s)
GP	91.2	124,000	92,398	62,461	57,264
FP	79.4	108,000	78,083	52,940	48,414
IM	72.1	98,000	79,082	53,855	49,747
ORS	39.7	54,000	19,671	13,455	11,192
RHEU	9.6	13,000	16,961	11,449	10,904
OB/GYN	86.0	117,000	51,312	33,969	29,065
DERM	36.8	50,000	26,598	14,178	12,081
ALLG	10.3	14,000	3,434	2,146	1,559
ENT	8.8	12,000	5,561	3,459	2,956
Total	433.8	590,000	373,100	247,910	220,382

SSM Recommended Policy

Allocation to	Number of Reps	Sales Calls	Sales ($000)	Gross Profit ($000s)	Net Profit ($000s)
GP	116.0	157,818	103,915	70,246	63,632
FP	108.3	147,273	92,624	62,799	56,627
IM	78.6	106,909	81,586	55,560	51,079
ORS	36.1	49,091	18,622	12,737	10,680
RHEU	10.4	14,182	17,273	11,660	11,065
OB/GYN	70.4	95,727	47,120	31,194	27,181
DERM	0.0	0	12,767	6,805	6,805
ALLG	0.0	0	584	365	365
ENT	8.8	12,000	5,561	3,460	2,956
Total	428.7	583,000	380,052	254,825	227,590

Key:
GP	general practice	OB/GYN	obstetrician/gynecologist
FP	family practice	DERM	dermatologist
IM	internal medicine	ALLG	allergist
ORS	orthopedic surgeon	ENT	ear, nose, throat
RHEU	rheumatologist		

*Optimal allocations are only computed for sales force sizes in a step (see Exhibit 6.38). A consequence of this is that allocations are not available for every sales force size and thus allocated sales force sizes don't exactly match the current level.

Exhibit 6.40   Comparison of Existing Policy with Recommended Policy at (Near) Current Levels (1985)

Allocation to	Number of Reps	Presentations	Sales ($000)	Gross Profit ($000s)	Net Profit ($000s)
		Present Policy			
Naprosyn	96.8	358,000	214,400	150,000	144,565
Anaprox	142.4	527,000	36,500	20,075	11,956
Norinyl 135	52.7	195,000	21,200	15,264	12,260
Norinyl 150	24.1	89,000	37,200	26,784	25,413
Lidex	27.3	101,000	38,000	20,140	18,584
Synalar	29.7	110,000	14,600	7,738	6,043
Nasalide	56.8	210,000	11,200	5,824	2,589
Total	429.7	1,590,000	373,100	245,905	218,610
		Recommended Policy 369 Reps			
Naprosyn	246.3	911,272	306,526	214,568	200,530
Anaprox	0.0	0	5,475	3,011	3,011
Norinyl 135	57.5	212,727	22,019	15,854	12,576
Norinyl 150	28.4	105,181	38,049	27,394	25,774
Lidex	37.2	137,727	41,222	21,847	19,726
Synalar	0.0	0	8,614	4,565	4,565
Nasalide	0.0	0	1,680	873	873
Total	369.4	1,366,909	423,585	288,115	264,257
		Recommended Policy 499 Reps			
Naprosyn	246.3	911,273	306,527	214,569	200,530
Anaprox	129.5	479,091	33,708	18,539	11,159
Norinyl 135	57.5	212,727	22,019	15,854	12,577
Norinyl 150	28.4	105,182	38,048	27,395	25,774
Lidex	37.2	137,727	41,222	21,848	19,726
Synalar	0.0	0	8,614	4,565	4,565
Nasalide	0.0	0	1,680	874	874
Total	498.9	1,846,000	451,819	303,644	272,405

sales reps, but no report on the current size of 433. The SSM indicated that the current allocation of sales effort across products was even more suboptimal than it had been across specialists.

Finally, with both optimal sales force size and optimal deployment, FY 1985 sales and contribution (see Exhibit 6.41) would be dramatically larger than with the current sales force size and optimal deployment (see Exhibit 6.42).

Management Implications

Robert Nelson had expected the study to show that the sales force was too small and that Naprosyn

Exhibit 6.41 Optimal Sales Force Policies

Based on Specialties

Allocation to	Number of Reps	Sales Calls	Sales ($000)	Gross Profit ($000s)	Net Profit ($000s)
GP	198.9	270,545	118,680	80,227	68,888
FP	173.3	235,636	104,067	70,558	60,682
IM	131.0	178,182	90,700	61,767	54,299
ORS	61.4	83,454	22,818	15,608	12,110
RHEU	16.5	22,454	18,327	12,371	11,430
OB/GYN	117.3	159,545	55,389	36,667	29,980
DERM	43.4	59,091	27,551	14,685	12,208
ALLG	12.2	16,546	3,667	2,292	1,599
ENT	13.6	18,546	6,506	4,047	3,270
Total	767.6	1,044,000	447,706	298,221	251,665

Based on Products

Allocation to	Number of Reps	Sales Calls	Sales ($000)	Gross Profit ($000s)	Net Profit ($000s)
Naprosyn	263.9	976,363	309,379	216,565	201,524
Anaprox	168.3	622,818	39,847	21,915	12,321
Norinyl 135	76.7	283,636	24,068	178,329	12,959
Norinyl 150	37.2	137,545	39,060	28,123	26,004
Lidex	49.6	183,636	43,155	22,872	20,043
Synalar	29.7	110,000	14,600	7,738	6,043
Nasalide	82.6	305,455	15,802	8,217	3,512
Total	708.0	2,619,454	485,911	322,761	279,606

Exhibit 6.42 SSM Predicted FY 1985 Sales and Contribution from Optimal Deployment

According to:	Sales Force Size	Sales	Net Contribution
Specialty Model (current)	434	$373.1mm	$220.4
	429	380.1	227.6
	768	447.7	251.7
Product Model (current)	430	$373.1	$218.6
	369	423.6	264.2
	708	485.9	279.6

probably needed more emphasis, but he had not anticipated such a large difference. When he received the SSM analyses, Lewis decided four major conclusions could be drawn:

1. Until the size of the sales force approaches 700 general representatives, profitability will not be a constraint to adding representatives.

2. From the FY 1981 base of 430 representatives, Syntex Labs should grow to an optimal allocation of sales effort rather than by redeploying the current sales force. This could be done by devoting additional sales resources largely to the primary-care audience.

3. Naprosyn was the largest product in Syntex's product line, the most sales-responsive, and highly profitable. Thus Syntex Labs should make it the driving force behind nearly all deployment and allocation decisions.

4. Syntex should consider itself a major generalist company, since optimal deployment would require the greatest portion of a large sales force to be devoted to the generalist physician audience.

Although enthusiastic about these conclusions, Lewis added a note of caution to their acceptance.

A significant change in the marketplace that would decrease the ability of any of our products to compete would challenge the validity of the model output. Such phenomena as a product recall or a revolutionary new competitive product might act to reduce the value of this model.

Significant error in the sales response estimates of either products or specialties could lead to reduced validity of model output. The similarity between the two model outputs derived from independent response estimates hints at the low likelihood of significant error in the sales response estimates. The model would be most sensitive to significant error in the estimate of Naprosyn's sales responsiveness.

Lewis concluded his presentations of the study results by stating that Syntex was faced with two choices if the sales force was not expanded to an optimal size:

1. Optimize the physician sales call allocation with a smaller than optimal sales force by dramatically reducing coverage of specialists to increase calls on primary-care physicians. This option would maximize sales for the number of sales reps by leading to large gains in Naprosyn at the expense of sales losses in oral contraceptives and topical steroids.

2. Limit Naprosyn's growth to substantially less than its potential, while maintaining the present contact levels with Syntex's traditional specialist physicians and older products.

Preparation Questions

1. What is the nature of the market in which Syntex competes? What role does the sales force play in the marketing mix for Syntex?

2. What are the important managerial issues that must be considered in determining the sales force policy for Syntex?

3. Be sure you understand how the sales force strategy model described in the case works.

4. Describe and evaluate the research process.

5. What was learned from the research?

6. What should Nelson do about next year's sales force size and allocation of sales effort?

7. What longer-term sales force policy do you recommend?

8. How does the decision model in the Syntex I spreadsheet differ from the model used by the consultants? Why do those differences exist?

Syntex Laboratories Sales Force Strategy Model

The sales force strategy model (SSM) in the Syntex I case was developed by Professor Leonard M. Lodish of the Wharton School and is the property of Management Decision Systems (MDS) of Waltham, Massachusetts. That version of the model, which resides on a mainframe computer, features procedures that estimate the response functions from judgmental estimates, find the optimal sales force size, and produce a set of optimal sales effort allocations for sales force sizes in a range specified by the user. A number of report-generating programs are also part of that system.

Professor Lodish and MDS have authorized the preparation of this Lotus 1-2-3 model using a modification of their algorithm.* This model computes the sales and profit that will result from an arbitrary allocation of sales force effort. Using it, you can change the planned effort level, the planned sales response, and the judgmental responses. It also computes the marginal net contribution from adding one more sales rep. See Exhibit 6.43.

The basic computational concept is that the S-shaped judgmental response functions in the case are approximated by two simple exponential functions, one curved upward and the other downward, and that the parameters of these functions are estimated from the distances between various pairs of judgmental estimates. Exactly how the parameters have been estimated and when to switch from one function to the other has not been specified, but that isn't necessary to understand how it works.

It is very simple to use the decision model. For each product or specialty group, input the planned sales effort and the forecasted sales response that you want to serve as the base level (corresponding to 100% in the judgmental estimate); and input the number of sales reps. The model computes the sales response and the profit. The values already in the model correspond to those in the case, so you only have to input those values that you would like to change. This decision model actually consists of two separate worksheets—one for product allocations and the other for physician-specialty allocations. The format of the program is much like the others in the book: [Alt]M will bring up a menu that you can use to move around the spreadsheet. [Alt]P will raise a print menu so that you can choose the spreadsheet that you want to print.

A feature of the model that you will find useful is the "Marginal Net Cont" (marginal net contribution to profit) column at the right of the spreadsheets. This column contains the net contribution to profit that would result from adding one more sales rep. These values are key indicators of the direction to change the allocation to improve profits. The optimal number of sales reps for a given product is found when the marginal net contribution to profit is zero. The optimal sales force size, if there are no constraints on the number of sales reps, is the sum of the optimal number of sales reps for each product. If you want to allocate a less-than-optimal number of sales reps optimally across products, the marginal net contribution should be the same for each product.

Syntex Laboratories Spreadsheet

The Lotus 1-2-3 model consists of four parts:

1. A menu program reached by [Alt]M that directs you to choose whether you want to make a prod-

---

*Permission to use this adapted version of the model is granted by Management Decision Systems for use *only* to analyze the Syntex cases. Note that the response functions at the heart of the model contain a number of constant parameters that have been derived from other expressions not included in the 1-2-3 model; these parameters are unique to the Syntex cases and will not be appropriate for other applications.

Exhibit 6.43 Specialty Allocation Model

```
Syntex Laboratories (I); Speciality Model

Sales Force Strategy Model: Specialty Model Assumptions
```

	-----Strategic Plan-----			Allocation		Marginal
	# reps	Revenue	Net Cont.	# reps	Net Cont.	Net Cont.
Gen Prac	91.2	$92.4	$56.7	198.9	$68.2	($0.007)
Fam Prac	79.4	$78.1	$47.9	173.3	$60.7	($0.007)
Int Med	72.1	$79.1	$49.3	131.0	$54.3	($0.008)
Orth Sur	39.7	$19.7	$11.0	61.4	$12.1	($0.003)
Rheu	9.6	$17.0	$10.9	16.5	$11.5	($0.006)
OB/GYN	86.0	$51.3	$28.5	117.3	$30.0	($0.007)
Derm	36.8	$26.6	$11.8	43.4	$12.2	($0.005)
Allg	10.3	$3.4	$1.5	12.2	$1.6	($0.007)
ENT	8.8	$5.6	$2.9	13.6	$3.3	($0.010)
Total	433.9	$373.2	$220.4	767.6	$253.8	

```
Allocation Plan Sales Management:          $2.8           End of Inputs
```

Performance forecast

	Gen Prac	Fam Prac	Int Med	Orth Surg	Rheu
Strategic Plan Input					
Number of reps	91.2	79.4	72.1	39.7	9.6
Effort share	21.0%	18.3%	16.6%	9.1%	2.2%
Planned revenue	$92.4	$78.1	$79.1	$19.7	$17.0
Unit contribution	$62.5	$53.0	$53.9	$13.5	$11.5
Net Contribution	$56.7	$47.9	$49.3	$11.0	$10.9
Allocation Plan					
Number of reps	198.9	173.3	131.0	61.4	16.5
Allocated/Strategic	2.181	2.183	1.817	1.547	1.719
Effort share	25.9%	22.6%	17.1%	8.0%	2.1%
Sales management					
Net contribution	$68.2	$60.7	$54.3	$12.1	$11.5
Marginal net cont.	($0.007)	($0.007)	($0.008)	($0.003)	($0.006)
Operating Results					
Revenue	$118.7	$104.1	$90.7	$22.9	$18.4
Gross contribution	$80.2	$70.6	$61.8	$15.6	$12.4
Net contribution	$68.2	$60.7	$54.3	$12.1	$11.5
Marginal revenue	$0.079	$0.078	$0.077	$0.084	$0.080
Marginal net cont.	($0.007)	($0.007)	($0.008)	($0.003)	($0.006)

Exhibit 6.43   (continued) Specialty Allocation Model

OB/GYN	Derm	Allg	ENT	Total
86.0	36.8	10.3	8.8	433.9
19.8%	8.5%	2.4%	2.0%	100.0%
$51.3	$26.6	$3.4	$5.6	$373.2
$34.0	$14.2	$2.1	$3.5	
$28.5	$11.8	$1.5	$2.9	$220.4
117.3	43.4	12.2	13.6	767.6
1.364	1.179	1.184	1.545	1.769
15.3%	5.7%	1.6%	1.8%	100.0%
				$2.8
$30.0	$12.2	$1.6	$3.3	$251.0
($0.007)	($0.005)	($0.007)	($0.010)	
$55.4	$27.5	$3.6	$6.6	$447.8
$36.7	$14.7	$2.3	$4.1	$298.3
$30.0	$12.2	$1.6	$3.3	$251.0
$0.081	$0.104	$0.086	$0.082	
($0.007)	($0.005)	($0.007)	($0.010)	

uct allocation or a specialty allocation and then retrieves the spreadsheet you've chosen.

2. Two separate spreadsheets for making product and specialty allocations.

3. A working area and a report area for each of the spreadsheets. All of the inputs are put into the work area and it provides the marginal net contribution figures that indicate the direction of change that will increase profitability.

4. Two sets of graphs that display the response functions. One set shows the product response functions; the other shows the specialty response functions. The graphs are reached from the main menu by choosing the **Graph** option.

When you are satisfied with your allocation and want a printed copy, type [Alt]P to raise a print menu from which you choose the spreadsheet you want to print. Since the spreadsheets are too wide to fit on the paper using the normal IBM printer print size, the report is printed on two pages. The format of the specialty spreadsheet is presented in Exhibit 6.43.

Most of the work you will do with the worksheet will be to determine the revenue, contribution, and net marginal contribution that will result from a particular sales force allocation. This is done by simply changing the number of sales reps in the fourth column. You can shift the whole response curve by changing the revenue in column two. You would only want to do this if you were questioning the manager's judgmental estimates of the response curve or if you were interested in investigating the effect of some global change in the market environment, such as a drastic decrease in the sales of one of the products due to new competition.

CASE: Syntex Laboratories II

This case focuses on implementing the strategic recommendations obtained from the strategic analysis in the previous case. The emphasis in this case is on reconciling the sales force allocation of the optimal product and the specialty recommendations, and in determining how to achieve the desired sales force size.

Robert Nelson's proposal to increase the number of new sales reps from 40 to 100 during fiscal year 1983 had been approved on the strength of the analysis submitted to support the request, despite the fact that the request had been made midway through the corporate budget cycle.*

Subsequently, Nelson had formed a task force to develop a plan for implementing the sales force expansion. This task force included himself; Frank Poole, national sales manager; Laurence Lewis, manager of promotion analysis; and Martha Drummond, sales force deployment analyst.

Lewis, who had been Syntex Labs' liaison to the outside consultant for the project so far, was directed to spend full time on the task force and act as a consultant to Poole.

Lewis's initial recommendations, which were the basis of Nelson's proposal, and which would be the starting point for the task force, included:

1. Expand Syntex Lab's general sales force as quickly as possible.

2. Apply all new sales resources to the primary-care physician (PCP) audience. Deploy new reps to areas of high PCP concentration.

3. Allocate one-half of all sales presentations to Naprosyn.

4. Institute a four-week call cycle for all targeted physicians across all specialties.

5. Redefine physician targets in terms of prescribing potential and target the heaviest prescribers first.

6. Refine the sales force strategy model (SSM) as quickly as possible and develop its on-line use by Syntex personnel. Refinements should include: (a) maximum and minimum call and presentation limits, where appropriate; and (b) response function estimates by product by specialty to generate one comprehensive output.

The sales force strategy model (SSM) had been developed as a result of a research project executed by Management Decision Systems (MDS) of Waltham, Massachusetts, to determine: the optimal Syntex Labs' sales force size and allocation of effort given the current product line and market conditions. There were two versions of the SSM, one based on the allocation of sales presentations to products, the other on the allocation of sales calls to physician specialties.

These two models computed the optimal sales force size to be 708 and 768 reps based on the product allocation and the specialty allocation, respectively.

Development of an Initial Implementation Plan

As Lewis began to develop his initial recommendations to the task force, it became apparent that a number of important issues had not been adequately addressed in the SSM model. Since the

---

*See the Syntex Laboratories I case.

This case was prepared by Darral G. Clarke.

Copyright © 1983 by the President and Fellows of Harvard College, Harvard Business School case 9-584-034.

SSM, like all models, was only a mathematical abstraction of Syntex Labs' actual situation, the model's results needed to be translated into implementable plans. Major issues that emerged from Lewis's analysis and his discussions with Syntex Labs' managers were:

1. Reach vs. frequency. The SSM allocated presentations or sales calls, but did not directly address the breakdown between how many (or which) physicians should be visited and how often. For example, if three visits were to be made, the SSM did not address whether one visit should be paid to each of three physicians or three visits should be made to one physician. This ambiguity was reflected in a need to determine the call cycle and the target physician audience.

2. The SSM did not consider the fact that Syntex Labs' sales reps had established relationships with numerous physicians over the years. Many of these relationships would be severed if the optimal allocations of a smaller rather than optimal sales force were implemented. This problem was especially acute with dermatologists and obstetricians.

3. The SSM did not consider the feasibility of finding, training, assigning, and managing new sales reps.

4. The SSM did not explicitly consider market growth, competition, or the new-product development plans of Syntex Labs or its competitors.

Call-Cycle Conversion

Lewis devoted considerable time to gathering available information and interviewing knowledgeable Syntex managers in order to determine the proper sales call cycle—that is, the time between sales calls on the same physician. Syntex had operated in the past on a six-week call cycle, except with rheumatologists and dermatologists, who were visited every four weeks.

Arguments advanced by various managers in favor of the four-week call cycle were:

1. The top drugs in any therapeutic class (TC, a family of drugs used to treat similar diseases) seemed to be supported by a sales force working on a four-week call cycle.

2. Marketing research survey results indicated that the average physician's perception of call frequency understated the actual number of visits. The average physician underestimated how often a Syntex rep was actually seen and perceived their calls to be less often than the reps of competitors' reps with four-week call cycles.

3. The actual number of visits to a physician was often less than planned. The percentage of the most productive physicians visited during a six-week call cycle had averaged about 50% during 1980 and 1981.

Nelson summarized his feelings about the four-week call cycle as follows:

At some point you just have to arbitrarily decide you are going to have to have enough people so you can schedule as many as ten visits per year, so your call plan will actually yield as many as seven or eight visits. It seems to me that this has to be better than to only expect three or four visits per year. Especially when your competition is visiting at the higher level.

The importance of maintaining competitive parity in call frequency seemed to be reinforced by the nature of the products in the industry. Stephen Knight, senior vice president for marketing, explained, "There are usually a number of competing drugs that are relatively equal in quality. If one drug dominated the other, it wouldn't be so important to maintain visit parity."

Finally, Lewis considered the results of the SSM analysis. The SSM had indicated that substantial profit increases would follow an increase in the number of presentations or sales calls, and as Lewis explained:

The decision to go to a four-week call cycle was forced upon us: there was no more room for sales reps if the call cycle remained set at six

Exhibit 6.44   Physician Prescription Productivity

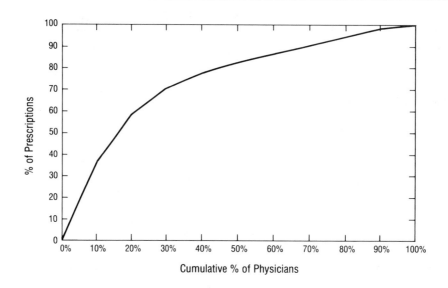

weeks. There are not enough doctors and not enough geographic territories. It works out that if you decrease your call cycle from six to four weeks, you increase the size of the sales force you need by 50%! The model didn't differentiate between frequency and reach, but we knew that our reach was pretty extensive already, and adding more physicians probably wouldn't have a significant impact—so we opted for increased frequency.

Define Physician Targets

Once the decision had been made that a four-week call cycle was to be the norm in planning sales force effort, attention was focused on defining criteria for determining which physicians should be visited. Research indicated that 25% of the physicians wrote 65% of the prescriptions, and 80% of the prescriptions were written by 50% of the physicians (see Exhibit 6.44). This observation, when combined with the number of physicians in various

specialties, led Lewis to target the top 50% of prescribers in each specialty. This target physician definition, a four-week call cycle, and the physician populations shown in Exhibit 6.45 indicated a need for 621 sales reps.

Other information Lewis had obtained that he thought might be valuable were the average value of physician specialties in terms of NSAIs and other relevant TCs (see Exhibit 6.46) and the market potential for the therapeutic classes in which Syntex Labs competed (see Exhibit 6.47).

Market Franchise

Since Syntex Labs' first products were steroids, its initial marketing emphasis had been with dermatologists and obstetrician/gynecologists. The relationship with these physician specialties had been developed over the years and was considered a valuable resource. While these two specialties accounted for only 3.2% and 14.3% of Syntex Labs' sales in 1981, an active research program to

Exhibit 6.45:   Total U.S. Physician Counts

Specialty	Total # in Patient Care	Total # in Office Practice	Target %	Total # in Target Audience
GP	27,382	25,404	50	12,702
FP	28,090	20,417	50	10,209
DO	18,826	8,826	50	9,413
IM	52,040	0,484	50	15,242
Total PCP	126,338	95,131		47,566
ORS	11,435	10,744	50	5,372
RHEU	1,216	1,110	100	1,110
OB/GYN	22,870	17,596	50	8,798
DERM	5,174	4,404	100	4,404
ALLG	1,385	1,354	50†	677
ENT	5,896	4,890	50†	2,445
Total	174,314	135,229	52%	70,372*

* 70,372 Drs. x 12 calls/year/Dr. = 844,464 calls needed.
844,464 calls/year ÷ 1,360 calls/year/rep. = 621 reps.

†Arbitrarily selected; 100% − 6 mos. of year.

Key:				
	GP	general practice	RHEU	rheumatologist
	FP	family practice	OB/GYN	obstetrician/gynecologist
	DO	osteopath	DERM	dermatologist
	IM	internal medicine	ALLG	allergist
	PCP	primary care physician	ENT	ear, nose, throat
	ORS	orthopedic surgeon		

Source: Clarke-O'Neill, March 19, 1982.

develop new products for the OB/GYN market was maintained.

Lewis felt that if the research effort in developing new drugs for dermatologists and allergists resulted in a breakthrough product or two, the economic potential of these two specialties would be greatly increased and the good relationships between the specialists and Syntex sales reps would be a valuable asset that could lead to rapid market penetration.

The SSM analysis, however, indicated that, at the present sales force size, neither of these specialties should be visited (see Exhibit 6.39) and even at considerably larger sales force sizes, they would not receive much attention under an optimal sales effort allocation.

He noted that the SSM recommendations had not recognized this franchise value, and felt it might call for some modifications:

We can approach optimal deployment in the short run in two ways. We can redeploy the current sales force along the optimal lines indicated by the SSM (and damage our present franchise) or we can grow more rapidly and dedicate incremental sales reps to the PCP markets. I think the more rapid growth alternative is less risky than damaging our specialty franchise.

Exhibit 6.46   Productivity of the Average Physician (1981)

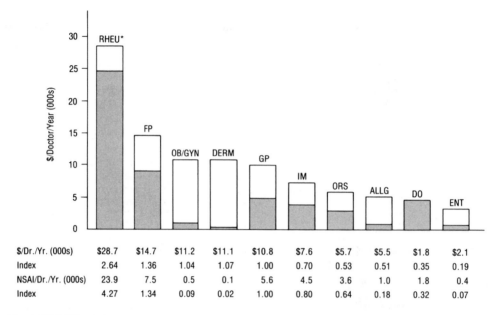

$/Dr./Yr. (000s)	$28.7	$14.7	$11.2	$11.1	$10.8	$7.6	$5.7	$5.5	$1.8	$2.1
Index	2.64	1.36	1.04	1.07	1.00	0.70	0.53	0.51	0.35	0.19
NSAI/Dr./Yr. (000s)	23.9	7.5	0.5	0.1	5.6	4.5	3.6	1.0	1.8	0.4
Index	4.27	1.34	0.09	0.02	1.00	0.80	0.64	0.18	0.32	0.07

* Projected from CY 1980.

Source: PDS

Exhibit 6.47   Physician Market Potential ($000s)*

	NSAIs	Analgesics	Oral Contraceptives	Topical Steroids
RHEU	$ 18,507	$ 1,251	N/A	$ 1,187
FP	127,974	23,519	$ 52,398	14,934
GP	167,998	37,934	55,230	21,814
DERM	620	399	568	44,041
OB/GYN	9,851	6,606	180,368	2,603
IM	132,184	25,564	12,472	13,179
ORS	36,174	11,077	1,490	280
DO	31,435	9,031	12,899	3,432
ALLG	1,626	769	90	1,796
ENT	1,912	2,304	690	1,257
Others	95,614	45,667	31,064	18,046
Total	$623,895	$164,121	$347,269	$122,569

*Projected from CY 1980.

Feasible Growth Rate

It was apparent to Lewis that the sales force could not be increased from 433 to more than 700 sales reps immediately. The realities of identifying, hiring, and training precluded such a rapid increase. A series of discussions with various sales management people indicated that 100 new reps were about the most that could be considered for an increase next year. It was further estimated that during the coming year approximately 20 reps would leave Syntex for one reason or another. As a result of his discussions, Lewis established the goal of recruiting and training 100 new reps during FY 1982 with a resulting net increase of 80.

Lewis recognized that assigning 80 new sales districts in a year would cause a great deal of reshuffling.

> There aren't 80 geographic areas out there that we aren't visiting that are just waiting for a sales rep. Each new sales district will have to be carved out of three or four existing sales districts, which will, in turn, then be unbalanced compared with other districts in the region. Very few districts would be left intact during such a process.

Frank Poole, the national sales manager, was especially concerned about the unsettling influence of the new districts:

> We have to recognize the trauma that could be caused. Some of our senior reps may lose physicians they've called on for years. You can't just dump that on a rep and tell him to give up an MD because we have a new rep that needs space or we've changed our physician targets. We'll really have to work with our reps to get them to see it's for their own good, as well as that of the company. It will take time!

Lewis found also that both Poole and Robert Nelson were concerned about the sales management organization's ability to handle an 80-person increase in the sales force in one year. Details of the sales organization and sales force composition are included in Exhibits 6.48 and 6.49.

Lewis was concerned about the strain on sales reps and sales management if this rapid growth continued for three years. Lewis had analyzed a number of sales force growth scenarios, including:

> The present growth rate—40 new sales reps/year, which would result in 120 new sales reps by FY 1985, for a total of 553 ($244.3 million net profit, using the specialty allocation).

> Forty new sales reps this year, but thereafter, 80 per year, for a total of 200 new reps and 633 on board by FY 1985 ($250.1 million net profit, using the specialty allocation).

> Eighty new reps in each of the next three years, for a total of 240 new reps and 695, near the optimal range by FY 1985 ($251.1 million net profit, using the specialty allocation).

During his analysis of the other major implementation issues, Lewis had repeatedly met concern over the "human element." Frank Poole expressed his concerns.

> Sales forces are composed of people, not chessmen that can be moved about at will by some grand strategist. You may tell them what to do, and they may even report they've done it—but they won't have done it unless they believe it.

> Being a sales rep is a tough job. There is a lot of rejection to it. Even an MD you've got a good relationship with can often be too busy to see you. Fatigue sets in from always talking about the same products. It's hard to see you've really accomplished anything—the physician doesn't buy anything from you. So personal relationships are important—important to getting results, and important to morale.

Market Trends and Competition

Most major drug companies competed in more than one TC. Within each TC there were generally a number of closely competing products. New products ranged from "me-too" imitations to major breakthroughs. The growth rates in the various TCs were closely related to the number of breakthrough

Exhibit 6.48   Sales Management Organization

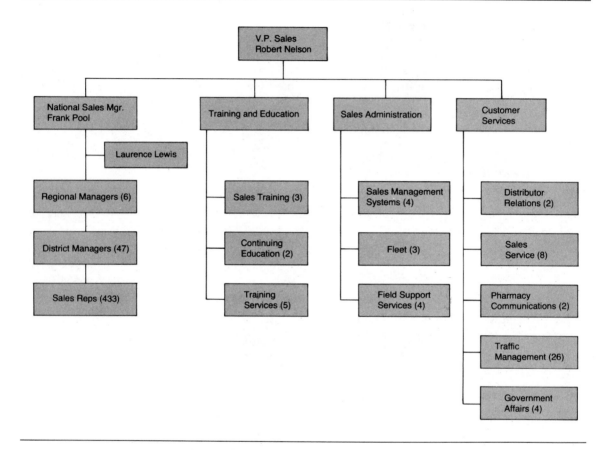

Exhibit 6.49   Sales Force Description

Age Distribution

Age	Number	Percent
20–30	133	25
31–40	204	42
41–50	97	20
51–70	55	11
	489	100

Experience Distribution

Year of Hire	Years of Service	Number	Percent
1950–1955	26–30	1	—
1956–1960	21–25	1	—
1961–1965	10–20	48	11
1966–1970	11–15	70	14
1971–1975	6–10	118	24
1976–1981	1–5	251	51

Growth Rate

	Sales (000s)	Sales Force Size	Sales Per Rep (000s)
1961	301.4	13	23.2
1966	10,841.4	190	57.1
1971	20,328.9	230	88.4
1976	63,506.0	325	195.4
1981	184,096.9	430	428.1
1982	227,400.0	465	489.0

Compensation

Regional Managers (6)	$50,533 (plus 15%)
District Managers (47)	$38,368 (plus 12%)
Sales Managers (12)	$32,100 (plus 11%)
Sales Representatives (433)	$24,116 (plus 10%)

Exhibit 6.50   Market Trends and Promotion Effort—NSAIs* and Analgesics

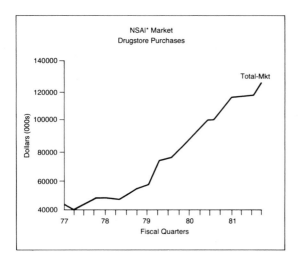

NSAI* Market
Drugstore Purchases

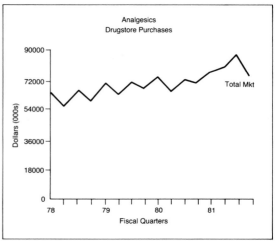

Analgesics
Drugstore Purchases

	Current 12 Months ($000s)					
Promotion	Details	Journal	Mail	Total	% Share	Promo/DSP
Naprosyn	3,244	1,593	262	5,099	11.8%	5.6%
Motrin	9,313	2,506	18	11,837	27.5%	8.7%
Clinoril	5,951	990	106	7,047	16.4%	6.8%
Indocin	2,095	775	97	2,967	6.9%	4.2%
Meclomen	8,317	1,291	18	9,626	22.3%	68.2%
Nalfon	2,902	170	1	3,073	7.1%	9.0%
Tolectin	2,753	772	179	3,704	8.5%	11.5%
Total	34,575	8,097	681	43,353	100.0%	9.0%

*NSAI: Nonsteriodal anti-inflammatory; antiarthritis drugs such as Naprosyn.

	Current 12 Months ($000s)					
Promotion	Details	Journal	Mail	Total	% Share	Promo/DSP
Syn. Non-Narcotics	22,357	7,038	895	30,290	75.3%	19.6%
Anaprox	4,745	4,571	292	9,608	23.9%	118.3%
Zomax	7,891	3,716	412	12,019	29.9%	50.0%
Darvocet-N	2,459	23	1	2,483	6.2%	4.6%
Darvon Comp	68	0	39	107	0.3%	1.1%
Total Propoxyphene	3,170	132	40	3,342	8.3%	4.1%
Talwin	2,055	343	0	2,398	6.0%	9.3%
Codeines & Comb.	5,654	3,348	943	9,945	24.7%	6.2%
Tylenol w/Cod.	401	976	382	1,459	3.6%	2.6%
Empirin w/Cod.	865	967	0	1,841	4.6%	10.0%
Total Market	28,865	10,386	1,838	40,235	100.0%	12.8%

products, and the size of each TC was related to the prevalence of the diseases they treated and the duration of treatment.

The NSAI market was the largest TC in which Syntex Labs competed and had the highest growth rate. The analgesic market, though large, was quite stagnant in terms of growth. Both oral contraceptives and topical steroids enjoyed moderate growth rates (see Exhibits 6.50 and 6.51).

The degree of marketing competition also varied across TCs and competing companies. Sales rep visits were the primary sales tool used by most drug companies, supported by medical journal advertising, direct mail, and the distribution of samples to physicians. Exhibits 6.50 and 6.51 also provide an overview of the relative amounts spent on these marketing activities by various competitors in the relevant TCs.

Preliminary Recommendations

Having gathered the supporting data about call cycle, physician targeting, model recommendations on sales force size, and the capacity of sales

Exhibit 6.51   Market Trends and Promotion Effort—Oral Contraceptives and Topical Steriods

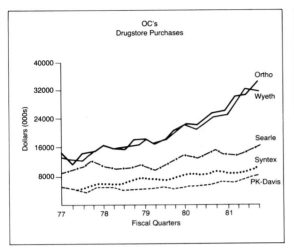

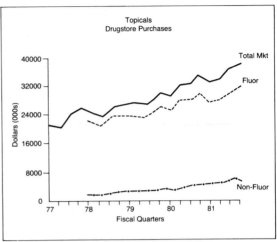

Promotion	Detail	Journal	Mail	Total	% Share	Promo/DSP
		Current 12 Months ($000s)				
Syntex	1,204	666	29	1,899	13.5%	5.1%
Ortho	3,960	1,078	313	5,351	38.0%	4.6%
Wyeth	2,567	1,019	27	3,613	25.7%	3.2%
Searle	1,095	559	59	1,713	12.2%	3.0%
Parke-Davis	159	353	28	540	3.8%	2.0%
Mead-Johnson	661	288	0	949	6.7%	11.4%
Total Market	9,646	3,963	456	14,065	100.0%	3.9%

Source: IMS Audits

Promotion	Details	Journal	Mail	Total	% Share	Promo/DSP
		Current 12 Months ($000s)				
Syntex	1,466	487	78	2,031	13.2%	6.5%
Schering	1,534	191	3	1,728	11.2%	5.6%
Squibb	1,295	161	56	1,512	9.8%	8.0%
Lederle	1,993	525	23	2,541	16.5%	19.5%
Hoechst-Roussel	2,004	293	13	2,310	15.0%	26.6%
Non-Fluor Total	3,905	430	59	4,394	28.5%	20.8%
Fluor Total	9,017	1,705	279	11,091	71.5%	9.3%
Total Market	12,922	2,135	338	15,395	100.0%	11.1%

management to absorb growth, Lewis addressed the coverage of the target market in the coming year if 80 new sales reps were added (see Exhibit 6.52). The correspondence between the model's product- and specialty-based optimal allocations of effort and the required number of calls defined by the desired call frequency and the target market definitions was quite close, in his opinion.

One final problem in allocating sales effort was that various specialists were interested only in certain Syntex Labs products—for example, rheumatologists have very little interest in oral contraceptives. Thus, the allocation of presentations to specific products had to consider which specialty was being visited. Lewis's initial recommendation for a primary presentation allocation, which assumes that approximately 80 sales reps had been added with 510 on board in FY 1982, is found in Exhibit 6.53.

The First Task Force Meeting

The first meeting of the task force began with Laurence Lewis's presentation of his initial recommendations. At the conclusion of this presentation, Lewis summarized the situation as follows:

Exhibit 6.52   Reach and Required Calls at 510 General Representatives

Specialty	Total U.S. Audience	Target U.S. Audience	%	Calls Required at 12x per year	%	Model % of Activity
GP/DO	48,000	17,300		207,600	31.3	26.8
FP	16,000	5,800		69,600	10.5	23.3
IM	27,000	9,700		116,400	17.5	16.0
Total PCP	91,000	32,800	36.0%	393,600	59.4%	66.1%
ORS	10,000	5,000	50.0	60,000	9.0	7.8
RHEU	2,000*	2,000	100.0	24,000	3.6	2.4
OB/GYN	18,000	9,000	50.0	108,000	16.3	14.8
DERM	6,000*	4,500	75.0	54,000	8.1	5.3
ALLG	1,600†	1,600	100.0	9,600	1.4	1.6
ENT	4,700†	2,300	50.0	13,800	2.1	2.0
Total	133,300	57,200	43.0%	663,000	100.0%	100.0%

* From internal call system.
† Seasonal promotion January–June.

Exhibit 6.53   Product Allocation of Primary Presentations (510 Representative)

Specialty	Total Calls	Naprosyn	Anaprox	Norinyl 135	Norinyl 150	Lidex	Synalar	Nasalide
PCP	393,600	2/3‡ 262,400	1/3 131,200					
ORS	60,000	2/3 40,000	1/3 20,000					
RHEU	24,000	3/3 24,000						
OB/GYN	108,000			2/3 72,000	1/3 36,000			
DERM	54,000					3/3 54,000		
ALLG	9,600*							9,600
ENT	13,800*							13,800
Total	663,000 100.0%	326,400 49.2%	151,000 22.8%	72,000 10.9%	36,000 5.4%	54,000 8.1%	0 0.0%	23,400 3.5%
Model Allocation†	695,971 100.0%	349,419 50.2%	177,967 25.5%	78,967 11.3%	38,876 5.6%	51,072 7.4%	0 0.0%	0 0.0%

*Seasonal promotion: January–June.
†Model output in "presentations" divided by 2.7 to yield "primary presentations."
‡Read "Two focus periods out of every three on primary promotion," etc.

A sales manager is required to make many major decisions. Some decisions can follow careful study, but often the time and resources simply aren't available for such study and the decision must be made based on judgment and experience. The recommendation to expand the sales force obviously followed in-depth research. I don't think we need that kind of research in making the call-cycle decision; it should be based on our current best assessment of the situation.

I don't feel we can put off implementation of these recommendations to do more studies. The results of the SSM show a big opportunity and I don't feel unsure enough about anything to wait for the results of additional studies. There is a commitment now to move—if we lose our momentum now, it will be very hard to start it up again.

Preparation Questions

1. What allocation of sales effort would you recommend for the current (510 rep) sales force size?

2. What sales force growth policy would you recommend?

3. How vulnerable is your recommendation to an erosion of Naprosyn's market position?

4. How good are the judgmental response functions?

5. What role should the sales force strategy model play in the determination of sales management strategy at Syntex?

Spreadsheet Models for Syntex Laboratories II

The Syntex Laboratories II case deals with the problems in implementing the recommendations of the SSM model, both qualitative and quantitative. You are pretty much on your own in regard to the qualitative ussues, but this note describes two 1-2-3 spreadsheets that you might find useful on the quantitative side. They are both simple little models that can be expanded with your own ideas, replaced with a model of your own design, or ignored entirely. As you use these models, make sure that the relevant managerial considerations have been a part of your analysis.

There are two rather obvious matching tasks that need to be performed in determining an implementation plan:

1. The number of presentations or sales calls made by a given sales force allocation plan should be compared with the target audience to see how well they match.

2. The primary presentations (featured presentation made on a sales call) should be allocated across *both* products and specialties.

Each of these tasks, though not challenging, are tedious and t ime consuming. They are also the kind of thing that can be nicely handled in Lotus 1-2-3 on a personal computer. Each of these worksheets is reached by typing [Alt] M, and they can be printed using [Alt] P.

Target Worksheet. The *Target* worksheet contains the data in Exhibit 6.45 on the number of physicians in each specialty. Input values include the percent of physicians to be visited, the number of visits per year, and the number of sales reps in your sales force plan. Using these values, the worksheet computes the number of sales calls required for your desired coverage of the target market, the number of sales calls that can be provided by the planned sales force allocation, and the ratio of the two. See Exhibit 6.54.

Allocate Worksheet. The *Allocate* worksheet is a simple program to allocate primary presentations to both specialties and products at the same time much as was done by Lewis in Exhibit 6.56. Inputs to *Allocate* are the number of sales reps allocated to each specialty, the number of sales calls planned per year, and the number of sales reps allocated to each product. The final set of inputs are the fraction of primary sales presentations to be made for each product while visiting each physician specialty. *Allocate* assumes you want to start from the number of sales calls made to specialists and then allocate those calls to the products. *Allocate* computes the share of effort across specialties and across products. See Exhibit 6.55.

Combining these two spreadsheets with the allocation model in Syntex I should provide you with adequate tools to make a rather detailed sales force plan without having to do too much calculation by hand.

Exhibit 6.54 Worksheet for Assessing Target Market Coverage

```
                    SYNTEX LABORATORIES (II)

Plan Coverage of Required Calls for Target Market
------------------------------------------------------------------
            Size of    Calls Target   Calls     Planned   Goal
            Speciality /year Mkt.(%)   req.     # of reps Coverage#
            ----------------------------------     ---------------------
Pri Care    95,131      12    50%     570,786    459.1    109.39%
Ors Surg    10,744      12    50%      64,464     54.1    114.14%
Rheu         2,000      12   100%      24,000     15.6     88.40%
OB/GYN      17,596      12   100%     211,152    101.7     65.50%
Derm         6,000      12   100%      72,000     40.1     75.74%
Allg         1,354       6   100%       8,124     11.2    187.49%
ENT          4,890       6   100%      29,340     12.8     59.33%
            ----------                -------   --------  --------
Total      137,715                    979,866    694.6     96.41%

Total Calls rep/year          1,360
# Calls available/calls required
```

Exhibit 6.55 Worksheet to Reconcile Specialty and Product Allocations

```
Specialty-Product Sales Plan                                                    Effort
             Calls  Calls                                                       Share
Specialty Reps /year (1000s) Napro  Anapr  N 135  N 150  Lidex  Synal  Nasal    Share
---------------------------------------------------------------------------------------
PCP's   459.1  12    624     416    208     0      0      0      0      0        67.3%
                            66.7%  33.3%  0.0%   0.0%   0.0%   0.0%   0.0%
ORS      54.1  12     74      49     25     0      0      0      0      0         7.9%
                            66.7%  33.3%  0.0%   0.0%   0.0%   0.0%   0.0%
Rheu     15.6  12     21      21      0     0      0      0      0      0         2.3%
                           100.0%   0.0%  0.0%   0.0%   0.0%   0.0%   0.0%
Ob/gyn  101.7  12    138       0      0    92     46      0      0      0        14.9%
                             0.0%   0.0% 66.7%  33.3%   0.0%   0.0%   0.0%
Derm     40.1  12     55       0      0     0      0     55      0      0         5.9%
                             0.0%   0.0%  0.0%   0.0% 100.0%   0.0%   0.0%
Allg     11.2   6      8       0      0     0      0      0      0      8         0.8%
                             0.0%   0.0%  0.0%   0.0%   0.0%   0.0% 100.0%
ENT      12.8   6      9       0      0     0      0      0      0      0         0.0%
                             0.0%   0.0%  0.0%   0.0%   0.0%   0.0%   0.0%
---------------------------------------------------------------------------------------
Total   694.6        928     486    232    92     45     55      0      8        99.1%
Share of effort             52.4%  25.0%  9.9%   4.9%   5.9%   0.0%   0.8%       98.8%
---------------------------------------------------------------------------------------
Share of effort (model)     37.8%  24.1% 10.3%   5.0%   6.7%   4.3%  11.8%
Reps    698.5              263.9  168.3  71.9     35   47.1   29.7   82.6
```

Measuring the Effects of Promotion

When they think of marketing, most nonmarketers focus on advertising, but insiders have recognized the importance of promotion for many years. Promotion has become an increasingly important part of the marketing mix for consumer products. During the period 1976 through 1983, promotion expenditures increased 12 percent per year, from $29.8 billion to $64 billion. Over the same time period, advertising expenditures increased 9 percent per year, from $19.4 billion to $35.7 billion. In 1976 promotion budgets accounted for 42.1 percent of the advertising and promotion budgets for American consumer products, but by 1983 it accounted for 62 percent. In terms of the marketing expenditures of U.S. consumer product firms, promotion is more important than advertising.

Pricing has always been understood to be an important determinant of consumer product sales, but despite its prominence in economic theory, it has been hard to measure its effects on consumer product sales with the aggregate data that was available (see Chapter 5).

Until recently, however, accurate measurement of promotion and pricing effects on sales of frequently purchased consumer products at the consumer level has been unavailable. This lack of empirical information about the impact of pricing and promotion left management to rely on folklore and mythology. The advent of accurate, detailed consumer product purchase data made available through sources such as BehaviorScan and the *Marketing Fact Book* (see the Information Resources, Inc., case) have provided much needed insight into the management of these two important marketing mix areas. This discussion is based on data and analysis developed by Information Resources, Inc., using BehaviorScan and *Marketing Fact Book* data. You will note that the discussion and exhibits shift from one product to another; this is necessary to protect the information provided about a particular product. Most of the effects that are discussed are typical, and it does give us a chance to look at more products.

Promotion is important not only because of how much is spent for it, but also for the magnitude of its effects on sales. Promotion is nearly ubiquitous for some product categories—59 percent of soft drink purchases are made on promotion, while the top ten promotion categories all sell at least 48 percent of their volume on promotion. Exhibit 6.56 shows that promotion's effect on the sales of 13 product categories is very powerful, ranging from a 600 percent increase for potato chips to 40 percent for frozen potatoes.

The Effect of Data Aggregation

The discussion of the effects of data aggregation on the measurement of price and sales response to price in Chapter 5 pointed out the importance of the methodology used to gather these data. The highly aggregated procedures used

Exhibit 6.56   Sales Response to Promotion

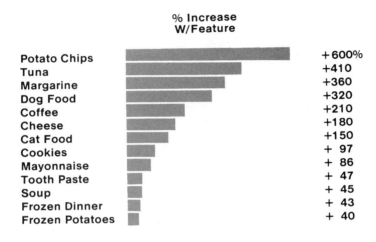

SALES RESPONSE TO PROMOTION

% Increase
W/Feature

Potato Chips	+600%
Tuna	+410
Margarine	+360
Dog Food	+320
Coffee	+210
Cheese	+180
Cat Food	+150
Cookies	+ 97
Mayonnaise	+ 86
Tooth Paste	+ 47
Soup	+ 45
Frozen Dinner	+ 43
Frozen Potatoes	+ 40

Source: Used with permission from Information Resources, Inc., Chicago, IL.

by Nielsen and SAMI to obtain reliable estimates of sales and market share were observed to mask the relationship between price and sales that is essential for developing price and promotion response functions. The highly disaggregated data collection methods used (on a more limited geographic scale) by BehaviorScan, however, provide a transaction-level matching of sales, price, and promotion that provides the data foundation for the development of more reliable price and promotion response functions.

Consider the data about sales volume, price, and promotion conditions for Crest toothpaste presented in Exhibit 6.57. A manager that had only the bimonthly or monthly aggregated data in the top two panels of this exhibit to influence pricing policy would conclude that the demand for Crest was highly price-elastic—small changes in price give rise to large changes in volume. With the weekly data on price and volume, one begins to see that the price decreases associated with the various increases in volume are larger than they appeared to be from the more aggregated data, and that the change in demand is more sharply focused. Based on weekly data, our impression is still that price has a very pronounced effect on sales volume. A manager faced with such data would assume that: (1) lowering the price would lead to large increases in volume and market share, and (2) raising the price would be disastrous.

Now look at the bottom panel in the exhibit, which is at the individual store level and includes promotional activity. It is no longer as clear that price is what

Exhibit 6.57   The Effects of Aggregation on Crest Data

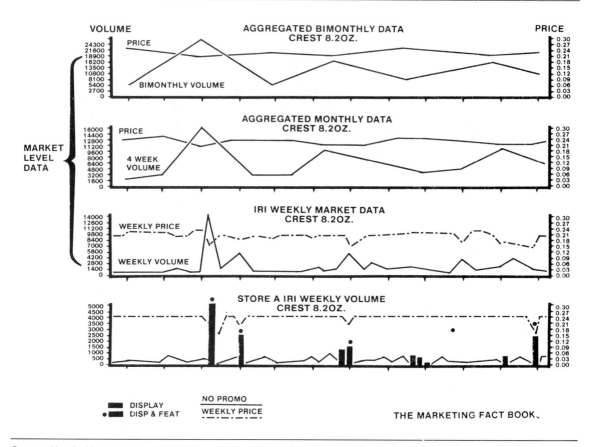

Source: Used with permission from Information Resources, Inc., Chicago, IL.

is driving the changes in volume. We notice two things: (1) Price is stable between promotions as compared to the upper panels—there are no small price variations, so the volume variations we associated with them in the top panel were due to aggregation across stores with different prices. (2) The large volume increases were all associated with *both* price decreases *and* promotion.

The effects of price and promotion can be separated if one has adequate transaction-level data—data matching the price and promotion conditions under which a purchase was made. Exhibit 6.58 shows the results of analysis of this kind of data for another frequently purchased supermarket product (not Crest toothpaste). We see from the flat slope of each of the curves that the price elasticity is very low. We also see from the vertical spread of the curves that the effect of the various kinds of promotion is quite large. The conclusion that one draws from this exhibit—and the data are very typical—is that the effect of promotion

Exhibit 6.58   Price Deal Sensitivity Regression Results (Brand A 48-oz. Size)

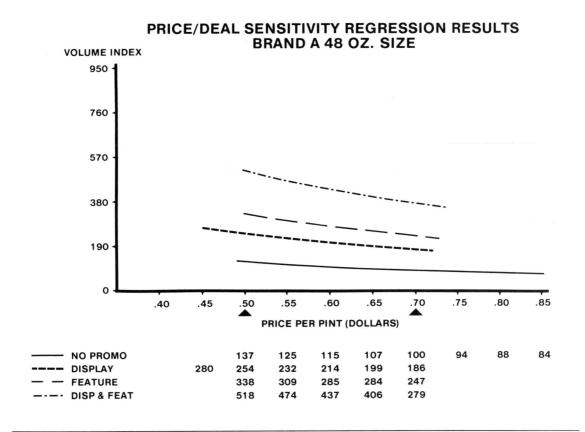

PRICE/DEAL SENSITIVITY REGRESSION RESULTS
BRAND A 48 OZ. SIZE

	.40	.45	.50	.55	.60	.65	.70	.75	.80	.85
NO PROMO			137	125	115	107	100	94	88	84
DISPLAY		280	254	232	214	199	186			
FEATURE			338	309	285	284	247			
DISP & FEAT			518	474	437	406	279			

Source: Used with permission from Information Resources, Inc., Chicago, IL.

on demand is much stronger than is the effect of price. Two factors are at work in this kind of analysis: promotion calls attention to the product, and it is more likely that there will be a price difference between the promoted product and its competitors than will normally be the case.

If the data in Exhibits 6.57 and 6.58 were for the same product, the product manager's earlier conclusions about price policy would have been incorrect and disastrous. Cutting price would probably not lead to increased volume and would result in smaller margins. The data in these two exhibits show that a better policy would be to stress promotion with the smallest price cut that would still make an impression.

A further example of the benefit of having purchase-level data is provided in the data on the market shares of Coca Cola and Pepsi Cola found in Exhibit 6.59. Looking at this data, one might conclude that the cola market is a zero-sum

Exhibit 6.59   City A—Share of Carbonated Beverage Market

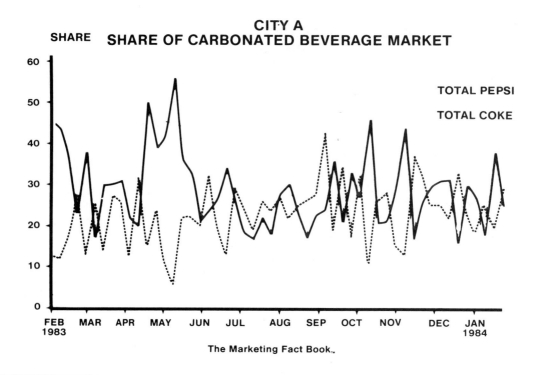

CITY A
SHARE OF CARBONATED BEVERAGE MARKET

TOTAL PEPSI

TOTAL COKE

The Marketing Fact Book.

Source: Used with permission from Information Resources, Inc., Chicago, IL.

game—what one cola gains comes directly from the franchise of the other. While this is certainly accurate to some extent, it isn't quite as true as it might at first appear. Exhibit 6.60 introduces promotion policy to the data and restricts the data to a single store. We see at once that Coke promotes much more frequently than does Pepsi, but we also notice that the promotion responses are very large compared with the base level of sales (at least for Pepsi, where we have a chance at saying what the base sales level is), and we notice that the volume obtained from the promotions didn't come from the base level of the other product. In other words, the large swings that we saw in Exhibit 6.59 probably didn't result from one brand losing loyal customers to the other, but rather from consumers that buy only if there is a promotion and don't care which brand it is. This type of a consumer market structure is not unusual. If one arrays consumers by their share of purchases for a given brand, one frequently finds that high brand loyalty is rather rare. Take a look at Exhibit 6.61. Only 26.9 percent of Crest customers buy Crest for more than 90 percent of their toothpaste purchases and the loyal consumers of the other three brands are an even smaller percentage.

Exhibit 6:60   Effect of Promotion and Price on Sales in One Store

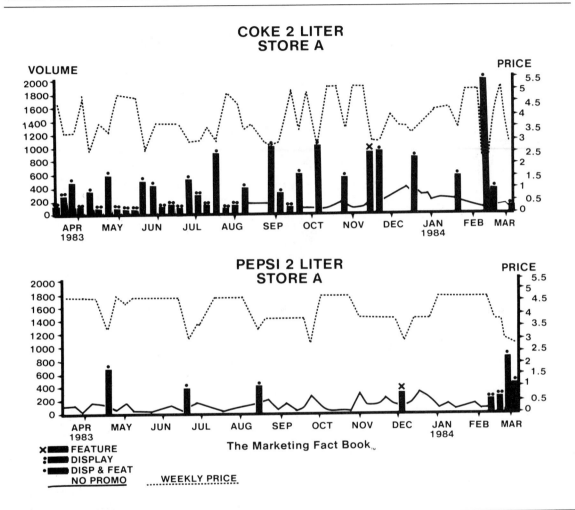

Source: Used with permission from Information Resources, Inc., Chicago, IL.

The Role of Switchers in Response to Promotion

A related analysis is to look at the source of the consumers that respond to a promotion. Consider the very large response to promotion for Ragu spaghetti sauce shown in Exhibit 6.62. Since the promotion sales levels are so much greater than the non-promotion sales levels, we feel that there must be a number of consumers that buy spaghetti sauce only when it is promoted. Exhibit 6.63 shows that for a promotion for another product—with much less dramatic promotion

Exhibit 6.61   Toothpaste Brand Loyalty Profiles

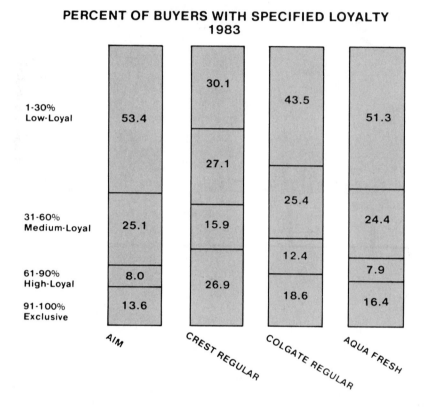

PERCENT OF BUYERS WITH SPECIFIED LOYALTY
1983

Source: Used with permission from Information Resources, Inc., Chicago, IL.

response than Ragu's—most of the incremental sales came from "switchers," consumers who were not loyal to any brand. Although the volume increase in the sales of brand A is dramatic (+238%), the damage done to the loyal customer franchise of other brands is fairly small and the increased volume due to increased purchasing by the brand's own loyal customers is quite modest. Exhibit 6.64 reinforces these conclusions and makes the allocation of promotion sales among customers more clear. More than 80 percent of the promotion sales of product A came from switchers, while only 2.7 percent of the sales came from customers that were loyal to other brands.

In these examples it seems clear that the companies would be better off if they didn't promote so much. Surely few consumers are so affected by promotion that they buy products they don't need or want just because they are promoted. It is

Exhibit 6.62   Sales Response to Promotion for Ragu Spaghetti Sauce

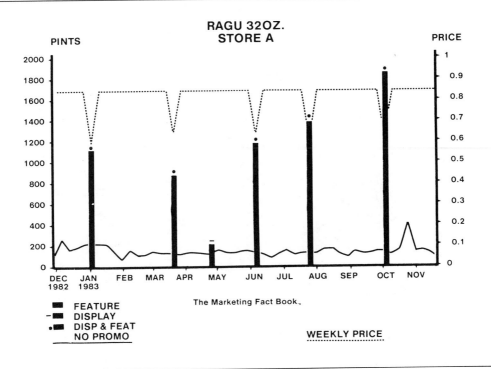

RAGU 32OZ.
STORE A

PINTS

PRICE

FEATURE
DISPLAY
DISP & FEAT
NO PROMO

The Marketing Fact Book.

WEEKLY PRICE

Source: Used with permission from Information Resources, Inc., Chicago, IL.

more likely that many consumers have come to expect that promotions will occur and so they plan on them and wait for them. When one recognizes that a large percentage of sales result from such consumers, it becomes very important to plan competitive strategies to win their purchases. The base of loyal consumers is rather stable, but it represents a minority of the available purchases and thus one must win the promotion purchases of switchers. Against this background, consider the toothpaste market again (Exhibit 6.65). It appears that if there were no promotion for any toothpaste brand, the category volume would be about the same as it is *with* the promotion. So why don't the companies stop promoting? First of all, this kind of data is relatively new and might not be known to all of the manufacturers. Second, a company that unilaterally reduced its promotion would lose its share of the switchers' purchases, which, as we have seen, is the majority of the category volume. It would be illegal for the companies to agree among themselves to eliminate promotion. Even if such an understanding could be achieved among the major brands through legal market leadership methods, it would be difficult to maintain, since promotion is viewed by smaller brands as

Exhibit 6.63   Switchers in Sales Response to Promotion

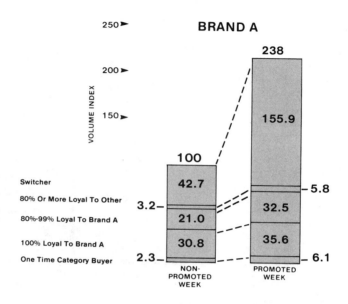

Source: Used with permission from Information Resources, Inc., Chicago, IL.

Exhibit 6.64   Sources of Promotion Incremental Volume—Brand A

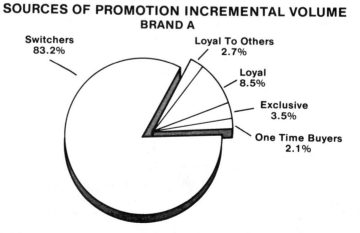

Source: Used with permission from Information Resources, Inc., Chicago, IL.

Exhibit 6.65   Effect of No Promotion on Toothpaste Category Volume

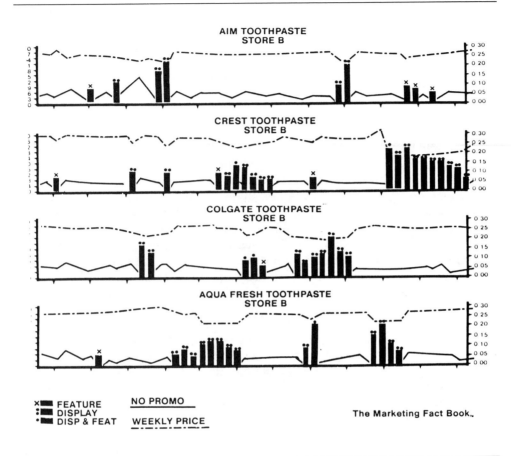

Source: Used with permission from Information Resources, Inc., Chicago, IL.

a means of increasing their market share, and they would be reluctant to quit. It is not surprising then that promotion continues at such high levels, since this is a near-classical example of the prisoner's dilemma.

Coupon Evaluation

A type of promotion that has become very popular in recent years is the coupon. Coupons are found in newspapers, magazines, at the point of purchase, and within packages of purchased products. Most coupons offer either a price or volume discount. Some coupons must be mailed to the manufacturer for redemption, while others can be "redeemed on purchase" (ROP)—used as cash at the time of the purchase.

Exhibit 6.66   Breakdown of Coupon Redemption and Repeat Purchasing

	Total	Trial	Repeat
% of households redeeming	3.5%	1.8%	1.6%
% of redeemers repurchasing	57.5	39.3	78.0

It should be recognized that the value of a coupon redemption to the firm depends on the consumer who redeems it. Imagine a consumer who has never tried our brand and has no intention of buying it. If, upon receiving a coupon, this consumer purchases our product, that redemption has an immediate value to our company of the unit contribution less the value of the coupon. Also, we may have won a new customer who will continue to buy our product in the future. Now consider what happens if a loyal customer uses the coupon. If the customer buys our brand every shopping trip, no matter what else is offered in the store, the value of that coupon redemption for our company is negative. Not only did the company just give away the value of the coupon, but there won't be any incremental volume from this consumer in the future either. In fact, we may have trained this customer to start waiting for future coupons or promotions before buying again—an even worse consequence for the firm.

These examples demonstrate that evaluating coupon success requires the consideration of more than just the total redemption rate. It is desirable to be able to examine the proportion of redemptions made by new triers and by repeat purchasers. For example, see Exhibit 6.66. We see that, for this particular coupon, slightly more than half of the coupons used were redeemed by households that had not purchased the product previously (1.8%). We also notice that only half as many of these trial households repurchased the product as did the households that had already tried it before they used the coupon. This breakdown is important, because it enables us to look at the degree to which a coupon served to expand the number of consumers compared with the number of consumers who used the coupon to save money on what they might have purchased anyway. The former effect increases the franchise, while the latter decreases profitability. Effective management of couponing and promotion in general requires that these two countervailing forces be carefully balanced.

Sample Package Evaluation

The availability of transaction-level data and longitudinal household purchase histories also makes it possible to evaluate the effectiveness of trial-size packages. Separate repurchase rates can be computed for consumers who first tried the product in a trial size rather than purchasing the product in a regular-size

Exhibit 6.67   Average Price and Promotion Impact (50 packet Equal)

| | Average % Change in Volume | | |
% Price Change	No Promotion	Display Only	Feature Only
+10%	−4%	+134%	+127%
+ 5	−2	+138	+128
0	--	+143	+130
− 5	+2	+147	+133
−10	+4	+152	+134
−15	+6	+158	+135
−20	+9	+164	+137

package. One would expect such consumers to be less frequent users of the product category or less convinced they need the product on the basis of the advertising. It is reasonable to expect that the repeat-purchase rates for such customers would be less. We observed this in the ASSESSOR test of Enhance in the Johnson Wax cases, in the G.D. Searle I case in the previous chapter, and it reappears in the G.D. Searle II case that follows. Additional information about the repeat-purchase rates of the consumers who bought the trial-size carton of Equal is provided. While the trial-size packages contributed to the largest trial rates in the BehaviorScan test periods, the G.D. Searle II case shows that, similar to coupons, the households that tried Equal with the sample-size packages had a lower repeat-purchase rate than did households that first tried Equal in the normal package sizes.

Display, Featuring, and Price Analysis

The G.D. Searle II case provides a summary of the results of display and featuring activity for Equal similar to that shown in Exhibit 6.58. The data in Exhibit 6.67 (which are abstracted from Exhibit 6.81) provide measurements of the effects of price, display, and featuring on the sales of Equal 50-packet cartons. They are repeated here to demonstrate how a response function can be derived from such data. Exhibit 6.67 provides the percentage change in sales volume that was observed for various percentage changes in price under three promotion conditions—no promotion, featuring, and display. Each of these promotion conditions existed for a period of time in various stores and the data were derived by aggregating the sales results by promotion condition and calculating the average response. The impact of price is observed to vary considerably with the display and feature conditions in the store.

As we saw in Exhibit 6.58, the effects of both display and featuring are much stronger than price effects. It is not at all clear from these results, however, what

Exhibit 6.68   Ratios of Percentage Changes in Price and Sales

% Price Change	No Promotion	Display Only	Feature Only
+10%	−0.4	−0.9	−0.3
+ 5	−0.4	−1.0	−0.4
0	—	—	—
− 5	−0.4	−0.8	−0.6
−10	−0.4	−0.9	−0.4
−15	−0.4	−1.0	−0.3
−20	−0.45	−0.82	−0.35

the marketing policy should be. It is apparent that great sales gains could be achieved in individual stores that cooperate in features and displays. The managerial problem is to determine what has to be done to achieve retailer cooperation on such programs, how much it would cost, how often promotions can be offered, and what degree of cooperation can be expected.

The concept of *price elasticity*, which we encountered earlier, relates the percentage change in volume to the percentage change in price. If we recast the data in the previous exhibit in terms of the ratios of these two percentage changes, we get the measures of the price elasticity at various price levels that appear in Exhibit 6.68. Examination of the ratios of the sales and price percentage changes show that they are relatively constant. A constant elasticity indicates a response function that exhibits diminishing marginal returns (concave downward), and we can easily develop the response functions for the various promotion situations directly from the definition of the price elasticity:

$$\text{Elasticity} = (\text{Change in Sales}/\text{Sales}) \times (\text{Price}/\text{Change in Price}) \qquad (6.9)$$

We can then solve for the change in sales due to a price change for a particular promotion condition:

$$\text{Change in Sales} = \text{Elasticity} \times \% \text{ Change in Price} \times \text{Sales}. \qquad (6.10)$$

A simple response function that includes both the price and the promotion effect can be constructed by modifying "sales" in equation (6.10) to reflect the change in the base level of sales due to promotion. For example, the response function for "display only" would be:

$$\text{Change in Sales} = \times 1.43 \text{ Elasticity} \times \% \text{ Change in Price} \qquad (6.11)$$
$$\times \text{ Base Sales}$$

The numerical values are found in Exhibits 6.67 and 6.68.

When combined with an estimated advertising response function and the estimates of the base sales level forecast by the BehaviorScan model, a decision model can be developed that greatly expands the value of the basic BehaviorScan results.

CASE: G.D. Searle II

This, the final case in the book, addresses the problem of determining a profit strategy for Equal low-calorie sweetener. The scope of the decision concerns most of the major elements of market strategy—target market, product position, price policy, advertising, distribution, and especially promotion. Through the BehaviorScan test, some interesting results about the effectiveness of display and featuring have been obtained. Other data provide the results of a number of couponing variations. The case summarizes our analytical approach in both the scope of the marketing decisions considered and the nature of the decision model developed to address the problem.

July 12, 1983, found Norris Frederic, director of marketing research for the consumer products division of G. D. Searle & Co., considering promotion and pricing policy for Equal. So far Equal had been an overwhelming success: 1982 retail sales were $7.4 million, and through May 1983 sales had been $23.5 million. Equal enjoyed a 40% dollar share of the low-calorie sweetener market nationwide. Both the southeastern district and the rest of the United States were doing well in rollout. Equal's May 1983 unit share in the southeast was 26.8%, and its unit share in the rest of the country was 30.6%. Distribution had been attained nationwide in nearly 90% of both drug and food stores.

Frederic observed that Equal's southeastern share was down slightly in July, to 24.3%. He found it hard to think of Equal as a mature brand only one year after it first hit retail shelves, and only six months into national distribution, but the trial rates in the BehaviorScan tests had indicated that repeat sales accounted for more than 80% of Equal's sales volume after only seven periods,* and less than 1% of households per period had made an initial trial of Equal after the 11th period!

Frederic wondered whether these test market results and the observed slowdown in growth in the southeast could signal the need to change Equal's

marketing strategy from trial to repeat purchase stimulation.

Extended Test Market Period

Although in October 1982 Frederic had been dubious about the value of additional price-level testing in the same two BehaviorScan cities, he was interested in the information BehaviorScan could provide on the four promotions that had been run since August if the test were extended. He succeeded in gaining management support to continue the BehaviorScan test for another seven periods and to schedule three more promotion events:

1. During the week ending October 31, 1982, half of the stores in each market would display Equal's 50s and 100s with a price reduction of about 10%. In addition, there would be an in-store product tasting during one day that week. The remaining stores would not have either a promotion or a price reduction.

2. Equal 50s and 100s were to be displayed at a reduced price (approximately 15%) in half the stores in each market during the week ending January 16, 1983. The remaining stores would also reduce their Equal retail price by 15%, but would not feature a display.

3. A $1.00 tear-off coupon pad would be placed in half the stores in each market during the week

---

*The BehaviorScan test results were presented in periods of four weeks.

This case prepared by Darral G. Clarke.

Copyright © 1985 by the President and Fellows of Harvard College, Harvard Busines School case 9-586-023.

Exhibit 6.69   Equal Volume per 1000 Households (10/26/86–5/8/83)

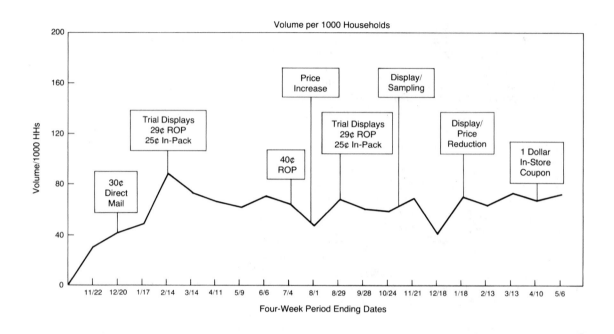

ending April 24, 1983. There would be no further price reductions or displays in any of the stores.

Exhibit 6.69 presents an overview of the sales volume and timing of promotional activities throughout the 20 test market periods.

BehaviorScan Results

Through May 8, 1983, Equal had achieved a 22.4% share of the low-calorie sweetener equivalent teaspoon volume, and over 25% of the households had tried Equal. Equal's cumulative average household buying rate was 4.8 50s, compared with 12.8 50s for sugar substitutes as a whole. Equal made 13.8% of its sales on deal—a considerably higher propor-

tion than that of the rest of the category; Equal's average price through 20 periods, while nearly 2.5 times the category average price, was $0.15 lower than the planned price (see Exhibit 6.70).

Although Equal had achieved rapid market penetration and substantial repeat rates, the penetration rate had slowed and repeat purchasing accounted for over 90% of purchases (see Exhibit 6.71). Equal's market penetration had outstripped its competitors', but the brand still lagged Sweet 'N Low in repeat (see Exhibit 6.72).

Forecasts based on the BehaviorScan data predicted unadjusted sales of 5.43 million cases during the first year after introduction and 5.44 million cases in the second year (Exhibit 6.73). Forecasts adjusted for expected market conditions indicated

Exhibit 6.70   Total Equal Purchasing Summary (Total Panel)

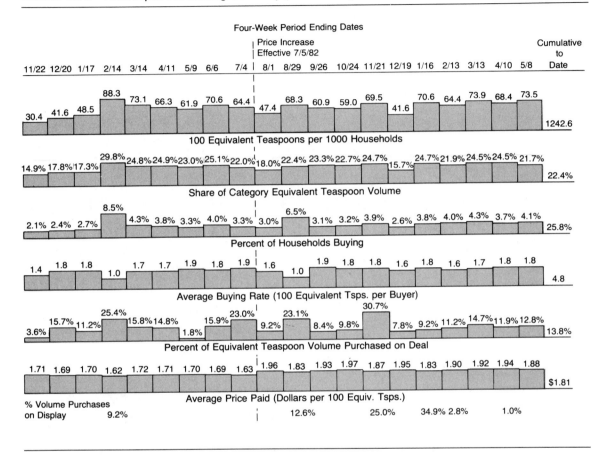

sales of 2.83 million cases in the first year after introduction and 4.1 million cases in the second year. The adjusted forecast for 1982 was 920,000 cases; 4.22 million cases were forecast for 1983, and 3.94 million cases for 1984.

The fact that the 1984 forecast was essentially the same as that for 1983 reinforced Frederic's interest in marketing actions that might buoy future sales and profits. As a result, he and Phillip Watson, director of sweetener products, met to discuss actions that would increase market share and profit by stimulating repeat purchase, and designed additional BehaviorScan tests to explore their effectiveness. They were particularly interested in list price, promotion, and merchandising (that is, samples, trial-size packages, coupons, price promotions, and store displays).

List Price

The initial test market had been designed to investigate two price levels, $1.99 and $1.58, for the 50s. On July 5, 1982, however, price in the test market had been increased to $2.19 in the high-priced

Exhibit 6.71   Total Sugar Substitutes Purchasing Summary (Total Panel)

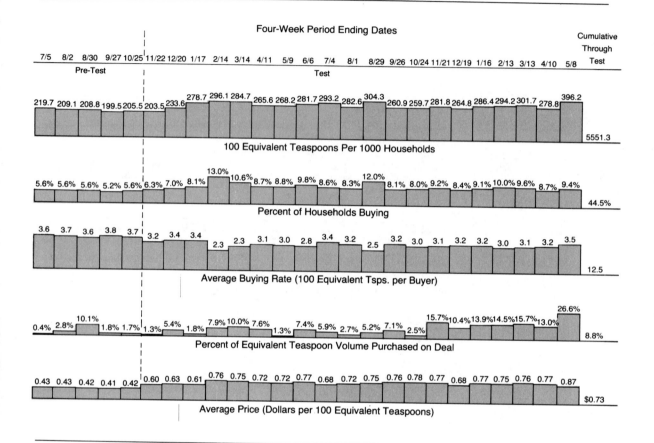

stores and $1.79 in the low-priced stores. The prices of the 100s had been increased from $2.99 and $3.49 to $3.69 and $4.29 respectively. The difference between Equal's market shares in the high- and low-priced stores had increased from 17% in the period before the price increase to 38% in the period of the increase and had generally remained greater than 30% thereafter. The price effect appeared to be concentrated in the 100s, where the share difference between high- and low-priced stores had risen from 29% before the price increase to 55% immediately thereafter and subsequently had generally remained higher than 60% (see

Exhibit 6.74). Watson felt that the $4.29 price of the 100s had exceeded a psychological price point.

Trial-Size Analysis

Trial-size cartons containing 10 packets and priced at 29¢ had been offered during the weeks of February 14, 1982, and August 29, 1982. During the February promotion a newspaper advertisement featuring a 29¢ coupon had accompanied the store display. Trial in those two periods was the highest during the test, and the trial size accounted for 78%

Exhibit 6.72   Total Equal Trial and Repeat Components of Four-Week Period Volume (100 Eq. Tspn. Volume per 1000 Households)

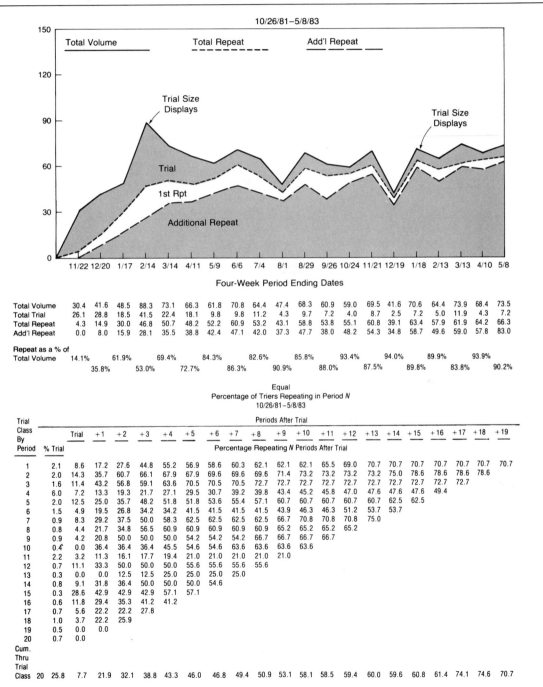

10/26/81–5/8/83

Total Volume / Total Repeat / Add'l Repeat

Trial Size Displays

Trial Size Displays

Trial

1st Rpt

Additional Repeat

Four-Week Period Ending Dates: 11/22 12/20 1/17 2/14 3/14 4/11 5/9 6/6 7/4 8/1 8/29 9/26 10/24 11/21 12/19 1/18 2/13 3/13 4/10 5/8

Total Volume	30.4	41.6	48.5	88.3	73.1	66.3	61.8	70.8	64.4	47.4	68.3	60.9	59.0	69.5	41.6	70.6	64.4	73.9	68.4	73.5
Total Trial	26.1	28.8	18.5	41.5	22.4	18.1	9.8	9.8	11.2	4.3	9.7	7.2	4.0	8.7	2.5	7.2	5.0	11.9	4.3	7.2
Total Repeat	4.3	14.9	30.0	46.8	50.7	48.2	52.2	60.9	53.2	43.1	58.8	53.8	55.1	60.8	39.1	63.4	57.9	61.9	64.2	66.3
Add'l Repeat	0.0	8.0	15.9	28.1	35.5	38.8	42.4	47.1	42.0	37.3	47.7	38.0	48.2	54.3	34.8	58.7	49.6	59.0	57.8	83.0

Repeat as a % of
Total Volume	14.1%		61.9%		69.4%		84.3%		82.6%		85.8%		93.4%		94.0%		89.9%		93.9%	
		35.8%		53.0%		72.7%		86.3%		90.9%		88.0%		87.5%		89.8%		83.8%		90.2%

Equal
Percentage of Triers Repeating in Period N
10/26/81–5/8/83

Trial Class By Period	% Trial	Trial	+1	+2	+3	+4	+5	+6	+7	+8	+9	+10	+11	+12	+13	+14	+15	+16	+17	+18	+19
								Percentage Repeating N Periods After Trial													
1	2.1	8.6	17.2	27.6	44.8	55.2	56.9	58.6	60.3	62.1	62.1	65.5	69.0	70.7	70.7	70.7	70.7	70.7	70.7	70.7	
2	2.0	14.3	35.7	60.7	66.1	67.9	67.9	69.6	69.6	69.6	71.4	73.2	73.2	73.2	75.0	78.6	78.6	78.6	78.6		
3	1.6	11.4	43.2	56.8	59.1	63.6	70.5	70.5	70.5	72.7	72.7	72.7	72.7	72.7	72.7	72.7	72.7	72.7	72.7		
4	6.0	7.2	13.3	19.3	21.7	27.1	29.5	30.7	39.2	39.8	43.4	45.2	45.8	47.0	47.6	47.6	47.6	49.4			
5	2.0	12.5	25.0	35.7	48.2	51.8	51.8	53.6	55.4	57.1	60.7	60.7	60.7	60.7	60.7	62.5	62.5				
6	1.5	4.9	19.5	26.8	34.2	34.2	41.5	41.5	41.5	41.5	43.9	46.3	46.3	51.2	53.7	53.7					
7	0.9	8.3	29.2	37.5	50.0	58.3	62.5	62.5	62.5	62.5	66.7	70.8	70.8	70.8	75.0						
8	0.8	4.4	21.7	34.8	56.5	60.9	60.9	60.9	60.9	60.9	65.2	65.2	65.2	65.2							
9	0.9	4.2	20.8	50.0	50.0	50.0	54.2	54.2	54.2	66.7	66.7	66.7	66.7								
10	0.4	0.0	36.4	36.4	36.4	45.5	54.6	54.6	63.6	63.6	63.6	63.6									
11	2.2	3.2	11.3	16.1	17.7	19.4	21.0	21.0	21.0	21.0	21.0										
12	0.7	11.1	33.3	50.0	50.0	50.0	55.6	55.6	55.6	55.6											
13	0.3	0.0	0.0	12.5	12.5	25.0	25.0	25.0	25.0												
14	0.8	9.1	31.8	36.4	50.0	50.0	50.0	54.6													
15	0.3	28.6	42.9	42.9	42.9	57.1	57.1														
16	0.6	11.8	29.4	35.3	41.2	41.2															
17	0.7	5.6	22.2	22.2	27.8																
18	1.0	3.7	22.2	25.9																	
19	0.5	0.0	0.0																		
20	0.7	0.0																			
Cum. Thru Trial Class 20	25.8	7.7	21.9	32.1	38.8	43.3	46.0	46.8	49.4	50.9	53.1	58.1	58.5	59.4	60.0	59.6	60.8	61.4	74.1	74.6	70.7

Exhibit 6.73   Sugar Substitutes Trial and Repeat Purchasing

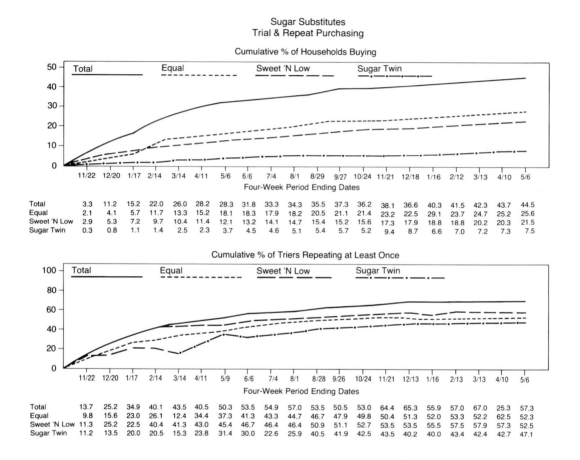

Sugar Substitutes
Trial & Repeat Purchasing

Cumulative % of Households Buying

	11/22	12/20	1/17	2/14	3/14	4/11	5/6	6/6	7/4	8/1	8/29	9/27	10/24	11/21	12/18	1/16	2/12	3/13	4/10	5/6
Total	3.3	11.2	15.2	22.0	26.0	28.2	28.3	31.8	33.3	34.3	35.5	37.3	36.2	38.1	36.6	40.3	41.5	42.3	43.7	44.5
Equal	2.1	4.1	5.7	11.7	13.3	15.2	18.1	18.3	17.9	18.2	20.5	21.1	21.4	23.2	22.5	29.1	23.7	24.7	25.2	25.6
Sweet 'N Low	2.9	5.3	7.2	9.7	10.4	11.4	12.1	13.2	14.1	14.7	15.4	15.2	15.6	17.3	17.9	18.8	18.8	20.2	20.3	21.5
Sugar Twin	0.3	0.8	1.1	1.4	2.5	2.3	3.7	4.5	4.6	5.1	5.4	5.7	5.2	9.4	8.7	6.6	7.0	7.2	7.3	7.5

Cumulative % of Triers Repeating at Least Once

	11/22	12/20	1/17	2/14	3/14	4/11	5/9	6/6	7/4	8/1	8/28	9/26	10/24	11/21	12/13	1/16	2/13	3/13	4/10	5/6
Total	13.7	25.2	34.9	40.1	43.5	40.5	50.3	53.5	54.9	57.0	53.5	50.5	53.0	64.4	65.3	55.9	57.0	67.0	25.3	57.3
Equal	9.8	15.6	23.0	26.1	12.4	34.4	37.3	41.3	43.3	44.7	46.7	47.9	49.8	50.4	51.3	52.0	53.3	52.2	62.5	52.3
Sweet 'N Low	11.3	25.2	22.5	40.4	41.3	43.0	45.4	46.7	46.4	46.4	50.9	51.1	52.7	53.5	53.5	55.5	57.5	57.9	57.3	52.5
Sugar Twin	11.2	13.5	20.0	20.5	15.3	23.8	31.4	30.0	22.6	25.9	40.5	41.9	42.5	43.5	40.2	40.0	43.4	42.4	42.7	47.1

and 50% of the trial in these periods respectively (Exhibit 6.75). For those who tried in these high-trial periods, however, the repeat rates three periods later were only 21% and 17.7%, respectively. The trial size had been purchased by 6.8% of the households and 26% of the Equal buyers. For 3.6% of the households, the trial size was their only Equal purchase. When these "trial size only" households were excluded from the base of triers, the percentage of triers repeating at least once increased from 52.3% to 56.4%, and the additional repeats per first repeat customer increased from 4.1 to 4.3 (see Exhibit 6.75).

A closer analysis of the consumers buying the trial size revealed that the first trial-size offering was much more effective in generating new customers than the second (see Exhibit 6.76).

Norris Frederic concluded that "the trial size had significantly expanded the Equal buyer base, although the relatively low repeat-purchasing level among the trial-size triers suggested they might represent somewhat marginal Equal buyers."

Exhibit 6.74 Equal Year-Two Fourt-Woodlock Forecasting Components (Unadjusted)

	Actual Through Year 1 (10/24/82)	Actual Through Period 20 (5/8/83)	Year 2 Forecast
Trial Volume			
Triers per 100 Households	21.40	25.81	28.0
100 Eq. Tspn. Volume Per Trier	.98	1.00	1.00
Total Trial Volume	20.94	25.79	28.0
First Repeat Volume			
Percent of Triers Repeating	49.92	52.31	55.4
First Repeat per 100 Households	10.68	13.50	15.0
100 Eq. Tspn. Volume per First Repeat	1.37	1.36	1.36
Total First Repeat Volume	14.68	18.34	20.4
Additional Repeat Volume			
Additonal Repeats per Repeater	2.84	4.09	4.8
Additional Repeats per 100 Households	30.34	55.29	75.0
100 Eq. Tspn. Volume per Additional Repeat	1.40	1.45	1.42
Total Additional Repeat Volume	42.47	80.16	106.5
Total 100 Eq. Tspn. Volume per 100 Households	78.09	124.29	154.9
100 Eq. Tspn. Increment	—	46.20	76.8
Total U.S. Case Sales Forecast (MM) (Unadjusted)			
83.5 MM Households — Year 1	5.43		
85.0 MM Households — Year 2			5.44

Adjusted Retail Sales Forecasts
(Million Cases)

	Adjustment	First Year	Adjustment	Second Year
Distribution Level/Build	.80	4.34	.89	4.84
Later Ad Start	.95	4.13	1.00	4.84
Distribution Quality	.85	3.51	.85	4.12
Promotion Activity	1.00	3.51	.96	3.96
National Rollout	.80	2.83	1.04	4.10
Adjusted Sales Forecast	1982	1983	1984	
Total U.S. Case Sales	.92	4.22	3.94	

Exhibit 6.75   Equal 100-Packet Volume Share—High vs. Low Price Stores

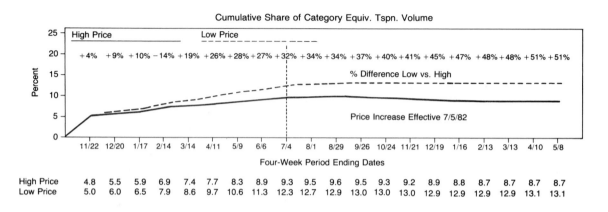

Cumulative Share of Category Equiv. Tspn. Volume

	11/22	12/20	1/17	2/14	3/14	4/11	5/9	6/6	7/4	8/1	8/29	9/26	10/24	11/21	12/19	1/16	2/13	3/13	4/10	5/8
High Price	4.8	5.5	5.9	6.9	7.4	7.7	8.3	8.9	9.3	9.5	9.6	9.5	9.3	9.2	8.9	8.8	8.7	8.7	8.7	8.7
Low Price	5.0	6.0	6.5	7.9	8.6	9.7	10.6	11.3	12.3	12.7	12.9	13.0	13.0	13.0	12.9	12.9	12.9	12.9	13.1	13.1

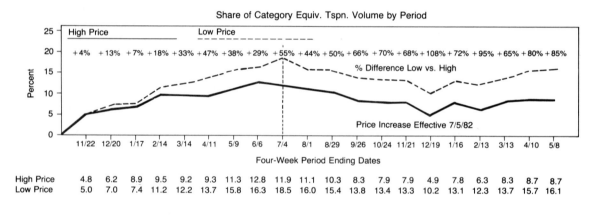

Share of Category Equiv. Tspn. Volume by Period

	11/22	12/20	1/17	2/14	3/14	4/11	5/9	6/6	7/4	8/1	8/29	9/26	10/24	11/21	12/19	1/16	2/13	3/13	4/10	5/8
High Price	4.8	6.2	8.9	9.5	9.2	9.3	11.3	12.8	11.9	11.1	10.3	8.3	7.9	7.9	4.9	7.8	6.3	8.3	8.7	8.7
Low Price	5.0	7.0	7.4	11.2	12.2	13.7	15.8	16.3	18.5	16.0	15.4	13.8	13.4	13.3	10.2	13.1	12.3	13.7	15.7	16.1

Advertising

By the end of the 20 periods, there was still no significant difference in purchasing between households exposed to the two ad weight levels. Cumulatively, Equal accounted for 21.2% of category volume in the high-advertising group, compared with 24.4% volume in the low-advertising panel. Watson maintained, as before, that the overall incremental advertising spending represented by the difference in the advertising weights was small in comparison with the total promotion spending on the brand.

Promotion Responsiveness

In addition to planned test market events, some price reductions and display/feature activity occurred in the test markets in connection with the national rollout of Equal.

Sampling.   Sampling appeared to have had a minimal effect on total Equal sales. By June 6, 1983, there was very little difference in purchasing between sample recipients and those who had not received samples (see Exhibit 6.77).

Exhibit 6.76   Equal Market Share—High vs. Low Price Stores

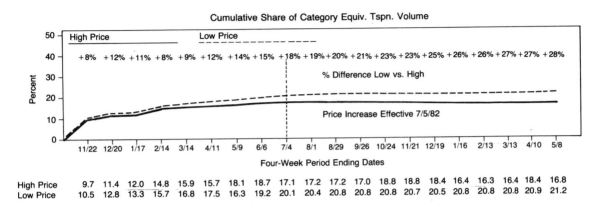

Cumulative Share of Category Equiv. Tspn. Volume

	11/22	12/20	1/17	2/14	3/14	4/11	5/9	6/6	7/4	8/1	8/29	9/26	10/24	11/21	12/19	1/16	2/13	3/13	4/10	5/8
High Price	9.7	11.4	12.0	14.8	15.9	15.7	18.1	18.7	17.1	17.2	17.2	17.0	18.8	18.8	18.4	16.4	16.3	16.4	18.4	16.8
Low Price	10.5	12.8	13.3	15.7	16.8	17.5	16.3	19.2	20.1	20.4	20.8	20.8	20.8	20.7	20.5	20.8	20.8	20.8	20.9	21.2

% Difference Low vs. High: +8% +12% +11% +8% +9% +12% +14% +15% +18% +19% +20% +21% +23% +23% +25% +26% +26% +27% +27% +28%

Price Increase Effective 7/5/82

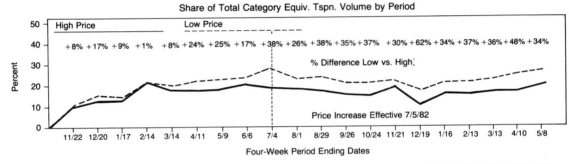

Share of Total Category Equiv. Tspn. Volume by Period

	11/22	12/20	1/17	2/14	3/14	4/11	5/9	6/6	7/4	8/1	8/29	9/26	10/24	11/21	12/19	1/16	2/13	3/13	4/10	5/8
High Price	9.7	12.8	13.2	21.3	18.1	17.8	18.2	20.3	18.9	18.4	17.3	15.5	15.0	18.9	10.8	15.9	15.8	16.9	17.0	20.1
Low Price	10.5	15.0	14.4	21.4	19.8	22.0	22.7	23.7	26.0	23.2	23.8	21.0	20.8	21.9	17.5	21.3	21.7	23.0	25.2	26.9

% Difference Low vs. High: +8% +17% +9% +1% +8% +24% +25% +17% +38% +26% +38% +35% +37% +30% +62% +34% +37% +36% +48% +34%

Price Increase Effective 7/5/82

*Based on 50- and 100-packet Equal only.

Display.   The October 31, 1982, promotion, which combined sampling and display, increased unit sales 117% over those in the control stores. The increase was greater on the 50s (180%) than the 100s (75%) (Exhibit 6.80). The January 16, 1983, period display was combined with a price reduction and achieved a similar net increase in sales of the 50s carton (Exhibit 6.81). During the April 24, 1983, period, a small store display that featured a tear-off coupon was tested. Sales in stores featuring the coupon display were approximately 70% higher for both the 50s and 100s than sales in stores without the coupon display.

Norris Frederic summarized his findings on store displays:

Equal has demonstrated considerable responsiveness to display events, with both events more than doubling sales. The coupon event was also successful at generating increased sales, although to a lesser degree than the highly visible displays. Moreover, given the

Exhibit 6.77   Equal Trial and Repeat Purchasing (10/26/81 - 5/8/83)

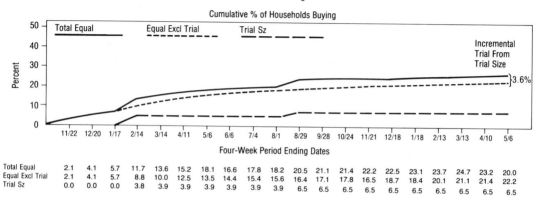

Equal Trial Purchasing
Cumulative % of Households Buying

	11/22	12/20	1/17	2/14	3/14	4/11	5/6	6/6	7/4	8/1	8/29	9/28	10/24	11/21	12/18	1/18	2/13	3/13	4/10	5/6
Total Equal	2.1	4.1	5.7	11.7	13.6	15.2	18.1	16.6	17.8	18.2	20.5	21.1	21.4	22.2	22.5	23.1	23.7	24.7	23.2	20.0
Equal Excl Trial	2.1	4.1	5.7	8.8	10.0	12.5	13.5	14.4	15.4	15.6	16.4	17.1	17.8	16.5	18.7	18.4	20.1	21.1	21.4	22.2
Trial Sz	0.0	0.0	0.0	3.8	3.9	3.9	3.9	3.9	3.9	3.9	6.5	6.5	6.5	6.5	6.5	6.5	6.5	6.5	6.5	6.5

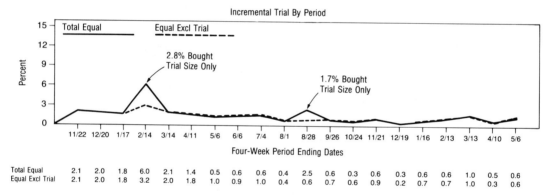

Incremental Trial By Period

	11/22	12/20	1/17	2/14	3/14	4/11	5/6	6/6	7/4	8/1	8/28	9/26	10/24	11/21	12/19	1/16	2/13	3/13	4/10	5/6
Total Equal	2.1	2.0	1.8	6.0	2.1	1.4	0.5	0.6	0.6	0.4	2.5	0.6	0.3	0.6	0.3	0.6	0.6	1.0	0.5	0.6
Equal Excl Trial	2.1	2.0	1.8	3.2	2.0	1.8	1.0	0.9	1.0	0.4	0.6	0.7	0.6	0.9	0.2	0.7	0.7	1.0	0.3	0.6

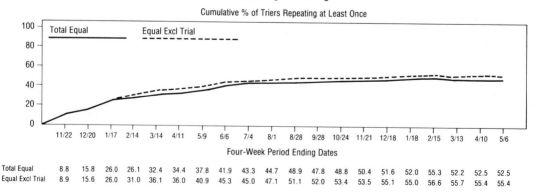

Equal Repeating Purchasing
Cumulative % of Triers Repeating at Least Once

	11/22	12/20	1/17	2/14	3/14	4/11	5/9	6/6	7/4	8/1	8/28	9/28	10/24	11/21	12/18	1/18	2/15	3/13	4/10	5/6
Total Equal	8.8	15.8	26.0	26.1	32.4	34.4	37.8	41.9	43.3	44.7	48.9	47.8	48.8	50.4	51.6	52.0	55.3	52.2	52.5	52.5
Equal Excl Trial	8.9	15.6	26.0	31.0	36.1	36.0	40.9	45.3	45.0	47.1	51.1	52.0	53.4	53.5	55.1	55.0	56.6	55.7	55.4	55.4

(continued)

Exhibit 6.77 (continued)   Equal Trial and Repeat Purchasing (10/26/81–5/8/83)

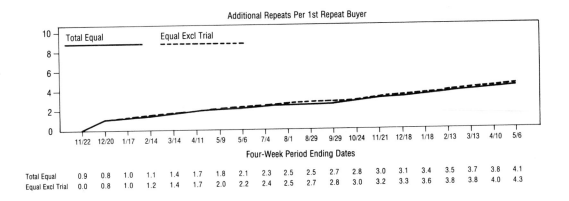

Additional Repeats Per 1st Repeat Buyer

Four-Week Period Ending Dates

	11/22	12/20	1/17	2/14	3/14	4/11	5/9	5/6	7/4	8/1	8/29	9/29	10/24	11/21	12/18	1/18	2/13	3/13	4/10	5/6
Total Equal	0.9	0.8	1.0	1.1	1.4	1.7	1.8	2.1	2.3	2.5	2.5	2.7	2.8	3.0	3.1	3.4	3.5	3.7	3.8	4.1
Equal Excl Trial	0.0	0.8	1.0	1.2	1.4	1.7	2.0	2.2	2.4	2.5	2.7	2.8	3.0	3.2	3.3	3.6	3.8	3.8	4.0	4.3

Exhibit 6.78   Comparison of First and Second Trial-Size Sales

10-Count Trial Size Sales

February 14, 1982	Total	Trial Purchases	Repeat Purchases
% of Households Purchasing	3.7	2.9	0.8
% of Trial Pack Buyers Repurchasing	45.1	37.5	72.0
August 29, 1982			
% of Households Purchasing	3.4	1.7	1.7
% of Trial Pack Buyers Repurchasing	31.6	8.3	55.3

Exhibit 6.79   Effect of Sampling on Sales

	Recipients	Nonrecipients
Cumulative percentage of household trial	25.5	25.9
Cumulative percentage of triers making at least one repeat purchase	56.0	51.9
Cumulative share of category equivalent teaspoon volume	25.2	21.8

Exhibit 6.80   Total Equal Unit Store Sales--Display vs. Non-Display Stores (9/27/82-11/28/82)*

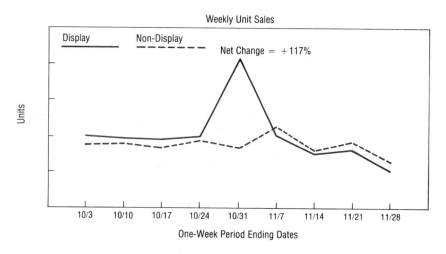

Weekly Unit Sales

Combined Markets Display vs. Nondisplay Stores

	% Change	Net % Change
Total Equal		
Display	+114	
Nondisplay	− 3	+117
Equal 50-Pack		
Display	188	
Nondisplay	+ 8	+180
Equal 100-Pack		
Display	+ 5	
Nondisplay	− 18	+ 75

*Results have been disguised.

minor changes in Equal sales during the post-promotion weeks, it appears that these increased sales primarily represented incremental sales.

Coupons. Consumers in the BehaviorScan test market received two types of coupons. Although they were indistinguishable to the recipients, the coupons were carefully coded so that researchers could determine who had received them, and within that group, who redeemed them and who did not. It was not known which households received coupons as part of the national rollout. Thus only those who redeemed the coupons could be identified. The test market coupon redemption rate could be precisely determined, whereas the redemption rate for the national coupons could only be approximated. Exhibit 6.82 presents the redemption rates of various coupon drops.

Promotion Analysis

The short-term responsiveness of Equal to price and promotion activity was estimated by IRI using

Exhibit 6.81   Total Equal Unit Store Sales--Display vs. Non-Display Stores (12/13/82-2/13/83)*

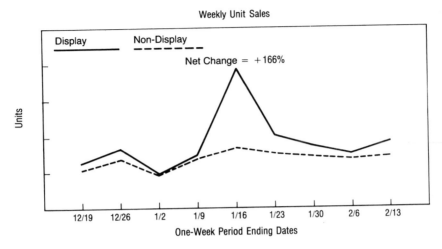

Weekly Unit Sales

Combined Markets Display vs. Nondisplay Stores

	% Change	Net % Change
Total Equal		
Display	+226	+166
Nondisplay	+ 60	
Equal 30-Pack		
Display	+240	+199
Nondisplay	+ 41	
Equal 100-Pack		
Display	+238	+147
Nondisplay	+ 91	

*Results have been disguised

multiple regression analysis. This analysis related weekly brand sales to price and promotion activity, treating each store-week as a separate observation. The analysis used data from all thirteen BehaviorScan stores in Marion and Pittsfield over the one-year period ending May 8, 1983. In all, 661 store-week observations were available.

In interpreting the results of this analysis, IRI cautioned that all effects were stated for a given week in a particular store, and were valid only within the range of observed prices. Furthermore, since the retail prices were generally fixed and the number of promotion events limited, the results of the analysis were suggestive rather than conclusive. In a report to management, Norris Frederic summarized his findings as follows:

Both the 50s and 100s exhibited only minimal sales variations due to changes in price alone; for example, a 10% price reduction alone resulted in increases of only 4% for the 50s and 8% for the 100s (see Exhibit 6.81). Furthermore, the amount of the price reduction when on promotion had a minimal short-term effect relative to the display effect.

Exhibit 6.82 Coupon Redemption*

	Total	Trial Purchases	Repeat Purchases
30¢ Direct Mail Coupon (11/81)			
% of Sample Recipients Redeeming	8.5	6.1	2.3
% of Redeemers Repurchasing	56.9	50.0	75.0
29¢ ROP Coupon (1/82)			
% of Households Redeeming	3.5	1.8	1.6
% of Redeemers Repurchasing	57.5	39.3	78.0
25¢ In-Pack Coupon (1/82)			
% of Households Redeeming	.5	.1	.5
% of Redeemers Repurchasing	75.0	50.0	78.6
40¢ ROP Coupon (6/82)			
% of Households of Redeeming	2.5	.4	2.1
% of Redeemers Repurchasing	58.4	30.8	64.1
29¢ ROP Coupon (8/82)			
% of Households Redeeming	2.9	.9	2.0
% of Redeemers Repurchasing	47.5	20.8	58.9
25¢ In-Pack Coupon (8/82)			
% of Households Redeeming	.6	.1	.5
% of Redeemers Repurchasing	76.5	100.0	73.3
$1.00 In-Store Coupon by Store (4/83)			
Coupon Stores			
% of Households Purchasing	1.1	0.2	0.9
% of Households Redeeming	0.4	0.1	0.3
Noncoupon Stores			
% of Households Purchasing	0.5	0.1	0.4

*Results have been disguised and are subject to round-off errors.

These results seemed to suggest that it is necessary to coordinate a display and/or feature activity with a promotion to generate a significant sales increase. Price reduction alone would have only a minimal impact.

These results are indicative of short-term price responses in a given store-week. Price testing conducted since the introduction of Equal has demonstrated that a long-run price sensitivity exists, at least for the 100-packet cartons.

Recent market data reflected many of the trends Frederic had observed in the test market during the time that advertising support had been weak. Sales had been slow to develop but had increased rapidly after the advertising began, especially during the periods in which a Carol Wright cooperative coupon mailing had taken place. The sales pattern had been generally increasing, but it had slowed somewhat during April and May. Although the market sales pattern appeared to be leveling off just as it had in the test market, Frederic was reluctant to conclude that Equal's introductory growth period was nearing an end.

Non-sugar sweeteners are still used on a daily basis by only 25% of American households. Advertising and brand awareness among sugar users were only 28% and 17% respectively in our November tracking study, and for sugar-substitute users only 57% and 43% respectively. With this kind of unrealized potential, it is hard to turn our attention from increasing penetration to increasing sales volume to our current customers, but maybe the cost of gaining incremental trial would be too high.

Preparation Questions

1. What are the major stategic decisions that must be made concerning the future of Equal?

2. Evaluate the reasonableness of the estimates of the effects of promotion on sales volume and price sensitivity?

3. What was learned concerning coupon effectiveness?

4. Develop a five-year plan for Equal.

5. Discuss the problems and contribution of the Equal pro forma decision model.

G. D. Searle II Decision Model

The decision model for the G. D. Searle II case is a pro forma planning model based on the promotion response function discussed in the last text section of this chapter. It also features judgmental advertising and distribution response functions. The advertising response function is judgmental because no sales response to advertising was measured in the BehaviorScan test, but it is included in the decision model because advertising would probably not be eliminated from the marketing program. The advertising response function is defined in terms of an advertising elasticity. If you don't want advertising to have any effect on sales, choose the advertising elasticity to be zero. An elasticity greater than one will give a greater-than-proportional sales response to advertising, while an elasticity of less than one will provide a less-than-proportional sales response. The BehaviorScan test provided no insight on distribution except for the estimates of distribution build, so distribution is also entered into the decision model as an elasticity defined from a base level.

The promotion response function is defined as:

$$S_k = V^* \{a - b [(P - P^0)/P^0] \times (N_d/Y)U\} \quad (6.12)$$

where

S_k is sales for the kth promotion situation

V^* is the base sales volume

P is the price

P^0 is the base price level

N_d is the number of days that situation k is in effect

Y is the number of business days in the planning period

U is the proportion of stores offering situation k

a,b are parameters determined by a least-squares fit of the data in Exhibit 6.83.

Although no data were available for a situation in which both featuring and display were operational at the same time in the Equal test market, a response function for that situation was developed by analogy with the results of other BehaviorScan tests. A graph of the promotion response functions for the various promotion situations can be seen by typing [Alt]G. The coefficients of the response functions are shown in Exhibit 6.84.

The decision model is used by determining the prices for the 50- and 100-packet cartons, an ad-

Exhibit 6.83   Average Price and Promotion Impact*

Price Change	50-Packet Cartons Average % Change in Volume			100-Packet Cartons Average % Change in Volume		
	No Promotion	Display Only	Feature Only	No Promotion	Display Only	Feature Only
+10	−4	+134	+127	−7	+96	+149
+5	−2	+138	+128	−4	+102	+158
0	—	+143	+130	—	+110	+167
−5	+2	+147	+133	+4	+118	+177
−10	+4	+152	+134	+8	+127	+188
−15	+6	+158	+135	+13	+136	+201
−20	+9	+164	+137	+18	+147	+215
No. of store-weeks	642	14	4	640	14	6

Average no-promotion price = $1.93   Average no-promotion price = $3.74

Total store-weeks = 661; one week display and feature not reported.

*Results have been disguised.

vertising budget, distribution level, and a promotion policy for each of the five years in the planning period. A promotion policy requires the specification of the type of promotion, the promotion price to be offered during the promotion period, the length of time that the promotion will be in effect, and the proportion of stores that will participate. The decision model then computes the sales forecast, contribution to profit, and return on sales over the planning period.

The decision model is very straightforward and is an example of what can be developed, with very little programming effort, from the results in a written report. The response functions are only approximate since they are developed without access to the raw data, but they are probably adequate for preliminary planning purposes. More accurate and sophisticated response functions could be developed from the data if it were available. A simple model such as this one could be useful in determining what issues should be addressed in a more

sophisticated decision model development process.

This decision model is the last one in this book, and in many ways it summarizes the approach to marketing analysis recommended here. It is very simple, it utilizes as much of the information as is readily available, it merges the results of research with the manager's decision-making framework, and it makes it easy to explore the implications of various marketing plans.

The decision model follows the same format as the other models: [Alt] M will raise a menu to help you find your way around the spreadsheet, and [Alt] P will print the results. The format of the whole spreadsheet is shown in Exhibit 6.85. The menu has six main segments:

Common Inputs. In this section of the spreadsheet, the market size, base advertising level, and advertising elasticity are defined. Base price levels,

Exhibit 6.84 Promotion Response Function Coefficients

Promotion Situation	50's		100's	
	a	b	a	b
No Promotion	1.000	−0.421	1.004	−0.835
Display only	1.430	−0.993	1.109	−1.700
Feature only	1.300	−0.993	1.684	−2.178
Both	2.000	−1.200	2.000	−2.250

wholesale margins, cost of goods sold, distribution base level and elasticity, and the share size are also entered. These values remain fixed during a particular simulation.

Strategy Sections.   There are separate marketing strategy sections for the 50- and 100-packet cartons. The advertising budget is entered in the 50s strategy screen; otherwise, the two sections require identical input information. The planning horizon includes the last half of 1983 and full years from 1984 through 1987. Your marketing plan for each year should include:

Distribution level—percent of stores stocking the size

Average price—the average non-promotion price

And for each of the three types of promotion:

Promotion days by type—the number of days of that type of promotion

Price—the average price on featured days

Participation—the percent of the retail sales volume accounted for by retail stores that will participate in the feature program.

Projection Section.   The purpose of the projection section is to establish what volume will be generated from the base price and advertising levels. These estimates are derived from the BehaviorScan

experiment and projected into the future judgmentally. The initial estimates were derived by the author, rather than by Searle management, so they shouldn't be granted unquestioning acceptance. The estimates are developed from the BehaviorScan data on the percent of households buying/month and the average buying rate/buyer. The product of these two values is the projected base volume and it is a function of the base price and advertising levels only. The projected base volume is then split into 50- and 100-packet carton volumes using the share-of-sales value entered in the common section. These two values become our base volume estimates by carton size.

Forecast Section.   This section forecasts the volume by carton size that will result from the marketing program. The forecast begins with the adjusted base-volume forecasts from the previous section and then modifies it, first for advertising and distribution and finally for the promotion program. The adjusted market volume becomes the V^* in the promotion equation (6.12). A final estimate of the volume per 1000 households is developed by summing the sales levels resulting from the four promotion conditions (including no promotion) and this value is multiplied by the number of households to compute the forecasted case sales volume.

Financial Section.   The final section of the decision model computes retail sales, factory sales, contribution to profit, and return on sales using standard financial conventions.

Exhibit 6.85 G. D. Searle II Decision Model

```
                    G. D. SEARLE & CO. (II)
                        Assumptions
                        -----------
Households:                     National Advertising:
   1983 (mm)        85.0           Average Elasticity              0.6
   1984 (mm)        86.0           Annual Base Level (000's)    $4,200
   1985 (mm)        87.0
   1986 (mm)        88.0
   1987 (mm)        89.0

                        50 packet           100 packet
Retail Margin             25.0%               25.0%
Wholesale Margin           7.0%                7.0%

Cost of Goods Sold        $0.89               $1.78
Tested Price              $1.93               $3.74
Share of Factory Sales    44.5%               55.5%
Distribution:
   Average Elasticity      0.9                 0.9
   Avg Annual Base Level   90.0%               90.0%

              Marketing Strategy (50 packet cartons)

                    83II      84       85       86       87
Advertising         -----    -----    -----    -----    -----
   ($x1000)         $2,100   $4,200   $5,000   $5,500   $4,000

50 Packet Cartons
Distribution         90.0%    90.0%    90.0%    90.0%    90.0%
Ave Retail Price    $1.93    $1.95    $1.99    $2.05    $2.10
Display only days      5        5        5        5        5
   Price            $1.89    $1.89    $1.89    $1.89    $1.89
   Participation      40%      40%      40%      40%      40%
Feature only days     10       10       10       10       10
   Price            $1.89    $1.89    $1.89    $1.89    $1.89
   Participation      40%      40%      40%      40%      40%
Disp & Feat days      10       20       10        5        5
   Price            $1.79    $1.89    $1.75    $1.79    $1.79
   Participation      30%      35%      40%      45%      50%
```

(continued)

Exhibit 6.85   (continued) G. D. Searle II Decision Model

```
                   Marketing Strategy (100 packet cartons)

                   83II        84        85        86        87
                   -----     -----     -----     -----     -----
Distribution       90.0%     93.0%     94.0%     95.0%     95.0%
Ave Retail Price   $3.34     $3.40     $3.45     $3.50     $3.55
Display only days     10        15        15        20        20
 Price             $3.29     $3.19     $3.19     $3.19     $3.10
 Participation       30%       35%       40%       50%       60%
Feature only days     20        30        35        35        35
 Price             $3.29     $3.25     $3.19     $3.15     $3.15
 Participation       35%       40%       50%       60%       70%
Disp & Feat Days      10        10        15        15        15
 Price             $3.10     $3.10     $3.10     $3.10     $3.10

Participation        40%       40%       40%       40%       40%
```

```
                        Volume Projections
          (100 equivalent teaspoon volume per 1000 households)
                   Input average values per month
                      83II      1984      1985      1986      1987
                      -----     -----     -----     -----     -----
Based on Exhibit 2
Percent of HH buying/mo
 Percent of HH Buying/mo   2.10%    2.40%     2.75%     3.00%     3.50%
Average Buying Rate (100
 Eq. tsp. per HH-month)    1.80     1.90      2.00      2.10      2.20
Projected Base Volume (a) 226.80   547.20    660.00    756.00    924.00
--------------------
Note:    (a) Based on tested price, base advertising, base distribution,
             and no promotion.
```

```
                        Volume Projections
                 (In 100 equivalent teaspoons/1000 HH)

                         83II      1984      1985      1986      1987
50 Packet Cartons        -----     -----     -----     -----     -----

  Projected Base Volume   100.93    243.50    293.70    336.42    411.18
  Advertising Effect        1.00      1.00      1.11      1.18      0.97
  Distribution Effect       1.00      1.00      1.00      1.00      1.00
  Adjusted Base Volume    100.93    243.50    326.09    395.50    399.32
  Price and promotion effects
     display only           1.87      2.26      3.02      3.67      3.70
     feature only           3.40      4.11      5.50      6.67      6.74
     display/feature        4.02     11.03      8.80      5.93      6.66
     no promotion          95.17    232.45    311.65    375.13    374.19
                          -----     -----     -----     -----     -----
  Adjusted Promo Volume   104.46    249.85    328.98    391.40    391.29
  Cases (1200eqt/1000HH)    8.71     20.82     27.41     32.62     32.61
```

(continued)

Exhibit 6.85   (continued) G. D. Searle II Decision Model

```
                    Volume Projections
              (In 100 equivalent teaspoons/1000 HH)

                      83II    1984    1985    1986    1987
100 Packet Cartons    -----   -----   -----   -----   -----

  Base Vol(100eqt/1000HH)  125.87  303.70  366.30  419.58  512.82
  Advertising Effect         1.00    1.00    1.11    1.18    0.97
  Distribution Effect        1.00    1.03    1.04    1.05    1.05
  Adjusted Base Volume     125.87  312.79  422.93  517.86  522.86
  Price and promotion Effects
    display only             3.16    7.13   11.02   22.49   28.07
    feature only            10.92   23.62   47.39   70.45   82.98
```

References and Background Readings

Farris, Paul W., and Robert D. Buzzell. "Why Advertising and Promotion Costs Vary: Some Cross-Sectional Analysis." *Journal of Marketing*, Vol. 43, No. 4 (Fall 1979), pp. 112-122.

Lilien, Gary L. "Keeping Up with the Marketing Joneses." *Industrial Marketing* (March 1980).

Lodish, Leonard M. "CALLPLAN: An Interactive Salesman's Call Planning System." *Management Science*, Vol. 18, No. 4 Pt. II (December 1971), pp. 25-40.

7

An Approach to Analytical Marketing Decision Making

The most surprising conclusion that emerges from the analysis of the cases in this book is not that poor research makes no impact on decision making, which is obvious, but rather that a lot of *good* research also has little impact on decision making. Most of the cases feature state-of-the-art marketing research and model building done competently—certainly at the better levels of current practice. The cases provide strong evidence of the wide range of research capabilities available to the decision maker who wants objective information about the marketplace. During our study of the cases, however, it became apparent that in no instance did the decision makers utilize research information to its full potential. The marketing research in the cases, while good and soundly conceived, was subject to some recurring problems:

1. The researchers and decision makers failed to develop an explicit, detailed conceptualization of the decision situation that included both marketing and financial considerations, defined the research needs, and integrated the research results into the decision-making process.

2. The research was not completed in time to impact the decision.

3. The results of the research were not integrated into the decision maker's quantitative decision-making framework and so were not presented in a form that was useful to the decision maker.

These problems are often caused by two basic shortcomings: (1) inadequate managerial participation, particularly at the stage of problem definition, research design, and implementation; and (2) a research design that is not appropriate for the decision situation in terms of the scale of the effort and/or the time required to do it.

This author believes that it is possible for most managers, even if they are not technically trained, to overcome these problems through effective managerial involvement in the research and analysis process. A few key concepts, tools, and considerations emerge from the discussion of the cases that suggest an approach to marketing analysis that would allow a decision maker effectively to use the resources of marketing research, marketing science, and economic theory to expand greatly the analytical power available to them. In this summary chapter we will integrate the experience gained in the case situations into a general analytical process.

The analytical process recommended here is very simple and straightforward. It is important to recognize that, even though many research techniques are quite sophisticated, the technical demands on the decision maker in helping to design the research and integrate findings into the decision-making process are relatively minor. The analytical process proposed in this chapter is based on a few fundamental, nontechnical concepts that are easy to understand and within the reach of most marketing managers, regardless of the level of their technical training:

1. The managerial analysis of a decision situation must integrate both the financial and marketing considerations into a single conceptualization of the deci-

sion situation, one that explicitly connects marketing action, market response, and financial success criteria *before* substantial research is undertaken.

2. The goal of research should be to develop market response functions. The nontechnical manager evaluates market response functions by considering specification, estimation, and data foundation.

3. Research should result in the development of an analytical tool that provides the decision maker with the capability to explore the implications of alternative marketing strategies.

4. The scope of the decision model should be appropriate for the decision situation.

5. Using the decision model in concert with its developers, the decision maker should develop his or her own decisions rather than relying on recommendations by the researchers.

In other words, a sound analytical process must pay special attention to defining research needs, integrating research results into the decision making process, and providing an analytical *tool* rather than an *answer*. (See Exhibit 7.1.)

This analytical decision making process is more extensive conceptually than that used in any of the cases, but it does not require substantial increases in expenditures for technical support. In particular, although substantial changes are suggested in the type and scope of activities that both precede and follow a market research project, the development of the preliminary and empirical decision models are quite small development projects.

Each of the research studies featured in the cases was preceded by some consideration of what information was needed, how that information could be obtained, and how the information would be used, but there are some major differences between the process shown in Exhibit 7.1 and what happened in the cases. None of the decision makers in the cases had decision models like the ones in this book available to them, for example. Decision models are the critical element in the decision-making process recommended here, and a number of procedural and philosophical assumptions are implicit:

Research can best achieve a direct impact on decision making if the results of the research, in particular response functions, are integrated into the manager's existing quantitative decision making framework in the form of a decision-model.

Decision models should be simple enough that the decision maker can personally investigate those issues that are important.

Decision models must include those factors that are important to the decision maker, whether or not they have been researched.

The development of decision models should *precede as well as follow* marketing research.

Exhibit 7.1 Analytical Marketing Decision-Making Process

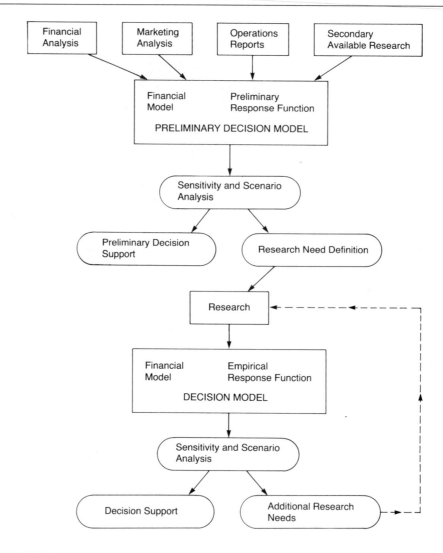

The decision model is used to define future research needs as well as to provide decision support.

Market research and decision models should affect decision making through the process of analysis and the learning that results from it, rather than by providing recommendations.

These are very important assumptions if market research is to have an impact on marketing decision making.

The Preliminary Decision Model

Our case analyses revealed a general inadequacy in situation analysis, defining the research needs, and planning how the research results were to be used; and we observed that, as a result, the research had less impact on decision making than would have been desirable. Therefore, one of the major considerations in designing a more advanced framework for analysis must be a more comprehensive and practical approach to problem definition and market research design, and at the same time the revised process should not add appreciably to the cost and time required for research projects. This need can be met by developing a preliminary decision model that integrates the marketing and financial considerations, and by doing sensitivity analysis before undertaking substantial marketing research or model building. The essential features of a useful preliminary decision model are:

It integrates the marketing plan with a financial model that expresses the decision maker's decision criteria.

It uses explicit, though largely judgmental, mathematical expressions of the relationships between the marketing plan and market response.

It uses readily available information to estimate parameters for the judgmental response functions.

It is used to determine what information is necessary to choose between alternatives and define the marketing research needs.

The purpose of the preliminary decision model is to explore the decision process *before* extensive commitments are made to specific alternatives, expensive primary research, or substantial model development. The amount of time and effort devoted to developing the preliminary decision model should be modest.

The CableShop case provided a dramatic example of the need for preliminary decision model development. It featured an extensive marketing research project, possibly the most expensive of any in the book, but unfortunately, the research was designed and executed before the essential information requirements for the success of the business were defined. The CableShop financial spreadsheet model detailed the costs of operating the business, but provided no marketing insight. Reconsidering our analysis of this case in the light of the analytical process proposed in Exhibit 7.1, we see that some essential steps were omitted and others occurred in the wrong order. As a result, when we tried to develop a marketing plan, we did not find the information that we needed in the research results and found no use for the results that *were* available.

Using the analytical process defined in Exhibit 7.1, the key elements of the CableShop marketing program and the advertisers' buying process would have been identified in order to define an explicit, conceptual link between marketing action and market response. This market response conceptualization would have identified the advertiser's wants and needs from CableShop, compared Cable-Shop with existing media alternatives, and provided the foundation for a preliminary decision model. If this decision model had been used for scenario and sensitivity analysis, the CableShop marketers would have identified the important information needs, and the research could have been designed to obtain the information.

Development of a preliminary decision model would have taken only a few hours, and the insight gained through its development and use would have shaped the development of both marketing and marketing research plans so that they addressed the essential business questions. This was not done in the Cable-Shop case, however, and marketing, finance, and research considerations were never integrated and neither the research nor the financial spreadsheet had an impact on decision making.

Using the Preliminary Decision Model

If the marketing, financial, and research considerations in a decision situation are integrated into a single conceptual model, the resulting preliminary decision model is a powerful decision-making tool with a wide range of applications. The development of the preliminary decision model forces the decision maker to approach analysis of the decision situation more rigorously and to be more disciplined in thinking across functional areas that are too often treated in isolation.

The use of the preliminary decision model for sensitivity and scenario analysis to determine the key success factors in a decision situation results in a better understanding of a decision situation, even if no further research or model development is undertaken. Sensitivity and scenario analysis using the preliminary decision model also have the critical effect of demonstrating the need for future research and for the development of a more rigorous model.

Using the Preliminary Decision Model for Decision Support.   The preliminary decision model is used to identify those issues in a decision situation that are critical to making a decision and to the development of rigorous, integrative thinking; however, one should be careful not to attach too much credibility to the forecasts made with it. It is very easy to fall into the trap of thinking that the neatly arranged figures that so easily emerge from a preliminary decision model are real. The goal of preliminary decision analysis is to determine what is important rather than to forecast.

There is a strong contrast between the CableShop's naive financial planning model and the preliminary decision model in the ODI case. The Cableshop model neither integrated the marketing and financial aspects of the business plan nor was it based on objective information from the extensive marketing research program. It provided no valuable input to decision making. The Optical Distortion, Inc. model, which was based only on secondary data about the size and number of chicken farms and a conceptualization of the adoption process, involved no primary research at all, but still provided considerable planning insight. The ODI spreadsheet was a preliminary decision model, while the CableShop spreadsheet, despite the extensive marketing research done by the company, remained only a naive financial model. Using the ODI decision model, we were able to learn a lot about the importance of customer acceptance rates, the size of the sales force, and the marketing policies that would be necessary for this product to be successful.

There were, of course, many inputs to the ODI decision model that could only be guessed at, but through sensitivity analysis, the profitability associated with various levels of these inputs could be identified. The ODI model incorporated a judgmental marketing response function that integrated the marketing plan and the financial analysis of the decision situation. The decision model was useful for decision making and was useful in defining research needs.

Using the Preliminary Decision Model to Define Research Needs.   A second use of the preliminary decision model is to define the need for marketing research, how the information gained from the research will be used, and to determine the value of the research. Using a preliminary decision model that explicitly anticipates market research information, one can be sure that the research will provide the estimates that are needed to make decisions and the importance of the information can be determined through sensitivity analysis.

This process is very similar in spirit to the description of algebra that we all heard in high school: "In algebra you try to find out a number by first calling it X and then pretending that you know what it is." Developing a preliminary decision model based upon the anticipated output of a market research project doesn't require the particular measurements that will be obtained by the research; it only requires the conceptual model upon which the research is based. To evaluate the potential value of a particular marketing research project, all we have to do is incorporate the conceptual model in a preliminary decision model and pretend that we know the values that will be estimated by the research. If we express the decision situation and the market research needs so clearly and precisely that a preliminary decision model can be built that incorporates them, then through sensitivity and scenario analysis we will be able to see what factors strongly influence the choice between alternatives. As a consequence, we will only research critical decision factors and we will know in advance exactly how the research data will be used and how they will affect our decisions.

It was not difficult in our discussion of the ODI case to determine ODI's most important information needs. Our use of the preliminary decision model had shown us clearly what we didn't know and what was important to determine. We needed to know how much effort it took to sell to a farm, what our success rate would be in obtaining trial, what proportion of farms would become adopters, and how long it would take. Considering ODI's limited resources and the type of information that was needed, it was clear that the best thing for ODI to do was to begin a limited market introduction and gather the necessary data from preliminary operations. An expensive marketing research project to determine farmer acceptance levels would have been too expensive and too time consuming to have been feasible. Keeping careful sales records would provide the information that was needed, and we knew exactly how we would use the information when we had it. This information would have provided better estimates of the transition matrices and a more empirically based decision model. Using this decision model, early indications of success or failure and of problem areas in the selling process could have been identified, their results forecast, and more realistic plans developed. A great deal of decision support was obtained through this simple preliminary decision model and the means of upgrading the quality of its estimates was readily apparent.

This approach is valuable in evaluating more formal research projects. Suppose we were considering using one of the research techniques described in the cases for another product—for example, a product sold by the company that will give you your first job after graduation. The case decision model could be used as the basis for a preliminary decision model to evaluate the importance and potential value of the research for the new product. All that would be required would be a modification of the financial model to express your new product situation. You could then use the conceptual model to see whether or not that research would help you to choose between the alternatives being considered.

This could easily be done, for example, in deciding whether or not the ASSESSOR model would be useful for Equal, or Tang, or any other frequently purchased consumer product. The important thing in determining whether or not the ASSESSOR model would be useful for any particular product situation is that market share can be estimated reasonably and usefully as a function of trial, first repeat, and retention; not what particular values might be obtained for the parameters from the actual research. This discussion suggests a general method for deciding whether or not to undertake any research project:

1. Integrate the response function that will result from the research into a financial model of the decision situation, thereby producing a preliminary decision model.

2. Define scenarios that express each of the alternatives you are considering.

3. Perform a sensitivity analysis for the judgmentally estimated parameters for each of your alternatives.

4. Using the results of the sensitivity and scenario analyses, determine whether or not the estimates that will be obtained from the research will enable you to choose between the alternatives.

If you can't complete the first step for any reason—because you don't have the financial model expressing your marketing plan, or you don't know the response function underlying the research, or the research doesn't fit your conceptual framework—then either you're not ready to undertake the research or it doesn't suit your needs.

If you *can* build the preliminary decision model, the next level of inquiry is whether or not the research will provide information that will allow you to choose between the alternatives that are being considered. This analysis should probably include the expected performance of the alternatives under different possible market scenarios. If the sensitivity analysis performed on the values to be estimated by the research doesn't discriminate between alternatives, then the research (which after all only provides estimates of the parameters rather than any new conceptualization), will not provide information that will allow you to decide between the alternatives and should not be undertaken. If the sensitivity and scenario analyses *do* discriminate between alternatives, you can determine both the range of alternatives that should be tested and the accuracy of the parameter estimates that will be required. The potential value of the research can be estimated by comparing the financial payoff for each of the alternatives across the reasonable range of values that the estimated parameters could be expected to exhibit. The difference between the highest and the lowest payoffs in this analysis is the most that the research is worth to you. This step will also provide insight into the range within which the estimates must be accurate, since the research must discriminate between the alternatives or it has no value. Suppose, for example, that alternative A is preferred to alternative B if the trial rate is 15% and alternative B is preferred if the trial rate is 20%. In order for research on the trial rate to be of value, it must discriminate between 15% and 20%, and it must do so at a cost that is less than the difference between the payoffs that will result from these two trial values. If it can do both things, then the research should be undertaken. If not, either the research costs more than it is worth, or the research that can be afforded will not allow you to make the decision that needs to be made. In either case, the research shouldn't be undertaken.

Design and Execution of the Marketing Research

If all the steps we've described in developing and using a preliminary decision model have been rigorously followed, it is relatively simple to decide whether or not a particular marketing research program will provide the necessary information. It is also very likely that the results of a marketing research study, thus defined, will have a significant impact on decision making, since the research was undertaken in the first place to provide information that was identified as critical in the decision process. It is not always possible to define marketing research needs so precisely, since a certain amount of research is necessary to develop a basic understanding of the market and consumer needs, but it is safe to say that far too much research is done without adequate preparation and the impact of the resulting research on decision making is destined to be informal and vague at best and, more often than not, inconsequential.

Since the preliminary decision model expresses both the decision framework and the framework for utilizing the research, the manager can easily see how the research will be used and what information needs to be obtained. If the problem and research definitions have progressed to this stage, the managerial functions required in designing the research have been completed and the remaining research design problems are technical and require the work of a technically competent research staff or consultant. Perhaps the most readily apparent example of the use of this design philosophy is associated with research projects that use a simple, explicit conceptual response function like the ASSESSOR model, but even in the CableShop case, for which it was not reasonable to expect a formal response function to emerge from the exploratory research, it is still easy to see how the research could have been more useful.

The two keys to effectively using market research for decision support are to obtain market response functions and to integrate them into decision models.

The details of the technical development of the market response function are generally beyond the capability of the non–technically trained decision maker, but there are three basic areas in which the decision maker can evaluate the appropriateness and reliability of research:

Analyzing the decision situation, including both marketing and financial considerations, while sensitive to the importance of the decision, the available time to analyze the situation, and the value of the information.

Evaluating the model to ensure that it mathematically expresses the relationship between marketing action and market response at a meaningful level. The managerial considerations for evaluating models are: *specification*—the shape of the response function; and *estimation*—how the parameters of the response function are determined.

Understanding the data foundation; that is, the nature of the data from which the models are estimated.

In the course of analyzing the cases, you were introduced to some of the more prominent commercially available research services. While this experience will not make you an expert, the introduction is certainly more extensive than you could obtain short of buying their services yourself.

A broad exposure to marketing research and model development in different marketing decision situations was also provided by the case collection. The case situations were organized according to the stage of the new product development process because of the similar nature of the decisions to be made at each stage, the similarity of the types of data that were likely to be available, and the type and amount of effort appropriate for decision model development. An overview of the types of models and databases covered in the cases is provided in Exhibits 7.2 and 7.3.

Exhibit 7.2   Types of Models Featured in the Case Discussions

Model Type/Case	Model Description
Naive Marketing Models	
CableShop	Financial spreadsheet
Heuristic Models	
Optical Distortion, Inc.	Modified Markov adoption model
G.D. Searle II	Response functions based on price elasticity measurements
Econometric and Statistical Models	
General Foods	Econometric models
UDIA	Experimental design (ANOVA)
G.D. Searle I	Experimental design (analysis of covariance)
Johnson Wax Company	ASSESSOR, factor analysis, perceptual mapping
Descriptive Decision Calculus Models	
Johnson Wax Company	ASSESSOR
Clark Equipment Co.	Market simulation analysis based on trade-off analysis
Convection Corporation	ADVISOR (cross-section regression)
Normative Decision Calculus Model	
Syntex Laboratories	"Strategic level" CALLPLAN

Development of the Empirical Decision Model

If you have followed the steps of developing a preliminary decision model, using it to define the information needed, and doing research to obtain the empirical estimates that were identified in the sensitivity and scenario analysis, then the upgrading of the preliminary decision model to an empirically based decision model can be extremely simple. Sometimes it only requires the substitution of the objective, research-based parameter estimates for the judgmental estimates in the response function. For example, if we had modified the Johnson Wax ASSESSOR decision model for use as a preliminary decision model for G. D. Searle's Equal, the development of an empirical decision model would only involve entering a few values into the response functions: advertising-based trial, first repeat, and switchback, as well as the same values for samples.

Exhibit 7.3   Types of Data Featured in the Case Discussions

Types of Data/Case	Data Description
Judgmental Data	
Optical Distortion, Inc.	Personal judgment
Syntex Laboratories I	Group judgments gathered in a Delphi-type process
Secondary Data	
Optical Distortion, Inc.	Government industry data
CableShop	Industry association data
Syndicated Survey and Audit Data	
General Foods	Nielsen retail audits
Convection Corporation	ADVISOR project, cooperative industry research
Syntex Laboratories II	IMS syndicated pharmaceutical industry data
Custom Survey Data	
CableShop	Extensive consumer survey
Johnson Wax Company	ASSESSOR (mall intercept, controlled environment questionnaire)
Clark Equipment	Trade-off analysis questioning
Designed Experiment Data	
UDIA	Multiple-city store audit data
Adtel, Ltd.	Split-cable, consumer diary panel
Information Resources, Inc.	BehaviorScan (targetable household experiment, electronic scanner data)
G.D. Searle I–II	BehaviorScan

Frequently, however, research has revealed more about the decision situation or additional issues have been raised that need to be considered, so that it is often desirable at this stage to modify or add to the scope and capabilities of the preliminary decision model. Also, the intention of the preliminary decision model is to provide a useful tool with minimum time and effort. It may prove useful at this later stage to make the decision model more powerful analytically by: (1) adding a more user-friendly interface so that managers not intensively involved in the development process can use the decision model, or (2) including more sophisticated ancillary mathematical capabilities such as optimization or goal seeking. It might also be necessary to move the decision model from a personal computer to a mainframe computer with greater computational capabilities, although the power of personal computers is evolving so fast that this may not be necessary for long.

Occasionally the response model derived during the research will need to be modified because the decision model must address issues different from those addressed by the research model, or because the research version of the decision model won't fit on a personal computer. We saw both of these situations in the decision model developed for the Clark III case. The trade-off analysis program for this case would not fit on a commonly configured IBM/PC (although it does fine on an IBM/AT). The research version was much too cumbersome to investigate the various price policy, product line, and competitive response scenarios that we wanted to consider, so the decision model featured a set of response functions that were derived from simulation runs of the research model. The decision model that was developed addressed a much smaller set of possibilities than did the research model, but it addressed the managerial issues that had been identified as important much more conveniently.

The sales force strategy model (SSM) described in the Syntex Laboratories I case is quite different from the decision model we used in analyzing the case, even though the same response function specifications were used. The sales force strategy model was designed to find efficiently the optimum sales force size and allocation, but it could not be used to evaluate a non-optimal sales force allocation. Since the SSM model did not incorporate all of the decision maker's considerations, it is reasonable to expect the decision maker to want to modify the optimal solution to the mathematical problem to recognize these other considerations. The SSM model couldn't be used in this way, so in order to incorporate the results of the research into the Syntex decision model, the SSM model had to be modified. Since the optimal solution was not of primary interest to us (and it was available in the case), it was not necessary to use the algorithm used by the research model to find the optimal solution in the personal computer decision model. The marginal response to change in the sales force allocation for each product and specialty was substituted for the optimization algorithm to make it possible for the decision maker to see what the economic impact of changes in the sales force size and allocation would be. Using this decision model, the decision maker could see what the most economically efficient changes were, but was not forced to make them if there were other factors to consider.

A final key point to remember is that even though we are terming this decision model an *empirically based decision model* (in contrast to the preliminary decision model), it probably still contains a number of judgmentally estimated response functions and parameters. In fact, it may well be that additional research could further improve the decision model. The empirical decision model, even after research findings are incorporated, should be used, just as the preliminary decision model was used, to define the need for further empirical research as well as for decision support.

The decision model that accompanies the Johnson Wax II case is actually a second-generation decision model. The first version of this decision model did not include a response function connecting gross rating points and awareness, which meant that the user had to guess what that relationship might be. Use of that model demonstrated the need for an advertising response function. Professor Subrata Sen of Yale University provided the graph found in Exhibit 4.49, which provides the basis for the informally estimated advertising awareness response function in the Johnson Wax II decision model. While the inclusion of this response function in the decision model is a great improvement, a logical next research project for Johnson Wax would have been to determine a more accurate, empirically based advertising expenditure-awareness relationship based on their past product introductions.

Using the Empirical Decision Model

Like the preliminary decision support model, the empirical decision model should be used for two purposes: (1) for decision support through scenario analysis, and (2) to define what information needs to be obtained through further marketing research and model building. Our analysis of the cases and use of the decision models enables us to say something about the most effective way to do these two things.

Sensitivity analysis using the preliminary decision model is primarily done to determine what the important factors are that influence a decision. When used for this purpose, sensitivity analysis involves varying both parameter values and expected "states of the world." This type of sensitivity analysis is not a very intellectual activity, since one simply plugs in a reasonable range of values and observes the response. A systematic collection of the results of such runs across parameters can lead to an estimation of the importance of each variable if all else remains equal. What one hopes to find in such analysis is that the decision to be made does not depend too strongly on the particular value that some of the variables might take on, even though those variables seem important in the conceptualization of the decision situation.

This sensitivity analysis can easily be relegated to the computer to do, using various simulation routines. In programming languages like BASIC or Fortran, a simple "do" loop will work; and even using Lotus 1-2-3, it can be done with the "table" commands.

A major limitation of sensitivity analysis is that if the various factors do not operate independently, you should not expect sensitivity analysis on one variable at a time to provide a definitive understanding of the possible situations in which the decision will be made. We observed this situation in the Clark Equipment I case, in which a sensitivity analysis had been performed on each of the product attributes separately (see Exhibit 4.66), but the consultants cautioned Clark management about placing too much emphasis on these results. That sensitivity analysis, although not definitive, was very important because it reduced the variables we needed to consider to price and type of transmission.

However, it soon became apparent that the sensitivity analysis did not provide the necessary information to develop a product line and pricing strategy in a competitive environment. What was required was the thoughtful definition of a number of situation descriptions in which the values of the different parameters and market conditions were coordinated. We called this kind of thoughtful situation definition *scenario analysis*. It is a very powerful analytical tool because the definition of the situations demands rigorous thinking so that analysis can provide us the opportunity to explore the implications of our decisions. The difference between sensitivity analysis and scenario analysis is illustrated by the experience of a prominent financial analyst who was called by a client to discuss a serious cash flow problem:

> I asked my client how they could be in such a serious situation when they had such extensive cash flow models. Hadn't they done sensitivity analysis on factors X, Y, and Z? They replied that of course they had, but they hadn't expected all of these factors to take on unfavorable levels at the same time! In fact, those three factors were closely related and could be expected to respond similarly to environmental conditions in general.

This anecdote illustrates one of the problems with sensitivity analysis and one of the reasons that scenario analysis is so important. Because the marketplace consists of complex, interrelated forces, one must consider what the likely ranges and relationships between important factors will be.

Scenario analysis consists of conceptualizing the decision situation as a whole and deciding how the important variables will vary *as a set* in different situations. This technique was used to generate the collection of simulation runs that provided the exhibits in Clark Equipment II. If we had wished to investigate three different market sizes, four Clark product lines, and five competitive environments using sensitivity analysis, we would have needed 60 simulation runs instead of the 20 we used. Forty of those runs would have been unreasonable, and if we had used their results, they would have been misleading. For example, Clark's highest contribution to profit would probably have resulted from a simulation run in which the market size was the largest, the Japanese had not entered the market, Hyster had not expanded its product line, and Clark's prices were high. Such a scenario isn't reasonable, since the large market size would have occurred only if the Japanese entered the market at the same time Clark and Hyster lowered their prices and introduced new products.

Scenario analysis is the most useful kind of simulation analysis because of the thought that goes into the design of the scenarios. The process of deciding what market conditions will be, what competitive response to expect, and so on, forces us to consider different strategies and market situations and keeps our thinking from becoming stale and rigid.

Above all, one should keep in mind that both scenario and sensitivity analyses are primarily done to learn about the decision situation. If after the analysis has been done, a strategy emerges that appears to be superior to the others, so much the better. But if the decision maker makes a decision that is not exactly like any of the alternatives considered, but that emerges from his or her enhanced understanding of the situation, the research, model development, and analysis effort has still been successful.

The Importance of Estimation

One of the key things to learn about the creation of decision models is that time spent on providing reliable estimates for model parameters greatly reduces the amount of sensitivity analysis that needs to be done and increases one's confidence in the results. It's also true that conceptual frameworks that relate one variable with another greatly reduce the amount of sensitivity analysis and scenario analysis that needs to be done. In general, time spent thinking about the problem, defining the approach, and obtaining estimates for model parameters is much more productive than time spent in sensitivity analysis. The proper use of sensitivity analysis is to estimate the sensitivity of a decision to those conditions that cannot be predicted; it is not a substitute for thinking.

Consider, for example, the last case that we analyzed, G. D. Searle II. Did you spend most of your time looking for estimates for the parameters using the BehaviorScan test data, or did you spend your time doing sensitivity analysis, looking for the best advertising budget or the optimum price discount? Sensitivity analysis on the advertising elasticity to find the optimum advertising level was a useless exercise for two reasons: first of all, the advertising function was a simple constant elasticity model that was judgmentally estimated—no advertising effect was found in the BehaviorScan test, so there was no empirical basis for the elasticity used. Secondly, given the elasticity and the unit profit margin, you could directly compute the optimal advertising budget. Similarly, the optimal price cut on promotion can be computed given the elasticity, so you don't need to do sensitivity analysis to find that either. You were better off to look for estimates of the base response levels and obtain other parameter estimates from the research. The most interesting sensitivity analysis I've seen in this case was to determine the value of a unit level of store participation in a promotion, since knowing this allows you to put a value on a sales force push to obtain retailer cooperation.

The Decision Model Development Process

One of the key features of the process outlined in Exhibit 7.1 is the dual use of decision models for decision support and for designing research to improve the decision model. These two roles are shown as outputs of both the preliminary and empirical decision model, together with a feedback loop to research design, research, and the empirical decision model. None of the cases that we studied utilized this entire process. However, considering the body of the cases as a whole, we can identify research and decision model development efforts that were representative of the different stages of the process, and that, when considered together, demonstrate a rational development process.

Beginning with the CableShop case, which displayed a reasonable financial cost model of the decision situation, we would observe that, although that model did not provide marketing insight or the foundation for research, it did provide a reasonable starting point as the existing quantitative framework of the manager. The ODI decision model provided an example of the next logical step in the development of a stronger analytical approach by:

1. Expressing a marketing plan, the consumer's response to it, and a judgmentally based market response function

2. Integrating the response function into the existing quantitative framework to provide a managerially useful tool

3. Using modest research on secondary data to provide initial parameter estimates

4. Giving the manager a model that provides an extensive understanding of the decision situation and initial estimates of the initial price, sales force size, sales policy, and critical success factors

5. Providing a decision model that clearly defines information needs for future planning and model development

These two cases together demonstrate the development of the preliminary decision model. The remainder of the cases all dealt with the research step and the acquisition of objective marketing research information. The amount of research, the time and money spent doing it, and its appropriateness for the decision-making task were considered in all of our discussions. A market research survey like the one done in the CableShop case (but addressing the right issues), the econometric models of the effect of advertising on sales in the General Foods case, and the use of the ADVISOR model in the Convection Corporation case were all examples of marketing research efforts that gathered valuable information that increased the objectivity and reliability of the preliminary decision model. The latter two of these research efforts were quite inexpensive, quickly done research efforts that provided estimates of important factors in the decision model.

Some of the other research efforts provided stronger conceptualizations and more precisely defined market response functions than the previous research efforts. The ASSESSOR model in the Johnson Wax cases and the trade-off analysis model in the Clark Equipment cases required more time and expense than did the types of research just mentioned, but the strong market response conceptualizations are easily adapted to decision model development. It is likely that, having performed an ASSESSOR test at the pre–test market stage, the need for accurate trial and repeat measurements for various market segments would be developed and would become a next priority, and a BehaviorScan test market similar to that in the G. D. Searle I case could provide them.

A final step in this developmental sequence might be to recognize that the decision models discussed so far were descriptive rather than normative. That is, the decision models provide an estimate of what the results of a marketing plan would be, but they do not provide optimal marketing plans or even information about the best direction of change. The sales force strategy model (SSM) for Syntex Laboratories was a normative model that provided an optimal sales force plan through the use of economic theory. Both the research version, which found the optimal sales force size and allocation, and the managerial decision model, which provided the optimal direction for change, greatly reduced the need for sensitivity analysis through the application of economic theory. Using these models, one could reallocate sales force efforts to improve performance and could know when the best possible allocation had been found. In other words, the theory in these models provided both the best direction of change and a stopping rule. We knew when we were finished in using the SSM model, while we just stopped analyzing when we were satisfied (or worn out) with the other models.

This composite scenario of the development of an analytical approach to decision making provides an example of how a decision support system might evolve in natural steps from a simple financial spreadsheet to a powerful analytical tool. The evolution occurs in modest increments that, while strengthening the power of the decision model, still provide valuable decision support at each step. This developmental scenario is presented in an overview schematic in Exhibit 7.4.

A final example of how a decision support system might grow is apparent if we reconsider the Syntex Laboratories case. As you know, the personal computer decision model that we used was developed *after* the research model described in the case. Let's suppose, for the sake of demonstration, that both the personal computer and Lotus 1-2-3 had been available at the time that Syntex was deciding whether to undertake the development of the SSM model. The PC Syntex decision model can easily be developed in a version that estimates the parameters of the response functions from managerial estimates. This version of the decision model would have provided a preliminary decision model that could have been used to determine whether or not the SSM approach would have value at Syntex. This little model could have been developed in only a few hours. Sensitivity analysis using this preliminary model would have shown that substantial profits were available from an increased sales force size over a wide range of possible response functions. Uncertainty about the response functions would then have led to the research approach that provided response estimates representing the consensus of managerial judgment described in the case. Having obtained these consensus judgmental response functions, the parameters would have been plugged into the preliminary PC decision model, providing the decision model that we used.

Considerable uncertainty about the judgmental response functions still existed in our discussion of the Syntex I case, so an attempt was made to compare them with empirical response functions that could be derived from secondary data in the Syntex II case. Further development of the decision model would result from the development of a sales call reporting system, and perhaps an experiment could be designed to provide the necessary data to estimate the response functions using empirical data. Following this process, the decision model would be strengthened over time while still providing the best available decision support at all times during the process.

Exhibit 7.4   Developmental Sequence of the Case Studies

Decision Model Stage	Case	Incremental Contribution
Naive financial model	CableShop	Manager's existing quantitative framework
Preliminary decision model	Optical Distortion, Inc.	Judgmental response function, marketing plan integration
Preliminary empirical model	General Foods, Convection Corporation	Parameterization of basic response function using operations and secondary data
Empirical decision model	Johnson Wax, Clark Equipment	Strong conceptual model parameterization using secondary experimental data
Empirical decision model	G.D. Searle	Extensive, time-consuming experimental research for marketing mix testing
Empirical decision model	Syntex Laboratories	Normative decision model providing direction of optimal change based on economic theory

Summary

The analytical decision process outlined in this chapter provides a powerful design for the use of marketing research for decision making that is innovative, evolutionary, and pragmatic. By following this analytical process, a decision maker can both strengthen the sophistication of marketing analysis and improve the quality of decision making.

This analytical decision process is a straightforward procedure that will improve the effectiveness of research design and increase the impact of objective research on decision making. The process is simple and quickly executed and does not represent a substantial increase in either the cost of research or the time required to do it.

The increase in the potential value of research for marketing decision makers in the last decade has been dramatic, but the gap between potential and realized value has increased even more dramatically. The approach developed in this book will allow marketing decision makers, regardless of their level of technical training, to increase their analytical power and make better and more profitable decisions.

Index